Contested Paternity

Contested Paternity

Constructing Families in Modern France

RACHEL G. FUCHS

The Johns Hopkins University Press
Baltimore

© 2008 The Johns Hopkins University Press
All rights reserved. Published 2008
Printed in the United States of America on acid-free paper
2 4 6 8 9 7 5 3 1

The Johns Hopkins University Press
2715 North Charles Street
Baltimore, Maryland 21218-4363
www.press.jhu.edu

Library of Congress Cataloging-in-Publication Data
Fuchs, Rachel Ginnis, 1939–
Contested paternity : constructing families in modern France /
Rachel G. Fuchs.
      p.   cm.
Includes bibliographical references and index.
ISBN-13: 978-0-8018-8832-8 (hardcover : alk. paper)
ISBN-10: 0-8018-8832-8 (hardcover : alk. paper)
1. Paternity—France—History. 2. Parent and child (Law)—France—History.
3. Domestic relations courts—France—History. I. Title.
KJV894.F83 2008
346.4401'75—dc22   2007040084

A catalog record for this book is available from the British Library.

*Special discounts are available for bulk purchases of this book. For more information, please contact Special Sales at 410-516-6936 or
specialsales@press.jhu.edu.*

The Johns Hopkins University Press uses environmentally friendly book materials, including recycled text paper that is composed of at least 30 percent post-consumer waste, whenever possible. All of our book papers are acid-free, and our jackets and covers are printed on paper with recycled content.

For Norman

CONTENTS

Acknowledgments   ix

Introduction   1

1 Families and the Social Order from the Old Regime to the Civil Code   16

2 Seduction and Courtroom Encounters in the Nineteenth Century   59

3 Find the Fathers, Save the Children, 1870–1912   109

4 Courts Attribute Paternity, 1912–1940   160

5 Families Dismantled and Reconstituted, 1880–1940   200

6 Paternity and the Family, 1940 to the Present   240

Epilogue   278

Notes   289
Works Cited   325
Index   345

ACKNOWLEDGMENTS

My work on this book began a long time ago, and one of the pleasures at the end is the opportunity to thank those who gave unstintingly of their time and energy to provide encouragement and assistance along the way. I am profoundly grateful to so many.

Institutional support has been invaluable. The National Endowment for the Humanities supported this project with a year-long Fellowship for University Professors. The Camargo Foundation provided a semester to write. Summer Research Grants from Arizona State University College of Liberal Arts and Sciences for 1996, 1998, and 2000 greatly facilitated my research trips to France.

This book would not have been possible without the services of the staff at various archives and libraries in Paris. I owe an especially warm thanks and much appreciation to Brigitte Lainé, Philippe Grand, and Alain Grassie at the Archives de Paris, not only for helping find invaluable archives for me, but also for their good cheer and dedication to the *patrimoine*, as well as to history and historians. At the Bibliothèque historique de la Ville de Paris, Geneviève Madore's kindness has made working in that exquisite building even more pleasant. When Mary Lynn Stewart first introduced me to the Bibliothèque Marguerite Durand decades ago, she described it as a "feminist haven for historians." It remains so, and I warmly thank Annie Metz and her staff for creating such an accommodating environment in which to work. I also thank the staffs at the Archives nationales de France and the Bibliothèque nationale de France for their assistance.

From this project's inception, I have presented drafts of chapters at conferences, and I welcome the opportunity to express my gratitude to receptive audiences and other panelists at meetings of the Social Science History Association, the Western Society for French History, the Society for French

Historical Studies, at the International Congress of Historical Sciences in Oslo, and at the George Rudé conference in Melbourne. I have also presented portions of this work at the following institutions, and I thank them here (in reverse chronological order of my presentations): Symposium on Reproduction in the Nineteenth Century at the Center for Humanities at Temple University; the Department of History of the University of Washington; Northwestern University's French Interdisciplinary Group's Institute on Family, Sexuality, and the Law; the European History Colloquium at UCLA; the Department of History at the University of Southern California; the European History Seminar in the Department of History at Cornell University; Universidade de Lisboa / University of Lisbon; Universidade Aberta, Lisbon, Portugal; Histoire des femmes, Centre de recherches historiques, École des hautes études en sciences sociales, Paris; and the University of Chicago Workshop on Inter-disciplinary Approaches to Modern France.

I am indebted to a great many people for invaluable feedback on my work. I greatly appreciate the invitations, constructive comments, important questions, conversations, and friendship of Linda Clark, Anne Cova, Dena Goodman, Sandra Ginnis, Jan Goldstein, Nancy Green, Steve Hause, Ray Jonas, Steven Kaplan, Sara Kimble, Cheryl Koos, Cynthia Koepp, Peter Logan, Michael Lucey, Pat Mainardi, Judith Miller, Jean Pedersen, David Sabean, Vanessa Schwartz, Chips Sowerwine, and Elizabeth Veron. My warm thanks to Suzanne Desan and Martha Hanna for stimulating conversations and for their reading of penultimate drafts of particular chapters; I have benefited from their expertise. Karen Offen, whom I first met in 1978, has helped me understand French feminism and women's history. I have deeply appreciated her incisive comments and intellectual rigor since then, most recently when she read Chapter 3. A portion of Chapter 3 appeared in a somewhat different form as "Seduction, Paternity, and the Law in Fin-de-Siècle France," in the *Journal of Modern History* 72 (December 2000): 944–989, and is used here with permission from the University of Chicago Press.

I am fortunate to have colleagues who have also been good friends for almost thirty years, and it is with profound pleasure that I can now publicly thank these very special people who have read this entire book manuscript. They have so graciously and generously given of their time and shared their sensitivities to French history. They have shown me how to live our lives as historians without losing sight of our humanity to others. They have read and offered expert critiques of almost every article and book I've ever tried to publish and offered insightful suggestions with style and grace on this manuscript, helping to save me and my readers from what we have good-naturedly called my "wretched excess" and "repetitive redundancy." Ever since I met Lenard Berlanstein in 1977, he has been an inspiration to me. He has shown by example what it means to be an exemplary scholar, friend, and colleague. His reading of this manuscript for the Johns Hopkins University Press provided affirmation of the project and encouragement. Just a few years later, I met Elinor Accampo, Leslie Moch, and Mary Lynn Stewart. They have become not only firm friends and colleagues but also collaborators and comrades. I met Bob Nye about a decade later. He also has read all my work with kindness and generosity. His own pathbreaking work has influenced me and many other historians to think in new ways. I am very grateful to all these scholars for their keen intellectual insights, friendship and understanding; they have enriched my work and life in countless ways. Uncharacteristically, *les mots me manquent.*

The History Department at Arizona State University has been enormously enriched by hiring Kent Wright and Victoria Thompson. Kent has spent numerous hours over lunch with me sharing his knowledge of eighteenth-century intellectual history and discussing natural law. I first met Victoria Thompson in Paris when she was a graduate student. I am delighted that she has since become my colleague, friend, and collaborator. She read this entire book manuscript and offered kind words along the way. The History Department and I have significantly benefited from having Richard S. Hopkins as a graduate student. I greatly appreciate the opportunity to work with him, and I cannot imagine a better young scholar and research assistant. He found newspaper articles, verified footnotes, and worked with me on many aspects of this manuscript, including the index—all with incredible research skills and good spirits.

At the Johns Hopkins University Press, Henry Tom had confidence in me and the patience to tolerate my missed deadlines for this manuscript as I wrote other books that took longer than I had anticipated and assumed administrative positions that involved an unexpected amount of time and energy, all further delaying completion of this book, and I sincerely thank him. I have enjoyed his wit and good humor since working with him on an earlier book. My thanks to Claire McCabe Tamberino and Julie McCarthy for their welcome advice and calm as they worked with me in the final stages of manuscript preparation, and to Peter Dreyer, copy editor extraordinaire, for his meticulous assistance.

I am deeply appreciative of my family and friends for their forbearance and understanding when I neglected them during the last year of writing this book. My love, admiration, and gratitude go especially to my two children, Daniel Fuchs and Mindy Fuchs Lokshin, and their families, and to my husband, Norman Fuchs. I would like to promise them all that I won't neglect them again for another book, but I'm not sure I could keep that promise. I will try.

Contested Paternity

Introduction

"Why are you writing a book on paternity?" some friends have asked—often adding, somewhat suspiciously: "But I thought you worked on women's history?" This book owes its conception to an earlier one I wrote on the poor and pregnant of Paris. As I was editing that manuscript, I eliminated ten pages on paternity searches and decided to write an article based on the material from the cutting-room floor. I soon realized, however, that it would take more than one article to understand why the Code Napoléon—the French Civil Code of 1804—expressly forbade paternity searches (*recherche de paternité*), and why that law remained unchanged until 1912.[1] Studying legislative discussions of recherche de paternité at the end of the nineteenth century, I found references, not only to judicial decisions of the preceding one hundred years, but to debates about the subject under the ancien régime of the late eighteenth century. Upon finding the judicial archives for civil suits, I quickly realized that they would be significant for understanding how women and men thought about their relationships and about paternity during the twentieth century. Exploring the question further led me to archives on paternity denials, deprivation of paternity, and adoption, inspiring me to place paternity in the context of reconstituted families.

Those ten pages from the cutting-room floor are now somewhere in the third chapter of this book. My response to the second question reflects how I view certain aspects of women's history. I do not see paternity as independent from women's history, nor do I envision women's lives as separate from the world in which they lived. That world included men—as part of a family, as the "author of the pregnancy," as fathers, as members of the state apparatus—either as part of women's intimate lives or as outsiders making decisions about women's lives or commenting on them. I also situate women's history within gender history, looking at gender as the culturally, socially, and politically negotiated roles of men and women in society and in relationship to each other. Gender relationships within families and the interaction of families with the state are critical to understanding history, societies, and culture.

I have chosen to study the French family by concentrating on those who fell outside the conjugal unit. Two of my earlier books focused on abandoned children and single mothers. In this book, I turn my attention to fathers and to paternity outside legal marriage. Conjugal families, sometimes referred to as traditional families, or more appropriately as heterosexual reproductive families, however, are not entirely absent from this study. They are present mainly as a referent, because until late in the twentieth century, the dominant French culture regarded these idealized families as the social core and sought to protect them from intrusion and competition by other family forms and outside individuals. I pay attention to families that did not follow an idealized model, revealing society's increasing acceptance of other family forms by the end of the nineteenth century. I examine the complex notions of paternity and fatherhood, placing paternity within the nexus of changing notions of the family. Paternity is not a fixed entity; it is a historically contingent one—one that is constructed by men, women, their social milieu, the courts, and the state.

Focusing on paternity as a category of family history reveals the importance of fatherhood, the family, and the law within the greater context of changing attitudes toward parental responsibility, the development of state welfare, constructions of the family, the rights of children, and women's agency. At the intersection of the social and political, of the public and the private, issues of paternity and the family have broad implications for an understanding of how private acts were matters governed by laws of the state and adjudicated by civil tribunals. I examine the development of the modern idea of paternity and the family in France. Defining paternity was not, and is not, a simple matter. As one French legislator said in 1883, "paternity is as mysterious as the source of the Nile."[2] Neither is now as shrouded in mystery as in 1883, but paternity remains problematic. Paternity was long based on the biological, but it was also socially constructed on the basis of behavior. Medical science could not determine paternity by blood types until after the mid twentieth century, and genetic testing came even later. Biological paternity was therefore difficult to prove or disprove, although people tried. Behavior construed as paternal included providing for the child's food and education, participating in child rearing, and expressing concern for the child.

In this book, I seek to address the contested definitions of paternity and of acceptable families, how public policy toward paternity and the family shifted, and what individuals did to facilitate or hinder their personal and familial ideals and goals. The issue of paternity is at the core of the controversial terrain of the construction of a family as an entity formed by a legal marriage between a man and a woman, and entails competing cultural, social, and political values about gender, class, and the family. Moreover, paternal responsibility involved different, and often contested, notions concerning male sexual domination and female sexual vulnerability, bourgeois respectability and working-class companionship, and gendered notions of sexual honor—all exhibited in the public arena. I explore the debates, tensions, and changes in how individuals, communities, society, and the law constructed families, but my focus is outside the idealized model of the heterosexual reproductive family. The historical literature on the family is vast, although much of it tends to focus on women and children, placing paternity primarily within the context of the conjugal family.[3] Scholarly works that feature fathers and paternity in France, with two recent notable exceptions, are general surveys covering the history from early medieval times to the present in one volume, and only marginally treat those issues of paternity and the family on which I focus.[4]

Throughout much of French history, the vast body of laws, literature, religious writings, and official state pronouncements defended the French heterosexual reproductive legally married and usually patriarchal family as the basis of French social and cultural life. Transformations in the family took place privately and informally. Although people lived in a variety of family arrangements, such as mother-child, consensual unions, same-sex, and adoptive, these arrangements did not always receive legal sanction; nor did family members always live under the same roof. As Michael Lucey has described, "numerous conflicting family forms exist in uneasy proximity to one another. Different social groups, different classes, different regions are all likely to think differently about what a family is, or, one might better say, they are likely to enact the concept of the family in different ways. . . . Within and between different social groups, attitudes toward the evolution of family forms will be different and often in conflict."[5] Throughout most of the nineteenth century, change in the cultural and legal acceptance of a variety of family forms was slow and unsteady. Fathers long held authority within the conjugal family and served as intermediaries between the family and the state. Although many in positions of authority viewed the legally married conjugal family as the guarantor of social stability, I argue that influential men in politics and law began to accept heterosexual consensual unions as early as 1900 because they resembled marriage, and indeed were a type of marriage for many. In the interwar years of the twentieth century, fathers' authority and power in the family diminished, only to have a brief recrudescence in the 1940s and then decrease again after the 1960s. By the end of the twentieth century, those dominant views about the preferred conjugal family adapted, although not without resistance, to include a more open system of family life and a multiplicity of families. Examination of recherche de paternité from 1804 to 1993 sheds light on how paternity was defined and how it functioned in the culture and experiences of individual men and women.

An investigation of the fluctuating and controversial concepts of paternal responsibility and of the legalization of paternity searches that delineates the complex and multilayered interrelationships of gender expectations, the family, law, politics, and the state goes beyond the important issue of paternity, I suggest. In the courts, the legislature, the popular literature, and the press, the debates over the rights and responsibilities of parents for each other and for their extranuptial children indicate gradually changing attitudes and policies toward the family, property, seduction, and paternity, and the role of the state in these private matters. They reflect social and cultural shifts in assumptions about how to safeguard the legal family, while at the same time protecting children born outside of marriage. As reformers and politicians debated the issue of paternity outside of marriage, they maintained the centrality of the legal conjugal family to the well-ordered state. Yet as they (re)negotiated the social construction of the French family, they faced the fact that extranuptial children required material support. Furthermore, although conjugal families may have been the ideal, the reality was that men and women lived their lives in common—eating, drinking, and sleeping together—outside a marriage established in law. Realizing that parental responsibility existed within and outside legal marriage, judges and legislators focused on the degree of the father's accountability external to marriage.

Law validates the existing power structure and communicates established ideas about proper behavior; it embraces widely shared social assumptions designed to reflect and protect the values of the polity, even when the polity consists of a small elite to the exclusion of others. According to the legal historian André-Jean Arnaud, the aim of the Civil Code in 1804 was to sanction social order as conceived by the bourgeoisie.[6] By the twentieth century, that perception of the social order had changed. Law, nevertheless, is culturally bound, created according to certain rationales, and it has only a limited capacity to reconstruct social and intimate lives according to certain general norms and principles. Law lagged behind social and cultural change, because people found their personal and intimate lives too important to be left to the dictates of the written law. Given this discordance of the law with how people lived their lives, and with society and culture, individuals and judges ignored or transgressed the letter of the law until the law eventually changed. Modification of law results from the interaction of ruling groups attempting to legislate their desires and of popular movements altering attitudes to effect legal change. I argue that jurisprudence, defined as a body of judicial decisions, revealed a greater diversity of attitudes toward paternity and the family and kept pace with the changing society and culture better than did the law.

Paternity, jurisprudence, and family law in modern France revealed cultural shifts that reflected multiple renegotiations of relationships between the family and the individual, the individual and the state, women and men, and parent and child. Those cultural shifts involved redefinitions of the family, adjustments in the balance between individual rights and the social good, as well as expanded applications of individual rights to women and children. Although men and women probably did not think of the law as they lived their private lives, law made its presence felt, with all its tensions. As Michel de Certeau has argued, everyday life and the law were mutually defining and "mutually constitutive processes." Certeau's "investigation of the ways in which users—commonly assumed to be passive and guided by established rules—operate" is particularly relevant as a framework for understanding civil litigation involving family matters. By initiating paternity suits, women, who are usually considered to have been among the powerless, used the law and courts as tactics of resistance to "reappropriate" space, power, and resources. Those women who initiated civil suits were habitually "consumers" rather than producers of the cultural forms that law and the powerful imposed upon them. Nevertheless, by filing suits they engaged in a "combat" to "invent" or deal with everyday life "by *poaching* in countless ways on the property of others." In doing so, they made the "rituals, representations and laws [that had been] imposed on them something quite different from what their [originators] had in mind." Their narratives began a series of "contingent social actions," resulting in legal decisions about their families and personal lives.[7] Men and women may not have been conscious of the law, but the law in some ways circumscribed aspects of their lives. It had the inherent capacity to structure power relationships, relationships that were sometimes disputed and disrupted. I am well aware, however, of the limitations of law in people's lives, agreeing with Pierre Bourdieu: "Law does no more than symbolically consecrate—by recording it in a form that renders it both eternal and universal—the structure of power relations among the groups and the classes that is produced and guaranteed practically by the functioning of these mechanisms."[8] As men and women tried to negotiate the law, they drew on it tactically and differently from each other and from the intentions of the legislators and judges.

The courtroom served as the arena for the struggle between laws and private behavior and between men and women. In adjudicating family matters such as paternity searches, judges interpreted and enforced a body of laws, but those laws left them much leeway as they weighed the evidence from men, women, and their lawyers. Michel Foucault called doctors the new confessors in a secular age. While not denying that doctors perform that function, I would suggest that judges and lawyers also served as confessors.[9] When men and women went before lawyers and judges to seek approval and win their cases, they likely minimized their sins and transgressions and emphasized their virtues, hoping to give their lawyers and judges the information necessary to win their cases. Judges could not grant the men or women spiritual absolution, but they could absolve men of paternal responsibility; they could likewise grant or deny women what they had requested. Women held power in presenting their legal cases; men held the power to bring countercharges, usually alleging the women's lack of virtue.

Judicial archives provide the major sources for this book. They contain legal decisions that illuminate the dark recesses of private lives, allowing us to discern the intimate relations of men and women who themselves left no written records. Judgments in civil suits also allow us to see how judges interpreted the law, and how the law affected private lives, moving the law out of the realm of public political discourse and into that of private practice. These court records depict the interaction between the state and the individual, but the voices of the men and women are mediated and heard only indirectly through the judicial decisions, unless letters are included in the files, which was infrequent. The letters, moreover, are only those that the men and women chose to submit to their lawyers and judges, and that those judges chose to include in the files. Men and women tell their stories with gender-specific language, which I call "creative nonfiction," according to what they thought their lawyers and judges wanted to hear. They built their narrative strategies, however creative they might have been, using concepts of morality and rights. To initiate a legal suit demanding one's rights in court is one of the rights of citizenship in a democracy—an active citizenship that women did not officially have in France until 1944. Individual autonomy is also an aspect of active citizenship, a trait normally associated with masculinity.[10] I suggest, however, that women were also exercising a type of autonomy and citizenship when they filed legal suits, despite the interdiction against paternity suits during the nineteenth century and the complications and delays in these proceedings during the twentieth. Since women could not exercise their autonomy based on their rights as individuals or citizens, they went to court as innocent victims and good mothers—one or the other, preferably both.

Gender was performative in legal suits involving sexual behavior and paternity.[11] Before their lawyers and judges, women created their identities to fit their particular personal needs, but also, by necessity, according to the moral and cultural imperatives of their time. The Rousseauist feminine ideal of women as virtuous, faithful, self-sacrificing, modest mothers persisted into the twentieth century, but not without some changes. In the nineteenth century (see Chapter 2), women appeared as young, innocent, vulnerable, seduced and abandoned good mothers. In the twentieth century (Chapter 4), because it would help them win their suits, they frequently continued to present themselves as young, innocent, and vulnerable; but they also appeared as more independent, engaging in voluntary heterosexual relationships, either living with a person without marriage or having a more fleeting love affair. Nevertheless, they still had to demonstrate that they were good mothers according to the standards of the time. In no case could they present even a hint of sexual promiscuity. Writers, politicians, and magistrates of the Third Republic lauded bourgeois reproductive conjugal families and held up marriage as the ideal, but they inconsistently and hypocritically acknowledged and often accepted voluntary heterosexual relationships outside of marriage. Women, their lawyers, and empathetic judges challenged and helped change laws and definitions of proper behavior. Poor young women, as well as those with property, "rebelling against conventional womanhood," challenged their traditional roles.[12] They rebelled by their sexual behavior and in pursuing paternity suits in court. At the same time, they presented themselves as having conventional behavior as good mothers in order to have their somewhat unconventional nonmarital sexuality accepted.

Men based their successful performances as defendants in paternity suits on appearing to have acted honorably, usually by having provided some material support for the women and children. They justified their having ceased to provide support by charging that the women had behaved dishonorably. When a woman named a particular man as the putative father of her child, his best defense was a good offense—accusing the woman of having many lovers and thus casting doubt on his paternity. Men's acceptable self-representation was culturally complex and time-dependent. Libertinage may have been acceptable behavior through the first half of the nineteenth century, but starting at the end of that century, men were expected to act responsibly. After the devastating loss of the Franco-Prussian war in 1870, French politicians became obsessed with the specter of a smaller and weaker population compared with Germany. Providing evidence of masculinity by fathering children now came to demonstrate virility and the performance of a man's natural duties. When men behaved irresponsibly by abandoning women with whom they had had a sexual relationship and failed to provide for the children of that relationship, they lacked not only a sense of duty but also of honor. Jean-Jacques Rousseau's ideas resonated in the twentieth century. If women were still supposed to be good mothers, à la Rousseau, then according to the same ideology, men were to be good fathers and provide for their children's education and material support—unless they could prove non-paternity. As Robert Nye has magnificently argued, the bourgeois paterfamilias was a man who aspired to honor and status, and who developed particular family strategies dependent on marital fertility and the control of sexuality—not only his but also that of his family members. Women's indiscretions could result in loss of honor, and having an extranuptial child could create problems of inheritance.[13]

"[T]he transformation and fragmentation of knowledge and values beginning in the eighteenth century assisted the diffusion of sexuality, and all of this change was associated with the ascendancy of the bourgeoisie," Foucault argues. The bourgeois family, he adds, was "an agency of control."[14] The concern with sexuality entailed a bourgeois male's anxiety about strengthening his control of the family and, by extension, of the polity. Men's discourse on paternity and sexuality therefore involved male protection of the family and the nation, which centered on men's property and concern for the social and moral order—an order that involved attempting to control women's sexuality. Although the bourgeoisie, according to Foucault, sought to reform and organize the sexuality among the poor, particularly the poor women, to form them according to the conventional conjugal family, these attempts largely failed. Foucault's analysis may speak to aspects of nineteenth-century discourse, but after 1918, his analysis breaks down, because men's and women's sexuality is less under the moral microscope of medical and state authorities and more open and acceptable.

Inherent in histories of heterosexuality are questions of domination and power. In the nineteenth century, laws and culture gave men dominant sexual power not only within the home but also outside it. A woman could exert her power in the courtroom by requiring that the magistrates condemn a man to pay for his sexual actions. To do so, however, took time, money, and energy; her success was far from guaranteed. Moreover, a woman's power was based on her weakness. She had to show that she was a virtuous victim of a man's sexual power. In the twentieth century, with consensual unions accepted as partial proof of paternity, men and women had greater equality in the sexual arena. Unmarried mothers, although economically and socially weak, had power over their children that married women lacked. Single mothers held parental authority, because they recognized those children. Even when judges ruled that men should be responsible for their sexual acts, those men did not have paternal authority over the children, a power that belonged to the mothers in France until the very end of the twentieth century. Sexual behavior is usually private and intimate, but going to court for paternity and child support entailed providing proof of sexual relations, thereby making one's love life and sex life public and pushing the boundaries of the right to privacy. In particular, the bourgeoisie cherished this right to family privacy, and fear of having it abridged was one of the obstacles to permitting recherche de paternité. Family relations and sexuality became very public issues when relations between men and women broke down, in divorce, disavowal of paternity, or paternity searches.

Laws and judicial decisions on standards of parental responsibility were constituent elements in the growth of state intervention in matters regarding women and children toward the end of the nineteenth century. As "the provident state" assumed a more active role in the family lives of poor women and children through various child-centered welfare measures, legally sanctioned paternity searches became another aspect of public involvement in the family, along with efforts to preserve the lives of babies and counter depopulation by public assistance and other means of legal and moral persuasion. French politicians attributed many of their nation's military and social woes to what they perceived as national depopulation. Maintaining that national depopulation derived from cultural degeneration and the failure of men and women to do their parental duty, politicians sought ways to provide for the children; having biological fathers contribute to the support of their children was one way to do this.

※

This book explores five themes. The first involves the power of judges, demonstrating that activist judges are not a recent phenomenon. I had not anticipated finding the roles of judges and the courts so important. The judiciary was closer to the people than the legislature; this was important when at least half the population did not yet have the right to vote. Decades ahead of the law, bending and stretching it as they saw necessary, judges reflected local mores and morals, demonstrating a degree of empathy with the private situations of both men and women. Judges and civil tribunals also represented the state, making the courts sites of confrontation between state policies and the intimate lives of individuals, with judges often functioning as intermediaries.

The second theme is the idea that paternity was divisible in terms of responsibility. When I began this study, I equated paternity searches with a demand for child support. How wrong I was. During the nineteenth and twentieth centuries, magistrates, mothers, and putative fathers divided paternity between a man's obligation to supply only a subsidy for food and his obligation to endow the child with full filiation that went beyond material child support. Filiation required that the father provide his child with his family surname, a portion of his inheritance, and assimilation into his family lineage with all the rights and responsibilities of belonging to that family; it could also include adoption. Filiation was not the equivalent of paternity based on biology, and did not necessarily include social fatherhood. Marriage, however, usually involved full filiation, and a husband was usually the biological father as well as the social father. For "natural children" (a term I prefer to "illegitimate children"), filiation tended to be the judicial determination of paternity that involved placing a child within the father's family. Providing full filiation to a natural child had an impact on the cherished bloodline of the bourgeois family, something men, families, and most legislators sought to avoid. Therefore, filiation of a natural child was the focal point of debates about paternity and was fundamental to consideration of the law that prohibited and then permitted recherche de paternité. But in the practice of everyday lives, filiation was not essential, even to women who filed paternity suits. Because full filiation was so problematic and controversial, judges divided paternity between filiation and provision of child support.

Paying a pittance for child support only until the child's majority, at which time all obligations ended, minimally affected a man's family property. It did not entail a name, family association, or inheritance, as filiation defined. Paternity was also divisible between a biological connection and social fatherhood. The latter required "acting as a father" by helping rear the child and providing for the child's education, in the French sense of upbringing. The "author of the pregnancy," or genitor, was not always the social father; biological paternity did not automatically result in a fatherly relationship with the child. This was a particular issue when the child was born outside of a legal marriage and there were no biological tests of paternity. In the twentieth century, with modern technology, the social father was not always the genitor. Paternity might be considered a symbolic liaison conferring an inheritance and lineage, while fatherhood also involved emotional and social ties. The culture and the courts were redefining paternity and what it meant to be a good father.

What are the boundaries of acceptable familial and extrafamilial behavior, and when and why did they change? The third theme traces the idea and practice of cohabitation, or consensual unions, what the French call *concubinage*, without any pejorative connotation. *Concubinage* was not only practiced among the urban poor throughout the nineteenth century, but the 1912 revision of the article in the Civil Code pertaining to paternity searches accepted it as a lifestyle providing a possible proof of paternity. At the end of the nineteenth as well as at the end of the twentieth century, legislators, judges, and reformers were quoting with approbation the aphorism of Antoine Loysel (1536–1617): "Boire, manger, coucher ensemble, c'est mariage ce me semble" (Drink, eat, sleep together, that's marriage it seems to me), while blithely ignoring its ironic qualification: "mais il faut que l'Eglise y passe." At the end of the nineteenth century and into the twentieth, it was applied to heterosexual couples; at the end of the twentieth century, it included same-sex couples as well. Nevertheless, *concubinage* is not a legal marriage. Heterosexual couples have the right to choose between *concubinage* and a legal marriage; homosexual couples do not. To recognize, describe and understand how, why and under what circumstances the French accepted *concubinage* as a family form is part of the third theme.

Fourth, this book studies the change in sexual mores from the assumption that women who had natural children were immoral to some recognition in the twentieth century of a woman's sexual independence, without casting aspersions on her morality, as long as she had only one sexual partner. Because barrier contraception was unknown, illegal, or not readily available until 1967, a woman's sexuality was not separate from reproduction, and if there was a child, she was expected to behave as a good mother. The representation of women who had a child outside of legal marriage went from that of seductress to that of one innocently seduced, and from sexual sinner to victim. At the beginning of the nineteenth century, women had to present themselves as innocent victims in order to have judges hear their cases and perhaps award in their favor. By the twentieth century, that was no longer always the case. What happened? I suggest that a new and overwhelming concern with the lives of children, in part out of the national interest, occasioned the change. This book traces the shift in the moral values that served as the basis for preserving social order.

Along with a transformation in perceptions and representations of women's sexuality came a modification of how men were expected to behave, involving new concepts of responsibility and honor. Men's exercise of individual freedom in their sexual activity and acknowledgment of paternity came to have some limitations. As its fifth theme, this book analyzes how paternity came to encompass voluntary social and emotional fatherhood, involuntary judicially declared paternity, and biological paternity in many variations.

Observing a generally chronological approach, the first chapter details the debates on seduction, sexuality, paternity, adoption, natural law, and the family during the successive stages of the Revolution, culminating with the Napoleonic Civil Code of 1804. Following the maxim that in order to protect children, "whoever creates the child must provide for it," Old Regime custom and courts permitted the naming of the father for the purposes of obtaining child support. During the course of the Revolution, legislators abolished paternity searches. Struggling with a conflict between the natural rights of children and those of fathers, they argued that paternity searches were against natural law and would interfere with a man's liberty. By 1804, the men who framed the Civil Code sought to guarantee the sanctity, tranquility, and property of the family under the husband's authority. They designed a code to calm men's fears that a woman (assumed to be working-class) would seduce a middle-class family man and accuse him of fathering her child in order for her to obtain money or introduce that child into his family's inheritance line. Legislators declared that all children were fatherless at birth and "only marriage makes a father." By forbidding paternity searches, the Code protected the legally married heterosexual reproductive family and confirmed marriage as a public act, placing family behavior firmly in the public discourse. This framework provided by the Revolution and the Napoleonic Civil Code would last for at least the following two centuries.

Chapter 2 examines how men, women, and judges managed to live and work within the confines of the Civil Code during the nineteenth century. Politicians upheld the letter of the Code, avoiding decisions that might have impinged on the honor and power of the male head of household and the transmission of his family name and property. Since reformers and politicians privileged marriage and the transmission of the family name and property over paternal responsibility for extranuptial children, they regarded permission for a single mother to sue a putative father for paternity as an endangerment of the conjugal family. The social order depended upon the family and the containment of woman's sexuality. Honor and property were integrally connected and conferred status. Yet a tension existed between the law and family practices, and during the second half of the century, parents and judges attempted to reinterpret, or even bypass the laws to accord with their lived experiences. Using an article of the Civil Code pertaining to property damages, judges let unwed mothers demand civil damages from putative fathers despite the prohibition of paternity searches. This chapter narrates these stories within their cultural context, demonstrating how judges considered paternity divisible between full filiation and mere provision of child support.

Legislative debates from 1878 to 1912 take center stage in the third chapter. The reversal of the 1804 prohibition of paternity searches was less than absolute; it exempted married men from paternity suits, thereby revealing legislators' inclination to preserve the rights and property of married men and their families, even when the preservation of those rights threatened the welfare of fatherless children. Nevertheless, the 1912 law demonstrated a cultural shift that involved a limited redefinition of the family, an adjustment of the balance between individual rights and the social good, as well as an expanded application of individual rights to women and children. The historical tapestry of thirty years of legislative debates, court decisions, and feminist positions over the complex topic of paternal responsibility was woven from contrasting threads of debate. This chapter examines several major developments leading to the passage of the law.

Chapter 4 recounts how paternity functioned within social and cultural parameters from 1912 through 1939. Although the legally married two-parent family remained fundamental to French ideology, in the twentieth century, acknowledgment of *concubinage* as a basis for paternal child support indicated a reconfiguration and expansion of the social construction of the family. I sampled the hundreds of paternity suits women brought before the civil courts of Paris between 1912 and 1939 in order to determine the situation of the women who filed paternity suits, their reasons for doing so, the nature of proof and evidence, the characteristics of the couple's relationship, and the judges' decisions in declaring paternity with full filiation or just mandating child support. The court records reveal public attitudes about good parenting, acceptable sexual behavior, and how men and women fashioned their cases. The courts were sites for generating paternity and fatherhood and for constructing families, as women and men reconceptualized gender relations and male responsibility.

Chapter 5 breaks with chronology and the focus on recherche de paternité; it examines different aspects of contested paternity and family constructions from the last decades of the nineteenth century to 1940, including disavowal of paternity, deprivation of paternity, and adoption. Although this book does not engage with paternity issues surrounding divorce, I sampled court records on divorce in which a father disavowed paternity of his children born within marriage, as well as all other court cases for disavowal of paternity based on a woman's adultery. The judicial dossiers on mothers and fathers whom officials sought to deprive of parental authority provide the details of how the critical legislation of 1889 depriving fathers of their *puissance paternelle* (paternal authority) functioned. The third, and longest, section of this chapter discusses families reconstituted by adoption. I loosely define adoption to include foster parentage and kinship care networks; these were ways of creating families of choice, even without the law, which did not permit legal child adoption until 1923. The archives containing confirmations of adoption in Paris for the 1920s and 1930s provide evidence that paternity and families based on emotion coexisted with families based on blood and property.

The last chapter functions as a coda, taking the history of paternity and the social construction of the French family from the Vichy era through the beginning of the twenty-first century. An analysis of several cases of family disputes and paternity searches under Vichy demonstrates some consistencies with the end of the Third Republic and illuminates important aspects of the relationships between politics and the family. In the post-1945 period, new laws regarding paternity and the family rapidly broadened the grounds for paternity searches and family formation. For example, after 1972, a man who had a child as a result of his adultery could be brought to court on paternity charges; since 1993, DNA tests have been the legal base for determining paternity, thereby forcing a reconsideration of both its biological and social basis. By 2000, Loysel's "Boire, manger, coucher ensemble . . ." still did not define a legal marriage, but it had come to represent a legal family.

CHAPTER ONE

Families and the Social Order from the Old Regime to the Civil Code

Families are adaptable forms of private and public relationships. As men and women fashion their families, private passions frequently conflict with an ideal family form. From the eighteenth century through the formulation of the Civil Code in 1804, the legally married family remained the political and social ideal, the bastion of social order. As authorities sought to safeguard it from disruption, they had to grapple with the results of private passions that threatened their ideal.

Seduction and sexual love outside of marriage have been facts of life from time immemorial, and essentially, women bore the consequences—pregnancy and the responsibility for childcare. Until the last decades of the eighteenth century, customs, laws, culture, a sense of duty, and judges' decisions could compel a number of men to accept some financial liability for their sexual activity, especially if it resulted in the birth of a child. If a mother named the putative father or "author of the pregnancy," magistrates could order him to pay child support or repair the damage to the woman and her family, but those same magistrates disallowed introducing the illegitimate child into the legitimate family. The child had no legal inheritance rights from the father or his family, although people always found ways around the law. Magistrates, however, decreasingly granted reparations or child support to the mother, only reluctantly giving credence to a woman's sworn testimony designating the putative father. Revolutionary upheavals at the end of the century, paying heed to the natural, civil, and individual rights of men, resulted in legal and social modifications to eighteenth-century practice. Family formation and the nature of paternity became more inextricably linked to family property—notably that of men, with the Revolution marking a transition in relationships between the family and the state. The 1804 Civil Code set the course for the legal construction of paternity and the French family for over one hundred years. Throughout the nineteenth and twentieth centuries, scholars, magistrates, laws, culture, and the individual behavior of men and women hearkened back to eighteenth-century concepts as they sought to maintain the sanctity of the legally married family. How individuals and authorities dealt with seduction and paternal responsibility underwent subtle, and sometimes drastic, shifts.

Seduction and Paternal Responsibility in the Eighteenth Century

To protect property transmission along bloodlines and to reinforce male dominance, men wanted women to be chaste outside of marriage.[1] Yet those very men seduced women outside of marriage, and women succumbed to seduction, passion, and love. Eighteenth-century seduction included gifts, sweet words, promises of marriage, and sexual activity. In addition, it often included fraud, rape, and other forms of violence against women. Although fraud and violence were usually criminal misdemeanors, courts tended to ignore a woman's complaints and even sometimes blamed her. Magistrates were more likely to entertain her complaints if she brought evidence that the violence had been extreme and she could show scars, or if she had visibly and publicly resisted, or if she were of a higher status than her seducer, or was of impeccable virtue, or if abduction had accompanied the seduction or rape.[2] Age was also important, especially when the woman was a legal minor. If a man seduced her with a promise of marriage without her father's consent to the marriage, authorities might consider it *rapt*. Although *rapt* could include rape, it usually indicated nonviolent seduction against the wishes of a woman's father. Writing in 1781, Jean-François Fournel, a leading legal authority, distinguished *séduction* from *rapt de séduction: séduction* was against the woman alone; *rapt de séduction* involved a man abducting a young woman from her parental home, usually with the avowed intent to marry her without her father's permission. Legal authorities considered *rapt de séduction* an injury to the authority, honor, and property of her father and a crime against the family, state, and society.

Laws proscribing *rapt de séduction* were intended to protect the property and pedigrees primarily of aristocratic families and to ensure the stability of society by preventing unworthy marriages and the corruption of social mores.[3] With *rapt de séduction,* a stranger in effect intruded on a father's control over his property, in this case, his daughter and any offspring she might have who could inherit his material property.[4] The Ordinance of Blois in 1730 established the death penalty for *rapt de séduction* without a marriage promise, although that sentence was rarely imposed. In practice, the social status of the perpetrator relative to the victim's family determined the severity of punishment. The lower the station of the person responsible for the seduction and the higher the station of the victim, the harsher the punishment. A man could avoid the death penalty if he and the woman agreed to marry, and, more important, if this marriage had the consent of her family as well as his. Eighteenth-century literature and moral codes are inconsistent about whether a man should be allowed to marry the women he had seduced or abducted, even if her father eventually consented.[5]

Valid marriages based on individual will, with the consent of family and community, formed the foundation of society. Secular law considered marriage as a contract, perpetuating the family for generations; canon law viewed it as a sacrament. To both secular and ecclesiastical authorities, marriage needed the free and unfettered agreement of all the parties, particularly the parents. Seduction by fraud and violence, especially *rapt de séduction*, was against the will and consent of the woman and her family; therefore, according to legal theorists, she should not be allowed to marry the seducer or rapist. Even seduction without force or fraud, but without consent of the families, reaped social disapproval. If the young woman were a minor, the situation for the man who seduced her, and even married her, without her father's permission was particularly grim, constituting an abuse of her father's family authority. Law courts could declare such a marriage null and the man guilty of *rapt de séduction*. The penalty for seduction was less severe if a woman who had reached the age of majority (adulthood) married without parental consent. Then the man was not liable for prosecution for *rapt de séduction*, but both the new husband and wife had to leave their parental property and could be disinherited for failure to do their duty to their families.[6] After *rapt*, a woman of any age became damaged goods to her family, especially if she became pregnant. Therefore, both sets of parents might ignore the law and consent to the marriage to save their honor, if not the life of the young man.

Contradicting the theoretical need for free and unfettered consent to marriage, judges acting on their own sometimes ordered the seducer to marry the woman, despite laws and customs proscribing such a marriage. The law may have said one thing, but families, public opinion, and some magistrates argued that the mother and father of an out-of-wedlock child should be allowed, if not actually encouraged, to marry. Progeny sometimes led to a shift in views. In 1722, the law court of Burgundy "convicted Jean-Baptiste Bailly de Bailleuville... of *rapt* against Jeanne Caulnier de La Noue, the underage and seven-month-pregnant daughter of an *avocat* at Charolles... ordering Bailly to marry the young woman within three months or pay her father in her name 4,000 livres in damages, plus 400 livres to cover the costs of childbirth expenses, plus unspecified expenses for raising the child to the age of fourteen, when he was to learn a trade suitable to his status." Allowing, or ordering, a seducer or the person guilty of *rapt* to marry the woman was "thus subverting the notion that *rapt* per se was an impediment to a valid marriage." Knowing that some courts were ordering men to marry the women they had seduced, the women may have gone to court in order to marry a man they loved without their father's approval and used *rapt de séduction* to get their own fathers to allow them to marry the men who had supposedly kidnapped them.[7]

A formal engagement created a mutual obligation to marry and constituted a pact that a person did not break without consequences. In his monumental and widely accepted treatise on eighteenth-century law, Robert-Joseph Pothier considered an engagement as a contractual agreement, part of the social and political order.[8] In a culture in which marriage was as much about the community as about the couple, a marital engagement was publicly acknowledged and customarily approved, making private matters public among the community. To be valid, a marriage promise had to have been officially executed before official witnesses; sometimes four close relatives of both parties sufficed. Since marriage was supposedly based on free consent, if a person ruptured an engagement, parents or judges could exhort, but not force, that person to marry. Breaking an engagement prevented the greater evil, that of a coerced marriage. Considering a marital engagement as a contract, a wronged party (most often the woman) could sue for damages if the other person broke the contract.[9] The jilted person had to appear before a judge in the hometown of the person who broke the engagement. The judge would then decide on the compensation (*dommages-intérêts*) the person breaking the promise must pay. The amount would depend on the cost borne for the upcoming wedding, the affront to the injured party resulting in loss of material or symbolic capital, and whether the jilted woman was pregnant. Secular judges determined whether the rupture would result in reparations to the wronged party, but ecclesiastical officials could pronounce the dissolution of the engagement and impose penitence, such as prayers or giving alms. In 1791, as an anticlerical move, the Legislative Assembly made marriage a civil contract, but this law and the subsequent Civil Code of 1804 remained silent on the contractual nature of an engagement. Legislators resisted forcing marriage on a man, but disagreed on whether a pregnancy should increase the reparations a man could owe a woman for breaking an engagement.[10]

A person could find several acceptable grounds for breaking an engagement. Most often a man accused his fiancée of having had sexual relations with another. Although his language emphasized her alleged lack of virtue, related legal treatises underscored a man's need to be sure a child was his in order to secure the family's lineage. Since the principal goal of marriage was procreation, other acceptable, but less frequent, grounds for breaking an engagement included his sexual immaturity, impotency, lack of reason, an already existing marriage to someone else, belonging to a religious profession requiring celibacy, *rapt de séduction*, and close degrees of consanguinity.[11] A man's sexual relations with another woman during the engagement were not an issue; her relations with another man were. The proven validity of the marriage promise was of paramount importance to winning the suit.[12] If the woman were pregnant, whether or not she had been engaged to the putative father, she had some recourse to law and social practice to try to repair her honor and claim some child support.

From the sixteenth through the eighteenth centuries, an unmarried woman or widow was supposed to file a declaration of pregnancy (*déclaration de grossesse*) informing a local noble, notable, clergyman, or midwife that she was pregnant and naming the "author of the pregnancy." By an edict of 1556 (reiterated in 1708), Henri II confirmed this procedure as a means to prevent abortion and infanticide, based on the supposition that if the woman could obtain monetary assistance from the responsible man, she would not have to resort to these desperate measures. Equally important, the edict was intended to reduce the economic drain of illegitimate children on the royal, seigniorial, and community treasuries by affixing responsibility on the author of the pregnancy. These *déclarations de grossesse* had never been obligatory, but if the baby were to die at birth, having previously publicly declared the pregnancy was one way for a woman to avoid the charge of infanticide, which could lead to the death penalty for her. Women also filed a declaration naming the putative father in order to collect reparations for the material and moral damages he had caused them. They wanted their seducers to bear the cost of their lying-in and to provide some sustenance to the child. Neither Henri II's edict nor subsequent decrees fixed the form and format of the declarations. With much variation in regional custom, the *déclarations de grossesse* provided the first step in paternity suits, but their usefulness rested on authorities' confidence in the woman's word. In some areas of France, they were rare and filed late in the pregnancy. Women would wait as long as possible, until they were sure that their seducer would refuse to help or marry them. Marriage had become the woman's obsession during her pregnancy, but by the time of childbirth, she had lost hope and would name the father, under oath, in the presence of a midwife or priest, during her labor pains. Already dishonored, with little expectation of marriage, she hoped for a miracle by naming the father.[13]

Clandestine liaisons come to light in the *déclarations de grossesse*. The women rarely mentioned rape by a person unknown to them; when a woman did mention that she had been taken by force, she identified someone she knew, such as her boyfriend, her sister's boyfriend, or a neighbor who had found her alone. If she were a domestic servant, she sometimes named her master or his son. Declarations by women who were recent migrants to a town or city indicate their naïveté and vulnerability to seduction. These sexual relationships were of both long and short duration, but the women making the declarations were young—in their early twenties. The declarations provide voices to women constructing narratives that would be credible to the local officials as well as to their relatives and neighbors, who were also judging them. Rarely did an older woman name a younger man. Few women named a married man; most named unmarried men who had promised to marry them. A fourth of the women were domestic servants, and many of the men were valets. Women tended to specify seducers of the same social level; they only rarely designated nobles because they feared losing their jobs if they named their employer. Moreover, employers reputedly expected domestic servants, of a lower social level and away from their families, to give their sons their first sexual experiences.[14]

Men and women constructed gendered narratives about love and a ritualized set of practices in courtship or seduction. These stories reveal contending realities, codes of ethics, concepts of self, and what people thought constituted culturally approved behavior. Women may have been seduced against their will, but they were also capable of discernment, passion, and love, which their own personal narratives could not mention without public opprobrium. Fictional comedies, dramas, and judicial archives are replete with instances of young couples in love facing parental opposition to their marriage.[15] Yet they managed to find ways to be together; sexual relations ensued, based on the desires of both the man and the woman. Sometimes, through the couple's cunning or the parents' love for their children, a father would acquiesce to the marriage. Perhaps more often, parental approval was not forthcoming, but pregnancy was, both in life and in fiction. Then the man might leave the woman, whose dreams of a happy marriage turned into a nightmare of abandonment and dishonor. When a relationship went awry, a woman could not admit her willing compliance in a sexual relationship. A woman's account typically involved tales of courtship, sometimes with words of love openly spoken in public or in letters. Her family and neighbors knew of the couple's relationship, and she always insisted that he had promised marriage, avowing that she had succumbed to carnal love only after placing her trust in his verbal expressions of love and promise of marriage. Her narrative was usually one of passivity and being overcome by his entreaties. Some women insisted that the man had forced himself on her. The acceptable female narrative reflected a culture that permitted sexual relations between a man and women upon a marriage promise.

The man's narrative in such cases was, conversely, that the woman seduced him by her wily ways, seeking to trap him into marriage. He denied having been interested in marriage; he had just been out for a good time, which he had thought he was entitled to take from a willing woman, especially one beneath his social station. Whether he was engaged in a long-term or short-term relationship with the woman, he would allege that she had had several sexual partners. Only rarely did a man deny having had sexual relations with the woman, or did the woman invoke the sleeping-beauty trope of having been unconscious when raped.[16]

Communities sympathized with a woman's sexual intercourse outside of marriage as a result of fraud or force, or if she consented after a marriage promise. Women sought to protect their own honor, as well as that of their virtuous friends. As women engaged in market activity and neighborhood traffic, going to and from shops, laundries, and markets, they had a degree of sexual freedom. Their working and social lives may have provided them freedom from the gaze of their families, but not from that of others in the community. Many a vulnerable young woman would believe a man's professions of love and succumb to his sexual advances. Some rural cultures condoned sexual activity and pregnancy before marriage, but the community enforced marriages, resulting in frequent prenuptial pregnancies. In urban areas, community enforcement was reduced, resulting in more children born out of wedlock. With the expansion of the market economy of the later eighteenth century, more men moved to cities, leaving pregnant women behind to bear the consequences of their seduction. Nonmarital cohabitation was regarded as "debauchery contrary to religion and good morality"; although not sanctioned, it was also not penalized, unless accompanied by scandal.[17]

Paternity Suits

Eighteenth-century courts, custom, and law allowed legal recourse to some women who had been victims of seduction by occasionally awarding reparations to them or to their parents if the seduction resulted in the birth of a child. A paternity suit almost always included a request for money to help provide for the child, as well as reparation for the damage the man had done to the woman's honor by seducing her. However, bringing a paternity suit was not a simple procedure.[18] A woman could act in her own name for damages to herself and could act in the name of her baby to claim child support. She could bring a civil or penal suit. Furthermore, taking a man to court for seduction and charging him with paternity was a costly remedy, not accessible to all.

The success of paternity suits depended on male authorities' willingness to take a woman's word. Eighteenth-century legal scholars argued that during the pains of childbirth, as in torture, a woman would reveal the truth. Furthermore, they contended, if she feared dying in childbirth, she would not want to die with a lie on her lips. "Creditur virgini parturienti": a young woman giving birth had to be believed. Furthermore, jurists and magistrates argued that both mothers and fathers had responsibility for nourishing their children, even those born of illicit unions.[19] "Qui fait l'enfant doit le nourrir" (He who makes the child must feed it), they held; to save the child, one must therefore find its father. With variation by locality, some notables who heard these declarations were inclined to believe the woman and condemn the putative father to pay, especially early in the eighteenth century. In other areas, increasingly toward the end of that century, notables would not take the women's word without additional evidence. Authorities worried that false declarations and abuses might arise from believing a woman; they averred that women did not always tell the truth and would even lie under oath during childbirth. Nevertheless, Fournel maintained that it was in the public interest to assign paternity to a man who would then contribute to the child's basic needs. But, he insisted, this was only to provide for material sustenance, not to give an extranuptial child a father. When a woman had sexual relations with several men, the biological father was in doubt. Yet one of them was the father, and the child needed support. Fournel therefore enjoined magistrates to search for the father from among those who were known to have lain with the mother, and to charge him with paying child support.[20]

A woman's moral virtue and elevated standing in the hierarchy of feminine honor were major criteria for the magistrates' confidence in a woman's word. Even if local officials believed witnesses who reported a mother crying out the father's name while under oath during the pains of childbirth, they still required other testimonial proof. Finding that proof was difficult in intimate matters. If a woman could show that the seduction had been aggravated by fraud, violence, abuse of authority, or kidnapping, and if she were young and innocent, she had a better chance of winning her paternity suit. Although widows and older women stood little chance, because they were supposedly sexually experienced and lacked innocence, age was not a barrier if the man were older and more experienced than the woman. A 42-year-old single mother, Chaubert de Beaugency, filed a paternity suit against Gourdineau, a doctor, aged 52. In March 1776, the magistrate condemned him to pay for the rearing of the child and 2,000 livres in dommages-intérêts to Chaubert. In effect, the magistrate believed that the pregnancy had come about after a marriage promise, and that she had had every reason to expect that the marriage would take place.[21]

Having a valid marriage promise was usually necessary evidence for the success of a woman's paternity suit. This emphasis on a marriage promise derived from ecclesiastical attitudes that condoned sexual relations after an engagement, but at the same time stipulated that the man had to keep his part of the bargain and marry the woman.[22] A woman might insist that she consented to sexual relations only after this promise, but magistrates preferred the written word from the putative father in which he acknowledged paternity or promised marriage. Such written evidence that would seal his fate was rarely produced. Magistrates also accepted conjectural evidence in which a mother presented witnesses who testified to her habitual intimacy with the alleged father. These witnesses could be friends, relatives, or neighbors—part of her all-important community connections. Witnesses testified about how often the couple had been together, whether they had seen another man with her, and if her sexual conduct was beyond reproach. Rumor and neighborhood gossip was admissible evidence in court. Some courts looked for proof in physical resemblances between the putative father and the child. If a domestic servant sought reparations for a pregnancy and child, magistrates usually assumed that her master or his son was responsible.[23]

It was up to the putative father to prove that the child was not his, which he usually did by alleging that the woman had engaged in "bad conduct" or "illicit commerce" with other men. The language was harsh. Using tropes associated with accusations of prostitution, a man would allege that the woman was dirty, stayed out all night, dressed indecently, talked to soldiers, and routinely became drunk. In referring to a woman in these terms, the man implied that he would never promise marriage to such a person. Sometimes, a man accused a woman of bringing paternity charges only to get his money and good name for the child, saying it was physically impossible for him to have been the "author of the pregnancy" because he had been nowhere near her during the possible time of conception. Proving these allegations was another matter. Even when testimony established that a woman had had sexual relations with several men, if there was sufficient proof that she had had sexual relations with the man she brought to court, her bad conduct was not always sufficient to free him from child support; it only freed him from paying damages.[24] Local magistrates needed to reconcile the custom of taking the mother's word with the argument that women abused their confidence, producing scandals, lies, and blackmail.

If the magistrate decided that a mother had sufficient and valid proof, he could condemn the father to pay the cost of childbirth and provide for the child's sustenance—sometimes up to the child's legal adulthood. The judge might also charge the father to provide funds to raise the child in the Catholic religion and to give the child a trade or a dowry, according to his means and the mother's position. But the child had no inheritance rights from the father's family, and neither the mother nor child could legally try to claim them. Aside from paying, the man had no fatherly role in raising the child, nor was he obliged to marry the mother. If the father could not provide for his offspring, then the mother was expected to rear the child by herself or with help from her family. Magistrates also declared that some women did not have a valid paternity suit because of their immorality, their willing compliance in the seduction, or the lack of sufficient evidence pointing to the putative fathers. Magistrates rarely focused on the child's rights, subsuming them under the morality of the mother; hostility toward her redounded on the child.

Courtroom testimonies were as gendered as *déclarations de grossesse* and other public discourses. Women constructed sexual narratives in the courtroom to maintain their honor in front of the magistrates and for their friends and relatives. They formulated tales of passivity and victimization, unlike male stories that featured the language of liberty. Men were free to seduce and abandon women. When women went to court for child support or reparations, they would not admit to consensual relations based on love or passion; rather, they insisted that they had been seduced after a promise of marriage. Women had to prove good conduct and victimization—or at least that they were less guilty than their seducers. Men would claim that the woman had consented, which she denied, or else confessed that she had only given in after he promised marriage. In one typical case, a woman attested that she had met a man who declared that he had suddenly "fallen" for her. He had then "obtained her favors" with forceful caresses and a promise of marriage. When she announced that she was pregnant, he left, telling her that he was going to obtain parental consent to marry her. He never returned.[25] It is also quite likely that women freely consented to sexual relationships outside of marriage, and also "fell" for a man, but they rarely admitted this. Such an admission would subject them to questions about their virtue.

Women such as prostitutes, actresses, and barmaids could not expect to win reparations as a result of seduction. Magistrates would not accept a woman's argument that she had had a legal marriage promise if they suspected her morality or if there was a suggestion that she had had sexual relations with several men. Judges and jurists maintained that she was not an "honest girl," and no man would promise marriage to an immoral woman. Judicial attitudes rested on the assumption that men's motives in marriage were to wed a sexually pure woman to protect the male lineage and his status. Servants in cabarets and hotels also suffered a low status and association with prostitution. If one of them brought a paternity suit, it would be limited to charging the man with the cost of rearing the child.[26] This judicial attitude implies not only that working-class women, such as servants and barmaids, might be expected to have loose morals, but also that a man of status and property could freely sexually exploit them without resorting to a false marriage promise.

Court procedures allowed considerable power to the magistrates. When a woman first presented her case, the judge ordered an inquiry to establish the reasonableness of her accusations and to see if there was sufficient evidence to proceed. If the inquiry warranted, he issued a decree against the alleged seducer, who was often arrested. Then there was another inquiry, with depositions, interrogations, and testimony under oath from a variety of witnesses on behalf of the woman and man. If magistrates demanded written evidence, it is improbable that women received reparations, since not many men would have admitted their seduction or paternity in writing. Some magistrates emphasized the importance of public oral testimony, such as the women naming the father under oath or in childbirth pains, or if a promise of marriage had been made before witnesses. Finally, after deliberating in camera, the judges rendered the sentence. The judicial issue involved a man's duty to provide for the mother and child and to redress the wrong he had done; judges did not declare him the father, with all that fatherhood entailed in terms of responsibility and property transmission.

Toward the end of the eighteenth century, seduced and abandoned women no longer had broad social support; they increasingly became victims of social reprobation. Their word was no longer sufficient or necessary proof of men's paternity and increasingly had to be supported by other proof; the idea that a parturient woman must be believed had lapsed. With some regional variation, both the law and the judges' opinions were hardening, trusting less in the mother's word and further restricting conditions of proof.[27] Reasons for the change remain speculative. The *déclarations de grossesse* and the maxim "Creditur virgini parturienti" coincided with the idea that if the mother named the father, he would be financially responsible for the child, thus removing that burden from the community or local nobility. With the intensification of capitalistic practices and movement to the cities, it is possible that local notables no longer feared a drain on their revenues, and therefore had no reason to believe the women. Extracting confessions under torture, long associated with religious conflicts, may also have appeared anachronistic in a society that prided itself on being more secular, tolerant, rational, and enlightened. Reason, however, was gendered male; it guided men, not women, and therefore men considered it unreasonable to take women's word. Furthermore, the notion that women's words and activities posed dangers to male authority became part of a new political philosophy, with the corollary that women's public confessions would disturb the stability of the body politic. As the bourgeois propertied brotherhood rose to public power during the Revolution, and as men sought to define themselves through their public voices, they relegated women's voices to the private realm, not to be heard in public—even in declarations during childbirth. Moreover, in men's increasing desire to control women's fidelity and assure their families' lineages, they feared that women might soil their own and their families' virtue by their words. The view of women as "violators of family property, as well as sexual transgressors" arose even before the 1794

Thermidorian reaction. "Creditur virgini parturienti" might have been discredited as a principle, but judges and other public authorities had never unquestionably accepted a woman's word even earlier in the century, and women continued to name the fathers.[28]

To gain some compensation from the man, either for the child or for herself, a mother increasingly had to show financial need and an inability to provide for the infant on her own, thereby threatening her community with an added financial responsibility. She was judged less harshly when the paternity charges came not from her but from the family and community, who would likely bear the costs of raising the child. In a form of gift exchange, a woman and her family could form a veritable parade to the putative father whom she had named under oath, presenting him with the gift of the baby and welcoming him to the baptism ceremony. He, in turn, could refuse the gift of the baby but was expected to provide a gift in return in the form of financial help in rearing the child. His refusal to participate in this exchange could lead to tension and conflict with the woman's community. In practice, the number of paternity suits, never very large, declined. In Cambrai, in the north of France, the number of women who lost their cases doubled from 1760s to 1780s.[29]

As a young lawyer, Maximilien Robespierre pled the cases of two unwed mothers who filed paternity suits in his hometown of Arras in 1782 and 1785. In the spirit of the time, Robespierre argued that "bastards" should have a right to support from their fathers, but that it would be mistaken to count on the laws to compel an egotistical man to do his duty. One should appeal instead to a man's honor and the force of public opinion to make him support the child of the unfortunate woman whom he abandoned without pity. Robespierre opposed *déclarations de grossesse*, contending that to "force a girl to declare her pregnancy before a magistrate is to force her to publicize her shame; it is an outrage to modesty and to laws of nature." It would be better, Robespierre argued, if young women approached someone of their own sex, a close friend or relative, to tell them their secret and have them help raise the child. In 1786, he favored a law that would require the father to provide monthly child support, and that if the father refused, the courts should fine him in proportion to his circumstances. To Robespierre, it was a matter of honor, justice, and humanity for a father to do his duty and help nourish the child he had helped create. This would help prevent infanticide and child abandonment.[30]

In legal procedures, private sexual and family matters came before the public, and public authorities, such as magistrates, searched for proof of the most intimate relations. Canonical and Old Regime culture that endowed the husband/father with power over his wife and children remained the overarching principle. This was not a public invasion of family privacy brought without the families' consent. Rather, individuals and the family exercised the liberty of bringing their most intimate matters before judges. Families made their private lives public when the birth of an illegitimate child had already shamed their daughters. Going to court and blaming the male seducer was the means to redeem their honor and reputation, and more than coincidentally receive financial assistance for rearing the child.

No suits for damages or paternity were possible if the child was the product of an adulterous relationship.[31] Adultery for men was accepted, but it was a crime for women, demonstrating glaring inequalities in private lives. A husband, as head of the family, dominated his so-called weaker wife in law and social practice. He had the right to "correct" his wife if she committed adultery; he could confine her to a convent for two years (upon the agreement of the family council), and then he had the option of taking her back. If he chose not to, she could remain in a convent for the rest of her life—shaven, veiled, and dead to the world. Her property would be divided among her children, her parents, and the convent. These practices were intended to protect the man's paternal authority, his property, and his bloodline by eliminating any possibility of his wife introducing a child that was not his into his family. Only with the law of 20–25 September 1792 on civil marriages, which attempted to achieve some equality between husband and wife, did a husband lose the right to send his allegedly adulterous wife to a convent and confiscate her property. Although a man could commit adultery with impunity, if his adultery was accompanied by abuse of his wife and a scandal, it could lead to a marital separation.[32] Yet adultery involved shame as well as male property rights. To some extent, a man valued his property rights more than the dishonor he would suffer by publicly acknowledging his wife's adultery. Quite likely, however, her adultery had already dishonored him because it had become public knowledge. He had to take action to repossess his honor, much in the same way a seduced woman brought her private life to the public courts to salvage her honor by blaming the man.

Unwed mothers, and children whom an adulterous man had fathered, suffered materially and legally. These children could neither assume the adulterer's name nor partake of his property or family inheritance. Their doing so, lawyers argued, would result in a breakdown of the family. This fear of the adulteration of a family's estate became a major obstacle to permitting paternity searches from the end of the eighteenth century through the nineteenth. Children of adulterous women posed problems to society when they entered the family of a man who was not biologically their father and contaminated his bloodline. A husband could renounce paternity if he could prove his wife's adultery. Children of an adulterous relationship suffered more than children born to two parents not married to each other or to anyone else. Although canon law did not recognize the difference, Roman law did, referring to those born of adultery as "spurious." Those born of sexual relations between consenting adults who were not adulterers were "natural children," who had natural rights according to natural law.

Natural children were unequal to legitimate children in inheritance and social status, but they were not always pariahs. Some legal scholars in the eighteenth century invoked theories of natural law in which legitimate children born within marriage were indistinguishable from natural children. Natural children had a right to demand sustenance from either or both parents until their majority, but they could not automatically inherit, although fathers could recognize their illegitimate children and choose to bequeath something to them. During the Old Regime, grandfathers and other family members may even have provided something to illegitimate children of legitimate sons.[33] Yet a continual tension persisted between a desire to provide for the natural child and the urge to preserve the family blood lineage.

Revolutionary Changes in Paternity and the Family

From the early days of the Revolution to the framing of the Civil Code, questions about the nature of the family, the rights of man, the rights of children, natural rights, and paternity rights were enormously complex, as legislators tried to reshape and stabilize the family, separate the needs of the child from the rights of the father, define the father's role under the law and moral code, and reconfigure power relations. Intense legislative debates on issues of paternity and the rights of the natural child led to the abolition of paternity searches before the time the Civil Code was finalized in 1804. Although legislators sought to protect the natural child, they were unwilling to permit paternity searches; however, they approved of a father voluntarily and freely legally recognizing his out-of-wedlock child.[34] They did not want the rights of the natural child to impinge on those of the father. Reformers, all men, jettisoned their belief in the equality of all children when it came up against their stronger sentiment for men's authority and their freedom to engage freely in sex outside of marriage. Designs for the Civil Code evolved in two stages, from 1789 to 1794 and from 1795 to 1804, as legislators sought basic principles for their new regimes. In breaking with the past, many looked to some of the principles of natural law, but modified their interpretations of it to suit their social and political interests.

In the first period of debate, roughly from 1789 to 1794, key legislators interested in issues of children, the family and paternity, most notably Jean-Jacques-Régis de Cambacérès, Théophile Berlier, and Charles-François Oudot, were influenced by the school of natural law derived from ideas of figures such as Hugo Grotius, Samuel Pufendorf, and John Locke in the seventeenth century, which gained general diffusion as the moral philosophy of the Enlightenment at the end of the eighteenth. Locke envisioned man and his property as closely interrelated; property was his "Life, Liberty and Estate."[35] Revolutionary legislators invoked the philosophy of natural law as their moral standard and as a body of principles transcending divine law and the conventional laws that the authorities of the ancien régime had imposed. In these early years of the Revolution, they drew on the concept of the natural rights of all individuals, including all children.[36] In an attempt to build a new regime of equality and liberty, in part by destroying the inequalities and privileges of the old, legislators used natural law as a basis for declaring that all children were naturally born equal and entitled to equal natural rights. Nature did not differentiate between children born within or outside of wedlock.[37] Nor did nature differentiate between natural children born of single parents and those who resulted from adultery. To emphasize their point, these legislators thought to abolish the word "bastard" (*bâtard*) and substitute "natural child" (*enfant naturel*), or "child born outside of marriage," thinking that language change would induce cultural change.

Relying on sometimes vague and conflicting concepts of natural law proved to be difficult in the design of civil codes pertaining to paternity and progeny, especially when revolutionaries attacked paternal authority over adult sons but also wanted to preserve the legal family based on marriage. Legislators postulated a difference between the laws of nature and the laws of civil society. All children might be equal, but the family was a natural unit that preceded civil society, and the aim of civil society was to preserve the family. By those same laws of nature, there was no such being as a child without parents, and Cambacérès argued that a natural child should have a family in conformity with natural law. Although legislators such as Cambacérès, Berlier, and Oudot revered the institution of legal marriage, they did not vehemently condemn free unions, and Oudot established the notion of private marriage, which encompassed concubinage, or nonmarital cohabitation.

Internal contradictions beset the arguments of these theorists, which changed during the course of the Revolution, especially after 1793. As adherents of one aspect of natural law, they stated that natural children and children born within a legal marriage had equal rights, but they also wanted to protect legal marriage. They borrowed from Montesquieu in stating that while natural law requires that fathers feed their children, it does not oblige them to make those children their heirs. Only civil and political laws, not natural law, oblige fathers to give the right of inheritance to their children. Nevertheless, the natural child had always legally belonged to the mother and could inherit from her and her family, since the child's relationship with the mother began in the womb. Legislators exacerbated the tension between the rights of the natural child and those of the legal family as they passionately debated the rights of the natural child versus those of the family, even the future family of an unmarried father, assuming that he would marry and have children. Faced with this tension, legislators attempted the difficult task of separating the rights of the natural child from those of the family and of the father. This distinction created legal ambiguity that would plague society for at least two centuries.

From 1789 to 1794, the issue of whether to give legitimate and natural children equal rights was the subject of debates, especially in 1791. Article 1 of the Declaration of the Rights of Man stipulated that all men are born free and equal in rights. Although some revolutionaries averred that this included natural children, others contended this article did not include natural children unrecognized by their fathers. In the 1791 Assembly, Isaac-René-Guy Le Chapelier proposed that a child born of concubinage be able to inherit from the father. However, other Assembly members challenged this position on the question of proof; "the child may be able to prove that he is the son of a given woman; but he will not perhaps be able to prove so easily that he is the son of a given man," one argued. "Gentlemen, this would mean the overthrow of our social foundations."[38] In September 1791, a decree designed to protect unmarried women from unfounded accusations of infanticide, and implicitly to prevent a mother from trying to prove that her child was the offspring a particular man, made *déclarations de grossesse* less compelling and paternity searches more difficult, although women continued both—to the dismay of some.[39] Conflicting attitudes toward increasingly vigorous concepts of liberty for young unmarried men and a decreasing willingness to believe the woman's word sparked further debates on paternity.

Revolutionary rhetoric and the influence of women revolutionaries prior to 1794 gave a temporary but resounding voice to the idea that the rights of women should parallel the rights of man. In enumerating women's rights in 1791, Olympe de Gouges (Marie Gouze, 1748–1793) argued that the free communication of ideas is one of the "most precious of women's rights since this liberty assures the recognition of children by their fathers." She declared that each citizeness (*citoyenne*) must therefore speak freely, saying, " 'I am the mother of a child who is yours,' without any barbaric prejudice that would force her to conceal the truth, except if she were to abuse this liberty in cases determined by law." Women were not to lie about the paternity of their children. Free communication constituted a social contract between men and women, giving credence to women's word. De Gouges argued that all illegitimate children should have the right to a stipend for food and necessities, but those whom their parents had acknowledged should also have the right to inherit. As she said in the postscript to her 1791 *Déclaration des droits de la femme et de la citoyenne* (Declaration of the Rights of Woman and Citizen), "A married woman can give bastards to her husband with impunity, as well as a fortune that does not belong to them"; however, what de Gouges calls "our ancient and inhuman laws" refuse a married man's bastards the right to his name and property. She continued, "We must recognize that our property belongs directly to our children, no matter which side of the bed they were born on, and that all without distinction have the right to bear the name of their fathers and mothers who have acknowledged them."[40] The key phrase here, one that aligns de Gouges with many male revolutionaries, is "who have acknowledged them." To protect women, de Gouges also wanted a law that would advantage widows and young women deceived by false promises of marriage. This would hold a fickle man to his engagement, or else force him to pay an indemnity to the woman in proportion to his wealth. She also wanted the law to be "stern against women who had the audacity to appeal to this law that they themselves had transgressed by their loose living, if there were proof of that misconduct." The guillotine silenced de Gouges on 13 brumaire year II (3 November 1793), but not the impact of her voice.

From 1791 to 1804, Jean-Jacques Cambacérès's voice was the loudest in preparing legislation regulating the family, but he shifted his position over the years according to the political climate. His ideas reveal the *mentalité* of the Revolution regarding paternity and the family. In 1792, he argued for the principles of natural law against those who maintained that paternity was established only by marriage.[41] To Cambacérès, a child, although born weak and powerless, still had rights; he belonged to those who had created him and needed family support from a father and mother.[42] The law of nature, Cambacérès argued, established paternity for children born outside of marriage as well as within it, as long as the children were born of "free persons" and not of prostitution or of an adulterous or incestuous relationship. Children of these corrupt relationships should only be able to claim their "rights of alimentation."[43] However, by 1793, even Cambacérès and his colleagues who appealed to natural law in proclaiming the equality of all children saw nothing "natural" about inheritance rights or the "right" of a child to paternity, because that would interfere with a father's liberty and pursuit of property. They believed that recherche de paternité was odious, contrary to natural law, and should be abolished. The child born outside of marriage had the right to a mother, and the mother had a responsibility for the child. Unless the father acknowledged paternity, however, he should not be made responsible for that child.

In principle, a man's liberty and his right of inheritance were separate from the child's natural right to nourishment and support. This 1793 viewpoint contradicted earlier statements that children belonged to those who had created them. Legislators now maintained that it was difficult to know the identity of both partners in that creation, because an "impenetrable veil" of secrecy covers conception. Childbirth was different from conception; one knew who the mother was.[44] Cambacérès and others contended that to force a father to accept a natural child or to recognize and rear a child that he had denied would be inconsistent with individual liberty. In designing civil laws in 1793, Cambacérès and his cohort downplayed natural law and held sacred the rights of liberty and property. Class, however, was critical. Cambacérès contended it was not fair to refuse the paternity claims of a "well-born woman who might have had a weakness."[45]

The law of 12 brumaire year II (2 November 1793) was an attempt to balance the rights of men to individual liberty with the natural rights of children, and also to protect marriage and the family. It allowed recherche de paternité if a father voluntarily recognized his child, but disallowed it for natural children whose father failed to recognize them legally, disadvantaging natural children and their mothers more than supporting them. Embodying Cambacérès's ideas of that year, it did not contest the principle of equality of children. "In a government based on liberty, individuals should not be the victims of the fault of their fathers," Cambacérès insisted. "What crime has a child committed [to be denied the rights of paternity and inheritance]?"[46] Only if the father had freely and voluntarily legally acknowledged the child as his, and the mother confirmed his paternity, did this law give the natural child the rights of a legitimate child. The law allowed *recognized* natural children the right to partake of a full equal share of their fathers' inheritance, but limited children of adultery to one-third of the amount legitimate children received. It excluded natural children born of prostitution or debauchery, demonstrating that not all children were born equal. An unmarried father could acknowledge paternity by public or private written records, providing continuous childcare that established bonds of affection, or furnishing evidence of long-term cohabitation with the mother.[47] Other legislators, such as Berlier, demonstrated more compassion for natural children, referring to them as "innocent victims of their parents' offenses." Even Berlier did not, however, support paternity searches, unless the father had voluntarily recognized his child, demanding "what bonds can ever be established between a child who enters a family only through the wretched auspices of a court case and the man who will be his father only because a tribunal has said so?"[48] The 12 brumaire law deprived natural children *unrecognized* by their fathers of the right of inheritance and even the right to child support in the form of food. Although the deputies intended the law to deprive a mother of her right to obtain the costs of childbirth or reparations from the father, that intent was only implicit and was worked out in practice through the courts. Thus, the law granted some rights to recognized natural children, but took away others, namely, the right of the unrecognized to file paternity suits.[49] Supporters of the law declared that it avoided scandals being created by women who lied, and that it was thus in the interests of morality and the tranquility of families. They did not mention how they expected single mothers to support themselves and their children, but a previous decree of the same year established foundling homes to permit these mothers to abandon their children to the state, which then assumed a type of paternal authority. This law did not stop some women from attempting to use the courts to obtain child support from putative fathers, however, and although the Civil Code superseded this notoriously vague law, it had repercussions for over a century.[50]

    The Revolution emphasized the voluntary nature of contractual bonds, which the 12 brumaire law supported by its protection of men's voluntary recognition of their children, and their sexual liberty outside of marriage. A married man was forbidden to recognize his extranuptial children, and children of his adultery were excluded from equal rights of inheritance. Jurists were far less likely to take a mother's word than they were to argue that accepting a mother's word would result in scandals, lies, and extortion. Proof of paternity was still an issue; however, now it had to come from the father, not the mother. Changing the nature of proof from belief in the mother's word to requiring the father's admission of paternity took basic rights away from the mother and gave them to the father. Nevertheless, women took matters into their own hands, battling it out before magistrates, just as they had been doing for decades.

Opposition to the law of 12 brumaire year II came from some who may not have understood it, believing that it gave all natural children the same rights as legitimate children. A petition to the National Convention demonstrates the intensity of emotion against recherche de paternité and the prospect that natural children might be able to inherit from their fathers. The signatories complained that they would be ruined if children born outside of marriage could inherit. They perpetuated the myth that poor women and their children would make claims on propertied men and their families. This petition referred to numerous families having been "plunged into pain and anxiety" as a result of this law and called for its abolition or modification. As a result of this law, it asserted, an enormous number of heirs—direct and collateral—who had given everything for the Revolution to "combat the tyrants" would, upon returning from defending their country, see their property bestowed on outsiders. Referring to laws of nature, the petitioners argued, "in the natural order a father owes nothing to his natural son." Civil law, not natural law, existed to regulate and distribute property rights, and the way to do this was through marriage. Therefore, "marriages must be honored and protected because they are incontestably the foundation of civil society and public morality." Petitioners maintained that to admit natural children to an inheritance from their fathers would destroy the institutions of marriage and the family and lead legitimate families into indigence because of the excessive claims of natural children. Families should have the right to maintain their justly and legally acquired property.[51]

Man's sexual freedom loomed more important to the signatories than the rights of unwed mothers and natural children. "Man naturally tends toward sexual license," the petition stated, but men are obliged to live with their wives and to raise their children, and wives are obliged to submit to their husbands. "Many husbands forget their sacred duties, give in to their passions and dissipate their fortunes, leaving their legitimate children to the horrors of destitution," the petitioners continued. If a man were not yet married, his "impetuous passions" would lead him to have a mistress and even legally to acknowledge the child resulting from his "shameful sexual pleasure." Then, "several years later, that child of a cook, comes to claim an inheritance from a rich man. In essence, nothing is certain, nothing is confident in the world of men. . . . Thick clouds cover births: [with this law] the ties of blood, the sacred relationships that form the base of society would be called into doubt or abolished. There are too many people who give in to passion." Therefore, the petitioners argued, "do not admit natural children to family inheritance." The signatories allowed only food and sustenance to natural children. To allow them to inherit would wreck the civil order and marriage and legitimate the excesses of "libertinage." In conclusion, the petitioners avowed that mothers and their illegitimate children were "driving legitimate families to tears, hopelessness, chagrin, and especially destitution."[52] They ignored the point that the mothers and their extranuptial children were the ones in misery. Neither the Convention nor the petitioners were interested in the rights of the unwed mother. Natural children and their mothers were marginalized from the legal family and hence from society, since the legal family formed the basis of society.

The Thermidorian backlash from 1794 to 1804 against the Convention of 1793 further defined the individual in relation to the family and reinterpreted natural law. Legislative proposals during that decade, ending with the Civil Code, placed the rights of the legally married family and especially the inviolability of the individual rights of the father, including his inalienable right to liberty and property, ahead of the rights of natural children. Some legislators interpreted Rousseau to argue that the purpose of civil law was to preserve the family, which had already existed in nature. Those who followed this version of Rousseau envisioned a natural law reconfigured by justice and reason, whereby man passed from a state of nature to a civil society. To them, the social contract, the foundation of civil society, was based on family, lineage, and paternal authority in order to preserve property.[53] Rousseau was inconsistent about this, but some of his followers derived their argument from his idea that the social contract served to bring property into the service of the family, which had existed in the state of nature. As a corollary, the natural rights of an illegitimate child became subsumed under the natural rights of the legal patriarchal family and its property. When natural law conflicted with civil law that emphasized liberty and property, natural law lost; family property and the individual rights of man triumphed. Women were critical in transmitting lineage and inheritance, and it was incumbent on them to help protect the property of the patriarchal family from outsiders, including illegitimate children.

Cambacérès shifted his views in 1794, emphasizing civil law and civil rights. In September of that year, placing the sanctity of legal families above the rights of natural children, he argued: "All civil rights can be reduced to the rights of liberty, of property, and the right to make contracts." It was thus necessary to affirm relationships between fathers and sons for the sake of liberty and the transmission of property. Laws should not bring disorder into the families by introducing outsiders. Although Cambacérès did not ignore natural law, he asserted: "Nature produces everything; but it is up to men to produce men." He referred to marriage as "the primitive law of nature," or "nature in action," but said that "personal liberty is the first order of nature and it must be respected." To reconcile the natural law of personal liberty with the natural law of marriage, he favored divorce, and to maintain a man's liberty in his relationships, he rejected paternity searches.[54] Berlier, who did not follow Cambacérès's change of sentiment, countered that he was not proposing to introduce the illegitimate child into the family, only to provide that child with some financial support for sustenance (a *créance alimentaire*). Cambacérès struggled with the conflicting notions that all children are equal and entitled to a family but that "the tranquility and perpetuity of families" must also be maintained. He finally declared that illegitimate children did not have exactly the same rights as legitimate children. Arguing counter to his position of 1792, he now maintained that only marriage fixes paternity.[55] Following the Roman law principle "Pater is est quem nuptiae demonstrant," the Convention, and Cambacérès, affirmed in May 1794 that "the mother's husband is the father of the child." The only exception that Cambacérès allowed was for children born before the seventh month of marriage, or more than ten months after dissolution of a marriage, or after the husband had departed for war. In those cases, the child did not necessarily belong to the mother's husband, who could disavow paternity.[56]

Legislators argued that under certain circumstances, the law should permit other proof of paternity, because unmarried women had children, and someone had to father them. Yet the fear that a spurious or natural child would interfere with the legal family of a married man obsessed legislators, who failed to focus on the unmarried father. This fear led them to pass a decree on 19 frimaire year III (9 December 1794) explicitly abolishing paternity searches. Although this decree did not take effect until the Civil Code of 1804, the Legislative Committee informed local magistrates that they should not consider paternity suits by unwed mothers. When the law forbade paternity searches, women went to court for dommages-intérêts for seduction.

In 1796, as Cambacérès was drafting measures of the Civil Code relating to the family, he maintained that "the best legislation is that which favors the general interest of society and the progress of public morality. It is not important if some individuals are deprived of their rights to a family and are raised at the expense of the state if, by this sacrifice, libertinage is proscribed, domestic tranquility is assured, and legitimate unions are encouraged." Opting for the rights of fathers over those of children, Cambacérès saw a need to outlaw paternity searches in order to maintain the social order of property and inheritance. Without paternity searches, he added, "women would become more reserved, and the men would become more attentive and less deceitful when they see that promises made by emotion are no longer a game. [Men] would be held to paternal duties only toward those children whom they will have acknowledged as the fruit of an engagement contracted under the double guarantee of honor and love."[57] The key phrase, as in the law of 12 brumaire year II, is "those children whom they will have acknowledged." Cambacérès had confidence that man was by nature honorable. He believed that an unmarried man who had contributed to the creation of a child would obey his basic natural sensitivities and fulfill his paternal duties. With this assumption, Cambacérès could rationalize his objection to recherche de paternité, since the prohibition of paternity searches would only apply to adulterous men; Cambacérès wanted to preserve the families of those adulterers. The question of how the law and the courts could make the dishonorable behave honorably pervaded discussions throughout the nineteenth and twentieth centuries.

At the turn of the nineteenth century, civil law trumped natural law, at least as it pertained to children and the family. The aspects of natural law that civil law incorporated were Locke's ideas of individualism and protection of individual property. Legislators maintained that they were behaving morally in creating the laws. In 1792, morality had sided with natural law in declaring all children equal with equal rights. By 1798, legislators decided that such equality would create immorality; they thus created civil laws that preserved the legal family. Echoing the refrain that "Only marriage makes a father," they stated, " 'Paternity is Nature's secret, and Nature is silent; it is also the mother's secret, and the mother's evidence is interested, lack[ing] the innocence of candor.' Nature that once made all children equal at birth, now made them all fatherless by cloaking paternity in mystery... Nature makes any assumptions unjust and inaccurate."[58]

Despite these debates and decrees, women continued to seek material help from fathers through the courts, with judges throughout France often awarding in their favor. Getting a putative father to pay childbirth expenses and provide for the early basic needs of the infant is not the same as attributing paternity. Some civil suits that had begun before the Revolution were only resolved years later. In 1778, the fifteen-year-old Marie Levacher, daughter of a former inspector of roads and bridges, came to Paris from a small town in Franche-Comté. There she met a young law clerk, Jacques Dubois, who charmed her. She had a child by him, whom she baptized, but in this baptism, the godparents provided a fictitious name for the father. Jacques Dubois became a lawyer but never abandoned this child, oversaw his upbringing, and visited his son when he was sick. Then Dubois died. Levacher wanted to amend the baptism certificate to reflect the biological father so that her son would be entitled to some of his father's inheritance. Dubois's mother, however, had different ideas. She stated that she had only heard of this child after her son had died. She claimed that Levacher was an immoral young woman who had had a long list of lovers, from which she had chosen Dubois. Mme Dubois refused to recognize and accept a child whose paternity was so uncertain. Levacher produced letters from Dubois, written at the time of their sexual relations, which established their intimacy. Levacher also offered to have witnesses prove that Dubois had given the child uninterrupted care. The tribunal ordered an inquiry, a normal procedure, but the case was settled out of court in 1792 when Mme Dubois took it upon herself to provide for the boy. In another instance, in 1791, in Paris, a young girl of seventeen made a *déclaration de grossesse* against a prominent man, who admitted sexual relations with her. Based on what he considered sufficient evidence, the judge declared him the child's father and condemned him to pay child support and reparations to the mother. Furthermore, the declared father had to provide the child with a trade in proportion to his means and the disposition of the child. If he did not provide for the child directly, he had to pay the mother a sum of money for rearing the child until he was twenty-five. The putative father appealed the decision and lost.[59]

After 1793, some judges denied women paternity suits, but others still allowed child support or reparations to the mother, ignoring the 12 brumaire law. For example, when a young woman brought a claim against Mouchet, an architect, the tribunal rejected her demand for child support, saying that she had engaged in "bad conduct," and that it was therefore impossible to prove that Mouchet was the father. In cases involving married men, the courts usually refused reparations to the women, but some asked the putative fathers to pay child support, notwithstanding the law. In April 1794, Marie Bertrand brought a suit against Alexis Bigot, a dyer and cleaner of fabrics. The tribunal condemned Bigot to provide for rearing the child, but refused Bertrand reparations. The court claimed that she, her father, uncle, and family had known that Bigot was married, and that therefore she could not have hoped for a marriage promise from him. Finally, a leading Jacobin deputy to the Convention, François Chabot, was hit with a paternity suit from the nineteen-year-old Julie Conpry. He denied paternity of the child, but a tribunal of Paris on 6 February 1794 ordered him to pay Conpry for the costs of childbirth as well as damages (*dommages-intérêts*). As he was preparing to mount the scaffold in April 1794, at the same time as the Dantonists, he asked his parents to aid in the education of Conpry's son until the boy was fourteen. He also asked his parents to console his widow for his weaknesses during his life.[60]

If judges and the law were unwilling to allow a single mother to pursue the putative father of the child for support, a mother's alternatives were to commit infanticide, abandon the infant, or provide for the child themselves—with help from parents, relatives and friends. Giving the baby up for adoption was not usually an option, but it was a critical issue in debates about what constituted father and families.

Adoption

Lawmakers sought to protect both natural children and the legally established family, but these two aims often clashed, and debates raged over who constituted the family of a natural child. During times of war and revolution, arguments in favor of child adoption increased along with the number of homeless and orphaned children whose fathers had been killed in service to the nation. Natural and legitimate children may have been equal in the eyes of lawmakers who believed in natural law, but the case for adoption was easier insofar as there were also legitimate children without fathers. Like other aspects of family life, however, the issue was not a simple one. Adoption was inextricably involved with the overlapping material and emotional interests of families and the intense desire for the stability of families and the state.

In their fierce protection of the legally married family against intruders, many couples scorned adoption, even if they were infertile or all their biological children had died. Blood kinship and paternal authority dominated Old Regime family matters. The nobility and upper bourgeoisie used the concept of lineage to define their position in society and justify their families' positions at the apex of the political and economic hierarchy. They emphasized the importance of the purity of their bloodlines and did not want them tainted by allowing their property and name to pass to someone of a different, and presumably inferior, blood. Permitting adoption and recognizing natural children would challenge the natural order and dissipate family fortunes, preventing them from going to collateral heirs or to blood children who might be born later. Furthermore, fear of potential incest when the time came for adopted children of unknown parentage to marry deterred many. Some couples may have believed that adoption went against God's will that they should remain childless. The Church and jurists opposed to adoption feared that it would encourage concubinage and illegitimacy—both scourges to family and national stability.

Despite legal opposition, both related and unrelated children had been adopted among all social classes for centuries, although in a somewhat fluid fashion. Many adoptions were informal arrangements, although usually officially notarized. Some adoptions were associated with a marriage contract, permitting children of a widowed mother to inherit from the mother's new husband. These adoptive ties did not, however, take precedence over the rights of legitimate children, thereby preserving the sanctity of the biological family as well as ties with the birth parent. Adoptions were often a means to transmit inheritance. The most disparaged form was when a father adopted an illegitimate son to allow him to have a share of the inheritance, thus introducing an "intruder" into the legitimate family. For centuries, law and custom had labeled families formed by adoption as "fictive," considering them imaginary families, not real or even natural, and discouraged their formation.[61] Families with adoptees did not have the approval of canon law because of the perceived threat to the so-called legitimate family and emphasis on material inheritance. Customary and Roman law sanctioned some forms of adoption, but prohibited adopted children from inheriting at the same level as blood relatives. Popular practice did not always abide by the laws, however, because some childless couples chose to adopt, either from friends, neighbors, or relatives or from public charity hospitals and foundling homes.

In Lyon and Paris, for example, charity hospitals allowed individuals and foster parents to adopt children who had been abandoned there. Many of these adoptive parents were foster parents, mostly artisans or peasants, who had taken in an abandoned or orphaned infant from the charity hospital. Then, through love, attachment, the desire for an heir, or a need for labor they chose to make this parenting relationship official. As part of the adoption act, parents agreed to support the children and provide them with a trade or craft. Sometimes the adoption contract even designated them as heirs. In instances when the adopted child had known living relatives, they, and the child's family council, consisting of male members from the mother's and father's side, had to approve the adoption. In Paris, private individuals adopted orphans or children who had been abandoned near Notre-Dame or in the public hospital, the Hôtel-Dieu. The numbers of official adoptions were few. More frequently, domestic reconfigurations through adoption allowed for transactions between two sets of parents in a type of gift exchange in which the biological parents transferred their children to neighbors, friends, or relatives, for reasons either of kinship, god-parentage, emotion, or material interest. In other areas of France, a system of guardianship (*tutelle officieuse*) captured the essence of adoption, giving a guardian the right to administer the child's property and the duty to provide for the rearing, protection, and education of the orphan as if that child were the guardian's own.[62]

In 1786, responding to the needs of natural children even before the Revolution, Robespierre proposed some fundamental principles of adoption, which he saw as benefiting both abandoned children and society. However, in the interests of society, laws should limit the adopted person's rights to the inheritance of property from the adoptive parents, although the latter could voluntarily leave a considerable part of their fortune to the adoptee. To preserve family inheritance, only married couples without children should be permitted to adopt. Robespierre recommended that the children adopted be "bastards" of "good and happy disposition" raised in hospitals and foundling homes established by the government. They should be capable of honoring the families they joined. However, whenever possible, authorities should facilitate the return of an abandoned child to "the hands of those who have given him the light of day."[63] Unsurprisingly, others insisted that once a mother had abandoned her "right" of parenthood, she should not get the child back. Oddly, Robespierre was silent when the National Convention later debated adoption.

In 1793, deputies to the Convention, such as Michel Azema and Cambacérès, thought of the nation as the father of children whose biological fathers had died in the service of the Revolution, and they advocated national adoption of those orphans. All citizens are united as brothers, Azema suggested, so the nation (*patrie*) should adopt orphans and abandoned children. The Convention issued decrees of 4 July and 9 November 1793 declaring that abandoned children became children of the nation, raised and nourished by the Republic.[64] The Republic was represented as a female allegory, but the *patrie* was also the father of children who lacked one, giving the children metaphorically and symbolically a mother and father.[65] Lack of funding and a later change of heart made these decrees empty phrases.

These lawmakers and others also maintained that creating new families through adoption would regenerate the family and the nation, as well as advance the interests of the Revolution. Oudot referred to adoption as a "sacred duty ... for every childless citizen," declaring that it served primarily to save the children. If they were to become good citizens of the Republic, fatherless children needed consolation, education, and above all, protection. Although Oudot opposed paternity searches, insisting that paternity could not be proven, and that the mother should bear responsibility, he also contended that natural children whose fathers failed to acknowledge them would become "poor orphans whom the Republic would adopt and rear at its expense." Realizing that the state might protect the children, but could not actually rear them, Oudot advocated finding adoptive fathers for "the greatest number of orphans ... to protect and rear the children. ... Citizens who do not have children should regard adoption of a natural child as a natural duty." Adoption was not for purposes of inheritance, as it had been under the Old Regime, Oudot argued, but rather to provide proper love and protection of the child.[66] It was always a man's option, however, whether to accept paternity or to adopt. Paternity could not be forced upon a man, because it would limit his liberty. Oudot based his position permitting adoption on the premise that natural children had the same natural rights as those born of a legal union, and that illegitimate children should not be punished for the sins of their parents.

Azema, Berlier, Oudot, and Cambacérès attempted to set the conditions of adoption and proposed that any adult should be able to adopt one or more children. Adoption imitates nature, they argued, but it is also in the interest of social order. They stipulated that the adopting father should be at least fifteen years older than the child whom he adopted, and the mother, thirteen years older. They differed about whether those adopting could have either legitimate or natural children of their own, and whether women or single men could adopt. Cambacérès and Berlier advocated that both women and men who already had "children of their own blood" should be able to adopt, because it would be useful not only to the parents and the children, but also to society. All agreed that the child should be a young orphan or natural child before puberty, still needing protection and able to benefit from adoption. They did not deny adoption of older children or adults, but that necessitated the consent of the adoptee. Furthermore, if the child had living parents, they had to consent to the adoption. This would allow families to give a child up for adoption and permit interfamily adoptions.

Members of the Convention disagreed about whether the adoptee should have the same property and inheritance rights as legitimate children. Cambacérès was virtually alone in arguing that the adoptee should take the name of the father who adopted him and have the same rights as children of the father's own blood. Others advocated adoption of "unfortunate children" by consenting adult married couples only, but those children were not to have any inheritance rights. Advocates of adoption idealistically believed that it would minimize class differences and diminish the social hierarchy if the rich adopted the illegitimate, abandoned children of the poor and poor orphans. It would be for the good of the nation, of orphans, and also of childless couples. These adopted children would then be good siblings, sons, and citizens. Adoption would thus lead to greater equality of wealth for the greater good of society.[67] Azema and Cambacérès suggested reserving adoption primarily for children of poor families, in part to equalize family fortunes.

Those who opposed adoption complained that if adopted children were allowed to inherit, it would make them equal to legitimate children and would ruin the institutions of marriage, the family, and society. Furthermore, nothing would hinder an adulterous father from adopting a child of his adultery, who would then inherit his property. This attitude reflected their profound fear of disruption to legal marriage and the conjugal family.

In attempting to draft provisions of the Civil Code in 1793 and 1794, legislators strove to maintain the conjugal family's inviolability, which some feared adoption would destroy. Nevertheless, they also appealed to natural law, which allowed them to understand the creation of "fictive" families through adoption as a valid imitation of nature. Along with Azema and other deputies, Cambacérès stressed connections between adoption, strong conjugal families, and natural law, repeating, "adoption imitates nature. [It is] ... a living image of nature" and a "moral institution, a resource against sterility, a new nature that supplies what the first one fails to do. Rather than multiply the number of beings on earth, it multiplies families, augmenting relations by means of sentiment."[68] Supporters of adoption believed it would strengthen families, not weaken them, as critics asserted. For children under fifteen without fathers, Cambacérès proposed adoption, even by families who already had children, or by having the child's biological family appoint a guardian. Guardians or adopting parents would preferably be close relatives, approved by the family council. If the guardians or adopting couple were married, both husband and wife had to consent to the adoption. Above all, Cambacérès argued, children needed protection, a moral upbringing, and tenderness. They had certain natural rights, and one of these rights was to a family, or at least a mother and father to support them. Although parents who adopted could not reverse their decision, adoptees could renounce the adoption upon reaching their majority.

The critical issue remained that of inheritance. Cambacérès stipulated that an adopted child could not inherit from family members—grandparents or collateral relatives. Moreover, the adoptee could not inherit the same amount as the parents' biological children. If there were no biological children, the adoptee could still only have a portion of the inheritance.[69] Neither natural nor civil law permitted equality between adopted children and those born to a legally married couple. "Liberté, egalité, et fraternité" did not apply to all.

Debates on adoption were part of the larger discussion on paternity and families. They were an attempt to realize the revolutionary ideal of fraternity among all citizens, based on the belief that the bloodline could be rearranged and new familial bonds created. Yet a tension persisted between the natural rights of natural children and the civil rights of men to individual liberty and property. During 1793 and 1794, the Convention upheld natural law and viewed children as building blocks in the new nation. It decreed that all legitimate descendants had equal rights to inherit from their parents, abolishing primogeniture. Furthermore, it declared that natural children had the right to inherit from their parents provided the father recognized them. Finally, the government of the Convention adopted young children whose parents' property had been confiscated by the state.

All these measures attempted to come to terms with the vast numbers of natural and orphaned children and to fashion the nation on terms acceptable to men. As Suzanne Desan so insightfully argues, during the 1790s, the Revolution redefined the complex relationships between the family and the state.[70] A few years later, however, in a more conservative era (1799 to 1804), members of the Council of Five Hundred, the Council of State (Conseil d'État), and legislature (Corps législatif) reacted against the radical measures of 1793 when they deliberated the all-important issues of paternity and the family in designing the Civil Code.

Framing the Civil Code

The men who framed the 1804 Civil Code sought to guarantee the peace, integrity, and property of the conjugal family under the husband's authority, while also reconfiguring notions of liberty and equality.[71] By 1801, legislators emphasized that in all measures pertaining to paternity and progeny, they were creating laws in the public interest, and nothing interested them more than protecting men's rights and family property, especially from poor women who might try to insinuate their illegitimate children into the families of propertied men. To the legislators, rights to property and the protection of one's family were the fundamental rights on which all social institutions rested.[72] Espousing Adam Smith's notions of the centrality of material self-interest, the men who framed the Civil Code based family law on their own self-interest. Like Smith, however, they realized that there was a contradiction between their material self-interest and the interests of young children, especially those of natural children. Smith acknowledged that "in the natural state of things... the existence of the child, for some time after it comes into the world, depends altogether upon the care of the parent."[73] He does not explicitly include fathers of natural children, but implies that "he who creates a child must nourish it"—a phrase that advocates of paternal responsibility often repeated. Since all young children need their parents' care, the child has certain rights to sustenance. These rights, however, could interfere with a man's liberty. Legislators' romance with the rhetoric of liberty and equality did not usually extend to natural children or to their mothers. Yet, as legislators deliberated, a few recognized that orphans and natural children had material and emotional needs, some of which adoption might address, but paternity searches would not.[74] By 1800, the integrity of a man's property and the security of his own family had taken precedence over earlier humanitarian views toward orphans and natural children, especially those of poor women.

Debates on adoption and paternity involved consideration of nonmarital sexual relations, adultery, and the nature of marriage, as legislators sought to increase the number of marriages and the national population. It was not just a simple matter of allowing adoption of orphans and parentless children. Intense discussion revolved around whether to allow a single person to adopt and how to prevent a married man from adopting children born of his adultery. In 1801, First Consul Napoleon Bonaparte, who played an active role in framing the Civil Code that bears his name, advocated adoption only within families. He stated that marriage was for having children and that "adoption is only a fiction and a supplement to the effects of marriage. It should not be possible for a single person to adopt," because one should not have children without marriage. Some legislators feared that adoption would encourage concubinage, thereby diminishing the number of marriages. Proponents of adoption in 1801, as in 1793 and 1794, maintained that adoption would neither increase concubinage or the numbers of children outside of marriage nor reduce the number of marriages or promote depopulation. Marriages did not increase the population; to increase the birthrate, legislators quite presciently stated, there should be an increase in the means of subsistence. Jean-Étienne-Marie Portalis, one of the major authors of the Code, mentioned that only when the household was well organized by a married couple would the means to subsistence increase.[75]

To counter the earlier arguments that adoption would destroy the property and bloodlines of the legitimate family, Berlier now intoned that adoption should not depend just on the will of the man adopting; his parents and spouse must also consent. Instead of insisting that an adopting person be married, Berlier suggested that a person should be of an advanced age, implying that he would no longer sow wild oats. Others, such as Antoine-Claire Thibaudeau, argued that adoption, or "fictive paternity," was not a supplement to natural paternity. He stipulated that "legal paternity exists only in marriage.... [Adoption] should be a consolation to sterile marriages and not an encouragement to remain single and to the disorders that ordinarily follow." Cambacérès made light of these arguments: "The fear [that adoption would] impede marriages is a chimera. Marriage is enough in vogue because of its advantages." Cambacérès argued for a broad legal principle of adoption that would allow certain latitude in the application.[76] In 1801, proponents of adoption supported its dual role as a consolation to infertile couples and as a protection of orphans, appealing to the view of adoption as an "imitation of nature." Other members of the Committee of the Council of State feared the introduction of illegitimate children into the lineage of licit families and continued to oppose adoption as a threat to the sanctity of marriage and public morality.

In 1802, arguments shifted from parents' morality and marriage to the actual child and his relationship to his biological and adopting families. The legislator François-Denis Tronchet had always opposed adoption, arguing that it was "not necessary or even useful. It has no other effect than to flatter the vanity of those who wish to perpetuate their name, and the vanity [of seeking] to perpetuate one's name is tolerable only in the ancient system of the nobility. Although adoption has the advantage of allowing those who do not have children to enjoy having them, it is only a very imperfect imitation of nature. It disadvantages the father's blood-related heirs and is not even necessary for the children's happiness." He offered the following scenario: A couple do not have children; they find a child who pleases them and whom they adopt. Then one spouse dies and the other remarries. The new spouse does not want the adopted child, and the new couple have biological children. The discord that arises troubles the entire family. Adoption could only work if the adoptee and the adoptive parent remained free, Tronchet maintained. Otherwise, an adopted child was "a monstrous being," cut off from his natural family and not really belonging to his adoptive family because he was denied the right to inherit its property.[77]

Proponents of adoption, most notably Bonaparte himself at that time, argued against Tronchet, saying that it would not alter the moral customs of society, as Tronchet alleged; rather it would regularize practices that had already existed. Bonaparte favored adoption by childless married couples for the transmission of their name, property, and business. People had been doing this for years, he contemptuously remarked, and had never been accused of making the adoptee "a monstrous being in the social order." Moreover, adoption should not just present an adoptive father with an heir; "it should give him a son" within a family. He argued that if adoption did not include bonds of affection between father and son, it did not imitate nature and had no reason to exist. Bonaparte added that adoption would not only benefit the father by providing security in his old age but would also prepare fine, upstanding citizens for the state by supporting orphans and children born outside of marriage. However, if the entire family did not agree, and an adoption was without honor, it would be a gross injury. Adoption of those who had already reached their majority was bizarre, Bonaparte added, if the adopting parents had not raised the adoptee since early childhood. Speaking against Cambacérès's earlier position, Bonaparte opposed allowing a single person to adopt, because that would reduce the number of marriages and the population. He minimized the effects adoption would have on the other heirs.[78]

By 1803, Bonaparte had changed his attitude; he now opposed child adoption even by married couples. In an increasingly conservative French society, adoption became the mere transmission of name and inheritance between two consenting adults. This was the end of the revolutionary dream of an imitation of nature in fictive families that would benefit both the adopted child and adoptive parent; the dream reappeared in 1923. Official guardianship by kin and community, restricted to minors, was created to fulfill the needs of orphans.

Adoptions that had occurred between 1792 and 1804 remained valid. These usually involved fathers or mothers adopting their recognized natural children. Kin of the adopting fathers attacked these adoptions, claiming denial of their inheritance rights. Take, for example, Antoine Gentile's adoption of Jeanne-Antoinette, born in 1785 to an unmarried domestic servant, Jeanne Baron, who had declared her daughter's father as "unknown." After Jeanne Baron's death in 1800, her master, Gentile, recognized Jeanne-Antoinette as his illegitimate daughter. He had raised her in his own house and wanted her as his legal heir. In 1813, Gentile died, and two years later, Jeanne-Antoinette died, leaving her property to her children. Suddenly, in 1822, Gentile's nephews contested the adoption because it affected their inheritance. The appeals court of Paris refused to annul the adoption, as the nephews requested, because it was an authentic act signed between 1792 and 1804.[79] Redactors of the Code became obsessed with the idea that domestic servants such as Jeanne Baron might introduce their children into propertied men's inheritance line.

The Civil Code set the rules of adoption in the perceived public interest, to preserve the sanctity, stability, and well-being of legally married families and the maintenance of public order. According to the Code, the adoptee did not completely sever ties with the natal family and did not take the name of the adopting parent but merely added his surname to that one. In clear opposition to the 1793 principles that adoption should imitate nature and benefit orphans, the Code stipulated that there could be no adoption of minors. Moreover, when adopting an adult, the adopting parent must have provided for the adoptee for at least six years during that person's minority.[80] Adoption became a contract for the property transmission of a childless couple, and also to add comfort to the adopting parents in their old age. The adopting person had to be at least fifty years old and have no other children or legitimate descendants.[81] Lawmakers demonstrated their support for the legitimate family by refusing to permit children of poor women into it. Earlier proposals that envisioned the equality of children and advocated adoption of those who were orphaned or homeless were scrapped, and some of those children were left to languish. Legislators ignored orphaned or abandoned children in favor of fathers and their families until after World War I.

Adoption was only one facet of the Civil Code's definition of paternity and the family. As lawmakers sought to protect men's liberties and rights, they discriminated against women and children outside the conjugal family in forbidding paternity searches. Implicit, and often explicit, gender and class discrimination against poor women, treating their children as outsiders, marked a reversal from the revolutionary ideal of equality. Paternity searches proved more controversial than adoption, largely because they involved, not orphans per se, who were sometimes legitimate children, but children who were illegitimate and often the offspring of poor women. In a major attitudinal shift from 1793, in 1801, legislators declared that natural children were not to be treated as equal to legitimate children. The natural child became a "monstrous being," engendered by an immoral poor woman. Yet these "monstrous beings" were still children, who needed the care of the authors of their days.

In the social imaginary, the identity of the "author of the pregnancy" had undergone a shift. He was no longer necessarily an unmarried young rake who had seduced and abandoned a young girl; he might now well be a legally married, propertied man with legitimate children. This shift in perceptions of the fathers of illegitimate children led legislators to take what they deemed the appropriate measures to support the legally married father with his wife and property against the unwed mother, assumed to be of a lower class. Legislators feared that poor women might trick men of means into sexual relationships. Such a woman might shamelessly name a virtuous rich man in order to get money or some of his inheritance for her child, or seek to introduce her natural child into his distinguished family. Lawmakers also wanted to prevent adult natural children from arriving on the doorsteps of married putative fathers, which would diminish the latter's property, as well as that of their legitimate families. Yet the social imaginary also pitied young natural young children who needed nourishment and support. The responsibility for rearing them, legislators agreed, should belong to the mother, since her identity was clear. Consequently, they designed article 341 of the Code, which simply stated, "maternity searches are permitted. The child must prove that he is the mother's child."

The Code's redactors still paid lip service to natural law, but they now believed that it shrouded paternity in a veil of secrecy. To Antoine Bergier, for example, "Paternity is Nature's secret, and Nature is silent; it is also the mother's secret, and the mother's evidence ... lacks the innocence of candor."[82] Seeking to erect an orderly legal and social system, legislators declared that paternity searches would bring social discord by introducing a natural child into a legitimate family. Order in society, these men argued, was linked to marriage and legitimacy. In their ideal patriarchal marriage, each person would be in his and her proper place. Félix-Julien-Jean Bigot de Préameneu, among others, wanted to maintain the family blood ties uniting the conjugal family and protect men from attacks on their allegedly pure conduct by "impudent and calumnious women."[83] Propertied men such as he sought to avoid the supposed scandals of the Old Regime. They therefore no longer countenanced a woman's word because, they said, women would lie. "Creditur virgini" became an archaic Old Regime concept, symbolizing abuses of the past. These men paid no attention to the possibility that if a woman gave false testimony, it might not be from lack of scruples but from sheer distress. Rather than following the maxim that one should believe a parturient woman or the interpretation of natural law voiced by Cambacérès in 1792 that all children, including natural children, had a right to a family, the majority of men who framed the Civil Code (including Cambacérès, who had changed his opinion) appealed to an opposing law of nature. They declared that all children were fatherless at birth, and that the father was the person married to the child's mother. To maintain the social order, they sought to establish paternity beyond a doubt, which was done only by a man and woman living together in a legal marriage.[84]

Article 340 of the Civil Code forbidding recherche de paternité stated: "Paternity searches are forbidden. In cases of abduction, when the abduction coincides with the date of conception, interested parties may declare that the abductor is the father of the child." This article prohibited the mother from seeking paternal child support for children born out of wedlock, even in the case of a broken marital engagement or if the man had used force on her. It condoned the sexual exploitation of women while protecting male honor and agnatic inheritance lines.[85] To the Code's architects, the men had been the victims, not the women they seduced and abandoned. The Code did not officially abolish *déclarations de grossesse*; however, since the woman could not name the father to pin financial responsibility on him, those declarations fell into disuse—although they did not completely disappear.[86] Article 340 was a charter of liberties for men, giving them no incentive to behave honorably or responsibly. It made having illegitimate children women's moral failing. Framers of that article argued that if paternity searches were forbidden, women would be more reserved, cautious, and moral, knowing that they alone would be responsible for any resulting child. Article 340, in effect, left the single mother dependent on family, friends, or the state.[87] In 1811, a Napoleonic decree increased the role of the state in providing for children. It validated Cambacérès's 4 July 1793 decree that every child should have a family, and that natural children abandoned by their parents should become *enfants de la patrie*. The 1811 decree created public institutions for foundlings in major cities of France and made abandoned children wards of the state. The institutions sent these fatherless and familyless babies out to wet nurses in the countryside, thereby providing them with a state-supported foster family. However, approximately three-fourths of the babies died from malnutrition.

In drafting article 60 of the Code, which required the civil registration of all births, legislators debated whether a mother should be allowed to inscribe the putative father's name on the baby's birth certificate. The political philosopher Benjamin Constant (1767–1830), the author of the widely read romantic novel *Adolphe* and a founder of modern French liberalism, was one of the most outspoken of the many who said no. Constant acknowledged that fathers might help raise the children or pay reparations to the women they seduced—but only if they had recognized the child. Providing the father's name, Constant insisted, would harm the man and not help the mother, since a father named on the birth certificate would have no duties to help support the child or compensate the mother. It would just destroy his honor and integrity, and that of his legitimate wife and family, especially if the child of a prostitute were to seek him out some twenty years later, presenting him with that birth certificate. As a result, his legitimate wife and children would no longer obey him, thereby disrupting the family order, and, by extension, that of society. Constant acknowledged, however, that in seducing a woman and making her a mother, the man contracted obligations to her that the law must enforce, and that paternity searches might be a "salutary brake on disorderly passions." In the interests of the mother, of the child, and of morality, a woman should be permitted to name the putative father. To refuse weak, honest, young seduced girls the right to make this declaration would be a great misfortune. Furthermore, he argued, even children born out of wedlock had rights, and "society owes them assistance." The peace and tranquility of the legitimate family, however, overrode those concerns.[88]

The Civil Code attempted to legislate morality, but it treated men and women unequally, especially in terms of sexual morality. Moreover, when discussing unwed mothers, legislators focused on women of the working classes. Morality required that a woman remain in the bosom of her family, under her father's power, until she married and was under her husband's authority. Yet it also presupposed that women had the moral and physical strength and responsibility to resist seduction, and had sufficient reasoning facilities to know that if they failed to exercise restraint, they would have to pay the moral and material price. Broken marriage promises left women without recourse. Morality for men was far more lenient. Without a policy of establishing paternity for children of single mothers, fathers had no legal incentive to behave responsibly. Men could exercise liberty in their personal lives and also had moral and paternal authority in their family lives. Natural children seeking support from married fathers disturbed men's liberty and family order. At the same time, however, natural children needed sustenance, and some legislators thought seducers should provide partial support, but not an inheritance, for those children. A few even wished to punish men who seduced and abandoned young girls, considering this a moral outrage against the civil order, as well as against the fathers of those young girls they seduced. Marriage and paternal authority based on individual liberty for men remained a guiding principle of the postrevolutionary civil and moral order, but the place of natural children in this order had shifted. In 1793, morality and natural law declared all children equal; by 1804, morality and natural law obliterated notions of equal status between natural and legitimate children to preserve civil order and men's liberty.

The Civil Code confirmed marriage as a public act, placing family behavior firmly in the public discourse and legal public sphere, underscoring the importance of marriage to society. It reinforced the patriarchal character of society by institutionalizing the *puissance maritale*, subordinating the rights of women to the rights of man. Reaffirming the 1791 law establishing marriage as a civil contract, the Code further stipulated the marital duties and responsibilities of both husband and wife. When a woman married, her loyalty was to be to her husband. She assumed his nationality and had to live wherever he chose. She could neither file a legal suit nor serve as a witness to any civil act—including births, marriages, divorces, and deaths. A married woman had minimal economic independence. By law, her wages went to her husband, and she could not have a business without her husband's permission; her profits also became her husband's property. Reinforcing social discipline began at home, within marriage, with the reinforced role of the father. Furthermore, any man had the right to refuse to assume paternity outside of marriage, and no natural child could claim a portion of the inheritance from the putative father or his legitimate family. Laws absolved the father of all legal, fiscal, moral, and social responsibility if he were not married to the mother of his child, but a man could commit adultery with impunity and immunity, unless he brought his sexual partner into his marital home. Inherent in the Code were the integrity of marriage and the prevention of an outsider from intruding on the family bloodline and property.

Women's adultery was another matter. As Portalis intoned, "'a woman is destined by nature for the pleasures of a single man.' The duty of fidelity is therefore, for her, absolute."[89] If a woman committed adultery, the husband did not have to take her back. Because a wife's adultery threatened her husband's line of inheritance, the Code punished it by imprisonment and fines. The sentence was often at the discretion of the husband, who could reduce the punishment by taking his wife back. Bigot de Préameneu was so interested in protecting the male line of inheritance that he provided a variety of ways in which a husband could deny the paternity of his wife's child, including evidence of her adultery, his physical inability to father a child, his absence from her during the time of conception, or her departure from their conjugal home.[90]

The Code's interdiction of paternity searches reversed centuries-old canon and customary laws that required a father to support his child, whether he married the mother or not,[91] and installed what André-Jean Arnaud called the "Pax bourgeoise," primarily to reinforce social discipline in an effort to restore social order. Its provisions communicated a regulated system of exchange and ownership—that of property and children. The Code represented the individualism of bourgeois male aspirations, legislating relations between men, in which property rights were inviolable and honor was tied to family property, children, and inheritance. Establishing the bourgeois social order required a Civil Code to set the rules of the game; but certain people were excluded from the game, notably women, children, and indigents. Poor women were excluded on two grounds: gender and poverty.

Children needed the protection of men, but some children were more worthy than others: at the top of the hierarchy were legitimate children, followed by the natural children of an unmarried man, then those of an adulterous relationship.[92] This concept of a hierarchy of children eliminated natural law's emphasis on equality; it also made the children responsible for the sins of the father. To restore order to France after years of revolutionary upheaval, legislators sought to control the alleged disorderly sexual behavior of women, especially those of the working class, and reinforce the power of the fathers. Forbidding recherche de paternité thereby protected the bourgeois family's peace and property, especially that of the married man. However, the groundwork for the article forbidding recherche de paternité had been prepared since the days of the Revolution. In essence, men did not want women of an inferior social and economic status, or of questionable morals, marrying their sons and dissipating their wealth. Nor did they want natural children interfering with the inheritance of those born within marriage. That the interdiction of paternity searches existed throughout the nineteenth century demonstrates the persistence of a passion for property that marked the French bourgeoisie.

Similarly, laws in other Western European countries were designed fundamentally to preserve the property and liberty of men, with resulting disdain for unwed mothers. In England, rules of coverture governed women's subordination to their husbands, yet the so-called bastardy laws provided a mechanism whereby a woman might sue the father of her natural child for maintenance. But it was difficult both to sue for child support and to collect.[93] According to a law of 1733, reenacted in 1809, justices of the peace had the power to order a man whom a woman accused of impregnating her to pay the cost of child support. His obligation to her and the child, however, was strictly economic.

Paternity suits were more frequent in eighteenth- and even early nineteenth-century Italy than in France, because ecclesiastical courts were traditionally sympathetic to young women, especially if they had the backing of their families, which they often did. This changed with the adoption of the Napoleonic Code by united Italy. The Prussian Code (Allgemeines Landrecht) developed between 1750 and 1794, unlike the French Code, stipulated that an unmarried mother, if she had been engaged to the father, had the same rights to child support as a wife who was divorced though innocent. Paternity was established by a mother's sworn testimony, and although the child was declared legally unrelated to the father, he or she could claim a share of the father's inheritance if there were no legitimate children. As in eighteenth-century France, a mother's sexual fidelity to the alleged father was paramount. German law contained the phrase "exceptio plurium concumbentium" (except for those with several lovers), making it more difficult for women with more than one sexual partner to receive child support. Yet, in instances when she had more than one lover, all could be held financially responsible. A provision of the code also provided illegitimate children with a court-appointed legal guardian, ideally, the mother's male relative, who was to take the place of the child's father or to try to ensure that the father did not renege on child support. Many relatives did not want to serve as guardians of these poor wards and neglected their duties. Given the long delays in appointing guardians and in bringing paternity suits, fathers had ample time to disappear.[94] Laws in other countries were somewhat more lenient toward unwed mothers and their children than in France. However, French women worked around the law.

In a shift from the Old Regime to the Republic, the responsibility for a natural child no longer rested with the biological father. After having flirted during the Revolution with the idea of naming natural children as "children of the nation," the male-dominated community put the responsibility for that child squarely on the mother. Although paternity searches were forbidden, this did not stop women from filing paternity suits or suits for material damages in order to try to reclaim some shred of honor, if not financial aid, during these tumultuous times, or during the nineteenth century, as the next chapter will show. Community judgment continued to be vital, because kin and neighbors might testify to the mother's morality or the sexual bravado or marriage promise of the putative father.

From the Revolution through the finalization of the Civil Code, public politics based on a radical individualism intruded into the realm of intimate family matters in unprecedented ways to define paternity and the family. The Revolution marked a transition in relationships between the family and the state. The new social order emerging in the aftermath of the Revolution, in attempting to restabilize society, legislated gender inequities particularly in the delineation of parental rights and responsibilities. Embedded in the concept of the social order was the omnipotence of propertied men. The revolutionaries' creation of the Republic tried to balance the initiative for individual rights, including the right to decide if and when to be a father, which often worked against women, with the ambition to make the licit conjugal family a core underpinning of the state. They tried to reconcile the tension between the rights of an indispensable French conjugal family with the rights of illegitimate children. Revolutionary and Napoleonic policy toward the family was complex, and often quite different, but in structuring laws on nonmarital paternity, it injured women and children. The Code discursively and legally relegated women as passive citizens to the private realm of the home, where they refused to stay, while bestowing on propertied men the right to be active citizens in the public sphere. That public/private divide was a rhetorical distinction, but one that nevertheless had an impact on lives. The Code often established a legal fiction that people tested and contradicted in their daily lives. Men could debate the laws all they wanted, but life depended on personal and community relations—on the determination of mothers, lawyers, and magistrates. Laws cannot regulate intimate life.

The rhetoric of 1793 invoked the metaphor of the nation as a great family and the leaders as a fraternity of fathers. The nation as a family wanted to adopt *enfants de la patrie*. From 1794 to 1804, however, rather than the nation being symbolized as a family, France became a nation of families, with propertied families headed by an ideal paterfamilias.[95] The politics and culture of the new regime attempted to define concepts of paternity, the family, and citizenship. Within this concept of citizenship, the liberty and rights of fathers within their families, and also within the "great family" of the nation, were paramount. The Civil Code focused on defining the family, because politicians deemed a securely constructed family to be essential to a stable state. The definitions of fatherhood, motherhood, the family, patriarchy, and citizenship that evolved during this era would be contested in communities, courts, and legislative chambers throughout nineteenth- and twentieth-century France. Generations of women, men, magistrates, and jurists elaborated upon and interpreted that Code.

CHAPTER TWO

Seduction and Courtroom Encounters in the Nineteenth Century

Women went to court to try to collect child support for their children and reparations for themselves from men who had seduced and abandoned them, despite the Civil Code's prohibition of paternity searches and the towering emotional and financial hardships they faced along the way. Women were not all passive victims who lived unhappily within the laws that attempted to govern their most intimate lives. Quite savvy about legal procedure, some acted in public, using litigation in sometimes futile attempts to redeem their honor and that of their families, but primarily to obtain some financial benefit. Going to court illustrates women's agency, or assertion of limited power, within the male-dominated legal system. Motivated by moral outrage and economic need, they found ways in the law to reclaim their bodies from the inflicted wounds of seduction. Although women were deeply vulnerable, some used the courts to assert a form of citizenship, claim damages as a result of an injury, and further their economic ends, with help from their fathers, lawyers, and judges. Judicial decisions helped define the fluid public and private lives of men and women and enforced unwritten codes of honor and behavior. This chapter offers glimpses into people's complicated lives and strategies, through court proceedings, in an attempt to understand personal relations gone awry and what these meant for social constructions of paternity and the family. Missing from this view are the countless instances where the men assumed paternity, either by recognizing their children, marrying the mothers, or providing sufficient material and emotional support.

In courtroom encounters over seduction and paternity, men and women depended on magistrates and lawyers, who almost immediately called into question the provisions and presuppositions of the Civil Code. Public law courts proliferated in postrevolutionary France, and jurisprudence provided elasticity to the structured codified law. This elasticity, not without considerable tension, allowed judges to [re]interpret the law and to hear women's voices that the Code had silenced or disregarded. During the eighteenth century, laws tended to acknowledge unwed mothers' plaintive cries identifying the father; local judges, however, generally supported the patriarchal family and tended not to hear the women. In the nineteenth century, the Civil Code supported the patriarchal family, but some local judges managed their way around it with open hearts and ears to hear women's pleas. In general, nineteenth-century magistrates demonstrated more sensitivity to women, the community, and the culture than did the Civil Code and often took the lead in formulating legal policy. The law moves slowly, but eventually catches up to judicial rulings. In 1804, the Civil Code corresponded to late eighteenth-century judiciary practice. During the nineteenth century, jurisprudence prepared the stage for early twentieth-century revisions of articles in the Civil Code.

France had a long history of judicial activism, especially on family matters.[1] Starting in the late eighteenth century and accelerating in the nineteenth, with the increased publication of newspapers, legal treatises, and collections of judicial decisions, discussion of judges' decisions occurred in the public sphere. Reports of court proceedings in the popular press often helped garner public sympathy for the seduced young woman and her poor, fatherless child. Conversely, these narrative dramas sometimes supported men who claimed to be wrongly accused. To some extent, judges played to the public and took into account prevailing attitudes. Wide publicity about trials and judges' decisions facilitated the formation of public opinion, which led to further judicial action reflecting prevailing codes of conduct and previous decisions. Although there was no official system of precedence in French law, judges, lawyers, and litigants knew of past decisions in similar cases, often quoting them, thus forming a basis for legal precedence, although it was nonbinding.[2] Resorting to precedence, even informally, leads to an evolution in ideas and law. Judges were fortified by opinions in past decisions.

The law, magistrates, women, and men contested power. Judges had the power to challenge the Civil Code and change implementation of laws through their interpretation—interpretations that went to the very basis of the patriarchal order—while denying that they did so. For the first half of the century, the Code dominated in this power contest; magistrates tended to apply the letter of the law, especially adhering to article 340 forbidding paternity searches. After mid-century, however, the balance of power between the judiciary and the written law shifted, giving more weight to magistrates. Patriarchal law became increasingly obsolete in the face of cultural and economic shifts in society. In this relocated balance of power, women exercised some initiative and made some gains. But there was no greater sense of gender equality for women, qua women. Rather, women gained power as mothers, in the name of their minor children, or as victims of fraud and broken contracts.

All three levels of the judicial system considered women's civil suits. The civil tribunals, departmental appeals courts (*cours d'appel*), and the Cour de cassation (Court of Cassation), the highest court, sitting in Paris, were established between 1800 and 1810 and exist to this day. The minister of the interior or his delegates appointed all magistrates or judges.[3] Magistrates in the local civil tribunals, the lowest courts for civil procedures such as paternity searches and property damages, were selected from communal lists. Those serving in one of the twenty-seven (now thirty-five) regional appeals courts were appointed from departmental lists, and those sitting on the Cour de cassation were selected from national lists. Panels of judges, ranging from three in the local civil tribunals to eleven in the Cour de cassation, rendered decisions. Each panel had a presiding judge, or president. Normally, entrée into the magistrature required becoming a lawyer, practicing before the bar for several years, and passing an examination; until 1908, however, this examination was not a barrier against favoritism. In practice, sons of those already serving as magistrates or government ministers were generally named to the magistrature, creating a partially inherited tenured profession based on preferential treatment and nepotism. Yet there was some nuance; the sons of property owners and of professional men with no connection to the bureaucracy or magistrature also became magistrates.

Magistrates held tenure (*immovibilité*) in their profession and could progress within the judicial hierarchy to the next level, or to more prestigious courts in larger cities, with promotion often depending on personal and familial connections. To advance beyond a local provincial level, judges had to have a small fortune, or marry into one, since a judge could not live in appropriate magisterial style on his salary alone. Although some democratization of the magistrature from upper bourgeoisie to middle and even lower bourgeoisie occurred starting with the Second Republic, the need for years of study in the law put the magistrature out of bounds for poorer workingmen. Women were excluded until the second half of the twentieth century. Magistrates tended to come from the geographical region they served, so that they would have one foot in the soil—as the saying went—giving voice to the neighborhood culture or family power relationships. Opposition to this practice came from those who thought a judge could not be impartial when he knew everyone in the region, and many of those he served might belong to his own extended family. Serving as government appointees who could not lose their jobs (except for criminal offenses) magistrates were free to frame their decisions in accordance with their own scruples, in line with those with whom they wanted to curry favor, or in keeping with the culture and rituals of their area. Magistrates worked in accord with, or in opposition to, the government of the time. During the early decades of the century, magistrates were loyal to Bonaparte, the Restoration monarchy, or to Louis-Philippe. With the Second Republic, Minister of the Interior Adolphe Crémieux appointed a new breed of magistrates, especially to the appeals courts and the Cour de cassation. His appointees demonstrated an allegiance to the Republic—either as true republicans or as men who merely professed republican sentiments but were most interested in restoring social order after 1848.[4] Using the courtroom to advocate a political or philosophical position in the grand scheme of politics and society was not unusual for judges or lawyers, many of whom sought to use trials to teach people how to behave.

Men and women constructed different narratives in the courtroom to define their families and property, to demonstrate sexual independence, to press their individual rights and to determine responsibilities. Legal and melodramatic gendered arguments, not uncommon during the eighteenth century, continued in court procedures throughout the nineteenth and twentieth centuries; they tended to follow similar scripts presented to an audience of the public, the judges, and the press. As public sites, courts functioned as theaters. Those unable to attend as spectators could satisfy their voyeurism by reading accounts of these dramas in the popular press.[5] Generally, in the nineteenth century, as in the eighteenth, women, and their lawyers, designed their court briefs based on the man's false or unfulfilled marriage promise. Women's insistence that they had succumbed to seduction only after a marriage promise implies that having sexual relations after a marriage promise was socially acceptable. They based their cases on their role as innocents who had been seduced and abandoned, portraying themselves as having become good mothers who needed food for their children. Men brought to court on charges of seduction and paternity spoke of the women's loose morals and insisted that women's testimony be treated with skepticism. Women were weak, unstable, and suggestible, they alleged; they had a propensity to lie, gave in to temptation, and bore false witness. At issue were the definitions of duties and rights, each one gendered.

Court narratives reveal women and men working out a meaning to familial relationships and social interactions of power. They communicated the boundaries of the individual and community. The individual, so highly vaunted in the nineteenth century, was nevertheless constituted by his or her relationship to others—but this was gendered, especially for women. In civil proceedings, litigants, defendants, lawyers, and magistrates determined the margins of what was proper and what was not, what kept order in the society and what disrupted that order. Court proceedings also reveal community connections—both friendships and enmities. It is easy to overemphasize enmity in relations when using court records, which by their very nature reveal antagonism more than cooperation. Instances where scenes of seduction were followed by the signing of marriage contracts in the city hall or by the man's assumption of responsibility in providing support for his child do not appear in court or historical records, nor do out-of-court settlements. Plaintiffs, defendants, and magistrates interpreted and reinterpreted the Code as they negotiated their daily lives around issues of property, family rights, civil rights, and civil actions. The Code specified national law, but magistrates would interpret it according to regional norms.

Paternal Responsibility and Seduction

Over the course of the century, plaintiffs, defendants, judges, and social commentators struggled to define and implement concepts of paternity, the place of a natural child in the social structure, and the nature of a marriage promise—all key aspects of private lives regulated by law and jurisprudence. Nineteenth-century French society valorized paternity, but only within a conjugal family. Article 312 of the Civil Code, articulating the maxim that "the mother's husband is the father of the child," failed to address paternity outside of marriage.[6] Legislators and magistrates abhorred the idea of making a man pay the costs of the childbirth and subsequent childcare only to find out later that he was not the biological father of children born outside that idealized conjugal family. To make matters worse for the natural children, the notion that "the person who creates a child must feed it" sometimes fell by the wayside, not even always applying to mothers. With the establishment of foundling homes in major cities throughout France starting in 1811, and the encouragement of anonymous infant abandonment during the first half of the century, the state, exercising a paternal role through its institutions and employing a network of wet nurses, took over the paternal and maternal duty of feeding children born outside of marriage—often with deadly results for the babies.

To establish paternal responsibility for natural children, many magistrates based their decisions on the controversial concept that paternity was divisible. They took great pains to separate authorship of the pregnancy from social fatherhood and filiation; filiation endowed the child with the father's surname and entitled him or her to a portion of the paternal inheritance and assimilation into the paternal family.[7] A father exercised paternal authority and participated in educating the child. Filiation applied to children within marriage or to those outside of marriage whom a father legally recognized. It involved the voluntary consent to be a father; filiation could not be forced on a man against his will. The author of the pregnancy, or genitor, could avoid the responsibility of filiation and at most could be required to help feed the child. Because the Civil Code forbade paternity searches, magistrates sympathetic to unwed mothers and their children separated the requirement that a man pay child support from requiring the man to bequeath the child his name and a portion of his estate. In ruling that the author of a pregnancy need only help feed the child he had created, magistrates could still obey the letter of the law, protect married men and their families, and also help support the children. Other jurists and magistrates opposed this and insisted that paternity was not divisible. A man was either a father or he was not. They insisted that if a woman pursued the author of her pregnancy in court, she also pursued the father of the child, and that was illegal.[8]

Paternity consists of complicated sets of duties and rights, but by allowing for the divisibility of paternity, magistrates kept duties and rights separate. Men had the right to decide their own interests, which included their right to affirm or deny paternity outside of marriage. Rights were also coterminous with property. The Civil Code confirmed a man's rights to fatherhood of children born within marriage and to making them his heirs. Neither law nor the man himself could abrogate those rights. Duties were different and could be imposed; but duties, such as supporting one's children within marriage, also accompanied certain rights. During the century, women had to struggle against enormous odds to be individuals, but men asserted their status as individuals, with undeniable rights, especially with the right to dispose of their property as they willed. In making paternity divisible, magistrates began to limit men's individual rights by imposing certain duties. They issued legal orders for the genitor to feed his child as a social duty. Such juridical decisions, however, did not limit a man's right to exercise paternal authority or his right to decide whether to acknowledge paternity of a natural child.

The natural child remained a pariah with severely limited rights in the civil and moral order. Even those whom their fathers legally recognized could receive only a small portion of the inheritance, the portion dependent on the number of legitimate heirs. The animus against natural children was part of the overwhelming desire to defend the legal conjugal family against them, and society against errant couples who lived together without legal marriages. In demanding natural children's right to sustenance, reformers and magistrates bypassed article 340 prohibiting paternity searches and avoided any indication of supporting them. Although they conceded that the person married to the child's mother was legally the father, they also sought to make the genitor responsible for feeding the child. To do this without instituting paternity searches involved walking a legal tightrope, dividing paternity and applying tort law to seduction.

Definitions of seduction, the rights of men, and social responsibilities for sexual behavior remained critical issues in discussion of paternity and the family. Despite the prohibition of paternity searches, the discussion of what to do about the seducers and seduced continued, because helpless children were in evidence, some women refused to be victims, and some fathers protested the violation of their daughters, who were their property. Writers during much of the nineteenth century disagreed about who were the seducers and who the seduced. Many blamed working-class women, to whom they ascribed loose morals, charging them with seducing propertied men. Even if the women were not active seducers, they added, these women too easily succumbed to seduction, rather than exercising their moral responsibility to resist men's advances. Other writers clearly branded men the seducers and women their victims. Seduction involves inequality, and the contemporary literature abounds with dramas of young men seducing domestic servants in the household. In some fiction, as well as in court cases, male heads of households believed that their female domestic servants should supply their sons with their first sexual experiences. For some men, seducing a woman was symbolic of manhood, a rite of passage that gave them bragging rights and enabled them to appear more mature and accomplished in the eyes of other men. It was also an indicator of masculinity and an expression of passionate love that formed part of male culture.[9] Yet seduction was not just a manifestation of masculinity for the sake of male egos. Seduction could also involve pleasure, love, and a search for a cherished intimacy. For women as well as men, sexual intimacy may have marked a course to adulthood, and intimate relations provided some emotional and physical attachment.

Intimate relations came at a price for women—the loss of virginity. Appearance and reputation were vital, and virginity was a valued possession for a bride. Alexandre Dumas *fils*, for example, demanded that the "law protect the virginity of girls, which I call their capital."[10] Virginity constituted social as well as material capital, assuring a good marriage and commanding a better price on the marriage market. Nothing could replace this capital once it was lost or stolen. Nevertheless, not all agreed that seduction was theft of property. Moralists considered an unmarried woman's virginity more as a virtue than as capital. If it was a virtue, it could not be stolen, and property laws should not apply. This was not to say that moralists thought dishonorable men should get off scot-free. Rather, depriving a woman of her virtue should be treated as extortion, swindling, abuse of confidence, or inciting a minor to debauchery, and treated as such by the law.[11]

Nineteenth-century society was changing, however, making issues of seduction ever more complex. On the one hand, village restraints were weakening, giving men and women more sexual freedom; on the other, virginity and virtue were still prized among women and among those who judged them. After marriage, procreation in order to transmit a name and family property, as well as to supply young workers, became the goal. Moreover, having children was sign of sexuality and male potency. In childless marriages, sterility was always attributed to the women.[12]

Definitions of seduction depended on the age of the girl and the circumstances. Girls between the ages of 15 and 21 had more discernment than younger ones, but they still needed protection from fraudulent seduction. The seduction of minors was in any case different from that of women who had reached legal adulthood (which they did at age 21 in nineteenth-century France). "[A] woman of 25 or 30 years could defend her virtue herself, had sufficient experience to understand the consequences of a fault, and sufficient discernment to thwart or frustrate the insidious promises of a Lothario." If such a woman consented to seduction, she was knowingly at fault.[13]

What the law and magistrates defined as rape, or seduction with violence, and the extent of the crime, varied with the age of the woman and the changing culture of the century. Generally, rape was considered a violent form of heterosexual coitus against the will of the woman; the emphasis was on the violence. In June 1857, the Cour de cassation decided to leave the determination of the seriousness of the crime up to individual judges, according to the consequences for the victim and the honor of all the families involved.[14] It was less important to protect the well-being of the woman than it was to protect the honor of the families—both the man's and woman's—especially if the rape resulted in a pregnancy.

Laws protected children from seduction and rape. The abduction or kidnapping of minors under sixteen was usually considered rape, not simple seduction. It was a crime punishable by imprisonment in solitary confinement with hard labor.[15] If the abductor married the girl he had kidnapped, it constituted an offense against the family. The girl's father could have the marriage annulled and bring charges of kidnapping and rape against the man. If, however, the kidnapped or raped young girl was seventeen or older, it was not a crime, and the man escaped the law. The law also punished those who led minors to debauchery. Article 331 of the Penal Code stipulated that those convicted of rape "or any other attack on decency [*attentat à la pudeur*] attempted or committed with violence against individuals of either sex will be punished by *réclusion*" (solitary prison confinement), with the term of the sentence up to the judge. If that crime was against a child under fifteen, however, it was legally rape and punishable by hard labor for a term of five to twenty years (*travaux forcés à temps*). Legislation of 1863 changed the age to thirteen for an indecent assault on a person to be punished as rape and modified article 333 to specify that if those guilty were the parents or older relatives of the person on whom the crime was committed, or had authority over her (such as teachers or religious leaders), or were aided in the crime, they were to be punished by hard labor for life (*travaux forcés à perpétuité*). An attack on decency without violence, therefore, was not a crime unless it was perpetrated on a child under thirteen. Sexual violence committed on an adult was punished by an unspecified term of penal servitude. If fraudulent seduction was without violence or on an adult, it escaped legal repression. The Penal Code was mute on seduction when the woman was seventeen or older and the man twenty-one or older; those cases could come under the Civil Code's articles on torts, or wrongs to another. To institute a criminal charge of rape or seduction was extremely difficult, facilitated only if the victim were young or of a social position much higher than that of her attacker, and if there was evidence that she had tried to fight him off or scream for help.[16] If a man did not resort to rape or other forms of violence against the woman or young girl, he might have resorted to a promise of marriage in order to get a young woman to succumb to his seductions.

Narratives about marriage promises often rested on assumptions of class differences and fear of scandal. Male social commentators seemed terrorized by the possibility that poor women would seduce men of higher income or status to demand marriage or money. They especially feared scandals to a married man's family, privacy, and property brought about by a deceitful woman seeking redress for damages wrought by a man's youthful indiscretions or adultery. Men fervently sought to protect their family names and property from lower-class women, some insisting that they would not have promised marriage to or tried to seduce a young girl from a lower class, but rather that those women had seduced them by flaunting their sexuality. Extant court cases fail to provide a basis for the myth in a collective male memory that poor women would pursue rich men in the courts for money or status and create a scandal.

Most women who went to court were not pursuing men of higher income or status, or married men with families, although they might very well have succumbed to a marriage promise from a man of property and wealth, which would have fulfilled many a poor woman's fondest dreams. On the contrary, they were, for example, a laundress suing a cab driver, a domestic servant legally pursuing a valet, a female mechanic bringing a plumber to court, or a woman employee seeking damages from a co-worker. Only rarely was there an inequality, such as a domestic servant suing her master, a young delivery girl and her family suing a wealthy landowner, or a seamstress seeking damages from a medical student. These, however, became the focus of the popular press.

Women and their families, moreover, also suffered scandals. In court, attempting to mitigate the scandal of a nonmarital pregnancy and obtain some reparations so that they could resume a respectable life, they blamed the men for their dishonor. Shifting the narratives from paternity to property damage and broken contracts allowed women redress within the legal system.

Deciding on whether a verbal or written marriage promise was a civil contract with responsibilities incumbent on the person who broke that contract was a thorny issue and a focus of nineteenth-century jurisprudence. The Civil Code said not one word about broken marriage promises, indicating that legislators did not consider marriage promises civil contracts, but rather a matter of honor. Magistrates differed about whether a marriage promise was a contract entailing obligations to the wronged party from the person who broke it. Those who argued that a marriage promise was a contract that should not be broken added that the seducer had contractual obligations to the woman.[17] Other magistrates maintained that although marriage was a civil contract, a promise of marriage was not. Moreover, if intimate relations followed a marriage promise, some argued, the woman was at fault.[18] Even if men and their lawyers respected the contractual nature of a marriage promise, they tried to cast the blame on the woman for her lack of moral strength and virtue, in part to avoid the loss of honor that breaking an engagement would entail.[19] They argued that a man was entitled to break an engagement without compensating a former fiancée if she exhibited "bad conduct."

Legal narratives intertwined marriage promises with sexual seduction, since a promise of marriage was usually part of that seduction. Reformers, magistrates and social commentators also held different views about whether seduction, with or without a promise of marriage, was a civil offense, and whether seduction, a marriage promise, and a resulting pregnancy and baby allowed a judge to order a man to pay damages to the mother. Breach of promise and fraudulent seduction made men liable for damages. This fell under tort law, which arose from complications of social change in an industrial capital society. Paternity suits and repairing damages did not have the same beneficiaries. Paternity suits ostensibly benefited the child; repairing damages benefited the mother.

From 1810 to 1845

Questions of seduction, the contractual nature of a marriage promise, and paternal responsibility appeared in the courts almost immediately after the promulgation of the Civil Code. Starting as early as 1806, mothers used the courts to try to force the men who had impregnated them to make amends, despite the Code's prohibition of paternity searches.[20] They did not file paternity suits, but rather sought reparations (*dommages-intérêts*) for the wrong caused them by a false or broken marriage promise, abuse of authority, or fraudulent seduction. In 1808, in response to a plea by a young woman who said that a man had promised her marriage and food for the child, but then reneged, the civil tribunal of the Department of the Seine declared that paternity attribution was forbidden, but that on the basis of a marriage promise, she could obtain damages and food. That same year, however, the Cour de cassation declared that decision invalid, and that paternity was indivisible.

Thereafter, in all but a few cases before the 1840s, judges denied the mother's appeal; the "author of the pregnancy" had impunity for his sexual actions, bore no legal responsibility, and did not have to act as the father of the resultant child.[21] Between 1814 and the early 1840s, a conservative Catholic and royalist milieu dominated the political and legal world, which included eliminating divorce in 1816, upholding the letter and spirit of the law supporting the father's authority in the conjugal family, and prohibiting paternity searches. In part, the image of the ideal conjugal family was religious, held sacrosanct under the authority of the father/husband, and forming the base of society and the social order. During these years, jurisprudence rarely diverged from the Civil Code. Magistrates acted with extreme prudence.[22] They repulsed attempts by unwed mothers to file paternity suits against the putative fathers for child support (*pension alimentaire*).

Rather than focusing on the forbidden recherche de paternité, some more innovative magistrates and lawyers looked to contract and tort law in the Civil Code and applied it to intimate family relations. They discovered the applicability to issues of seduction and marriage promises of article 1382, which specified that anyone who wronged another person was obliged to make reparations for that wrong and must bear responsibility by paying an indemnity, or dommages-intérêts.[23] Article 1382 derives from John Locke's view of natural law and supports man's individualism. "The state of nature possesses a law which is reason, and reason teaches that no one should injure another's life, health, freedom, or property," Locke wrote. "Every human being, furthermore, should have the right to protect his prerogatives drawn from natural law, chiefly to remain in the free state of nature and not to be subjected to the political power of anyone else."[24] In drafting the Civil Code, lawmakers adopted article 1382 without debate, stating that it would preserve the principle of protecting property and public order. They did not expect the many ways in which magistrates and lawyers would use it to adjudicate paternity and family relations, and they failed to foresee that smart women and their lawyers would use this article to request damages for seduction, broken marriage promises, and abandonment from the author of the pregnancy or from his family if he had died. Women acted bravely or desperately as individuals in their own right by going to court against men who had broken a marriage promise to force those men to repair the injury to them, their children, and their families.

Magistrates who considered a marriage promise as a contract and seduction as a civil offense against a woman and her family were able to offer some assistance to mothers and their natural children while also upholding the injunction against paternity searches. Key judicial decisions in 1808, 1814, 1827, and 1838 tested the binding nature of a marriage promise. Issues of honor and property were critical, although open to judicial interpretation. Fathers brought cases in the name of their daughters, based on the assumption that young women were their father's property, which had been damaged by seduction and a broken marriage promise. Magistrates took into account testimony about the age of the woman at the time of seduction, as well as her reputation and that of her family. The "fault" of the man had to be manifest. Some magistrates considered a marriage promise, especially if it was a formal engagement, as a reciprocal contract between the two families, not just the man and woman, and breaking that promise would entitle the other family to reparations. Others disagreed. Both sets of judges based their decision on their interpretation of articles of the Civil Code involving damages. The Cour de cassation in 1808 declared that a woman abused by a false marriage promise or other fraudulent means had the right to claim damages from her seducer if she had at first resisted and he had overcome her resistance.[25]

The key was proof of her resistance. In 1814, a woman abandoned by her fiancé went to court for compensation, alleging that a marriage promise was binding. The civil tribunal declared that this was an erroneous interpretation of tort law, which applied to business contracts about things and not to contracts pertaining to people. More than a decade later, the court of Toulouse took a broad position when it ruled that a marriage promise was a bilateral contract; no party could break the obligations that he or she had contracted to without risking a suit for dommages-intérêts for the failure to uphold an engagement. In 1838, the Cour de cassation disagreed and stipulated that as a contractual convention, a marriage promise was "absolutely null, devoid of all effect"—invalid in civil law. It was a simple engagement of honor, a domain of conscience; breach of it was without any pecuniary result. Magistrates continued to use article 1382 to allow a woman to demand an indemnity from a man for the prejudice caused her by a brutal rupture of an engagement without legitimate motives. Although damages could be moral as well as material, as a general rule seduction and a broken marriage promise without a resulting child were not usually sufficient grounds for ruling in favor of a young woman. Significant damages would have occurred only if the marriage promise was followed by a pregnancy and the birth of a child. Magistrates had difficulty affixing the quantitative amount for moral damages; pain and suffering were hard to quantify.[26]

Broken promises as grounds for civil lawsuits were not limited to those for marriage. If a man had promised to help support a child by paying a wet nurse or providing money for the child's basic needs, he became liable for damages. This commitment could have been verbal or written. Nothing compelled him to make that promise, but if he voluntarily made it and then broke it, courts could decide that he had ruptured a civil contractual obligation to provide for the needs of a minor child. When a woman went to court to get him to honor his promise, some judges declared it a claim for damages resulting from a broken contract, and not a paternity search. Those judges pronounced that the "engagement to furnish food to the infant is not an obligation indicating paternity, but a natural obligation" based on the idea that "he who creates the child must feed it." That natural obligation could lead to a civil obligation. Judges insisted there was no obligation of legal paternity or fatherhood, such as providing a name and inheritance, but rather a civil obligation to provide for the young child.[27] Magistrates separated child support and compensation to the mother from filiation and inheritance; allowing a baby the right to nourishment and the genitor the right to his name and property.

Courts upheld the interdiction on paternity suits, allowing them only in cases of abduction—with or without violence, as article 340 of the Code dictated—when the date of the abduction corresponded to the possible time of conception (judged to be between 180 and 300 days before childbirth). In these cases, resembling *rapt de séduction* of the eighteenth century, the kidnapper could be declared the father of the child upon the request of the interested parties—usually the girl's father. Lawyers disagreed as to whether rape was a necessary condition of kidnapping in paternity suits. As a Parisian judge decided in 1821, "It is sufficient [to declare paternity] if the kidnapper seduced the young girl without the knowledge of her parents" and the abduction from her father's house had occurred at the presumed time of conception.[28] To win a paternity suit, the young woman had to have brought the pregnancy to term, and have been held by her kidnapper in a state of subjection, leaving no doubt about the genitor. Furthermore, her morals had to have been impeccable. For a man to escape paternity charges he had to show that the morals of the woman he abducted or raped were impure.[29] Although the Penal Code provided for criminal punishment of rape, it was difficult to declare the rapist the father of the child. During the nineteenth century, cases of recherche de paternité based strictly on the Civil Code were on the grounds of abduction against the wishes of the girl's father—the key was the violation of her father's authority, not violation of the girl. The victims were usually under fifteen, not adult women.

Magistrates showed increasing flexibility in their interpretation of the Code starting in the 1840s. In significant and widely publicized judicial decisions, they assigned some men moral and financial responsibility for the results of their sexual activity and broken marriage promises, sentencing them to pay damages to the mother as a result of the pregnancy and child. Magistrates tended to fault the man for seducing and abandoning the young woman, rather than morally blaming her for her sexual activity. Some judges interpreted article 1382 not only to make the genitor pay the mother an indemnity for the broken promise and wrong he had done her, but also to award single mothers child support for the results of that wrong.[30] These judges took pains to declare that they were not permitting paternity searches and carefully avoided mentioning paternity, merely allowing the tribunals to award a mother damages under article 1382. Judges drew a fine line between recherche de paternité and restitution for a civil misdemeanor.

A pathbreaking attempt to circumvent article 340 and award damages to a wronged mother came before the Cour de cassation in 1845. It first appeared before the civil tribunal in the town of Castelsarrasin in southwestern France in the early 1840s, when a father brought a case against a neighbor for seducing his daughter. Monsieur Labia frequently visited the home of Monsieur Baysse, and soon Baysse's minor daughter became pregnant. After the birth of the baby, Labia wrote to Baysse, acknowledging that he was the author of the pregnancy and promising to make amends. Words came easily, but action did not follow. Baysse then took Labia to court in Castelsarrasin to have him condemned for failure to keep his promises and to get him to pay reparations for the prejudice he had caused him and his daughter. The judges in Castelsarrasin declared that article 1142 of the Civil Code could be extended to the failure to honor a marriage promise, if there had been injuries such as a pregnancy and baby. They ruled that Labia had abandoned the young girl after he promised to marry her. Moreover, his frequent visits to her and her father had resulted in a sexual relationship, pregnancy, and motherhood. This was an injury to her honor, a moral prejudice. The judge therefore ordered Labia to pay Baysse 3,000 francs in reparations. Labia took the case to the appeals court of nearby Toulouse, which on 5 July 1843 upheld the lower court's decision, declaring that it was not a question of the civil status of the child, but only one of the damage Labia had caused Monsieur and Mlle Baysse. His failure to keep an agreement for marriage was a civil offense (*quasi-délit*). Not satisfied, Labia took his case to the Cour de cassation, which on 24 March 1845, in a landmark decision, rejected his appeal, upholding the lower courts' decisions and ruling that failure to keep a marriage promise made a man liable for dommages-intérêts when it resulted in damage to the woman and her family, such as a pregnancy and the birth of a child. This ruling of the supreme court of the land applied tort law and article 1382 to a marriage promise, making it, in effect, a contract; breaking it without basis after the woman had a baby caused her injury. These judges, under the presidency of Joseph Zangiacomi (1766–1846), a renowned magistrate and officer of the Legion of Honor who was reputedly close to power in the July Monarchy, insisted that it was not a question of recherche de paternité; the child was outside the terms of the legal debate. Rather, the man must repair a prejudice to the honor of the woman and her family. Although Mlle Baysse had been a minor at the time of her seduction, reports ignored this.[31] Moreover, reports only mentioned a marriage promise and not fraudulent seduction; fraudulent seduction after a marriage promise was implied.

By 1850, magistrates interpreted a marriage promise as an act of honor, having the force of a contract in civil law, but civil law failed to specify the obligations of a marriage promise. They were part of a social web of individual and familial rights and duties. It became incumbent on magistrates to delineate those obligations and the consequences of breaking that contractual promise. Judges decided that if a person broke that promise without due cause, thereby harming another, he would have an obligation to pay monetary reparations for that harm. Due cause for breaking an engagement occurred if the man could prove that the woman had had sexual relations with another man.[32]

Judges did not force a man to honor a marriage promise; that would impinge on his rights. By dividing paternal responsibility between child support and family filiation, judges took into account the conflict between a man's individual rights and his obligations to his children. In walking a legal tightrope that tested their skills, judges and lawyers declared that repairing damages and fulfilling an obligation to the victim of a broken marriage promise did not indicate paternity and transmission of name and property. These judges argued that a man had natural obligations to the woman he seduced and to the child. Other judges disagreed, declaring that making a man pay reparations was forcing paternity upon an unwilling man and hence a violation of his natural rights and civil law. They denied the contractual nature of the marriage promise.

An explanation of why change occurred in the 1840s rests in part on information about why judges made their decisions; however, they were not required to explain their decisions and no record of their reasoning exists. Ideas about the nature of a family and paternity were in a state of flux, and there was a great deal of disagreement that judicial decisions reflected. Judges did not operate in a vacuum, and society and culture might have influenced their decisions. Awarding damages to single mothers for the wrongs men had done them indicates a changing climate of attitudes toward seduction, honor, paternity, the family, and the rights of both men and women. Women began exercising rights as citizens, bringing those rights to public attention in a courtroom when they did not exist in written law. In considering a marital engagement as a contract between a man and a woman, magistrates acknowledged women's right to enter into legal agreements. This is not to deny the persistence of marriage contracts between the patriarchs of two families, but women began to assert a right to receive such promises in their own names. If a woman made a contract and went to court when someone failed to honor it, she appropriated rights that usually pertained only to male citizens. Furthermore, in suing for reparations for the material injury of pregnancy and a child, she was repossessing her own body, which the man had damaged. Men, however, had essential rights to family and property. As Joan Scott has astutely observed, "Paternity was the way in which nature (equated with maternity and sexuality) was transformed into social organization; in the process all visibility for the mother's role and any sense of its independent importance was lost. The rights to family and property were quite literally men's right to women; these rights enabled men of different means and social classes to recognize one another as equals and as citizens."[33] In the mid nineteenth century, men's rights remained sacrosanct, but women's performances in the courtroom allowed their voices to be heard, and they began to exercise some rights as women and mothers. Even workingwomen started to claim some rights, notably the right to work.

With the more rapid development of industry and the market economy during the 1840s, young women increasingly left their families for employment outside the home, struggling to make an honest living and accumulate a dowry to improve the chances of an advantageous marriage. Seduction, pregnancy, and children not only damaged these women's value on the marriage market but also damaged their ability to earn a living and their right to work. The right to work became part of the broader cultural rhetoric contributing to damage suits, as well as to judges' decisions to rule in the women's favor. With the economic depression of the late 1840s and declining job possibilities, the right to work became part of men's and women's demands. Furthermore, the language of a right to work, heard so loudly in the revolutions of 1848, extended to workers' rights to have some control over their jobs and their rights to have their day in court. The women who sued for damages were exercising their rights to court hearings and to make contractual agreements, as well as their right to work, which their seducer had taken from them, along with their virtue and honor. For social commentators concerned about the right to work, and for families whose daughters had to work for wages outside the home, the freedom to work also included the right to work in dignity, without degrading tyranny, and without supervisors abusing their authority and seducing impoverished young girls.[34]

The proliferating journalistic, academic, and legislative discussions of political economy, which included numerous essay competitions on the causes and remedies of poverty, may have had an impact on judicial decisions. Several authors faulted women who had natural children, especially the thousands who abandoned them at the state-run foundling homes each year. Others demonstrated greater sympathy for mothers trying to support their children alone, and for those poor and sometimes abandoned children. Moreover, the 1845 decision coincided with debates raging about reducing child abandonment. With influential politicians—among them the poet Alphonse de Lamartine—exclaiming in alarm about the abandonment of so many newborn children, worry about the expense to the state of caring for those children increased. Making fathers financially responsible may have played a role in the judges' decisions in 1845. Liberal judges with republican sentiments may have been influenced by desires to alleviate social ills by having men bear some responsibility for the plight of unwed mothers and their abandoned infants, whose numbers soared during the 1830s and 1840s.[35] Literature and art from the 1830s through mid-century portrayed poor, honest, virtuous women who had succumbed to seduction and were struggling alone. Dumas's *Le Fils naturel* first appeared in 1858. Victor Hugo brought home the plight of the poor single mother, Fantine, in *Les Misérables*, published in 1862. The well-known painter and caricaturist Honoré Daumier depicted a weeping mother leaving the Palais de Justice with her child (fig. 2.1).

Octave Tassaert's 1852 painting *L'Abandonnée* (The Abandoned Woman) is unambiguous; with a wedding about to occur in the background, a pregnant young woman faints against one of the pillars in the church (fig. 2.2).

Figure 2.1 Honoré Daumier (1808–1879), *Au Palais de Justice*. This watercolor and graphite scene dates from between 1848 and 1853. It is easy to imagine the woman and child on the right having lost a claim against the man strutting off on the left. The magistrates are up front and center. Bridgeman-Giraudon / Art Resource, New York.

Tassaert's success as an artist, especially in the aftermath of the 1848 revolution, rested on the popularity of his themes of economic or moral poverty, which often included young unwed mothers abandoned by their lovers.

Ernest Legouvé, a prominent author and member of the Académie française, whose major work, *Histoire morale des femmes,* appeared in 1848 and was reprinted nine times by the end of the century, spoke out vehemently against men who seduced women and reneged on responsibility for their actions. He excoriated society and not the women: "Among the workers, what group is most wretched? Women. Upon whom fall all the burdens of illegitimate children? Women. Who endures all shame of faults committed by passion? Women.... Is such subordination legitimate? Is it necessary? That is the question.... The moment has come to claim for women their share of rights."[36] Speaking to the issue women brought to court, he exclaimed: "Punish the guilty woman [the prostitute] if you will, but also punish the man! She is already punished, punished by abandonment, punished by dishonor, punished by remorse, punished by nine months of suffering, punished by the burden of raising a child: let him then be smitten in turn;

Figure 2.2 Octave Tassaert (1800–1874), *L'Abandonnée*. © Musée Fabre, Montpellier. Photo: Frédéric Jaulmes.

or else it is not public decency that you are protecting, as you say. It is masculine sovereignty in its vilest form: *le droit de seigneur*." He continued, "There should be a law against seduction. What form should this law take?... It's not for me to decide, but... it must exist: because it is impossible that a society should live with such a cancer at its heart;... all are stigmatized ... by this fatal doctrine of impunity. Impunity assured to the men doubles the number of natural children; half of the murderers and thieves are natural children. Impunity nourishes libertinage, and libertinage enervates the race" and is responsible for society's vices.[37] These words symbolize a cultural wind coming in from left field during the 1840s, which kept blowing with changing strength during the rest of the century.

Others on the Left, including moderate liberals, socialists, and feminists, raised their voices loudly and hindered conservative Catholics from reinforcing the code of domestic authority.[38] Saint-Simonians and Fourierist socialists, active in the 1840s, questioned the very structure of the conjugal family. To them, it served as a unit for reproduction and not as the basic constituent unit of society.[39] They argued for greater equality for women and natural children and criticized the Civil Code, including the article prohibiting paternity searches. Lawyers and magistrates did not opt for recherche de paternité, but it is likely that some of these criticisms encouraged their opinions.

Feminists contributed to the outpouring of republican and socialist publications. The Saint-Simonian feminist message, in particular, had widespread exposure. Writers such as George Sand, Pauline Roland, and Flora Tristan argued against social injustice, the sexual double standard, and the subordination of women in marriage, society, and the workplace.[40] Intense discussions, often with heated disagreements, typified debates among utopian socialists. The Saint-Simonian women, who for a short time published their own journal, *La Femme libre*, included workingwomen.

Some Saint-Simonian women, such as Claire Démar and Suzanne Voilquin, sounded like the men in arguing that "paternity is always in doubt and impossible to prove." But Démar wanted to do without it altogether, advocating free love and an end to the concept of illegitimacy. Voilquin and others argued for paternal protection of children, including those born outside of marriage, but Voilquin insisted that childcare was a woman's responsibility. Pauline Roland had three children, and took full responsibility for them, proudly giving them her name and working to support them without help from the men involved. At one point, however, she resorted to begging to support her children. Doing without paternity and filiation through the male line did not negate the need for child support. Divisible paternity was a solution. Furthermore, as emancipated women, they cherished the right to make contracts and hold men to those contracts. Fourierists also sought women's rights, objecting to the Code's requirement that women owe obedience to their husbands and that they live where their husbands lived. The feminist

Jeanne Deroin "argued that childbearers were rights-bearers according to prevailing moral and political criteria."[41] To Deroin, those rights included the right to work. The post-1851 repression silenced the feminists, but magistrates with republican tendencies may have remembered.

The Second Empire

The first decade of the Second Empire repressed much of the revolutionary and republican fervor of 1848, but the second decade in the 1860s was a period of contrasts. The voices of socialist and republican social reformers competed with Bonapartists and conservative Catholic voices who maintained that paternal authority was indispensable to men's liberty and the social order.[42] Social reformers returned to discussions of gender and poverty, pointing out how a workingwoman could not survive on her wages except by sharing living quarters or subsisting on bread. The birth of a child made her already dire circumstances even more severe. To these reformers, maintaining public order required that women live and work within families and that prostitution decline. Helping support these poor women so that they could avoid turning to sex work to feed their babies when they could obtain no other employment was a means of maintaining social order.

It was a short step from bemoaning women's inability to support themselves to declaring that the genitor should help support the child, but it was a step reformers did not take. Rather, as the moderate republican Jules Simon asked in 1861, "shouldn't society provide a refuge for the seduced girl, if not out of pity, then at least for the protection of her innocent child? Does not the mother herself, after all, deserve any compassion? Isn't she the least guilty? And when one leaves the seducer unpunished does that indicate a lack of pity for the victim? By forbidding paternity searches absolutely and without exception, does not French society incur a debt toward seduced girls?"[43] French society did not always pay this debt, but some magistrates tried to make the genitor pay.

It is impossible to determine how many women went to court in the 1850s to sue for damages resulting from broken marriage promises, the nature of their cases, or whether the judges decided in their favor. By some accounts, the numbers of women going to court declined in the 1850s, as did decisions in their favor. Magistrates may have been motivated as much by fear of opening the Pandora's box of paternity searches as by their moral disdain for the women, whom they accused of seeking payment for their libertinage. In keeping with the moral climate dedicated to achieving social order, some judges declared that such payment would only encourage women to debauchery. They criticized awarding damages under article 1382, declaring that such cases were really paternity searches, which had been forbidden.[44]

Some judges followed the Cour de cassation's 1845 decision, which faulted men for seducing and abandoning young women, and awarded them compensation on similar grounds to those cited in 1845. A woman had to show that she had not entered into the sexual relationship willingly until after she had a marriage promise. It would especially help her case if she had been young and innocent. Judges were in a difficult position. They had to deal with the reality of people's passions and also with laws protecting property. They had to decide what was a contract and what constituted material injury, while carefully avoiding any mention of paternity.[45]

In deciding to award damages but deny paternity suits, the child remained an issue, because if the baby were not the concern, as judges declared in order to avoid any taint of recherche de paternité, then the material harm to the woman was difficult to demonstrate. Without the birth of a child, the damage might have been the destruction of her honor and of her virginity, and hence the consequent reduction of her value on the marriage market. But it was difficult to win a case for damage to a woman's honor, her reduction in value on the marriage market, or for her pain and suffering. Moreover, had there been no pregnancy and child, it was unlikely that anyone would have known of her dishonor, even if she was no longer a virgin and the engagement had been broken. If no one knew, she would be unlikely go to court to tell the world of her sexual activity or expose her shame and broken engagement.

Judicial decisions ordering men to repair damages occurred throughout France during the 1850s, with no discernable regional differences. In 1851, a judge in Montpellier ordered S. to pay his former fiancée 1,200 francs in damages for the injury he had caused her by his failure to keep a marriage promise—a promise made in front of a notary. She had given birth to a daughter in February 1849 and named S. as the father, accusing him of causing her a "serious injury." She did not ask for paternal recognition of the child. In Bordeaux in 1852, a judge ruled that a man's promise of marriage as a means of seduction and then his abandonment of his fiancée was indeed an injury to her. Not only did his actions dishonor the woman, but she also had to live with the resulting misery. Declaring both at fault, however, the judge ordered the man to pay only 500 francs, less than was customary. Although she had been an "honest girl," the woman had given herself freely upon a promise of marriage and had not waited until their wedding, as she should have. A court in Douai in December 1853 decided that a man's letters, stating inter alia "I am obliged as much as possible, under my honor as an honest man, to pay damages and to give you the means to raise our child decently," were admissible evidence as a promise of child support. The judge ordered the man to pay damages.[46]

Other magistrates refused women's claims; decisions depended on the individual case and the judge. An appeals court judge in Caen in April 1850 overturned a lower court that had ruled in the favor of the woman, explaining that she had not made any preparations for marriage, and that because she was twenty-six, she was no longer innocent. Furthermore, allowing the pregnancy and child as evidence for damages would open the door to paternity searches, and he wanted to avoid ties between the child and the seducer.[47] A judge in Aix-en-Provence in 1853 found no evidence that the author of the pregnancy had promised to marry the mother or that he had ever paid for rearing the child. Her case rested on an 1850 letter in which he had said he was the father of the child that she had "just delivered." The judge said that this recognition was "non-authentic," however, since there were no official papers of recognition, and ruled that the letter could not obligate the man to furnish child support. The judge continued, "it is true that the obligation to furnish food to a natural child derives not from civil law but from nature; it is incontestable, [however,] that civil law has the right to determine the form of proof on which the execution of that obligation depends."[48] Civil law again trumped natural law. The judge did not find proof of a broken marriage promise, which might have provided reparations to the mother, and he denied her child support. To this judge, paternity was indivisible; without evidence of the father's legal recognition of the child, he ruled against the mother. In Bastia (Corsica) in 1854, another judge viewed a relationship as reciprocal, based on mutual passions, and ruled therefore the mother should not be rewarded for her weakness, dishonor, and "libertinage."[49]

In the subsequent decade, voices of republicans and feminists increased in volume. Yet even in the 1860s, magistrates were not eager to award damages to the mother, adhering to the indivisibility of paternity. In Nancy, on the eastern edge of France, in early 1865, a judge refused a mother's claim, merely asserting that paternity searches were forbidden. In Savenay, on the other side of the country, six months later another judge ruled a case inadmissible in court on the grounds that the object of the case was a paternity search, forbidden by law. Moreover, investigations in this case, he alleged, would reward the immorality of a woman and compromise the honor and peace of families. The appeals court in Rennes confirmed this decision the following year, adding that the law could not distinguish whether paternity was the primary object of the suit or a subsidiary portion of a suit for damages, but whichever it was, any effort to discover it was forbidden. In other, similar cases, judges added that the public order, good morality, the avoidance of scandals, and the security of families required forbidding paternity searches.[50] Nevertheless, several judicial decisions supported the woman and awarded her damages for fraudulent seduction, a broken marriage promise and even child support. In Colmar (in the east), Mademoiselle L. claimed that Monsieur C. had promised to marry her. After she had had two children, he left her to marry another. L. took him to court to request damages. C. alleged, however, that L. had had relations with other men at the time of conception, and that these men had brought her money and gifts, using the prostitution trope. However, in December 1863, the court decided against him, declaring that he had promised to marry her and that this fraudulent promise was a technical offense (*quasi-délit*) under article 1382. Furthermore, in his correspondence with her from 1851 through 1859, he had agreed to pay the cost of childbirth and child support. Therefore, the judge demanded that he pay 3,000 francs in damages.[51] To this judge, paternity was divisible.

Details of two cases that appeared in the popular press best illustrate jurisprudence of the 1860s. Mademoiselle Bloch, a poor worker, and Monsieur Mont, a shop assistant, had sexual relations from 1852 to 1858.[52] They worked in Paris, raising three children together. In 1858, he left for a more lucrative position in Lyon. When he returned to Paris, he started his own business and ended his relationship with Bloch. Almost immediately, she went before the civil tribunal of Paris seeking support for the children and reparations for herself. Although Mont never denied his relations with Bloch, the judge rejected her demand, basing his decision on the fact that Bloch and Mont were both adults and she had entered into the relationship willingly. Therefore there was no injury and thus no reparations. Moreover, the illicit relations "condemned by morality and law" could not serve as a basis for reparations to a person who was an adult. As for child support, the judge reiterated that although there might be a natural tie between a father and the children born outside of marriage, paternity searches were against the law. Since Mont had not legally recognized these children and had made no written pledge to provide for their necessary nourishment and education, he had no "natural obligation" to do so. In his decision, the judge declared that a man might have moral and emotional paternal ties to children born outside marriage, but that man had to have accepted them of his own free choice. There could be no official ties, no juridically declared child support, no recognition, no inheritance, and no legal responsibility.

Bloch and her new lawyer appealed this decision. Bloch probably took advantage of the 1851 law of *Assistance judiciaire*, which permitted those without resources to have the benefit of legal aid paid by the local public treasury. In such procedures, at an initial hearing, a judge decided whether a plaintiff had a valid case and qualified for *Assistance judiciaire*. Bloch's legal representative, Bertrand-Taillet, pled her case eloquently. He passionately defended the law that forbade recherche de paternité: "Until I take a stand against the grand principle of public order that forbids recherche de la paternité, I respect this principle on which the security of families rests. No, I do not attack Mont as a father; he has written several letters full of affection for Bloch and their children." Bertrand-Taillet then proceeded to reveal Mont's paternal interest in the children by quoting from a letter in which Mont stated: "I made a big sacrifice in taking charge of two of your children." When Bertrand-Taillet asked Mont why he had taken care of the children, Mont replied that it was to acquit his conscience. Bertrand-Taillet, basing his case on the contractual nature of a promise, retorted:

> You have well acquitted your sacred and natural obligation. You have obeyed the cry of your conscience.... But, neither justice, nor I, have the right to tell you that your paternity was the reason you made the commitment that you believed was your duty to make. For us, making this promise is sufficient to hold you to its execution.... Furthermore, I can say that you are a man without anyone accusing me of searching into your paternity. You have converted a natural obligation, over which civil justice has no authority, to a civil obligation, which justice can order that you fulfill.... The court can, therefore, without casting a slur on the law that forbids paternity searches, condemn you to fulfill a commitment that you have voluntarily and freely made.

Paying respect to the Civil Code, to religion, and to natural law, and to Mont's manhood, Bertrand-Taillet avoided a slippery slope that might lead to a paternity suit.

Mont's lawyer, Josseau, opened the male narrative by explaining that his client suffered from his youthful indiscretions, and then repeated the standard refrain alleging that Bloch had seduced Mont and not the other way around. Josseau portrayed Mont as one of so many "unhappy young people who let themselves get carried away by their passions and who are duped by their inexperience." As the story unfolded, Mont had met Bloch at a public ball, where many young men and women at the time had sexual and social encounters. Josseau continued: "She had the art to attach herself to him, despite the prayers, beseeching, and remonstrance of his family." The birth of children "increased her pernicious influence, and it was only after several years that Mont recognized his regrettable errors. His elderly mother asked him to come home to her in Lyon, and he left Paris to see her. He finally listened to his mother's advice, [but] ... Bloch obsessively pursued him. Happily, maternal solicitude tore away the blindfold that had covered Mont's eyes for so long. He resisted her pursuits, and it was then that demoiselle Bloch did not fear to unveil her shame before the justice system and to demand a *pension alimentaire* for herself and for her children." The tribunal had rightly refused her, Josseau continued, "applying the grand principles of morality and the law that buttress society and without which society can not exist." Josseau praised the civil tribunal's decision, quoting the judgment: "Your [Bloch's] illicit relations are condemned by law and by morality and do not constitute the basis for judicial action. As for your children, recherche de la paternité is forbidden, and you have not produced a written promise from Mont [admissible in court] to provide for the care of your children."

Bloch and Mont's gendered narratives typify those at the time. Bloch based hers on Mont's written obligation to provide for the two children, who he indicated were his. Her lawyer also invoked the natural law "he who makes the child must feed it," noting that Mont had never denied that he was the father of those two children. But there was no language of a marriage promise or fraudulent seduction and abandonment, so characteristic of other women's narratives. Mont's and Josseau's typical male narrative questioned Bloch's morality, introduced the notion of her shame, and said that her suit constituted an illegal paternity search. Josseau's narrative emphasized Bloch's motherhood, not Mont's fatherhood, in an attempt to distance Mont from a paternity search, and pointed out that his letters referred to the children as "hers," noting that Mont never wrote "my" (*mes*) or "our children" (*nos enfants*). As Josseau quoted from one of Mont's letters: "I have already made a big sacrifice in taking responsibility for two of *your* children [emphasis in original]." Furthermore, Mont's letter contained a veiled accusation of Bloch's infidelity: "Don't you see that this commitment was inspired by the affection that I had for you? That commitment toward your children disappeared along with the affection that was so undeservedly deceived [*indignément trompée*]." Mont fairly screamed in this letter: "What! Because I consented to take temporary charge of two of your children, am I then forced to provide them with a monthly *pension alimentaire?* No, no, your children are nothing to me; they cannot get a title from me from the commitment I made to them solely because of you, and that you yourself broke, forcing me to sever my relations with you." Josseau cleverly used Mont's words to hint that Bloch was unfaithful and, furthermore, by using the word "title," that she was filing a paternity suit. Bloch's lawyer argued that it was a matter of Mont fulfilling a commitment; Josseau countered that it was a paternity search. Josseau warned the judges: "Reflect well, sirs, before making your decision. I beseech you in the name of the law and of morality. My adversary comes close to basing the case on paternity, the pursuit of which is forbidden."

The attorney general, Oscar de Valée, summarized:

You have, messieurs, two questions to resolve: one question of fact [*fait*] and one of law [*droit*]. In fact, has Mont taken charge of the children born to Bloch? Has he made a written promise to do so? ... In his letters Mont speaks of Bloch's children as his own; he promises not to abandon her; ... he hopes that his family will let him do what he considers his duty. But, at the time of the rupture of relations in 1859, Mont wrote to Bloch, "I have made a great sacrifice in taking charge of your two children [*vos deux enfants*]." Here, the commitment is made, without conditions, freely, as the fulfillment of a duty of conscience. In law, must he, can he, honor this commitment? ... One says that an obligation to feed the children cannot give rise to avowal of paternity or a paternity search. ... Recherche de paternité is forbidden in the social interest, and no magistrate can fail to recognize that. ... Thus Mont, could have several children with Bloch, forsake them, leave them to a life of misery with their mother, and the law would not demand anything of him. In a word, he could profit by the protection that article 340 of the Code accords to those who do not want ... to submit to the weight of paternity in a life of licentiousness. But, alas, Mont should not make written promises. Since he has made one, the situation is changed, and article 340 does not apply. This promise does not have the effect of an avowal of paternity, but it is a question of ...

the execution of a natural obligation.... It may be possible to believe in his paternity. He baptized these infants; he provided for their earliest needs; he can be obligated to fulfill these promises. There is a basis in the Code Napoléon for these obligations.

Bloch won her appeal. The appeals court ruled that Mont had agreed to satisfy his natural obligations by legal means in these letters, where he "freely and formally" committed to provide for two of her children. Bloch did not bring proof that Mont had made these commitments for the third child. Therefore the judge condemned Mont to pay Bloch 400 francs annually for each of the two older children until each child reached the age of eighteen.[53]

Written promises and imputation of a woman's immorality constituted grounds for claiming damages, or avoiding them, while skirting a paternity search. In December 1860, Anna B. went before the civil tribunal of the Department of the Seine to try to force Henri M. to pay her reparations for seduction, a broken marriage promise, and abandonment.[54] Blondel, Anna B.'s lawyer, stressed her morality and her family's good reputation. He began, "In 1857, a family of honest artisans lived in Montauban. In that year, *un sieur* M., an officer in a regiment garrisoned in that town was introduced to these good folk, became a friend of their son, and soon was received as a member of the household," where he met their daughter, Anna. Blondel emphasized that M. "loved Anna and had announced his intention to marry her. Then, under the pretext of obtaining his mother's consent, he left for Paris. A few days before his departure, the poor young girl gave in to his pleas for sex. The day arrived when she could not hide her fault. She confessed to her mother, and as often occurs in certain classes of society in similar circumstances, she was beaten." Blondel produced a certificate from the mayor of Montauban alleging Anna's mother's good morality and certified that Anna B., her pregnant daughter, had exhibited good conduct before her "fault."

Blondel furnished Henri M.'s letters as proof of his commitment to Anna and her family. In a letter of April 1858 to Mme B., Henri wrote: "You say that you want to speak frankly with me and have nothing to hide. I want to do the same. I have loved Anna since my arrival in Montauban. She responded to my love, but did not give in to my entreaties until several days before my departure. I promised to marry her and never to marry any other woman. I swear to you again that I love you like my second mother . . . I love your daughter to distraction and I will do all that is humanly possible to realize the dream of happiness that we have formed." On that same day, he wrote to Anna: "I swear to you that I will not have any other wife than you. Come here without hesitation. I will make you as happy here as you could wish. I will keep all my promises and I will repay you in love and happiness for all the torments that you have endured since my leaving. Until then, have patience, gentleness, and resignation in the name of our love and of our [*notre*] child." On 14 May 1858, he wrote again: "I did not reply to you for a month because I did not want to influence your head or heart at the time when you are making such a serious decision. No one can make you stay in Montauban if your intention is to come to me. It would be a great joy for me to have you here and I await, with courage and patience, the day which must reunite us forever." Blondel added: "My client went to Paris where she gave birth. A short time later, Henri's mother died; he obtained his portion of the inheritance and married another woman. Anna lost all hope, and when Henri rejected her request for help, she thought to go to court."

Henri's story, narrated by his lawyer, Lachaud, put a different spin on the issues. "The process before us is initiated by a young girl, a victim of seduction. We already understand that reparation is due to Mlle B., and my client offered her what he thought was reasonable [6,000 francs]. She refused it and preferred to plead her case in court, less concerned to safeguard her honor than to claim dommages-intérêts." Lachaud built his case on the superior social level, material position, and morality of his client compared to Anna and her family. Lachaud pointed out that Henri had only a modest military position, but had a fortune of 100,000 francs in inheritance from his mother. Lachaud cast aspersions on Anna and her family: "But what was this family? ... I ... want to call to the attention of the tribunal that Mme B., separated from her husband, was a merchant of bric-a-brac, and her daughter went out to do housework." The phrase "merchant of bric-a-brac" had a pejorative connotation, lacking the cachet of "furniture dealer" or "honest artisan." Also, being separated from one's husband connoted a laxity of morals. Moreover, Anna's work as a domestic servant indicated a lack of maternal supervision, the poor economic circumstances of the household, and the difference in social class between the officer and the servant.

Readers of the report in the *Gazette des tribunaux* could well imagine the lawyer haughtily sneering:

The propriety of young poor girls must be respected ... but it is necessary to take their positions into account.... A young man of twenty-four and a young girl of twenty meet.... But ... seduction comes from both sides: it's a fact of daily life. But why didn't M.... marry Anna B.? I'll tell you.... This young man ... had a deep affection for his mother, who was vehemently against this marriage. This son ... willingly respected her wishes and vowed on her deathbed that he would never marry Anna B.... I can ... declare that he loved this young girl less as time went by. Why? ... The blindfold fell from his eyes.... He never considered marrying her, because in doing so, he would have given his name to a girl without riches. Mlle B. came to join my client in Paris. I can show you that M. did not beg her to come. A baby was born of the relations of these two people, that is true; but this infant does not exist today.... My client paid all the costs associated with the childbirth.... But Mlle B. is not content with that. I could contest the principle of her request, but I will not do so, although many kind spirits think that it is not good if abandoned girls can count on dommages-intérêts. But at least I contest the amount of the request. The tribunal will not forget that Mlle B. is twenty-one years old.... As to the injury that she has experienced, I say ... she earns as much in Paris, if not more, than she earned in Montauban. As to the honor that she has lost, it was in part her fault that she lost it. M. is twenty-seven years old, and must take care of the needs of his regular family.... He leaves this in the hands of the court. Your judgment will free him from a moral constraint that has weighed on him for a long time.

The issue was less his guilt in seduction or promising marriage; Anna's case was rather solid. It was a matter of how much he should pay. The tribunal declared that he had to pay 2,000 francs in damages to her, 4,000 francs less than what he had originally offered.

In this case, no one contested that he had fathered the child. Moreover, unlike Mont's letters, M.'s letters refer to "our" baby and not "your" baby. The issues were social class, her age, morality, and perhaps the fact that the child was no longer alive. The lawyers' speeches typify gendered narratives and social attitudes. Her story stressed her morality, emphasizing that her family was one of honest artisans, shamed by his seduction and unkept marriage promise. His story had him blinded, keeping him from seeing the error of his ways and the woman's seductive powers. His dramatic structure also emphasized her age as an adult, implying that she had known what she was doing. His clever lawyer mentioned that her parents were separated (and therefore not morally upstanding). Moreover, the nature of her employment changed from a girl from a family of honest artisans in her account to a domestic servant in his, implying, not only that was she poor, but also that she was not from a proper family. In part because the baby had died and he had paid the costs for the baby while it lived, the issue of the forbidden recherche de paternité never arose. Protection of his new conjugal family did. The key in his plea to have his payment to Anna B. reduced was the argument that he had to provide for his "regular" family and did not have a solid job.

Local magistrates increasingly admitted seduction and breach of promise as grounds for reparations, especially if the plaintiff was underage and the man had abused his authority over her. Judges were still careful, however, not to assign responsibility for paternity. Not all, however, agreed with these judges who listened to women's voices with their stories of seduction. Some argued that these judges, in hearing the women's laments, reaffirmed some of the worst abuses of the Old Regime whereby a woman who had many lovers could choose the richest one to support her and her children. Only a broken marriage promise gave grounds for awarding damages to a woman in a suit of this kind, they argued.[55]

An often cited 1864 landmark case involved a young girl seduced by an older man without a prior marriage promise. As was customary in small villages, bakers' daughters delivered bread to village notables. In the village of Vire in western Normandy, 15-year-old Mlle G., a baker's daughter, was delivering bread to Monsieur L., a 33-year-old married man of considerable property.[56] She claimed that he had seduced her after her initial resistance. Their relations continued, and when she was eighteen, she left for Paris. By the time she was twenty-six, she had six children. Then, in 1861, Mlle G. brought a case for dommages-intérêts against L. before the civil tribunal in Vire, asking for 70,000 francs from him. She produced his letters as proof of his paternity and also provided evidence that he had paid for the children's wet nurse. According to the judge in Vire, although she later went to Paris, where she became "lost on a bad road," she had "repented." It was difficult to pull herself out of her bad ways, the judge added, but she had "honest sentiments." L. had been responsible for the "fall of a young innocent girl," making it impossible for her to provide for herself and her children. The tribunal at Vire agreed to her claim for damages and awarded in her favor because the seduction had begun when she was only fifteen and she had gone to his house to deliver bread on instructions from her father. Furthermore, she brought "incontrovertible proof" of L.'s paternity. This case comes strikingly close to being a paternity suit. The tribunal did not want to award her the full amount she claimed, however, and thought her demands were excessive, since two of her children were *en pension* and two others were about to go out and earn an honest living.[57] Therefore, the court ordered L. to pay her 2,000 francs and an annual allowance of 500 francs, a sum she could live on, but not well. The children were to be placed where they could learn a respectable trade and receive a religious education, and he also had to pay 500 francs a year until adulthood for each of them.

L. appealed this decision to the court in Caen on the grounds that the letters G. had produced in the civil tribunal were inadmissible because they were his private property. The appeals court denied his claim since he did not disavow his authorship, of the letters or of the children. The judges, and the press, considered that she was his victim. She had been young, pure, and inexperienced—the daughter of poor, honest artisans—while he was more than twice her age, in a more elevated social and economic position, with greater resources. By overcoming her resistance, his maneuvers had led to her "fall from grace." The judge added that this was not an "ordinary seduction" when both adults might have consented. In this case, L. had committed a "real offense," for which he owed reparations. Moreover, as a result of her relations with L., the young woman's future had been prejudiced; "without having been victimized by the seduction she would have been able to have lived honestly and become an honorable '*mère de famille.*'" Her inability to learn a trade that would enable her to support herself and her children was not her fault; it was L.'s fault, because by seducing her, he had deprived her of resources that caused her "serious prejudice for which he must be responsible under the terms of article 1382." On 10 June 1862, the appeals court in Caen denied L.'s appeal. Furthermore, that court increased the amount he had to pay for each child and decided that the 70,000 she had requested—a huge sum for a workingwoman—was warranted.

Not content with the decision, L. appealed his case to the highest court in the land, the Cour de cassation, which issued a pathbreaking decision on 26 July 1864. Most significantly, the Cour de cassation addressed the critical concern about whether in condemning L. to raise and support the children of G., the lower courts had indirectly allowed recherche de paternité for these children and had not only violated article 340 but also article 334, which specified that recognition of a natural child had to be done through an official act, and article 335, which prohibited recognition of a child born of adultery. The courts insisted that L.'s paternity had never been at issue, only the damage he had done to her. L. was guilty of the seduction, judges said, and would have known about the serious consequences of his acts. The Cour de cassation let stand all the lower court decisions, ruling that none of them violated the injunction against recherche de paternité, and that "when the seduction is not a voluntary agreement, but consists of fraudulent intrigue and disgraceful methods by a rich and influential seducer to retain a young and inexperienced girl in a relationship that she would like to break, it can be considered as a technical offense [*quasi-délit*] or misdemeanor [*délit*] liable to serve as basis for dommages-intérêts (under article 1382)." To make sure that they were not authorizing paternity searches for children born of adultery, the judges formally declared that recherche de paternité, especially for children born of a man's adultery, was positively prohibited by law. L., however, had acted contrary to other laws, good morals (*bonnes mœurs*), and public order.

Several aspects of this case remain in the shadows. Had G. turned to sex work in Paris? One judge said that she had "fallen" but was now "repentant"—code words for prostitution. Was he echoing the male narrative, saying that she had loose morals? Declaring that L. had prevented her from making an honest living and being an honest mother was a trope for his actions having compelled her to turn to sex work. Had he taken her by force, a serious fault, for which he had to pay an indemnity? The discrepancies in age and wealth undoubtedly made a difference. Her father's reaction is unknown. Neither he nor she filed a suit for damages right away, and there is no indication of why not. Was this married, propertied man too formidable a presence in their small village? A few facts are significant: G. was a minor when L., an older married man, first seduced her. He wrote letters to her that she successfully used as a basis for her legal claim, and he paid some of the wet nurses' fees.

Themes of honor run throughout. It might have been a loss of honor for her father to admit openly that he had let his daughter deliver bread to this man. Although it was the custom, he could have been accused of inadequate supervision of his teenage daughter.[58] Judges repeatedly referred to "honor" when speaking of her. She could have been an "honorable mother" and good worker, if L.'s seduction had not prevented her. Furthermore, the judges declared that he had behaved "dishonorably" in seducing an innocent young girl whose honor had been beyond reproach. Judges could restore honor. Since he had behaved dishonorably, they restored his honor by making him do the honorable thing and repair the damage he had caused. The courts gave her back her honor by putting the blame for her condition on him, showing the world that she had been innocent and that her loss of virtue was not her fault but his. She was trying to do the honorable thing and raise her children. She could have behaved dishonorably and abandoned all of them at the foundling hospice in Paris, as so many in her position had. Finally, in ruling in her favor, the judge of the civil tribunal restored her family's good name in the village. Lawyers for the plaintiffs and defendants used tropes according to gender and culture. His narrative was based on the legal interdiction against paternity searches and on the inviolability of his private property. Her narrative detailed how she had been young and innocent and he had deprived her of an honorable life.

The 1864 Cour de cassation decision went beyond that of 1845, but in both rulings judges protested that they were not establishing the paternity of the children; they were only awarding damages to the mother and upholding public order. In 1845, the judges had decided that breaking a marriage contract without cause provided sufficient grounds for awarding reparations to the woman if there were a child. They were protecting unwed mothers and their natural children by giving legal force to formal engagements. The magistrates in 1864 decided that seduction through fraudulent means, even without a marriage promise, especially if the girl was young and innocent, was also grounds for reparations. In 1864, and for the next half century, judges argued that the legal process to repair the injury caused by the birth of an infant differed from recherche de paternité. Meticulously careful with their words, they frequently awarded in favor of the woman-as-victim but took pains never to ascribe paternity to the seducer, carefully using article 1382 to define personal injury, and not violating article 340.[59] Critics of judicial activists vehemently disagreed, insisting that the author of an injury was the same as the author of a pregnancy, and that making a man pay for the damages was the same as ascribing paternal responsibility. When judicial decisions moved from contract law in 1845 to the 1864 case involving support of the children, they came perilously close to allowing recherche de paternité. The 1864 case reverberated through the next half century, giving rise to a doctrinal shift. Women and their lawyers obtained some redress for wrongs against them, even in the form of child support, circumventing the interdiction against paternity searches. Judges' rulings also implied that fathers had a valid obligation to provide some sustenance for their children. The line between recherche de paternité and dommages-intérêts was indeed a tenuous one.

Women's court narratives portrayed woman-as-victim, yet in going to court as a plaintiff a woman operated from strength, or desperation, exercising rights of citizenship. Throughout the second half of the century, at least twenty-one court cases followed along the lines of this 1864 decision, using article 1382 to undermine the prohibition on paternity searches. Magistrates focused on tort law, requiring a man to repair the damages he had inflicted on a woman through seduction by means of a marriage promise that he later broke. As long as the man did not have to recognize, adopt, or rear the child, or give the child his name and a share of his inheritance, he was not a father, but he was still liable for the damage he had caused the mother. Yet the child, visible evidence of that very damage, was not in the spotlight. The woman was on center stage because of the injury to her body, honor, and ability to perform honorable work. Narratives frequently depicted the mother as a child herself, weak, inexperienced, and worthy of pity, victimized by the seducer.[60]

For the next several decades, an increasingly powerful judiciary demonstrated some sympathy for unwed mothers, as they and their lawyers argued for reparations for injuries resulting from broken marriage contracts and fraudulent seduction. Judges' awards in the women's favor, however, were not without opposition. Some critics insisted that magistrates were destroying the veil of privacy surrounding the conjugal family, as well as compromising cherished paternal rights. In essence, jurisprudence was "usurping individual liberty."[61] Moreover, these critics repeated the male narrative about women who went to court targeting married men, asserting that they were victims, not of seduction, but of their own malign instincts and covetousness.

Others defended the authority of the judges: "When private life tears through its wrapping and escapes outside, individual liberty encounters sovereign power, and man must account for his actions.... Without domestic virtues, there are no public virtues worthy of the name, and both are the essence of society and good morality [*bonnes mœurs*]." Moreover, the "magistrature ... is charged to sanction moral principles ... and to teach the masses or solemnly remind them ... of the first duties of public and private life." A mother had a right to ask the man to make good on a promise. It was not a question of paternity but of fulfilling a contractual obligation. Paternity based on inheritance and property differed from fulfilling a promise to help support a child and a man's obligation as the author of a pregnancy.[62]

Many who supported mothers' claims in the 1860s, republicans as well as conservative royalist Catholics, argued that paternal care, even of natural children, was a duty. The child was a member of the social body, they declared, and thus had absolute needs; natural law had designated the father and mother to provide for those needs. Paternal authority, inspired by nature, rested on the need to raise the children according to their interests and those of society. Relying on the divisibility of paternity, they stated that a father had a debt to feed his child, but no obligation to provide an inheritance to children of his born outside of marriage. If a father legally recognized a natural child, he had paternal authority over that child, but if he defaulted, the natural child came under the legal authority of the mother. Conservative Catholics strengthened their resolve to oppose paternity searches and preserve the conjugal family partially as a response to socialists whom they accused of trying to destroy the family and foment revolution.[63] To provide for natural children whose fathers did not willingly rear them, they favored state-supported Catholic foundling homes and wet nurses.

Lawyers and judges teaching and writing during the 1860s became outspoken. As Philip Nord has discussed, during this decade several elite republican members of institutions with autonomous traditions, such as the judiciary and the universities, advocated social reforms and furthered the development of a civil society. For example, Émile Acollas (1826–1891), an immensely popular law professor, republican jurist, freethinker, and vocal critic of the Civil Code, did not just argue for natural law and men's contractual obligations, but also sought legal recognition of nonmarital domestic arrangements and overturning the law prohibiting paternity searches.[64] Referring to the natural child as a "love child," he boldly argued that a mother should receive child support even when the baby was a result of consensual sex, and she had not merely been seduced by fraudulent promises of marriage. He viewed the high number of illegitimate and abandoned children partially as a consequence of the interdiction on paternity searches, adding that those high numbers were also a result of certain "vices" in the institution of marriage in laws and customs of the day, confounded by a new industrial society. Acollas taught that paternity searches would reduce abortion, infanticide and abandonment—all crimes against children. They would also be good for men, inspiring a sense of duty and responsibility. Since there could be no real proof of paternity, however, judges needed to look at the probability of a woman's fidelity during the time of conception. Like others before and after him, Acollas argued that concubinage in which a couple lived together for an extended period of time was similar to marriage. A married woman was presumed faithful to her husband, so a woman living in concubinage should be presumed faithful to her partner.[65]

During the early decades of the Third Republic, many cases of a marriage promise, seduction, and pregnancy received wide publicity. In an 1875 case, a judge ruled that a man had to pay damages and a *pension alimentaire* because the putative father had written to the mother promising support: "Whether or not my father approves of you as my wife, I will not be less the father of your child, and as a result I will contribute as much as possible to make you happy. Believe me, you can always count on my aid and protection." Although he said "your" child and not "our" child, the judge viewed these as spontaneous promises. Several lawyers faulted the judge's ruling in this case, complaining that the man had never promised marriage or seduced the woman fraudulently. Therefore, he violated neither article 1382 nor prior Cour de cassation rulings. Furthermore, given that she was one year older than he, and presumably not so innocent, he should not be liable for damages.[66] Other magistrates, in different courts, determined that although a man lived with the mother and admitted paternity in a letter, unless he legally recognized his child, he bore no responsibility for child support. Basing decisions on article 340 and not on article 1382, judges ruled that a man did not have to pay when he had a change of heart and left both mother and child. Although it is as impossible to quantify the number of judges ruling against women who claimed damages as it is to know the number who ruled in their favor, there is ample evidence that many magistrates argued that to award a woman damages in such a case amounted to paying her for her "libertinage" and so "encouraging her in debauchery."[67]

Judge Paul Magnaud (1848–1926), as president of the civil and criminal tribunals at Château-Thierry, became well known for his sympathy toward unwed mothers, believing that although they might be guilty of crimes such as assault and infanticide, society and the men who seduced and abandoned them were even more responsible.[68] Magnaud was called *le bon juge* first by Clemenceau in *l'Aurore* of March 1898 and then by Anatole France in *Le Figaro* of November 1900. Not all held him in such high esteem; some considered him subversive and a *mauvais juriste*. Born in Bergerac in the Dordogne, the son of an upper-level bureaucrat with a personal fortune, Magnaud entered the magistrature in 1880 at the age of thirty-two, arriving at the tribunal of Château-Thierry in 1887. His career resembled that of other magistrates; personal connections and republican credentials enabled him to obtain these positions at a time when clerical and nonrepublican magistrates were encouraged to leave the magistrature. With his own passionate view of the law and emotional regard for poor women, if he believed that a law was outmoded, he would acquit a guilty woman; if he could not acquit her, he would fine her only a few coins.[69]

In one of Magnaud's famous cases, a young worker, Eulalie Michaud, came before his court in 1898. She "had always been of good moral character," but when she was obviously pregnant, she was fired from her job, which had paid good wages at 50 francs a month, and forced to take a lesser one at one-fifth those wages. The opposing party, Louis Stievenart, son of one of the richest industrialists in the village, had promised to marry her. He had paid for the doctor at the time of childbirth on 7 November 1896 and purchased the layette and even a little carriage. Furthermore, he paid for Michaud's lodgings and gave her regular payments, "albeit quite modest in light of his wealth." Suddenly, in 1897, he stopped all child support, leaving her without means to sustain herself or their child. Refusing Eulalie's requests, he abandoned her for another. Meeting him on the street, and in a state of despair, according to Magnaud, she hurled stones at him, wounding his right eye. He brought charges of assault. Although she expressed regret that the behavior was inappropriate for a woman and mother, she had undisputedly thrown the stones and wounded him. Magnaud therefore found her guilty, fining her one franc (suspended) and ordering Stievenart, who had brought the charges, to pay court costs. In explaining his leniency, Magnaud faulted the social organization that "leaves an unwed mother the entire costs of the child she had conceived while allowing he who had made her pregnant to lightly disengage from the relationship and from all material responsibility." Magnaud advised Michaud to claim damages from Stievenart for "rupture of a marriage promise," and, since she had no money, found a lawyer to represent her pro bono. Michaud then sued her seducer for 5,000 francs in dommages-intérêts and monthly child support of 366 francs.

Stievenart hired a lawyer from Paris, who based his case on Michaud's allegedly bad conduct and loose morals, and on the fact that she was a year older than Stievenart and at the age of discernment. Stievenart admitted promising her marriage but said it was only after their intimate relations had begun. Alleging that she had had relations with others, he disputed his paternity. Magnaud based his decision not only on emotion, but on Stievenart's letters to Michaud during the five years of their relationship in which he said he sought to be worthy of her, complained of her "excessive modesty," referred to her as his "little wife," and asked after the child's health. He never contested her morality during all those years, promising to make her his wife and even signing those letters using both their names "Stievenart-Michaud." Magnaud concluded that Stievenart had acted as the father, especially since he initially contributed to the rearing of the baby. Echoing the concept of natural law of a century earlier, Magnaud insisted that Stievenart had a "natural obligation" to provide for the needs of the child and ignored hostile witnesses from the community who spoke of Michaud's immorality, saying that they were just jealous because Stievenart was the most eligible bachelor in town. Furthermore, he declared, Stievenart had failed to keep his promise of marriage. Therefore, basing his decision on article 1382, which required a person to make reparations for the damages he had done, Magnaud ruled that Stievenart had to pay the full amount requested, both in child support and reparations, citing seduction by fraudulent means, failure to keep a marriage promise, and a father's obligation to face the consequences of his acts and support his child, whether married to the mother or not. Although the monthly payments went to Michaud, upon her death they would go to the child until that child's majority.

Stievenart then appealed to the court in Amiens, saying he had broken with Michaud because of her immoral conduct, which he had only learned about after the birth of the child. He produced a witness who testified to seeing Michaud in the company of a "gallant" young man in a compromising position, but it transpired that Michaud had not been in town on the date given. Moreover, the young man accused of having relations with Michaud protested these "lies." Stievenart's witness was then brought before the criminal court for bearing false witness and condemned to prison for three months.[70]

Magnaud's most famous decision involved the 22-year-old Louise Ménard, who could not get regular work, yet had to support herself and her mother because her father had died. She met a young man who promised to marry her. At the time she discovered she was pregnant, he left for military service, promising to marry her when he returned. After the birth of the baby, she was without steady work and money, dependent on gifts of food from friends and neighbors. One day, after thirty-six hours when neither she, nor her mother, nor her little son had had a bite to eat, she stole a loaf of bread and was soon arrested. In March of 1898 she came before the *tribunal correctionnel* at Château-Thierry, with Magnaud presiding. Ignoring the law that stipulated a penalty for theft, Magnaud let her off without any penalty, stating in his judgment, "It is regrettable that in a well-organized society, one of the members of this society, especially a mother, can lack bread other than by her own fault.... An act, ordinarily reprehensible, loses its criminal nature when the person who commits it is pushed by the need for bread, a basic necessity."[71] The local and national press picked up this story, with praise for Magnaud's humanity coming from conservative Catholics as well

Seduction and Courtroom Encounters 99

La loi condamne « la fille-mère » qui vole un pain pour nourrir son enfant... et la même loi condamne également « la fille-mère » qui tue son enfant, parce qu'elle ne peut le nourrir !

Figure 2.3 E. Couturier. "The law condemns 'the unwed mother' who steals some bread to feed her baby, and at the same time equally condemns 'the unwed mother' who kills her baby because she cannot feed it." *L'Assiette au Beurre*, no. 89 (13 December 1902). Bibliothèque historique de la Ville de Paris.

as the political Left. The Parisian satirical journal *L'Assiette au Beurre* obliquely referred to this case in a special issue of 13 December 1902 by the artist Couturier devoted to poor unwed mothers. This picture (fig. 2.3) probably refers to an unwed mother who allegedly committed infanticide but illustrates the inequities in the law.

Although controversial, Magnaud was not alone. On 12 November 1901, the Cour de cassation reaffirmed that dommages-intérêts under article 1382 were appropriate for seduction and a broken marriage promise. Prior to that 1901 decision, numerous issues of the *Gazette des tribunaux* for the 1880s and 1890s contained dozens of reports with headlines such as: "Seduction—Pregnancy—Paternity of the Seducer—Damages." The key in having the courts award the single mother reparations was having her prove, usually by a written letter from the putative father, that he had seduced her after promising marriage, and that she had been virtuous until then. As a result of the seduction, she could no longer support herself and the baby. The mother and her lawyer (usually obtained from *Assistance judiciaire*) had to make clear that she was asking for damages for herself because of the seduction. If the mother asked for child support, the magistrates frequently denied her, observing the letter of the law, if not the spirit. In 1892, however, a Paris civil tribunal allowed a mother to have both dommages-intérêts and a *pension* for the child, in part because she was a 15-year-old domestic servant who had been seduced by her 41-year-old master, who had abused his authority over her. The appeals court in Paris partially overturned the lower court decision, awarding the young woman damages because she was a victim of her employer, but denying her support for the child.[72] Court decisions raised and only partially resolved thorny legal questions. Consensual nonmarital sexual relations did not entitle a woman to damages; they had to have been preceded by force, fraud, abuse of authority, or a written promise of marriage.[73] Some legal theorists and judges argued that if the woman entered the sexual relationship freely, even after a fraudulent promise of marriage, she should not have the right to sue for damages.

An unknown number of seduced and abandoned young women took their cases to court. Some sought other, more risky, ways to avenge their honor, such as hurling stones or shooting the man.[74] Some never lost hope that their lover would return to them and either marry them or continue to support them and their children. Some simply lacked the money, connections, and family to help them bring court action.

Why Women Went to Court

It took an enormous amount of time, money and energy—including emotional energy—for a woman to seek some compensation in court from a man who had left her with a baby to feed and support. She had to have been financially desperate, or else it was a critical question of honor—hers and her family's. Women entered the civic sphere of the courtroom with their private dramas and dreams, looking for public redress of private wrongs in intimate matters. They had to be particularly desperate, or their lawyers particularly ingenious, to claim the right to go to court when the law prohibited paternity suits. They also had to have had some indication that they might have a chance at success, which their lawyers could provide from reading legal commentaries and journals such as the *Gazette des tribunaux*.

Through their lawyers, women declared they had gone to court seeking material recompense for their pain and suffering from a broken marriage promise and for the injury the man had done to them by contributing to the birth of a child, which had in turn diminished their right to work or ability to make a good marriage. They also sometimes sought financial aid to feed their babies. Women did not often specifically mention that they sought to restore their honor; yet throughout the nineteenth century, courts were popular sites for defending family honor. In the 1820s and 1830s, fathers would go to court in the names of their daughters to try to salvage their family honor; after mid-century, women increasingly brought suits in their own names. At first glance, it would seem that the shame or loss of honor women incurred by making public their very private sexual behavior would have deterred them from becoming plaintiffs. Undoubtedly, the publicity of going to court and putting their sexual lives before a critical audience inhibited many. For others, desperate or emboldened by successes they or their lawyers had heard about, admitting their dishonor in court paradoxically enabled them to reclaim that honor and obtain indemnification for their loss. By going to court, they placed the dishonor on the men, thereby removing it from themselves and emerging with their honor, albeit not their virginity, restored. Some women had little shame in going to court to ask for money from the men who had seduced and abandoned them, seeking a restoration of honor as well as alleviation of their material need. Press reports of court cases fed the public's voyeurism and desire for melodrama. Women came on stage as victims, using the language of vulnerability—theirs and that of their children.[75] The fortunate who won their cases took their curtain calls as heroes. Those who lost possibly had poor or fraudulent cases; others became doubly victimized—by the men who seduced and abandoned them, and by the male-dominated legal system.

For a woman to have a chance to reclaim her honor in court, there had to have been a baby. An innocent young girl from an honorable family who had been seduced and abandoned, or who had had a premarital love affair after a marriage promise, might not want to publicize that relationship unless there had been visible signs of dishonor, such as a pregnancy. If she remained silent, the seduction or love affair could remain secret—unless the man bragged. But if a pregnancy ensued, there would have been no way to keep it a secret from her community. Even if she left home, as thousands did, suspicion, if not knowledge, of the pregnancy would remain. In these circumstances, it might have been in her interest to lodge a complaint and put herself under the aegis of the magistrates, believing, correctly or not, that she might receive public support, and that the law might punish a man who had betrayed her. A better alternative than suicide or infanticide as a means to reclaim personal and family honor, it would also help salve her wounds if judges could place the blame on the man who had violated her body, her heart, and her sense of reason by false promises, abuse of authority, or a broken engagement. He had behaved dishonorably by taking advantage of her; she, in turn, was behaving honorably by going to court to make him assume some financial responsibility.

Given the frequency of child abandonment in the nineteenth century, these women who went to court could also show the world that they were indeed honorable mothers; they were raising the children themselves. Women had codes of behavior and honor, usually involving community approval, regardless of what the Civil Code prescribed or proscribed. Women's ideal of honor among all social classes included marriage and family; they blamed dishonest men for keeping them from that ideal, and used the glare of courtroom exposure to avenge themselves. For poor workingwomen, the cost of childbirth and raising an infant were uppermost in their pleas. Financial desperation drove them to court.

Urbanization and industrialization created a group of workingwomen in the cities who struggled to define honor and respectability, regardless of the economy, seduction, or their own individual sexual inclinations. Among workingwomen, seduction and having a natural child were not always matters of shame; shame was the inability to keep one's children fed and clean. Communities self-regulated women's behavior. They sanctioned, condoned, and upheld neighborhood cultural standards of respectability based on shared information. Young women had reason to fear the watchful eyes of neighbors who observed when women kept company with certain men and whether they acted properly; they also noted with disapproval if women were slovenly, drank, had multiple lovers, or abused their children. In some communities of Paris, for example, it was less important if a mother were married than if she had sexual relations with more than one man or if she neglected or abused her children. To help maintain economic respectability and prevent women from the shame of community dependency, women risked a civil procedure to obtain reparations for damages resulting from seduction and abandonment. Some women deliberately publicized their intimate sexual lives in order to gain support for themselves or sanctions against the men. Women also had to protect themselves from malicious gossip, which could control their lives by ostracizing them from the community. Gossip about a woman's immorality might lead a man to leave her. When community policing was insufficient, such as an inability to enforce marriage upon a recalcitrant man, women turned to the courts in family disputes. A woman's reputation in the community as honest or as having loose morals could win or lose her case for her in court.

Men sought honor and dreaded shame, but their sense of shame was different; it involved a misalliance. A man's fear of shame may have been sufficient reason to leave his pregnant lover if there had been the slightest bit of gossip about her immorality. He could seize the slightest hint of a rumor about her loose conduct as a reason to flee from marriage. The trepidation over a misalliance may have arisen from an alarm over diluting his property with the blood of others; he had to be certain the child was his. Honor also entailed marrying someone of a similar level in society.

In court proceedings and in letters, men cited parental disapproval of their marrying women of lower social station. Such a marriage would entail a loss of honor, as well as a dilution rather than augmentation of family property. For both men and women, a good marriage entailed an increase of property or status. If a man broke an engagement at his mother's or father's request, it usually was not dishonorable; rather, he had demonstrated that he was honorable in sanctifying his parents' wishes and not giving in to what he, his parents, or his lawyer described as the wiles of covetous women. For a man, abandoning a woman was not dishonorable, because there were no community sanctions of honor to make him stay with a woman beneath his station, even if they had a baby. Accusing her of a lack of virtue would provide a sufficient and honorable excuse for breaking the engagement.

Concepts of property rights played into decisions to go to court, with property as important for women as for men. A woman's concept of property also involved her body. Making an advantageous marriage loomed large in the culture of both rich and poor, men and women alike; seduction of a woman, without marriage and without parental consent, diminished a woman's value on the marriage market, and hence family property. Thus, it was logical to go to court to make the seducer liable for the damage he had done. Property had not only a symbolic meaning but also a literal one. Protecting it from those who would harm or take it was critical, whether it was a man's material property or a woman's body. Although important, property was not everything.

In nineteenth-century France, people used the courtroom to seek recompense for a personal injury. Injuries were not only physical, although a pregnancy could be a physical wound when a result of abuse or force. Words also wounded, whether as an insult or unfulfilled promise.[76] People used words as instruments of power, to assuage guilt or expiate a fault. Men's words of seduction embodied power; men and women's words in court constructed gendered narratives of power. Women who were presumed powerless in a sociopolitical sense used the law as a tactic to claim agency and exercise control in their daily lives. In part, civil suits were also confessional narratives, varying along gender lines, in which both men and women confessed and tried to expiate their guilt. Women confessed to succumbing to sexual relationships only after promises of marriage; men confessed to being blinded by wily women's ways. Judges, lawyers, and community were the audience for these confessions. But this audience did not require truth.[77] As women and men confessed sins of seduction, they created a narrative, performing the drama for the judge and press, seeking approval or expiation. Appearance in court, with the lurid details reported for all to read, brought individual private shame to the public confessional and judicial arena. Nevertheless, plaintiffs had much to gain in terms of material support, regaining a sense of honor, or claiming rights of citizenship.

In going to court, women were making a noise, demanding attention and the right to be heard. Their court appearances were heroic acts in defiance of specific articles of the Civil Code. They had learned the tactics of using the law to their own advantage. Although many women were not acting from strength, and most were in deplorable and pathetic situations, by initiating legal suits, in general, women claimed and exercised certain fundamental rights of active citizenship, a citizenship that had been legally and formally denied to them. They were active participants in civil society, using the judicial processes and courts to settle disputes. After mid-century, they more often took legal action in their own names to redress wrongs that men had done them. Acting with male public authorities, such as members of the court and judicial system, was the first step to a more active citizenship. In this way, some women demonstrated that they were active participants in their own lives, rather than merely victims of a patriarchy. Moreover, the patriarchy was inconsistent; male judges increasingly awarded in women's favor. Women more and more acted as individuals with rights, suing their seducers in their own behalf and on behalf of their children, claiming rights as citizens to demand that contracts involving them be honored and that wrongs done them be remedied. This legal independence indicates not only a weakening of paternal rights and responsibilities but a lessening of families' control over their children's work and choices of marriage partners. Young women were increasingly outside the family circle, less the property of their fathers and more responsible for themselves. It required a sense of self even to contemplate taking legal action. Women's use of law also indicates some cracks in the law and legal system.

The Civil Code provided a blueprint for people's personal lives, which they used to construct a set of rights and obligations. Magistrates interpreted that blueprint, but not without ensuing power struggles along gender lines, with the courts as sites of contested power and paternity. Men still retained the power to give their name and bequeath their property, but women tried to exercise some limited power in their own right to rectify the injuries men inflicted on them, although their gains were difficult and small. Judicial decisions reflected nineteenth-century social and ideological disagreements about the nature of the family and paternity.

In the search for a moral order following the upheavals of revolutions, political discourse during the first half of the nineteenth century faulted unwed mothers for disturbing an idealized moral order; during the second half of the century, in the popular imaginary, disturbers of that desired moral order could also be the men who seduced and abandoned women, breaking contracts and leaving poor, abandoned natural children along the way. Like their mothers and fathers, these children in their turn disturbed the moral order, constituting a constant reminder of sexual secrets.

During the nineteenth century, judges sought a social use of jurisprudence as an alternative to written law. Both magistrates and the law were very clear, however, in not assigning paternity. Although at the turn of the twentieth century, judges might demand some child support, the male genitor had no legal responsibility to the child, and neither the child nor the mother had any right to claim a name or inheritance from him.[78] When tort law gained prominence in the mid nineteenth century, concomitant with the growth of an industrial society, it affected not just the parties directly involved but also the social fabric, involving the press and public opinion. It created rules of behavior that applied not only to business and capital but also to gender and women's bodies. Women appropriated male language pertaining to privilege and rights, as well as male forms of honor, in taking another person to court for breach of promise. They emulated male forms of contractual rights and property protection with respect to their bodies, their honor, and their children.

A complex web of social and sexual relationships involving family, inheritance, and property established a system of rights, obligations, and duties. In family matters, a series of lawyers, judges, fathers, and mothers constructed acceptable social relationships that formed the basis of society. Paternity was considered a sacred right, based on individual will. As Joan Scott has argued, paternity "was taken as a political relationship secured through institutions such as marriage and the social contract and through symbolic practices such as the naming of children." There was no place in this system for natural children, mothers outside of marriage, or involuntary paternity, such as would result from paternity searches. Therefore, paternity became juridically divisible, separating filiation rights from contractual obligations. Men had rights based on law and individual will to decide on their paternity and filiation; courts could assign duties and obligations to mothers and children. "Rights could be conceived abstractly as attributes of 'the individual'; duties were concrete practices of individuals," Scott observes.[79] If, as childbearers and mothers, women were seen as walking wombs, some judges viewed men as walking wallets, providing money for food. Moreover, in the liberalism of the nineteenth century, men believed they had a fundamental right to property. Allowing them the right to determine their heirs and maintaining the divisibility of paternity guaranteed them this right. Magistrates also could assign responsibilities; they acquiesced to natural law and ordered men do their duty to help support the children they had sired.

Courtrooms were also sites constructing the boundaries of acceptable extrafamilial behavior, while preserving the inviolability of the conjugal family. "The debate about laws is at once a debate about what kinds of sexual arrangements and forms of kinship can be admitted to exist or deemed to be possible, and what the limits of imaginability may be," Judith Butler remarks.[80] In the courtrooms, men and women envisaged acceptable and unacceptable forms of sexual behavior. Within the boundaries of acceptable sexual behavior, a man's adultery was neither shameful nor dishonorable; it was not thought to disrupt the conjugal family, unless he had a child from his adultery. Then that child might try to invade the sanctity and privacy of the conjugal family by staking a claim to the man's name and property. Therefore the Civil Code prohibited a child from doing so by proscribing paternity searches. A woman's adultery was always condemned, because she might bring a child that was not her husband's into his household to claim his name and inheritance, infringing on his rights to paternity and property. Adultery and the transmission of family property assumed paramount importance for constructions of the family. Law and jurisprudence prohibited paternity searches out of a desire to shelter scandals affecting the bourgeoisie from voyeurs and the public. They also sought to protect adulterous men from the claims those children and their mothers might make on them.

Men, women, lawyers, and magistrates explored, challenged, pushed and shifted the normative boundaries of acceptable social organization from the unacceptable. To some extent, changed sexual and social mores during the nineteenth century contributed to shifting the borders of families. Men continued to follow what they considered their prerogative—to obtain pleasure and sow their seed both within and outside the boundaries of the home. Women, however, were beginning to set some new boundaries and increasingly claimed some rights of their own. A marriage promise drew boundaries that men had to honor, and defining fraudulent seduction also set boundaries for proper behavior. Men had to live within these restrictions; failure to do so damaged not only the women but also society—damage that they had to repair. The political discourse against the "immoral woman" shifted to one in support of the "victimized woman" and against the "immoral seducer." Such a shift took a full century to be realized in culture and law. It is difficult for the state to engineer a profound transformation in private life and family law, but during the nineteenth century, magistrates took great strides in jurisprudence, especially during the last three decades, demonstrating the inadequacies of the Civil Code.[81] The Code was out of step with contemporary intimate relationships. It was giant steps behind the new concepts of rights and responsibilities in matters of sexual behavior and toward natural children.

CHAPTER THREE

Find the Fathers, Save the Children, 1870–1912

Demonstrating the power of the judiciary and of women, significant court rulings during the nineteenth century set the stage for enacting a law in 1912 to permit recherche de paternité. At issue were concepts of class, gender, the French family, and conflicting beliefs about duties and rights. The debates surrounding issues of paternal responsibility revealed a contest over male sexual domination and female sexual vulnerability, over ownership rights to female bodies, over bourgeois respectability and working-class companionship, over individual male rights to property and privacy, and over gendered notions of sexual honor—all played out in the public arena for political ends.

During the later nineteenth century, with women filing suits for reparations or child support and magistrates effectively legislating from the bench by interpreting the law in new ways, members of the Senate and Chamber of Deputies began to debate the possibility of permitting paternity searches. They argued many aspects of this complex issue, both symbolic and practical, and tabled proposals several times. As a result, passage of the law permitting paternity searches took more than three decades following the first significant legislative proposal in 1878. Jurisprudence formed a dialectic with legislative debates on the family, paternity, maternity, morality, and property. Legislative debates and opinions published in the reformist literature and legal tracts may have influenced court decisions, but jurisprudence took the lead in reflecting changes in culture and society. Although judges' language during the nineteenth century resonated in the 1912 law in many instances, judges and jurisprudence showed more sympathy to women than did legislators and the law. In general, the law of 1912 ignored the mother except as agent for her child.

During the first decade of the twentieth century, court cases involving reparations or child support differed little from those of the later nineteenth century. Judges did not require that the putative father provide the child with his name or a portion of his property, maintaining the divisibility of paternity that judges had long relied upon. Judges still required some written proof of paternity or evidence of fraudulent seduction or a broken marriage promise. Men's letters remained crucial evidence, especially when embellished with phrases such as "I am so proud of the trust you have in me and await the happy day when I can show you that I am worthy"; "I promise you that I'll make you very happy; fear nothing, my dear, I shall never abandon you"; and "Better days will come when we shall be united and not separated" (this one signed "your future husband").[1]

In an emblematic 1905 case, an unmarried domestic servant, Estelle Mahler, went to court to claim child support and damages from the putative father, Léon Girard. Mahler and Girard had been nineteen years old in 1900 when they began a relationship. They had a son in 1902, whom they both legally recognized at their local city hall. In 1905, she gave birth to a girl, whom she recognized but Girard did not. Nor by 1905 did he provide for the needs of either the boy or the newborn girl. Mahler submitted Girard's letters as evidence of his acknowledgment of his paternity. In 1903, when Girard was doing his military service, he had written to her expressing his great affection toward her and to the child. He even wrote to Mahler's father saying that he looked forward to being his son-in-law. Despite these letters of 1903, the judge refused damages to Mahler because she could not bring proof that Girard's marriage promise had led her to begin intimate relations with him. The judge determined that her relationship with Girard was purely voluntary, disqualifying her from winning a suit based on fraudulent seduction or a broken marriage promise. Furthermore, he denied her child support for the baby girl, since Girard had never acted as a father toward that infant. Girard's recognition of, and paternal affection toward his first child, however, inspired the judge to find Girard liable for child support for the boy.[2] The key in this case was Girard's recognition of the child.

Adèle Hartmann met Maurice Cohen on the street in Paris in April 1902. He was a medical student; she was a seamstress about ten years older. Intimate relations followed. They never had a dwelling in common, but in May 1903, they had a child. In one letter, he confessed that he had acted "in a regrettable caprice" and wanted to end the relationship. She then sent him a "menacing letter," leading him to seek police intervention to avoid a "scandalous situation." The judge refused her both child support and damages because Cohen had never acknowledged being the father, regretted his involvement with her, and had never provided anything for the child's needs; furthermore, she was older than he was. The judge did not comment upon her occupation or their different socioeconomic statuses, but one suspects they were factors in his decision.[3] A woman's age and alleged morality, based on occupation and social status, factored in judges' decisions. Seduction still had to have been based on a marriage promise, and the woman had to have been regarded as virtuous.

From 1909 to 1912, judges were awarding child support to worthy young women when a man had recognized the child, had made a written promise to do so, had previously provided for the child, or had written a letter indicating that he was the father, or if witnesses testified to his having acted as a father or that he and the mother had lived together as husband and wife, as the following three cases illustrate.

Marie Jaquemet met André Lalouette in March 1908, and they lived together, having twin daughters in December of that year. Lalouette monetarily aided Jaquemet and the twins, promising in writing to recognize the children and even to "regularize the situation" with her. Then he abandoned them completely. Because she could not work owing to her poor health and the needs of the twins, the judge ordered Lalouette to pay Jaquemet 50 francs a month in child support until the twins reached their majority.[4]

Marie Deniel, a charwoman (*femme de chambre*), did not succeed as well in her court case. Deniel declared that she had had intimate relations with Roux, a *valet de chambre* in the same household, only after he had made formal promises to marry her and had publicized the engagement. He then abandoned her when she was pregnant and without resources. Stipulating that Roux was the father of her baby girl, she demanded he pay child support (*pension alimentaire*) of 40 francs a month until the girl's age of majority. Roux did not deny promising to marry Deniel, but insisted that he had pushed back the wedding date because he had received some information on her past morality. He denied paternity. The court rejected her request for lack of proof of damages or of Roux's paternity, and his testimony as to her possible loose virtue.[5]

In 1911, the laundress Bataisse brought charges against Fleury, an automobile chauffeur, charging that in 1909 she had had intimate relations with him, resulting in the birth of a daughter in June 1910. Bataisse showed that during the pregnancy Fleury had written letters promising not to abandon her and their "future son." For some time after the child's birth, Fleury sent her money to pay a wet nurse, and according to witnesses expressed his affection for his "dear little girl." Nowhere in the correspondence did Fleury ever express any doubt about his paternity. Subsequently, since she could not both work and care for her daughter, Bataisse had abandoned the baby to the foundling institution of Assistance publique in Paris. She now wanted her daughter back and demanded damages and child support from Fleury. The judge decided in Bataisse's favor and declared that Fleury had to pay monthly child support of 40 francs, starting from the time that Bataisse reclaimed her daughter and until the child's majority or marriage. Fleury also had to pay Bataisse 1,089 francs for the midwife and doctors.[6] This judgment supported the arguments that recherche de paternité would decrease child abandonment and save the state money.

Prior to the Third Republic, few politicians or legislators sought to affix filiation to fatherhood; almost none wanted to change the Civil Code to permit paternity searches. Opponents of paternal responsibility for out-of-wedlock children argued on much the same lines as earlier critics. They wanted to protect men from women's allegedly immoral or duplicitous behavior. It was better, they asserted, to try to reform women's morality.[7] Working-class women's sexual morality was especially troublesome. Language and law granted a woman moral power, while restricting her legal options. Her abstention from sexual relations before a civil marriage was supposed to help moralize the working-class family. But should the working-class woman bear children outside of marriage, she became immoral; law and custom absolved the father of any responsibility and effectively prevented her from trying to form a two-parent family. Legislation and practice accepted a working-class mother-child dyad if naming the child's father might disrupt a bourgeois conjugal family. Most of the reformers who advocated paternal responsibility for out-of-wedlock children encouraged marriage, even proposing that the "guilty" man marry "his victim," but they did not usually have the mother's welfare in mind. They wanted to control her sexuality by preventing what they considered "immoral concubinage." Some rare reformers thought the men were as guilty as the women and deserved punishment of a year in prison or a fine.[8] Social reformers tended to ignore issues of paternal responsibility, focusing on the women's sexual immorality. A man could therefore seduce and abandon a young woman without any recognition of the consequences. However, women who succumbed to seduction, or worse yet, workingwomen who seduced men of a higher social and economic station, were deemed immoral and bore the consequences alone.

Revising the Civil Code to permit paternity searches was a thorny issue, because revisions would affect not only individual men, women, and children but also legally constituted conjugal families and men's rights. Unlike magistrates, legislators did not consider paternity divisible between child support and full filiation. Various legislative bodies during the nineteenth century upheld the letter and spirit of the Code, avoiding family legislation that might have impinged on the honor and power of the male head of household and the transmission of his family name and property. The social order depended upon the male-headed family and the containment of women's sexuality.[9] Legislators considered marriage as the foundation of the social order, and bourgeois marriage and property had primacy over paternal responsibility for extranuptial children. Legislators regarded any permission for a single mother to seek the putative father for child support as an endangerment of the family. They especially feared she might name a married man, thereby causing a scandal for the legally married wife and legitimate children. Furthermore, if such paternity suits were successful, they would obstruct the property rights of the legitimate children and besmirch family honor. Honor and property were integrally connected, conferring status. Forbidding paternity searches would protect that legitimate child and family from the claims of an "irregular" child, which might adversely affect the conjugal family and inheritance rights.[10]

The prohibition of paternity searches also involved issues of class. During the decades of debates, legislators' views of the working-class family were inconsistent. Reformers and politicians concerned about the poverty and alleged immorality of the working classes often employed rhetoric enjoining the working-class family to be more like the ideal bourgeois family: a married couple who delayed having children until after marriage and abstained from having more children than they could afford. Yet the civil procedure, requiring fees for the necessary certificates, made marriage prohibitively expensive for some working-class couples, while society condemned women for cohabiting and having extranuptial children. The required birth and marriage certificates cost approximately two day's wages for a woman. Then, if the man were under thirty and the woman under twenty-five, they had to provide written and notarized parental consent, or death certificates for a deceased parent. These involved further expense—the legal stamps cost a few francs—and sometimes travel and loss of several days' work. All this could add up to a month's wages for a poor workingwoman, who might earn some 500 francs a year.[11]

Legislative Proposals

Proposals to permit paternity searches did not arise in a vacuum. Not only had jurisprudence begun the groundwork, starting as early as the Cour de cassation decisions of 1845 and 1864, but lawyers, novelists, and playwrights also took up the question of paternal responsibility. Alexandre Dumas *fils* declared that a man "who put a child into the world voluntarily (and it is always voluntary) without assuring him the moral and social material means to live and without recognizing that he [the father] is responsible for all the disorder, is a criminal, classed between a thief and assassin." Dumas's highly popular play *Le Fils naturel* (1858) involves seduction, a resulting natural child, criticism of paternal irresponsibility, and bourgeois preoccupation with property and status. The young, innocent Clara succumbs to Charles Sternay's promises of love and marriage. After the birth of their baby, Jacques, Sternay leaves Clara to marry another woman, but before going, he gives her a house in the country and 3,000 francs. He does not recognize Jacques because of his family's disapproval. Aristide, Clara's good friend and godfather to Jacques, observes: "That's no reason for a gentlemen," and he advises Clara to remind Charles of the duties that paternity obliges him to fulfill. Clara refuses, saying that she wants Charles to esteem her as well as love her. Twenty years later, when Jacques is twenty-three and in love with Hermine, who is eighteen, Aristide tells Jacques that Hermine's uncle is his father. Jacques confronts his father and demands to know why he never married his mother and never recognized him. Sternay replies that he was "the slave of [his] mother and of social necessities," and later adds: "One does not marry a worker whose mother was a haberdasher [*mercier*] in the provinces, her father a road mender [*cantonnier*], and her aunt a charwoman." Dumas implies that a form of egoism and ambition prevents Charles from recognizing Jacques and giving him his name. Jacques, a successful man with a close, warm bond with his mother, exercises his right to refuse Charles's claim to recognize him at the end. This drama not only criticizes Sternay, and by implication others like him, but also accepts the mother-child family exemplified by the devoted and virtuous Clara and her son Jacques. No law or social custom compels Charles to recognize or provide for Clara or Jacques.[12] When Dumas wrote the preface to *La Dame aux Camélias* in 1867, he interjected: "Why does a man so easily dishonor a woman? Because nothing protects the woman! Why does he so easily abandon the child that he has made with her? Because nothing protects the child." This first degradation can lead to her prostitution. Dumas called for monetary penalties, according to his personal material circumstances, against "every man who violates a virgin." If unable to pay, he should be imprisoned for five years. If he made her a mother, and refused to marry her, then he could be condemned to prison for ten years. "Protect the woman against the man and then protect one against the other," Dumas concluded. "Place *la recherche de la paternité* in love and divorce in marriage."[13]

The number of didactic plays and novels calling for reform of the laws on seduction, marriage, and the family increased at the turn of the century. The Committee on the Reform of Marriage, comprising at least a dozen writers, called for laws that provided indemnities to seduced young women, the possibility of recherche de paternité, more equitable distribution of property, greater ease of adoption of minors, monthly pensions for pregnant women and nursing mothers, and other family reforms. The novelists Paul and Victor Margueritte may have thought that women were imprudent in letting themselves be seduced, but they did not think that they alone should suffer. Fathers should share responsibility for the children, who also suffered.[14]

Before the first proposal to permit paternity searches was introduced in the legislature, several authors of legal tracts promoted laws to make the seducer liable for child support when the seduction was based on false promises or abuse of a young woman's confidence, provided conception coincided with the time of seduction. They did not propose paternity suits or judicially imposed filiation, citing the lack of adequate proof and the possibility that a woman might have had sexual relations with more than one man. Rather than permitting paternity suits, the law should require the seducer to repair the damage he had done and assume responsibility by indemnifying the mother and by providing child support. As the influential lawyer Albert Millet argued in 1876, "it is not a question of civil status; it is the fact of seduction, the fact of a pregnancy, and the injury caused the woman by these double facts." Nor was it a simple question of damages under article 1382. Millet acknowledged that some "magistrates protect unwed mothers and give legal sanction to formal engagements their seducers made," but he blamed the Penal Code for being "mute on seduction" and leaving "the civil tribunals...to catch the seducers by relying on article 1382." He argued that laws against fraudulent seduction would protect women as well as "public morality"; they would not interfere with individual liberty, since private life between consenting adults would remain private. He asked, however: "Is domestic life really secret? ... Furthermore, doesn't individual liberty have its limits? Shouldn't the guilty person be punished? ... The tribunals daily lift the veil that hides individual manners to invoke justice." Millet sought a change in morals and laws to garner respect and protection for honest young women and not for the men who seduced them.[15]

Nineteenth-century penal laws condemned men for sexual violence against girls under the age of fifteen, but Millet urged extending the law in order to protect innocent girls aged from fifteen to twenty-one from seduction, whether aggravated or not. Opponents to legal changes argued that if women under twenty-one could marry (with their fathers' consent), they could also give their consent to seduction. Millet replied that the woman might have agreed, but she might have been threatened with "moral violence." Or she might have consented because she was fooled by false promises. Those opposed to paternal responsibility or penalties for fraudulent seduction described seduction as a combat in which it was impossible to know who the aggressor was, and where the vanquished and the victor were more accomplices than enemies. When opponents ranted about a poor woman seducing a rich man in order to get support, Millet replied that the "man is naturally disposed to attack; the woman to resist. Man is strong; woman is weak, timid, and reserved. The man is thrown into life's battles, has more liberty and experience; the woman is always occupied with the untroubled work of the interior." It was the woman who capitulated, not the other way around. Continuing the use of military metaphors, he declared: "We are firmly convinced that attacks [on young women] will be less frequent, less easy, and less forceful if the assailant knows in advance that after his victory, he will be obliged to indemnify the victims of war and to support the charges resulting from his conquests."[16]

To bolster his argument, he engaged in a type of international competition, invoking comparisons with the some of the United States and countries of Europe whose laws condemned forceful or fraudulent seduction and imposed a fine on the seducer. In England, if there were no aggravating circumstances to make seduction a misdemeanor (*délit*), it was at least a technical offense (*quasi-délit*). The father of the seduced girl could open a civil action against the seducer for an attack on his paternal authority.[17] Millet acknowledged that no law would stop libertinage, because the world was not perfect and there would always be seducers, but legislators should not ignore or condone such behavior. Not all agreed, arguing that legislation against seduction would insult private life and inhibit individual liberty, contending that personal and consensual relations should remain outside the law and public surveillance, unexposed to scandalous revelations.

The slow and arduous movement to change the law shifted to the legislature in 1878, but bills often languished in committees for years. Reflecting contemporary culture, arguments and positions varied over the long period of legislative debate, lasting a third of a century. In 1878, the prominent social reformer René Bérenger (1830–1915) and three other senators brought the first proposal for paternity suits before the Senate.[18] As a moderate Catholic and republican, Bérenger had the respect and support of senators across the political spectrum, from the conservative Right to the extreme Left. He had no tolerance for criminals and regarded men who seduced and abandoned women as libertines, whose behavior was illicit, if not immoral. Much of Bérenger's work was in the cause of exploited women and children in the interest of protecting public and private morality and combating government-licensed prostitution, which contributed to earning him the sobriquet "Pére la pudeur" ("Mister Morality"). Like other republicans of his era, he struggled to reconcile his battles against immorality with his liberal ideals extolling individual liberty. To him, permitting paternity suits with specified criteria could still safeguard the individual liberty of men and also protect exploited young women and their children. Bérenger and his cohort did not want to eliminate article 340, but merely to add more exceptions, allowing paternity suits for child support in cases of rape, fraudulent seduction, or if the father had legally recognized the child, similar to the terms that magistrates had employed in their decisions. This issue lay dormant in a Senate committee, although not in the press or courts, for five years.

Not until 7 December 1883 did senators consider Bérenger's proposal. Bérenger began by acknowledging themes of recherche de paternité in novels and in the theater, as well as in numerous legal treatises by prominent law professors, quoting Émile Acollas, who contended that the lack of recherche de paternité had a "regrettable influence" on morality and should be modified. Bérenger and his allies invoked the Cour de cassation's decisions in 1845 and 1864 as precedents. He and his supporter on the right, the monarchist Edmond Dufaure de Gavardie, further declared that since jurisprudence contradicted the law, the law should be changed. The proponents of recherche de paternité, however, significantly differed from some magistrates by maintaining the indivisibility of paternity. Bérenger asked: "How is it possible to ask an indicted man to give the woman reparations founded on the birth of a child without recognizing paternity? How is it possible to provide the children with a *pension alimentaire* without imputing paternity to that man?" He continued: "What proof is necessary to give a child the right to food from the father but is not sufficient to give that child the right to bear the father's name or claim a portion of the inheritance.... Either a child is someone's child or he is not." By implication, either a man was the father or he was not. "The situation of the child is indivisible," Gavardie asserted. "If he has a right to claim support for food, he can only claim that right by virtue of a natural right that creates filiation."[19]

Bérenger and his leading opponent in 1883, the left republican Jules Cazot, who argued from a position of power as minister of justice, sometimes appeared to talk at cross-purposes. Cazot feared a return to the Old Regime; Bérenger held certain aspects of his proposal as French tradition, which he left undefined. Cazot focused on filiation and the problems of imposing fatherhood on a man and making him give his name and inheritance to a "bastard," rather than on the poor natural child, who was in the spotlight of Bérenger's proposal. Bérenger never referred to the children as "bastards" or even as "illegitimate," but always as "natural," even when comparing them specifically with "legitimate" children. His focus was on the children, who would be out on the street because men had caused damage to the women and refused to support them and their children. Cazot concentrated on the need to avoid scandals involving the private lives of established propertied families. He admitted that other legal processes, such as marital separation and renunciation of paternity, exposed scandals, but the scandals in paternity searches would be greater, inasmuch as plaintiffs and defendants alike would introduce specific private information—and misinformation—to prove, or disprove, paternity. Furthermore, Cazot objected to arguments based on men's abuse of women through seduction: "I do not believe much in seduction; I believe that there are many more women who seduce than women who are seduced." Senators smiled at these words. Cazot further protested: "the attribution of paternity is not a penalty [for seduction]."[20] The Penal Code provided penalties for seduction, albeit of a minor child, and attribution of paternity was not one of them.

The senators debated the nature of the French family, of marriage, and of presumptions of paternity. They generally agreed that the family was based on a legal marriage between a man and woman. Bérenger stressed the importance of marriage for a woman, because in this "society a woman is something [*quelque chose*] only by marriage." For a woman of the "underprivileged classes," marriage was a form of "emancipation" and so vital to a woman that a marriage promise was a form of seduction. He further contended that a woman had grounds for legal action against a man if he promised marriage and then broke his promise. Therefore, article 340 should be changed to allow women some recourse if during the time of the engagement a pregnancy ensued.[21] Cazot maintained that men should have the liberty to form a marriage and also to break a marriage promise. Both Cazot and Bérenger acknowledged that many urban working-class women and men lived in consensual unions. To Bérenger, if a couple lived together and had children, and the man provided for the children, that made him de facto the father. Supporting the children was tantamount to acknowledging them, and he therefore should be liable for a paternity suit, and become the father de jure. Cazot, on the other hand, referred to such unions as "inferior marriage." To allow paternity suits in such cases would create and sanction another family construction, one that was second-rate. There was only one type of marriage and family in France, the legal family. Not surprisingly, the republican and socialist Alfred Naquet, often called the father of French divorce, took issue with Cazot on what constituted marriage and filiation. He agreed with Bérenger that there was a presumption of paternity when a man and woman had lived together as a family for a certain number of years, even without a legal marriage, if there were children, and if the man had provided for them as a father. It should not be up to the child to establish proof of paternity, but rather the man who should furnish proof refuting paternity, if that were the case.[22] Finally, after three days of debate, Bérenger sensed defeat and withdrew his proposal on 10 December 1883. Senators refused to send it back to committee and ended the discussion because they feared that recherche de paternité would favor cohabitation, a decline in personal and national morality, and lead to scandals for legally married families.[23]

Lawyers outside the legislature debated Bérenger's proposal in particular and paternity searches in general. They discussed seduction that occurred in factories and workshops and the increase in couples living together without marriage in what the French nonpejoratively call *concubinage*. Some praised Bérenger's proposal for attempting to deal with the sexual abuse of vulnerable young workers by their supervisors. Paternity searches, they contended, might diminish the immoral behavior of seducers, who had legal immunity for seducing a girl older than fifteen, except if kidnapping or violence were involved. Other social commentators asserted that only women of loose morals would consent to seduction, and that paternity searches would encourage women's immorality. Moreover, if a woman consented, then there was no issue of seduction, fraudulent or otherwise. They continued to declare that the honor of families depended on prohibiting paternity suits, so that private life would not be open to an "intolerable inquisition" and the danger of scandals. Moreover, paternity was difficult to prove, and filiation of natural children involving an inheritance should be avoided in the interest of social stability. These objections did not deny the duty of a natural father to the child, however. "It is an illusion," they concluded, "to believe that to prevent libertinage it is sufficient to threaten only the woman with the consequences." The man also must fear the consequences; granting impunity to the man invited him to seduce vulnerable women.[24] Yet these very lawyers who wanted some men to bear the consequences of their seduction still opposed paternity suits; they separated seduction with violence, which was a misdemeanor, from consensual sex and paternity searches involving filiation.

Coinciding with the defeat of Bérenger's proposal on 11 December 1883, Gustave Rivet, a Left Radical deputy from Grenoble (Isère), presented the Chamber with a much more radical proposal that recherche de paternité be permitted if there were written proof or sufficient witnesses to any of the following circumstances: cohabitation of the mother and putative father; rape at the possible time of conception; fraudulent seduction; or that the putative father had contributed to the care of the child. Prostitutes were not entitled to file paternity suits, and women who filed "in bad faith" were to pay a heavy fine. This legislative proposal, however, was never brought to the floor. In committee, Rivet's colleagues criticized it for being too broad and for providing insufficient proof of paternity. The terms of the debate were reminiscent of the debates of the Corps législatif almost a century earlier in which those addressing the topic of recherche de paternité had discussed the nature of proof, the value of the mother's word, contracts and obligations, and the rights of children.

Rivet submitted his second proposal to the Chamber in 1890. In addition to requiring written proof or sufficient witnesses to the couple's concubinage, he added six other provisions, detailing procedure, special circumstances, and time limitations. Although he worried about the mothers' morality, he was more concerned with their material needs. He contended that the father should marry the mother, and that if he refused, the mother should have the right to claim damages and child support. Furthermore, if a woman libeled or slandered a man by bringing a paternity suit in bad faith, she should be liable to punishment for defamation of character. This proposal went down in defeat.

In 1895, Rivet submitted his third proposal. In keeping with a strong national preoccupation in having the state take measures to prevent infant mortality and depopulation, he buttressed this proposal with data providing infant mortality rates according to the marital status of the mother. He showed that extranuptial children had a mortality rate almost twice that of those born to married couples. In addition to identifying three female crimes (abortion, infanticide, and child abandonment) as major contributing factors to depopulation, proponents of paternity searches argued that prohibiting them raised infant mortality. They couched their language in terms of the interests of the nation, those of the "innocent child," and the "rights of the woman." Furthermore, they argued that cohabitation constituted a presumption of paternity, because a couple lived as if in a state of marriage.[25] This time, Rivet had additional support from the official Catholic legal community on the Right and the socialists on the Left.[26] The same year, a group of socialist and Left Radical deputies submitted a bill not only to permit paternity suits but also to accord extranuptial children the same inheritance rights as those born within marriage; they referred to the measure as *recherche de la filiation*. The socialists collapsed the issues of paternity and inheritance and sought to make children born outside a legal marriage equal with legitimate children.[27] In 1897, the Chamber defeated both bills, despite a long and elegant appeal pointing out that the arguments against paternity searches were spurious.

Conservatives and Catholics, those primarily opposed to recherche de paternité, were divided. Although they pitied the innocent woman who had been raped, seduced, or kidnapped, they envisioned recherche de paternité as destroying the ties of legal marriage and the family. In the end, Catholic legislators decided that unpunished seduction was worse than acknowledged *concubinage*. After all, they said, *concubinage* resembled family life, and seduction was a moral sin (especially if accompanied by force or dissimulation). Social Catholics, sometimes sounding like centrist Radicals, couched their arguments in terms of encouraging morality as well as alleviating the women's misery and preventing the crimes of abortion or infanticide. They found that the limitation of paternity suits to a child's sustenance was a measure they could ratify. More conservative Catholics invoked the similarity with Old Regime canon law, which had permitted paternity searches.[28]

In 1900, the indefatigable Rivet, now a senator with strong backing from deputies and other senators, submitted his fourth proposal. The main advocates of the bill, the Radicals, who by 1900 were less radical and more centrist, stressed the need to help the poor innocent children and supported recherche de paternité as a means to save children's lives and counter France's depopulation. Socialists envisioned recherche de paternité as a step toward eliminating legal distinctions between legitimate and illegitimate children. If marriage were proof of paternity, they argued, cohabitation should also be proof. The socialists' language resembled that of the members of the Convention in the year II (1792–93) who had had the similar goal of eliminating legitimacy distinctions; the Convention, however, had tried to do it by decree and had disdained recherche de paternité.

Despite much support, the bill remained in committee until 1910, when the Senate finally debated it from 7 to 17 June. As in previous years, and in so many other legislative proposals, lawmakers fixated on depopulation and prevention of abortion, infanticide, and child abandonment. They discussed women's morality ad infinitum, especially protesting paternity searches, because prostitutes and other "immoral" women would bring any rich man to court to get paternity for their children; they sought language to avoid that. As they came to accept *concubinage notoire* (used nonpejoratively of cohabitation or consensual unions, which the community viewed as resembling marriage) as presumptive proof of paternity, they also regarded a woman's publicly viewed misconduct (*inconduite notoire*) as grounds for disallowing a paternity suit. They still feared the possibility of public scandals involving conjugal families. Some legislators declared that marital separation, divorce, and disavowals of paternity already made family scandals public; others replied that searching for proof of paternity would be more invasive. They settled on forbidding the press to report specifics of any case. In their endless discussions of the nature of proof, they allowed testimonial proof, presumptions of paternity, and written avowals, drawing on the experience of magistrates.

Senators finally approved all the measures on 11 November 1910 and sent the bill to the Chamber, which passed it in 1912 and then sent it back to the Senate, where senators debated the measure for the last time, passing it on 8 November 1912. It became law on 16 November 1912. After more than a quarter century of debate and seven legislative proposals, a range of conservative, Catholic, Radical, and socialist legislators had ultimately agreed that recherche de paternité was in the general interest of society, would safeguard the rights of the mothers, while affording justice to the fathers, and would protect the children. They modified article 340 of the Civil Code accordingly. Many legislators did not like the word *recherche*, since to them it implied that a woman could go into any household, make trouble, and name just any person as the father of an illegitimate child, thereby ending a man's right to privacy and property. Fearing the implications of paternity searches for all innocent men, legislators titled the final law "judicial recognition of natural paternity" (*reconnaissance judiciaire de la paternité naturelle*). Under proper conditions of proof, a judge could henceforth order filiation as well as child support.[29]

Article 340 of the Civil Code permitted paternity searches under specified conditions; most important, the man could not have been married to another woman at the legal time of conception, determined to be between 180 and 300 days prior to the birth of the baby.[30] A mother could take action only as plaintiff in the name of the child during the first two years of the child's infancy, or within two years after the father stopped supporting the child or their relationship ended. If she acted in her own name, the judge could disregard her request. Acceptable proof consisted of written letters from a father in which he indicated that the child was his. This was tantamount to his avowal of paternity.

Some authorities argued that the demand for written proof undermined the law, resulting in few cases of recherche de paternité being brought before the courts. Lacking letters, a mother needed to bring testimony of *concubinage notoire* in which neighbors, friends or relatives attested that she and the putative father had freely and openly lived together "maritally" during the legal time of conception.

The law also allowed a father's prior regular contribution to rearing the child, such as paying the wet nurse, as proof of paternity. Paternity suits were still justified in cases of rape or kidnapping when the time of rape coincided with the legal time of conception. Legislators generally argued that a younger man could not be held liable for "fraudulent seduction" of an older woman, but could be held liable for child support.[31] Women who reputedly engaged in public misconduct were prohibited from bringing paternity suits. Much of the debate revealed the lack of a clear separation between the public and private. *Concubinage* and misconduct had to be

Figure 3.1 Jehan Testevuide, "The Games of Love." —"Not him, he's too yucky! I don't want to call him papa!" *L'Assiette au Beurre*, no. 8 (23 May 1901). Bibliothèque historique de la Ville de Paris.

public; but to preserve the privacy of propertied families, all legal proceedings had to be behind closed doors.

Before bringing paternity charges, the mother had to recognize her child legally. If the mother did not file a paternity suit in the child's name within the specified time, the grown child could seek judiciary recognition of the putative father's paternity within one year after reaching adulthood. A mother bringing paternity charges in bad faith would suffer penalties—penalties that feminist supporters of paternity searches such as Maria Vérone and Victor Margueritte viewed as "appalling" and a "murderous obstacle to justice."[32] Finally, children of an adulterous or incestuous relationship could not bring paternity suits. But the imprecision of law provided for broad judicial discretionary power. Furthermore, the mother's appeal for judicial recognition of paternity could be bound up in court delays, often lasting more than a year, and then fail to reach a hearing because the judge deemed her immoral or out to blackmail the man; or the judge may simply have wanted more evidence. The most cautious and far-sighted seducers could still avoid paternal responsibility, especially if they were married, left nothing in writing, or could show that the woman had brought charges in bad faith or had other lovers.[33]

Discussion of paternity searches was loud and strong, not only in the legislature, but in the popular press, which parodied the legislators' arguments. In 1901, confronted by his young mother with an elderly gentleman in a cartoon in the satirical illustrated journal *L'Assiette au Beurre*, a small boy says, "Not him, he's too yucky!... I don't want to call him papa!"

A year later, *L'Assiette au Beurre* devoted an entire issue to unwed mothers, in which more sympathy is shown to the women than to the men, in favor of recherche de paternité, as figures 3.2 and 3.3 illustrate.

The July 1910 issue of *L'Assiette au Beurre* focused on recherche de paternité, lampooning the contradictions in some of the debates and also satirizing legislators' fears of what might happen after passage of the law. The cover illustration (fig. 3.4) depicts a blindfolded woman grabbing "just any man," precisely as opponents of paternity suits had feared. In another cartoon, titled "The Supreme Argument" (fig. 3.5), a male servant seeking to seduce a young female domestic tries to convince her that "if you have a kid, you can force the boss [*le singe*: that is, the "monkey"] to acknowledge it [as his]." Using language typical of men brought to court on paternity charges, he speaks of "you"—not "we"—having a child and takes it for granted that she has also had sex with her employer. A cartoon titled "A Legacy" (fig. 3.6) mocks scheming women and the use of written proof, caricaturing a dying mother who leaves her son a legacy of letters written to her by millionaires, from among whom, she says, he will be able to choose a father when he attains his majority. Critical of women's infidelity and of the validity of *concubinage notoire* as proof of paternity, in a cartoon titled "The End Justifies

Figure 3.2 E. Couturier, "Why should I care? *Recherche de la paternité* is forbidden!" (*top*) "The seducer wins again" (*bottom*). *L'Assiette au Beurre*, no. 89 (13 December 1902). Bibliothèque historique de la Ville de Paris.

Juste châtiment contre le séducteur, mais non un remède contre la séduction et l'abandon.

Figure 3.3 E. Couturier, "Just punishment of the seducer, but not a remedy for seduction and abandonment." *L'Assiette au Beurre*, no. 89 (13 December 1902). Bibliothèque historique de la Ville de Paris.

Figure 3.4 Maurice Radiguet, "*Recherche de la paternité*... Or the game of the Fish and Duck [blindman's bluff.]" *L'Assiette au Beurre*, no. 484 (9 July 1910). Bibliothèque historique de la Ville de Paris.

Figure 3.5 "The Supreme Argument." —"And then, if you have a kid, you can force the boss [*le singe*: that is, the "monkey"] to recognize it [as his]." *L'Assiette au Beurre,* no. 484 (9 July 1910). Bibliothèque historique de la Ville de Paris. Unsigned, but by either Juan Gris or Maurice Radiguet.

Figure 3.6 Juan Gris, "A Legacy." —"My son, take good care of these letters that I'm leaving you. Thanks to them, at your majority you will choose a father from among the millionaires who have written them to me." *L'Assiette au Beurre*, no. 484 (9 July 1910). Bibliothèque historique de la Ville de Paris.

Figure 3.7 Maurice Radiguet, "The End Justifies the Means." —"You think that I live with Gaston for my pleasure? It's necessary that my kid has a father!" *L'Assiette au Beurre*, no. 484 (9 July 1910). Bibliothèque historique de la Ville de Paris.

DIALOGUE DE COURTISANES.

— Épatante, cette loi !... Nous-mêmes, pourrons dénoncer l'un de nos clients comme étant le père de notre lardon, à condition de rester dix mois tranquilles...
— Oui, mais qui nous flanquera à bouffer pendant ces dix mois-là ?...

Figure 3.8 Maurice Radiguet, "Conversation of Courtesans." —"This law is great! Now we can denounce one of our clients as the father of our kid on the condition that we lie low [i.e., stay without work] for ten months." —"Yes, but who'll feed us during those ten months?" *L'Assiette au Beurre*, no. 484 (9 July 1910). Bibliothèque historique de la Ville de Paris.

Figure 3.9 Maurice Radiguet. —"Admirable law! The seducers will now have to think twice."
—"Those who have the dough, sure. The others still won't give a damn . . . what have they got to lose?" *L'Assiette au Beurre*, no. 484 (9 July 1910). Bibliothèque historique de la Ville de Paris.

— M. Victor Margueritte estime que seules les femmes irréprochables devraient avoir le droit de poursuivre.
M. Prudhomme. — Ce monsieur me plagie... Bien avant lui, j'ai dit : « J'admets qu'une femme ait des amants, à condition qu'elle soit de mœurs irréprochables... »

Figure 3.10 Maurice Radiguet. —"M. Victor Marguerite estimates that only women of irreproachable conduct will have the right to pursue a man." M. Prudhomme: —"That man plagiarized me. Well before him, I said: 'I admit that a woman could have lovers on condition that she is of irreproachable morality.'" *L'Assiette au Beurre,* no. 484 (9 July 1910). Bibliothèque historique de la Ville de Paris.

JUSTE RETOUR DES CHOSES D'ICI BAS.
— Nous avions jadis l'innocente enfant qu'un misérable avait rendue mère. Nous aurons maintenant le candide jeune homme qu'une vile séductrice a rendu père !...

Figure 3.11 Maurice Radiguet, "Just Rewards Here on Earth." —"We used to have an innocent young girl whom a scoundrel made a mother. Now we have a guileless young man whom a vile seductress has made a father." *L'Assiette au Beurre*, no. 484 (9 July 1910). Bibliothèque historique de la Ville de Paris.

the Means" (fig. 3.7), a woman says to her lover, "You think that I live with Gaston for my pleasure? My kid has to have a father!" In another cartoon (fig. 3.8), two "courtesans" on a streetcorner cynically discuss the merits and demerits of the law and how it would be quite difficult for them to use it to their advantage.

Not only critical of wily women but of crafty men as well, other illustrations satirize some men's reactions and loopholes in the law. Figure 3.9 sarcastically points out how men could seduce women and still avoid paternity suits. "Admirable law!" an elderly *flâneur* exclaims, standing in front of a sign in a park advertising an agency offering to help women with paternity suits. "Seducers will now have to think twice." —"Those who have dough, sure," his interlocutor replies. "The others still won't give a damn . . . what have they got to lose?" Yet another cartoon (fig. 3.10) mocks Victor Margueritte's idea that only women of irreproachable morality should have the right to bring paternity suits; "M. Prudhomme"—who may perhaps be the Parnassian poet René Sully-Prudhomme (pseudonym of René François Armand Prudhomme [1839–1907]), winner of the first Nobel Prize for Literature in 1901—gripes that Margueritte stole the idea from him: he said it long before. Finally, a cartoon (fig. 3.11) derisively depicts the world turned upside down as a result of the proposed law: yesteryear's innocent young girls impregnated by scoundrels have been superseded in the popular imagination by guileless young men trapped into paternity by vamps. For *L'Assiette au Beurre*'s cartoonists, except for E. Couturier in 1902, the women they depict are hardly victims of men's seduction; rather, the artists focus on the arguments against recherche de paternité and portray women as operating in bad faith and victimizing men; in part, these illustrations represent men's fears that women would abuse the law.[34] Public opinion was as shaded as some of these cartoons.

Why Did the Law Pass in 1912?

Legislative debates reveal the eventual resolution of conflicting attitudes toward seduction, sexuality, morality, and the rights and responsibilities of men and women. An evolution in public opinion, shaped in part by feminists, novelists, playwrights, philosophers, and lawyers, allowed for reconsideration of critical issues. On the broadest level, the cultural and political climate of the Third Republic regarding seduction and paternal responsibility shifted, in part as a result of an increasing number of court decisions awarding a mother damages for seduction and child support. These court decisions rendered old prohibitions ineffective. Moreover, by the turn of the century, a large number of republican jurists had been elected to the Senate and Chamber. The measure also passed in part because numerous and vocal feminists addressed the issue, in part because it was in keeping with a myriad of other social measures supporting children and national population growth, and in part because state intervention in personal and family lives had already increased, especially in the domain of legislation allowing for deprivation and disavowal of paternal authority. Moreover, the long period of legislative deliberations allowed interested politicians to state their positions and make their voices heard in the relevant debates on the respective rights of men, women, and children. All bands of the political spectrum exhausted their arguments, finally finding a common consensus. The passage of the law in 1912 was one of the crucial strands of the web of social welfare measures woven by the complex social and cultural forces of the Third Republic that began to accept some children's rights (especially the right to sustenance) as competitive with men's rights. In the conflict between the priority of children's rights versus men's rights, the cultural emphasis shifted to children's rights.

Passage of the bill required that legislators resolve the questions of whether to exempt married men and how to deal with women who lied. Whether to include children born of a man's incestuous or adulterous relationship involved prolonged and impassioned discussion, holding up passage of the bill, because it encompassed the fundamental issues of male sexuality, the responsibility of married men, and the possible introduction of out-of-wedlock children into the legally married family. Most legislators condoned married men's sexual infidelity. Yet the proponents of permitting children born of an adulterous relationship to file paternity suits argued that children born of such a relationship had the same rights to sustenance as other children. Gustave Rivet initially wanted to include children born of an adulterous relationship, because "that child is still a child. Why should he be deprived of his rights just because a parent was an adulterer?"[35] This argument is strongly reminiscent of Cambacérès's 1792 argument for the natural rights of all children. As in the decade from 1794 to 1804, most legislators a century later rejected the idea of an illegitimate child encumbering the inheritance rights and property of the legitimate children, or dishonoring the father's legal marriage and shaming his wife. Children of an adulterous woman were also problematic, but her husband could always disavow paternity in court. This argument against paternity searches involving married men supported the middle-class family strategy that called for the accumulation and preservation of wealth as a component of family honor, while at the same time allowing for male sexual permissiveness.[36] Legislators also wanted to avoid blaming the innocent natural children for their parents' sins. Thus they did not explicitly exclude married men from paternity suits, but effectively exempted them by letting stand the ban on children of adulterous relationships filing suits and inheriting. Although advocates of paternity searches placed less blame on the mother's immorality and put more emphasis on the child's rights and fathers' responsibility, it was still a far cry from having respect for, and confidence in, single mothers.

The most hotly debated issues were the fidelity, morality, and credibility of the unmarried mothers. Whereas questions of unmarried mothers' morality were largely absent from the debates of the First Republic, they stood front and center in nineteenth-century jurisprudence and the social controversies of the Third Republic. Within the moral climate of the late nineteenth and early twentieth centuries, legislators had to work out the nature of proof based on the honor and fidelity of men and women, with an eye to the preservation of the honor and property of married men and their families. When legislators discussed the nature of proof, in part they were considering women's fidelity. The most acceptable proof of paternity was a father's letter openly admitting his role. Lacking that written statement, however, *concubinage notoire* at the probable time of conception became acceptable proof. What was the difference, Rivet queried, if a woman said "I do" in front of the mayor or not, provided she had kept her virtue, her fidelity, her morality, and her dignity?[37]

Lawyers argued that when the friends and families of the couple knew of and accepted their liaison, the fidelity of the woman seemed probable. Many legislators called for the same rule for proof of paternity in *concubinage notoire* as in marriage. The married woman was presumed faithful, several reformers declared, unless proven otherwise, yet the woman living in concubinage was presumed unfaithful. It was time, they said, to end the contradiction and presume that a woman living in concubinage was as faithful as a legally married wife. It seemed logical that if concubinage resembled marriage, and a married man who divorced had to pay child support, then a man who left his partner should also have to pay child support.[38] The debate, however, was less about logical assumptions about the fidelity of women living in concubinage than it was about women's sexuality, which legislators equated with moral and social disorderliness. Proof of women's sexual fidelity, not men's, was at issue. After years of debate, legislators apparently accepted couples living together without legal marriage, but they left the determination of what constituted *concubinage notoire* to judges in the twentieth century.[39]

Arguments against paternity searches centered on preventing a scandal for an innocent married man and his family that a woman might create by bringing false charges. The rhetoric shifted from the eighteenth-century maxim "Creditur virgini"—trust the young woman on her childbed—already in disrepute by the time of the Revolution, to the late-nineteenth–early-twentieth-century idea that one should not believe a single mother without substantiated proof, because she would most likely lie and name a man in bad faith. The extensive debate over the "bad faith" clause was in part a response to a generalized fear of female sexuality, starting at the end of the eighteenth century and pervading the nineteenth. Although Rivet's proposals emphasized the difference between a woman living in concubinage and a prostitute, lawmakers obsessively feared that innocent men would be subjected to extortion by wily women or by women who engaged in sex for money.[40] For decades, this fear hindered passing a law permitting paternity searches. Debates over women's credibility continued until final passage of the legislation in 1912, when the cultural climate regarding morality and honor of men and women had come to recognize that many people of different social classes had relationships outside of marriage, and that paternity suits could be justifiable under the proper circumstances.

Even supporters of paternal responsibility wanted to protect men's honor and reputation by prohibiting women from bringing charges against a putative father in bad faith. They almost obsessively dwelt on designing legislation that would prevent a poor workingwoman, often considered as having loose morals, from seducing a man of some economic means, such as one of their sons, for her own profit.[41] Even Alexandre Dumas *fils*, whose plays and treatises supported paternity searches, wrote that any woman who pursued an innocent man to create a scandal should be subject to a penalty ranging from ten years in detention to twenty years of forced labor for bearing "false witness."[42] These were harsher penalties than he wanted for men who avoided child support or for those who violated a virgin. Some legislators, mostly of the political Left, opposed penalties for bringing charges in bad faith. Yet none could agree on what constituted proof of bad faith, or on the precise penalties; they left that to the judges.[43] Although some senators argued that criminal penalties were excessive, the Senate endorsed a penalty of five to ten years in prison and a fine from 500 to 3,000 francs for women who defamed, libeled, slandered, or blackmailed a man by bringing false charges, thus allowing passage of the law.

To answer those who feared scandal for a married man and his family, supporters of paternity searches argued that the possibility of scandal was no greater in paternity searches than it was in cases of divorce, disavowal of paternity, or adultery. Throughout the nineteenth century, fear of scandal neither deterred men who suspected their wives of adultery from disavowing paternity or seeking marital separation nor deterred women from demanding separation because of their husbands' adultery.[44] Before the 1884 law making divorce possible, a wife could demand legal separation if her husband's adultery had occurred in her marital home. Underlying paternity debates was the fear of scandal as well as the freedom of all men, married or not, to engage in sexual relations with women and avoid responsibility for any ensuing children. Accordingly, in addition to penal sanctions, the Senate and Chamber voted that there should be no publicity in paternity suits; paternity hearings were to be held behind closed doors, and newspapers were prohibited from printing details of the proceedings to avoid the public scandal, shame, and dishonor for "legitimate families."[45] When Senator Paul Strauss offered an amendment that would have the same measures applied to *recherche de maternité* as in *recherche de paternité*, because the honor of the putative mother was as important as that of the father, his colleagues met his amendment with stony silence, and he was reluctantly forced to withdraw it. To many of the legislators, women had already lost their honor when they became pregnant outside of marriage. The shouts of "Very good!" and strong applause were reserved for those senators who spoke about protecting men and instituting penalties for women who brought charges in bad faith. Finally, in November 1912, they all agreed, with strong applause, that it was "humiliating for France to be the only nation without a law allowing judicial recourse to paternal child support," and that children needed protection from poverty, degeneration, and death.[46]

With the nationalism and international competition that colored the beginning of the twentieth century, a nation's pride rested, not just on battleships and imperial conquests, but also on relative population strength. The health of children and the family, including paternity searches, became a national concern. Other nations did indeed have legislation enabling paternity searches. In Germany, to whom the French compared themselves, paternity laws were not as liberal as they had been in the eighteenth century, but paternity searches were still permitted. Jurists criticized an extranuptial child's entitlement to support from the father and limited mother's claims to the cost of delivery and some limited child support. The German Civil Code of 1896 (Bürgerliches Gesetzbuch, or BGB) stipulated that the unrecognized illegitimate child and his father were unrelated and made the illegitimate child a member of the maternal kinship group. However, it required the father to pay child support until the child reached the age of fourteen, according to the material level of the mother. It also included the earlier *exceptio plurium concumbentium* that excluded women who had several lovers from filing paternity suits, and more significantly provided a loophole by which men could escape financial responsibility. In practice, a child could claim support from the father, but these claims were usually unsuccessful because of the father's counterclaim that the mother had had several sexual partners. This law was predicated on the divisibility of paternity. The father owed the child maintenance, but no further relation was stipulated. The child did not have the right to inherit from him, and the responsibility for the child belonged to the mother alone, who sometimes bore heavy sanctions as a result, such as dismissal from the civil service. Some French lawyers at the time criticized the German law for harshness toward a man who had seduced a woman with fraud or used violence, the legal terminology for rape; if he were found guilty, punishment was six months' hard labor.[47]

Portugal (in 1867) and Spain (in 1889) also permitted paternity searches in cases of rape, or if the couple had lived together in a union resembling marriage, or if there had been a written avowal by the father. Paternity searches in these countries had limitations and exceptions comparable to those of Germany and the 1912 law in France.

In England, the right to pursue the father for child support belonged to the mother or the parish. The 1834 Poor Law Amendment Act gave the mother the right to bring a putative father to justice if he refused to marry her or to help raise the child. She had to bring proof of his paternity, such as written statements or witnesses to their relationship. It was up to the man to demonstrate that she had had relations with someone else during the time of conception, much as in German law. If the mother succeeded in her case, the man was condemned to help support the child until the child's teen years, depending on the situation. A child without support was charged to the parish. English laws of 1872 and 1873 fixed the sums the fathers had to pay.

It would be facile, yet correct, to conclude that the 1912 French law finally passed after a quarter century of debate in part owing to a strong turn-of-the-century political desire to protect children by allowing for paternal child support, as all the other nations of Western Europe had been doing for decades, if not longer. And it would be equally superficial, although correct, to say that it passed in part because it exempted married men and left the details sufficiently vague. By so doing, it preserved the legal family, which many, especially the leading Catholics, considered the basis of social order.[48] The legislature passed the law permitting paternity searches in 1912 in large measure, but not entirely, because the judiciary had been awarding in favor of single mothers for many decades. Judicial decisions had paralleled legislative indecision for almost half a century. Only at the turn of the century did a host of other social, cultural, and political pressures on the legislature join forces. The needs of state coincided with changing notions of the rights of men, women, and children, which the legislature and judiciary reflected.

French politicians across the political and religious spectrum became obsessed with demographics and societal degeneration toward the end of the century. Believing that population was power and that national strength depended on the well-being of children, they argued that holding fathers financially responsible for their out-of-wedlock children would increase the population by reducing the number of abortions and infanticides and by preventing infant mortality resulting from single mothers' inability to care for their children adequately.[49]

Using medical metaphors of degeneration, lawyers referred to natural children and their mothers as a "social cancer" or "gangrene." To rid society of these ills, France needed to institute paternity searches and protect young women who were victims of seduction, and, more important, their children.[50] Legislative debates, invoking leading statisticians and demographers, often focused on whether allowing paternity suits would lead to decreases in illegitimacy, in infant mortality, and in degeneracy, immorality, and crime.[51] Doctors as well as politicians argued in favor of paternity searches to decrease illegitimacy and infant mortality. In 1902, Dr. Gaston Variot, at a conference on maternal feeding, argued for changing the Civil Code to reduce infant mortality, rhetorically demanding, "Why should a mother alone be the victim of easy morals and improvident behavior, and why must she alone support the burden of raising her child?"[52]

Many social commentators thought the state had a problem. National leaders equated the decay of the family (evidenced by illegitimate children and absent fathers) with the decay of the nation. France needed solid, reproducing, republican families as the building blocks of the state. Absent fathers and incomplete families became symbols of degeneration. In their search for a moral order, legislators contended that the state needed fathers to regenerate the family and by extension to regenerate the state. In permitting paternity searches, the political and social became fused; a functioning family was needed for a functioning state.

Politicians advocated paternity searches as part of their larger objectives in the prevention of depopulation and degeneration. Rivet argued that if mothers had "the assurance of material aid, whereby ... the father must also contribute to rearing the child ... one would see a decrease in the alarming number of infant murders or abandonment. In the interest of the innocent child and in the name of the rights of the woman, it is necessary to assure the child and the seduced woman the natural protection of the father, a protection more efficacious and just than that of the commune or of the state." Rivet admitted that a poor seduced and abandoned woman who committed infanticide was culpable, but she was not the only one. He contended, "if she could only get the father of the child to pay a *pension alimentaire* ... she could have housing, a job and food for her baby and not have to commit infanticide or turn to prostitution to get enough to feed her baby." He added that infanticide, abortion, and child abandonment were rarer in the countries where paternity searches were permitted than they were in France, and those countries were not suffering from depopulation.[53] Many agreed with Rivet and prominent members of the Académie de Médecine who showed that the mortality of illegitimate babies was higher than that of legitimate babies, and that countries that legalized paternity searches had lower illegitimacy rates and lower infant mortality.[54]

"Seduction and libertinage jettison some 50,000 abandoned children annually on French soil," the social reformer Dr. A.-T. Brochard declared in the late 1860s.[55] He exaggerated only slightly, and his words were not lost on later legislators who thought that paternity searches would reduce the number of abandoned children and infanticides. Rivet and others further argued that granting immunity to men who seduced women not only led to national depopulation by increasing the number of abandoned children, abortions, infanticides, and extranuptial births with high infant mortality rates, but that those illegitimate children who lived tended to become thieves and murderers. Legislators as well as reformers assumed that women seeking child support would be poor, without resources.[56]

The concept that children, including misbegotten children, had their own rights gained increasing social acceptability toward the end of the nineteenth century. They were not at fault for being natural children; moreover, commentators did not distinguish between boys and girls. As Senator Pierre-Ernest Guillier, a republican lawyer who orchestrated Rivet and Bérenger's proposal in the Senate, succinctly stated, "We have sympathy for the woman, but our main concern is with the children. A child, no matter what his origin, has a right to existence, and he has a right to demand that of those who gave him life." Thus, a mother could pursue the putative father for child support only in the name of her legally recognized child, who had the right to seek its father for child support, and the man had the social obligation to provide that support. The abiding concern with depopulation, brought on in part by high infant mortality, meant that politicians believed that the most important right for children was that of survival. They extended this right to illegitimate children because their mortality rate was double that of legitimate children. Supporters of recherche de paternité argued that without a father's support, natural children became sickly, weak, and died. In a civilized society, children deserved protection. The natural father had rights, but he also had duties.[57] The natural child also had rights, and the most important was the right to life (*droit à la vie*); making the natural father do his duty was one way to assure the child a basic right. The nation must come to the aid of children born outside of marriage and should aid poor seduced women by permitting paternity searches.[58]

Permitting paternity suits marked another step in the history of state intervention in protecting children in France, following the regulation of wet-nursing and child labor laws in the 1870s, an 1889 law depriving parents who mistreated or abused their children of paternal authority, a series of measures to aid nursing mothers starting in the 1870s and developing throughout the decades, the limitation of women's factory work in the 1890s to prevent miscarriages, and a 1904 law further providing for abandoned children. For example, Paul Strauss, one of the leading advocates of state welfare for women and children, promoted recherche de paternité for the same reasons that he led the movement for child welfare: to protect the lives and health of the children in the national interest. In a seeming contradiction to increased state power over poor families, in this instance, instead of the state contributing directly to children's sustenance, officials stepped in to facilitate fathers' financial contributions, believing that almost any measure was better than none. Moreover, this would even save the state money, while limiting reluctant and absent fathers' actual authority over their children.

Politicians had come to believe that inasmuch as children had a social utility as workers and soldiers, their protection was in the interests both of the state and of society. Proponents of recherche de paternité argued that because of the suffering, poverty, and neglect they experienced, illegitimate children without a proper moral upbringing, as a result of paternal abandonment, would be "recruited to the army of vice and occasionally to crime; they became disinherited wretched pariahs," vagabonds, prostitutes, revolutionaries, and recidivist criminals—a burden, danger, and expense for society—in larger proportion than legitimate children. They became visible components of the generalized fear of social breakdown. Social ills, especially those of the cities, were discursively traced back to fatherlessness. Fears of juvenile delinquency, gangs, and adolescent nighttime marauders were all part of the sensationalism of the turn-of-the-century press. With paternity searches, the juvenile crime that threatened the public security would be nipped in the bud; paternal child support for these children would then make them socially useful citizens. If neither parent, however, were willing to recognize and nurture the extranuptial child, then, echoing the Convention's decrees of a century earlier, the state had the duty to support these children and make them useful.[59] Insecurities about juvenile gangs were part of the social milieu that contributed to the passage of the law permitting recherche de paternité, as well as that establishing juvenile judges and courts in 1912.

In fostering the rights of the child and children's social utility, the sexuality of their mothers became less important. To some extent, children's wellbeing became a symbol of national population strength and political power. Therefore, criticism of sexual relations—whether men's seduction of women, women's loose virtue in being seduced, or women's immorality in seducing men—became less important than the reproduction of society and achievement of social order. The child as a social being and the embodiment of the social political order needed protection, and whether the child was born within a legal marriage or not, some of that protection had to come from a father.

Rivet and others discussed children's "natural" rights to their fathers' protection and the duties society should accord them. In Albert Millet's words, "the child should have the option to search for the individual whom he considers his father and to force this man to execute his natural obligation that he had spontaneously contracted." If a man had declared himself to be the father of the child, had provided for the child and then stopped, the child had the right to ask for a continuation of aid.[60]

Others invoked children's victimization by the lack of recherche de paternité. A leading Paris appeals court lawyer, Henri Coulon, contended in his treatises on the family that the illegitimate child suffered through no fault of his own by not having a legal family. Coulon asserted, "In a government based on liberty, individuals should not be victims of their fathers' faults." Advocating paternity laws to "reconcile the sacred interests of the family with the situation of the legally recognized illegitimate child so worthy of pity and of justice," Coulon argued that humanity called for protection of the weak, especially children. He did not, however, want to assimilate illegitimate children to those born of legally constituted marriages, because that would be contrary to public order and social decency.[61] The children who were pitiable victims were only those fathered by single men. Arguments in favor of children's natural rights to their father's support and the father's responsibility to provide that support had been surfacing during the nineteenth century. By 1912, these concepts became more widespread, as the rights of children dominated much of the Senate discussion, buttressed, in large part, by the addition of feminist voices.[62]

A series of gains for women's rights in the 1890s also paved the way for further legislation.[63] Feminists advocating recherche de paternité did so to further women's equality as well as for the good of the children. They provided a new vocabulary for the debate on the rights of women and children that sympathetic men in government adopted. Rivet addressed the inequality between the mother and father in calling for equivalent rights. He declared that when "two human beings cooperate in a work such as the creation of children, there must be *equivalence* in the duties and charges that this work imposes; it is wrong to have, on the one hand, men who have the right to pleasure, and, on the other hand, women who have the duty to suffer." Taking a position in favor of the rights of the mother, Rivet echoed Victor Hugo's widely known declaration that "the eighteenth century has proclaimed the rights of man; it is necessary that the nineteenth century proclaim the rights of woman."[64]

The position of feminists on recherche de paternité varied over the course of the long debate. Olympe de Gouges was the first feminist to plea for the right of a woman to name the father of her child and receive child support from him. But she framed her petitions in the interest of the right of women to free speech and in strengthening the family with "shared responsibility for children." She did not want a man to get away with seduction, and demanded in 1791, well before nineteenth-century jurisprudence, that an honorable mother (i.e., one who was not a prostitute) be free to seek an indemnity in cases when the man deceived her into sexual relations with a marriage promise. She was the first to consider maternity a social function, a concept adopted by Jeanne Deroin in mid-century and by several feminists toward the end of the nineteenth century.[65]

Feminists' arguments often led those of men. Paternal responsibility was inherent in the "discourses of individualism, individual rights, and social obligation as used by republicans,"[66] some of whom were feminists. In 1890, many feminists called for the right of women to engage in paternity searches for their children. Even male writers bemoaned not having a law permitting recherche de paternité while there were a number of women who "cry in silence." Furthermore, the law permitted *recherche de maternité*; why not *paternité*?[67] René Viviani, an appeals court lawyer, Chamber deputy, minister of labor, and friend of a leading feminist, Marguerite Durand, pointed out inconsistencies in contemporary thinking whereby a man could be a father in fact but not in law. Unlike nineteenth-century proponents of paternal responsibility who based their reasoning on dividing paternity between filiation and child support, feminists did not envision divisibility, but rather wanted recherche de paternité to provide filiation. The feminist Léon Richer based his 1890 appeal for paternity searches as a means to limit the number of abortions. In addition, he considered "that each child should have a right to his father, just as he has a right to his mother, as is permitted by *recherche de maternité*."[68]

Numerous feminist congresses from 1878 through the early twentieth century discussed the issue of paternal responsibility. Their participants wanted to appear unanimous in support of recherche de paternité, although there were strong divisions among feminist groups and across that broad timespan, just as there were with other groups based on secular ideology or religion. The 1892 General Congress of Feminist Societies (Congrès général des sociétés féministes), after two hours of debate, declared that paternity searches were needed to remedy the misery that confronted the workers, especially unwed mothers.[69] The group Solidarity of Women (Solidarité des femmes) stipulated that the child was the product of a couple; since the mother had to support the child, the father should also. This group stressed the importance of keeping the unhappy single mother from committing infanticide, placing the debate in the context of depopulation, while keeping salient moral issues in the forefront. Within the decade, support for the bill advocating recherche de paternité became one of the major demands of the feminist journal *La Fronde*, which serialized a *roman à thèse* condemning article 340.[70]

The Second International Conference of Feminine Organizations and Institutions, attended by women of all political persuasions, met in 1900. Feminists, such as the journalist Marya Chéliga and the attorney Jeanne Chauvin, led the debate advocating the right of an unwed mother who had recognized her child to institute a search for the father, in the name of the minor child, in order to force the father to provide for child support. Most of the proposals at this 1900 conference supported both single and married mothers. Feminists emphasized the dignity of the mother more than the legislators did. Female attendees did not demand that the fathers legally recognize their out-of-wedlock children; they just wanted the fathers to share the financial responsibility of raising them.

Another speaker, Paule Vigneron, shared the views of many when she argued for protection of the legal wife and family of an adulterer. She commented that only unmarried men should bear full responsibility for natural children, and then only where there was sufficient proof. There was never a question of the father being forced to introduce the child into his "legitimate family. The natural child belongs exclusively to the mother." The father should help feed that child since he had contributed to its creation. If a single mother's search for child support would create a scandal for a married man and his family, Vigneron declared, allowing this search would be an excellent measure to prevent seduction of single women.[71] She separated filiation from child support, as had magistrates.

The more radical International Congress on the Condition and the Rights of Women also met in 1900. Members maintained that in the interest of justice, a man should materially provide for the children he brought into the world. The children had a right to subsistence, and the parents had the responsibility to provide for the child. Without parental support, the children became the victims of a situation they had not created. The poor woman had no source of income except her work, whether or not she had a child. "If she let herself be seduced by beautiful promises that a man made to her in saying he loved her, she is then often abandoned by this man when he perceives that she will soon have a child." The father must be made responsible for the situation he had created; it was a sacred trust. The participants at the Congress praised English law permitting paternity searches, especially since employers could withhold the wages of their employees for the child support they owed. "Why is *recherche de la paternité* still forbidden when the same law [the Civil Code] prescribes imprisonment for a woman guilty of marital infidelity and *excuses* the husband who surprises her in flagrant *délit* and kills her?" Marguerite Durand, the general secretary of the Congress, demanded. In 1900, this International Congress endorsed recherche de paternité when there had been cohabitation at the probable time of conception, or when there was written proof of paternity. In these cases, the father should pay the mother a pension, with a penalty if he defaulted. In cases when he did not pay, the Congress concluded, the state should provide the mother with a pension sufficient to cover the needs of the child.[72]

Other, more radical feminists viewed recherche de paternité as an insufficient, temporary measure, because mothers would lose their dignity in going to court and it would be hard to collect from the fathers. Maria Pognon, speaking on behalf of the League of the Rights of Women, opposed recherche de paternité on the grounds of practicality and equality for the women. Men who had abandoned the mother and child should not have rights to that child; moreover motherhood should be a source of "glory and honor" for women, entitling them to "respect and dignity." Men, she argued, would refuse to pay, just as married men sometimes refused to provide for their children, whether within marriage or after separation and divorce.[73] Furthermore, many women would have too much pride, in the first place, to apply to *Assistance judiciaire* (legal aid) and then, if it deemed them deserving of free legal support, to take their cases to court. And then the woman would have to pursue the man if he did not pay. This would be shameful for the mother, as well as impractical for child support. Even after the woman received a court judgment against the father, Pognon noted, it was unlikely that the man could be forced to pay; the present law entitled married women with children to receive child support from their husbands who had deserted them, but they were unable to collect. Furthermore, she demanded, what was to prevent a man from bringing witnesses who would support his denial of paternity? Pognon's goal was to help the single mother raise her child; the child was not the "bastard who dishonored the family," as Jacques Bonzon had alleged at this conference, but a "respectable little person."[74] By implication, that "little person" had certain rights.

Nelly Roussel, another leading radical feminist, subsequently spoke against the inadequacies of recherche de paternité. Roussel maintained that men should bear some responsibility for the consequences of seduction and pay the woman he had abandoned the indemnity that was her due. The child should also know the father who had helped create him or her. But, Roussel continued, recherche de paternité was not a remedy for all women who were victims of seduction; it would only be another insufficient palliative.[75] Proposing a radical solution, Roussel wanted women to be able to choose for themselves if and when they wanted to be mothers. Rather than recherche de paternité, she argued for "a fair salary for the noble task of motherhood, with motherhood [for single and married women] classified as an honored and remunerated social function, with the children bearing their mother's name."[76] To Roussel, recherche de paternité might be good, but a Caisse de la maternité, or national maternity fund as an endowment for motherhood, would be better, because it would enable a woman to be independent of her seducer.

In the interest of child support, Roussel, Pognon, and others advocated a national Caisse de la maternité, supported by a tax on all men, as a pension for all mothers, whether married or not. Children needed support to live and did not exist just for their mothers and fathers: "our children are reared for the entire society." Controversy about the *caisse* centered on the issue of paternal responsibility and whether all mothers should be entitled. The male politicians present at the feminist debates said that the state did not have the money for a such a *caisse*, and that all fathers would be contributing to this *caisse*. They suggested that only if the father could not pay after a woman won a paternity suit against him would the child have recourse to "M. Tout-le-Monde" ("Mr. Everyman"). There was disagreement as to whether only men, or both men and women, should contribute, and whether all mothers or only those in need should have recourse to the *caisse*. Feminists such as Pognon, Hubertine Auclert, and Pauline Kergomard wanted only men to pay into the *caisse*, since women were already victims and men needed to be taught a sense of responsibility. The 1900 International Congress on the Rights of Women voted in favor of recherche de paternité and for a Caisse de la maternité "in all civilized countries" for all mothers, according to need.[77]

Feminists influenced legislative proposals by having the ears and hearts of politicians who attended their congresses and spoke on their behalf in the Senate and Chamber. Deprived of the right to vote and legislative seats, women expressed their political agendas by promoting legislative proposals with politicians with whom they were ideologically in tune. René Viviani, Paul Strauss, Marcel Sembat, Gustave Rivet, Louis Martin, and other senators and deputies participated in feminist congresses and took up the cry for paternity searches, espousing feminist arguments. Feminists, through public meetings, campaigned to influence public opinion as well as the legislators. Moreover, parliamentary discussions included references to feminist ideas and proposals. The proposal that Marcel Sembat brought before the Chamber in 1905 was the verbatim recommendation for recherche de paternité that the National Council of Frenchwomen (Conseil national des femmes françaises) had approved in 1902. Viviani served as vice president and head of the Committee of Honor at feminist congresses in 1900, 1908, and 1910. He carried the majority opinion of those congresses in favor of recherche de paternité back to the Chamber and had worked with Rivet since 1900. Viviani's own arguments included complementary roles for the state and the father in child support. Although agreeing with the importance of a state Caisse de la maternité, he believed that the state should take charge of the children by instituting recherche de paternité. According to Viviani, a child had the right to know his father, and fathers bore responsibility toward their children, within and outside of marriage. If a poor mother without bread attempted abortion or infanticide, it was the father's fault. The Caisse de la maternité could provide needed financial assistance if both mother and father were indigent, but laws, such as one permitting recherche de paternité, would force men to exercise their responsibility to their children. In 1910, Rivet echoed the feminist concept that maternity should always be honored, and not considered shameful when the mother was unmarried.[78] Other writers and legislators also used the language of men's responsibilities to children.

New concepts of paternal responsibilities and rights, often couched in language pertaining to the natural rights of the child, also inspired the legislation. Proponents of recherche de paternité contended that natural law applied both to fathers and their children, requiring that if fathers had a child, they must feed that child and provide for his or her future. To Bérenger, paternity was a responsibility, a function, and not the individual right of a man. Rivet and his colleagues put paternal responsibility in the context of social rights more than that of the natural rights of man. Rivet argued that society had the right to impose responsibility for their acts on men and contended that a man had duties to a woman he impregnated and to their child.[79] In 1890, the feminist journal *Le Droit des femmes* similarly contended that the child, too, had rights—to support, to an education, to an inheritance, and to search for his father to provide them.[80] French legislators' notions of paternal responsibilities around the turn of the century echoed the views expressed earlier by Dumas *fils*, who had insisted that the father was responsible for his "fault," arguing that the man bore responsibility for the woman's loss of virginity, that the woman was less culpable than the man, and that the child was the least culpable of all. If the man were married and could not give his name to the child, or poor and could not provide the child with a means of subsistence, he should go to prison. Responsibility for the child existed irrespective of the father's individual rights. Most objected to Dumas's punitive terms for fathers who failed to provide for their children, declaring that the fathers would be faced with economic and social ruin; a few agreed to authorize punishment, but only in cases of kidnapping and rape resulting in conception.[81]

The legislators of the Third Republic did not only invoke the Declaration of the Rights of Man to support many of their general political and anticlerical arguments; they also used the language of natural law that their predecessors in the First Republic had drawn upon. But there were some new twists. Catholic opinion stressed an interpretation of natural law that concurred both with civil law and canon law in maintaining the responsibility of both parents to provide the essential needs of the child they created. In Catholicism, having a child, or even sex, outside Holy Matrimony was a sin for both the father and mother, but they could lessen its severity by supporting the child, Hector Lambrechts reasoned. If marriage were not possible, the father should not have complete rights over the child, only the duty to provide sustenance in compensation for the "moral sin" of seduction.[82]

To allow for some responsibility on the part of the putative father, and also to sustain the patriarchal legal conjugal family, much of Catholic opinion implicitly acknowledged the divisibility of paternity. Instituting paternity suits was not an anticlerical measure, since many Catholics supported it, and it also hearkened back to Old Regime canon law. Other proponents of paternity suits, in an inversion of the priorities of the period from 1795 to 1804, asserted that where the rights of the child impinged on the individual rights of the father, the father should relinquish those rights in favor of his duty to his children.[83] They complained that the existing laws allowed men to satisfy their passions without any risk, not sufficiently protecting the defenseless single mother or her child.[84] No longer could the rights of the father trump those of the child; rather, to many reformers, it was the other way around—but only if those fathers were unmarried.

Even reformers who argued that the lack of paternal responsibility for a child born outside of marriage led to male debauchery realized that forcing a child upon a recalcitrant father would not be good for the child. As a result of attention to the father's rights and responsibilities, the 1912 law called for the imposition of child support up to the child's majority, according to the economic position of the mother and the resources of the father. The law allowed the father no rights over that child without the mother's approval, since he had initially rejected the child; the child would not take the father's name. In a typically French semantic turn, the mother retained *puissance paternelle*. The majority of legislators stipulated that only the unwed male seducers should pay child support for the infants they had helped produce. Reformers thus protected the "natural legitimate family" (both the husband and wife) and at the same time appeared as champions of natural children. Marriage still permitted a man to escape the responsibilities of misconduct. Since paternity financially bound the fathers and limited some of men's freedoms, it had been difficult to pass the law. Married fathers needed reassurance that they would not suffer from a law permitting paternity searches.[85]

Some legislators and public assistance administrators, influenced by budgetary concerns as well as the welfare of the children, may have opted for paternal financial responsibility as a means of saving the state money. Expenditures for programs of aid to single mothers were growing, with allocations to infants tripling to 39.5 million francs between 1875 and 1910. If the state held fathers financially responsible for their offspring, then it would not have to spend so much supporting foundling homes, wet-nursing, and foster parentage, and the expanding programs of aid to single mothers with nursing infants.[86] Discussions about the rights of children and their social utility might have been a way to express the state's economic reasons for advocating paternal responsibility. Less budget-conscious public administrators also viewed the legalization of paternity suits as one more measure in the construction of a welfare system for mothers and children designed to reduce infant mortality.

Legislation prior to 1912 that modified laws of inheritance and property quelled some fears that paternity searches would dissipate family fortunes. The law of 25 March 1896 modified more than ten articles of the Civil Code and resolved many of the property and inheritance issues that had impeded paternity laws. Changing the provisions of these articles engendered almost as much debate as recherche de paternité, because the two were related. The key issue was protection of the legal conjugal family while also giving natural children rights of filiation, including an inheritance. This legislation gave only those natural children whom their fathers had recognized rights of inheritance when their parents died without a will, and it increased the portion a parent could allot to the recognized extranuptial child. Hereditary rights remained set by the Civil Code, but the 1896 measure increased the proportion a recognized illegitimate child could inherit to half of what legitimate heirs inherited. As with the law of 12 brumaire year II, the key was paternal recognition of the natural child. The 1896 inheritance law left unchanged the Code's article specifically prohibiting children born of adulterous or incestuous unions from inheriting property; they had to be content with food and vocational training, limited by the needs of their parents' legitimate children.[87] When the 1896 law limiting inheritance assuaged the fears that recherche de paternité would permit the assimilation of illegitimate children into the legitimate family, the 1912 law became possible. Debates hearkened back to the Convention in August 1793, when discussions of paternity searches involved the inheritance rights of natural children and the inherent primacy of the legitimate family.[88]

Finally, in 1905, 1907, and 1908, additional laws modifying the legal position of illegitimate children set forth in the Civil Code removed more obstacles to recherche de paternité. In 1905, recognized natural children could be allowed to take their father's name. The 1907 and 1908 laws dissociated paternal authority from child support by stipulating that parental guardianship over legally recognized natural children belonged to whoever recognized the child first—either the father or mother—thus satisfying feminist concerns about maternal authority over her children. In 1907, the Chamber voted in favor of a proposal providing some rights of filiation for children born of their father's adultery (*enfants adultérins/ines*), who were not the guilty ones. The Senate, fearing a legal sanction of bigamy, restricted filiation to certain categories of children born of adultery, but added possible filiation of children born of an incestuous relationship (*enfants incestueux/se*). In a fragile compromise, it authorized the legitimation of those children in only two cases: if the child were born more than 300 days after the separation or divorce decree, or if the mother married her "accomplice" after her former husband had disavowed paternity. Amid cries of "destruction of the family," a 1908 law in effect allowed for legitimation after marriage of children born of adultery.[89]

Thus, prior legislation, decades of jurisprudence, and gradual cultural and social transformations made legislation permitting paternity searches part of a package of turn-of-the-century reforms in how the state viewed seduction, sexuality, and the family. The paternity law of 1912 went further than these laws in allowing children whose fathers did not legally recognize them to have their paternity juridically declared. This limited a man's individual right to decide when to be a father, but also gave the child the right to partake of his inheritance and name.

The issue of recherche de paternité was both personal and political. The historical tapestry of thirty years of legislative debates, court decisions, and feminist positions on the complex topic of paternal responsibility was woven from contrasting threads of discourse: the construction of the family; men's sexuality and individual rights versus female sexuality, credibility, and a woman's ownership of her body; the culpability of men and women in seduction; the acceptance of male seduction of women; and women's consensual sexual relationships. The intimacies of adultery, seduction, and women's sexual behavior were all essential components of public paternity discussions. Allowing recherche de paternité also blurred private/public distinctions, because the courts and community publicly discussed people's private sexual relations and their domestic arrangements. It inspired fear of public intrusion into the private lives of families, with dread that their intimate life would be revealed to all. The concept of *concubinage notoire* destabilized conventional understanding of the boundaries between public and private. Moreover, the class component to family privacy was omnipresent. Bourgeois families prided themselves on their privacy, but legislators had no problem making the intimate lives of the popular classes public. Concubinage, long a family structure of the poor, was open to intense public scrutiny, as were many aspects of poor women's sexuality, honesty, and fidelity.

The subject of a woman's morality and fidelity was paramount. Legislators were terrified that immoral workingwomen would abuse propertied family men by seeking child support or filiation from them, but opponents of paternity searches paid little attention to men's abuse of women. They continued to believe that women were not to be trusted, and that single mothers were "immoral seducers" of men, reserving particularly virulent blame for working-class women. Sexual relationships were troublesome when they crossed class lines. In 1912, as in 1804, legislators did not want poor women pursuing rich married men, and they designed a law that would continue to protect the private lives of the propertied conjugal families.

The two concepts of women's sexuality and seduction (whether they were the dissimulating seducers or the victims of irresponsible seduction) could not be reconciled. Therefore, the legislators sidestepped the conflict and agreed to protect the children, but not to pursue married men. Recherche de paternité began with judicial attempts to protect young women seduced by fraudulent promises of marriage, coerced, or made victims of abuse of authority; it ended by protecting the unfortunate children, avoiding further contention over the rights of men and the immorality of women.

Although the legally married two-parent family remained central to French culture, by 1912, acknowledgment of *concubinage notoire* as grounds for paternal child support indicated a reconfiguration and broadening of the social construction of the family to include an unmarried couple living together. If presumption of paternity existed within marriage, then by extension the presumption of paternity could apply to consensual relationships resembling marriage. Senators invoked not only the Latin tag "Pater is est quem nuptiae demonstrant" (i.e., the father is the person married to the mother) but also employed a new one: "Pater is est quem concubitus demonstrant" (i.e., the father is the one in concubinage with the mother). In his speech of June 1910, Rivet quoted the sixteenth-century judge Antoine Loysel's aphorism: "Boire, manger, coucher ensemble, c'est mariage ce me semble."[90] Although the legal family and its property remained sacrosanct, legislators admitted other family constructions, but not those involving incest or adultery, because of the "absolute necessity to defend society and the [legal] family."[91]

A husband feared his wife's adultery because it would damage his honor and might introduce another man's child into his household, thus dispersing the inheritance to someone not related to him by blood. A man's adultery, however, was not a problem—to men—unless the mother of the resultant child tried to introduce that child into the married man's home, as legislators had feared she would. This fear that a child born of adultery might dissipate the family fortune and ruin the reputation of a bourgeois family had hindered legislation permitting paternity searches.[92] In the debate on inheritance, legislators sacrificed the natural child to the legal conjugal family, yet they also recognized "natural families" not sanctioned by civil marriage as a family construction for the purpose of fixing paternal responsibility for natural children. Legislators in 1912, as more than a century earlier, invoked natural law, arguing that to protect the natural child's rights, the authors of the pregnancy should also provide child support. Natural law remained an important rhetorical referent in debates on the family.

Recognizing concubinage also acknowledged women's voluntary heterosexual activity and some equality in heterosexual relations. The very concept of seduction, in contrast, implied inequality in relations. In the early years of the nineteenth century, a woman's body figured as the property rights of others. Starting with mid-century jurisprudence, a few judges allowed women some control over their bodies and began to penalize seducers. Then, in the later nineteenth century, advocates of recherche de paternité maintained that allowing immunity to seducers fed prostitution and weakened the nation, yet they did not insist that men legally recognize their out-of-wedlock children; they only encouraged financial responsibility. At the turn of the twentieth century, with the courts awarding damages for fraudulent seduction, a woman increasingly had some legal ownership of her body.[93]

This does not deny women ownership of their bodies prior to this time, but their success in the courts became consequential. The debates leading to passage of the paternity law of 1912 revealed that it was not necessary for a man to have taken advantage of a young woman or for her to have behaved imprudently in order for her to win in court. The nature of proof differed from that in the nineteenth century, because legislators now recognized and accepted a woman's consent to live with a man in concubinage. No longer did women have to be unwilling victims in order to collect damages for themselves. As willing partners, they might collect child support for their children. *Concubinage notoire* replaced seduction as a criterion for a monetary award—but the recipient changed from the mother to her child. By 1912, legislators recognized concubinage as a fait accompli. Furthermore, concubinage had the added advantage of allowing single mothers (still often deemed immoral) to raise their children "morally" in a "family."

Paternity laws were connected to the notion that the well-ordered state depended on the well-ordered family. With that logic, the revolutionaries of the 1790s, the crafters of the Civil Code, and nineteenth-century legislators argued against paternity searches: if marriage were the crucial moral and structural institution underpinning the state, then marriage alone must determine paternity. The fate of the mothers was secondary in this political logic. However, as more complicated notions of the relationship between the state and the family developed from the 1880s through 1912, the republican state tried to balance protecting the bourgeois family (the adulterous fathers, their wives, and legitimate children) and property, with a commitment to protecting all children, including the illegitimate. At the turn of the century, the state assumed a paternal or patriarchal role and increasingly entered into the private lives of the poor, while at the same time it sought ways for fathers to share some of the financial burden. Although a mother and child could take him to court to pay for the basic essentials of child support, a man had no legal authority in that family because he had abandoned them and denied his fatherhood; partitive paternity predominated in life and laws.

Male honor may also have involved supporting recherche de paternité. It was a question of honor for a man to repair his faults, and those faults came to include sexual misdeeds. In 1804, the concept of male honor entailed preserving a man's property; his sexual behavior was not an issue. By 1912, the courts and the law tried to enact procedures whereby a woman could file a legal suit to require a man to behave honorably and pay for his dishonorable deeds. Before 1912, the dishonor was seduction; after 1912, it was abandonment of his family. Moreover, with the "crisis of masculinity" of the fin de siècle, supporting the idea of recherche de paternité may have been a way for a man to show his virility and support the nation's children. The cultural shift in concepts of masculinity, now embodying nonmarital fatherhood, may have been part of the support given to recherche de paternité in the first decade of the twentieth century.[94]

Legislators believed in the influence of laws on people's morality, and identified women as guardians of the family's and nation's morality, while designing laws to try to ensure women's sexual restraint. The Civil Code's architects tried to control women's behavior and avoid what they considered abuses of the ancien régime when women had victimized men through false allegation of paternity. If women could not affix paternal responsibility for their children, legislators argued, the women would become more moral and sexually circumspect. After mid-century, jurisprudence sought to protect innocent young women from victimization by irresponsible and dissembling seducers. Then, at the dawn of the twentieth century, legislators argued that if recherche de paternité were allowed, men might not behave irresponsibly and immorally. The creation of article 340 in 1804 gave a blank check to male passions; the revision of that article in 1912 limited that blank check to married men. In turn-of-the-century France, responsibility for sexual morality shifted from the women alone to both women and unmarried men. Unable to agree on whether men victimized women or vice versa, legislators declared children to be the victims.

The 1912 law was a manifestation of a cultural shift that resulted from multiple reconceptualizations of relationships between the family and the individual, the individual and the state, women and men, and parent and child. That cultural shift involved a limited redefinition of the family, an adjustment in the balance between individual rights and the social good, as well as an expanded application of individual rights to women and children. The negotiations and actions of various groups, including the women who brought court cases for damages and the judges who ruled on them, the feminists, those who feared depopulation, and those who advocated a more interventionist state, caused this cultural transformation. Law lags behind social change. As Dumas *fils* so aptly declared: "Customs [*mœurs*] sometimes modify laws; laws do not modify customs."[95]

By 1912, the law had lagged so far behind that it had become obsolete; the law was in such vast discord with how people lived their lives, formed their families, and viewed their sexuality, honor, and independence that men and women ignored, transgressed, or tried to change the letter of the law. The Civil Code in 1804 sanctioned social order as conceived by propertied men of the time; however, that perception of the social order had changed. In written law, women remained passive citizens. They were far from passive, however, when they seized the initiative to collect from recalcitrant and evasive fathers, even though they acted, not in their own names, but perforce in the names of their minor children.

CHAPTER FOUR

Courts Attribute Paternity, 1912–1940

Jeanne Capbourg gave birth in Paris on 12 December 1908 to a daughter, Andrée Marie. Two weeks short of her child's fifth birthday, on 27 November 1913, she went to court to obtain 70 francs a month in child support from the putative father, Guislains, and reparations of 2,000 francs for his breaking a marriage promise. Guislains objected because the newly enacted law of 16 November 1912 stipulated that paternity suits had to be filed within two years either from the child's birth or from the time the father stopped supporting the child, or from when the parents stopped living in a consensual union or *concubinage notoire*. Guislains maintained that he had never lived with Capbourg or participated in rearing the child. Guislains further insisted that he did not owe Capbourg damages for a broken marriage promise because he had never made such a promise.

The judge considered this case as recherche de paternité under the terms of the new law. He carefully took into consideration the beginnings of written proof, such as letters Guislains had written between 1911 and 1913, when he was fulfilling his military service. In the earliest one, written to Capbourg's grandmother in 1911, Guislains praised Capbourg's morality, writing, "she has always worked very honestly and never went out with other young men in Paris except me." He stated that he was pleased that "she has the good fortune to fall back on a family who did not abandon her and who have made it a point of honor to concern themselves with her until this misfortune could be remedied, which will take place a short time from now." In this letter, which he did not write hastily to her in a moment of passion, but composed quite rationally to her parents, Guislains announced his resolve to "redress the unfortunate birth of the child." The judge interpreted these letters as unequivocal avowals of paternity, implying that Guislains would marry Capbourg and recognize the child. No one, and no law, could force him to marry Capbourg, but failing that, Guislains must help Capbourg provide for the child's needs. The judge thought the 70 francs a month that Capbourg demanded for child support out of proportion to the father's resources, so he fixed child support at 25 francs a month until Andrée Marie was eighteen—an amount that might keep her fed but probably not in shoes. In ruling in Capbourg's favor on paternity, he also acknowledged that the 1912 law permitting paternity suits was retroactive and covered children born before the law passed. Yet he did not consider this case one of recherche de paternité, indivisible and strictly interpreted: he did not require that Guislains give Andrée Marie his name or provide her with an inheritance. Capbourg also requested damages for a broken marriage promise, and this judge behaved much like those of the nineteenth century. He looked for cause to award damages, such as evidence of a binding marriage promise, and determined that there had been no such promise. Age was also an issue, as it had been in previous decades. Capbourg was five years older than Guislains, and because of this age discrepancy the judge found no proof that Guislains had coerced her into sexual relations. He therefore ruled against Capbourg's request for damages for fraudulent seduction and a broken marriage promise.[1]

The paternity law of 1912 delineated the time frame for filing such suits and the nature of proof: written letters with unequivocal avowal of paternity, having publicly lived together as a couple, or having provided child support. It also left much discretion to the judges, giving them vast powers of interpretation to bend the law in many ways. Although some judges had long been deciding that fathers must pay child support to their extranuptial children, the 1912 law finally enabled women like Jeanne Capbourg to go to court with a paternity suit against a putative father.[2] Magistrates' decisions addressed questions of honor, seduction, sexuality, and nonmarital sexual arrangements.

Courts privileged maternal bonds and the child's material interests, yet the 1912 law permitting paternity searches and the judges' subsequent decisions did not make the plight of abandoned women and children much easier, for it changed little with regard to the burden of proof expected of mothers. A woman had to bring letters from the father that the judges could interpret as proof of paternity; she had to have witnesses summoned and deposed attesting that she and the putative father had lived together maritally during the legal time of conception (considered 180–300 days before the child's birth), or supply evidence that the putative father had contributed materially and emotionally to rearing the child. Moreover, a woman's morality was still a central issue, but she no longer had to have been young and innocent—just sexually faithful to one man and a good mother. The putative father could bring countercharges against the mother, usually by summoning witnesses who testified that she had had sexual relations with others besides him, thus making his paternity uncertain. Furthermore, in almost every case, the judge thought the woman's monetary request excessive and reduced the amount awarded.

Judgments in civil paternity suits from 1912 to 1940 reveal issues of contested paternity and different family constructions. Courts mirrored society, and judges in the twentieth century, as in the nineteenth, were drawn from the middle and upper echelons of that society.[3] They were also agents of the state, and as such they represented what public authorities, state officials, and the general dominant cultural milieu regarded as acceptable behavior. They had the power and capacity to reconstruct social ties according to a certain number of general norms and cultural traditions, as they saw them, but within the parameters of the law. Judges limited the arena in which men were able to exercise choice regarding paternity; men could less easily avoid responsibility for the results of their sexual liaisons, unless they were married at the time of conception and thus by law exempt from paternity searches.

Paternal authority (*puissance paternelle*), which involved legal and parental rights and responsibilities with respect to rearing and educating children, belonged to married fathers and to unmarried men who legally recognized their children. Within marriage, biological paternity and fatherhood based on emotional care were linked. Outside of marriage, men could voluntarily legally recognize their children, have emotional ties to them, and, by virtue of a 1907 law, also have *puissance paternelle* over those children. If fathers failed to recognize their extranuptial children, as a result of the 1912 law, judges could attribute paternity to them. Judicially declared paternity, however, did not entitle the man to *puissance paternelle*, which was vested in whoever recognized the child first, usually the mother. A woman could not be deprived of that authority by a recalcitrant, or even hostile, genitor, whose paternal authority and active involvement might be detrimental to the children. With judicially declared paternity, these men were simply material providers. Neither judges, nor lawyers, nor mothers wanted to invest an individual who was ill disposed toward the child with paternal authority. The French perceived *puissance paternelle* as a right based on parents' presumed affection for their children. If, although a man may at one time have had some affection for the child, he later denied the child and shunned all connection, affection, and responsibility, he should have no authority over the child other than to provide a name, some inheritance, and some child support.[4] It is not clear that he would have wanted more than that, or even that much. In a twist of gendered language, paternal authority belonged to the mother of the natural child.[5] Prior to the discovery of biological proof of paternity based on blood groupings and DNA testing in the late twentieth century, judges used evidence of social fatherhood to indicate biological fatherhood, but judicially declared biological paternity did not entail social fatherhood.

Paternity remained divisible. Lawyers and magistrates interpreted the 1912 law to allow a mother acting in the name of her minor child to bring a case for a *pension alimentaire* alone, or for judicial recognition of paternity, or for both, either at the same time or in successive legal actions. The notion of sexual responsibility is inherent in declaring that men pay child support without declaring paternity with full filiation. The reasoning resembled that of the nineteenth-century judges in awarding reparations for seduction and abandonment, although in the twentieth century, most of the time, these awards were for the children. Following one of Antoine Loysel's aphorisms, "He who creates a child must provide for that child," judges could order presumptive fathers to provide the money to cover food for their children until those children reached adulthood (usually eighteen) and still decide against legal recognition of paternity and filiation. All depended on the nature of proof and on the judge. If the mother won her suit for judicial recognition of paternity, judges fixed a sum for child support, if the mother requested it, and also ordered the surname of the judicially declared father to be added to that of the mother on the child's birth certificate so that the child could take the declared father's name and inherit a portion of his property.[6] Neither the law nor the judges demanded that he contribute to rearing the child other than materially.

The social divisions between acting as father and being the biological genitor became blurred when women married someone other than their children's biological father. Some husbands took an "aversion to the child their wife had had with another man before their marriage and reproached her for having had a child when young."[7] Other husbands willingly acted as fathers to children their wives had had before their marriage. Prior to her legal marriage to M. Faure, Mlle Bourg and M. Orsoni had a daughter in

1917, whom they both recognized. Orsoni left her in 1918 for another woman and no longer contributed to rearing the child. After his departure, Bourg also married another. However, she still wanted child support of 100 francs a month from Orsoni, because she was in a "modest" situation, having had to take a job and pay a pension to the foster parent who looked after the girl. The relationship of Bourg's new husband to his stepdaughter is unknown; whatever the home situation between stepfather and daughter, however, the judge ordered Orsoni to pay child support because he had recognized the child and had initially acted as a father.[8]

Living in a consensual union could also indicate paternity and provide evidence that a man had acted as a father. The 1912 law took notice of *concubinage notoire* as one of the possible proofs of paternity but left its definition up to the judges. By 1920, judges decided that *concubinage* was not cohabitation, strictly speaking, since cohabitation included domestic servants or apprentices living in their employers' homes, and this was not the intent of the law. *Concubinage notoire* usually involved a man and woman living publicly in a domestic household as partners, having a continuous and constant life in common, sometimes called a second-class marriage. In such a relationship, a woman was presumed sexually faithful to her partner, just as a wife would have been toward her husband.[9] Moreover, a man in such an arrangement might have a sense of responsibility to his partner and their children. A woman in the twentieth century who brought paternity charges or a suit for child support could bring evidence that she and the putative father had lived in *concubinage notoire* during the probable time of conception; she did not have to claim a broken marriage promise or fraudulent seduction, as women had to do in the nineteenth century when claiming damages. As court cases shifted from the claims for damages for broken marriage promises and fraudulent seduction of the nineteenth century to child support and paternity suits in the twentieth, *concubinage notoire*, which had been an invalid basis for claiming damages and child support, became a basis of proof in determining paternity in the twentieth century. Loysel's definition of marriage, invoked by Rivet, "Boire, manger, coucher ensemble, c'est mariage ce me semble," became *concubinage notoire*, a socially acceptable family form, although only legally recognized in 1999, when it included homosexual as well as heterosexual couples.

Women and men thought about sexuality differently in the interwar period than in the nineteenth century, and were more open about it. Yet sexual freedom was an illusion, and sexuality still had consequences; it remained connected with reproduction, since contraception and abortion were outlawed. Furthermore, in the eyes of the community, women's sexuality was supposed to be confined to concubinage that resembled marriage. Reformers of the early nineteenth century denounced concubinage as immoral sexuality and linked it to the destruction of the family among the working classes in the cities. At the end of the nineteenth century, reformers condemned it less as an example of immorality and more as evidence of social disorganization. During most of that century, living in concubinage and having children in that relationship exemplified a type of family that had been widespread among the urban poor. For the women, it was often an alternative to marriage or a marriage strategy that failed, leaving women relatively powerless until after 1912.[10] Then, in the first half of the twentieth century, the law and a broad spectrum of society recognized and accepted concubinage, tolerating young couples of all social classes living together. Accepting concubinage implied new relationships between the sexes and recognition of women's voluntary sexuality. Despite the relative openness vis-à-vis the previous century, and the de facto if not de jure recognition of heterosexual consensual unions, legal civil marriage remained the foundation of the family and of the republic, considered to be the family form that best preserved the interests of the children and the nation. It continued to indicate a proper social position, implying property ownership and a good job.

Not only did judgments in paternity suits reveal perceptions of paternity, fatherhood, and sexuality, but courtroom mise-en-scènes reflected concepts of honor, integrity and decent behavior (*honnête comportement*) for men and women who used the courts as theaters as well as confessionals, involving family, friends and community on the proscenium with them. Friends and families testified that they knew of, and by implication approved of, a couple's consensual union. In other situations, community witnesses testified against women from whom they wanted to distance themselves. If a woman's sexual honor and fidelity, or her motherhood, were at all suspect, or if she were not a good community member, others would denounce her as lacking moral honor as a means to affirm their own honor. Court appearances also involved a form of citizenship. Although, as Joan Scott has shown, women as rights-bearing individuals were problematic in the political culture,[11] women could demand rights of social citizenship, if not political citizenship, by going to court, and also that society fulfill its duties toward them.

Going to Court

Women increasingly explored the new frontier of sexual and personal independence during the twentieth century. Although in doing so, they confronted obstacles—especially when they became pregnant outside of marriage—different paths now opened up to them in the courtroom. Seemingly powerless women used the legal system to improve their situations and those of their children when they sought child support and filiation for their children. Their courtroom narratives reflect a fashioning of themselves as virtuous women who had become good mothers, relying on notions of honor that had been the bulwark of court presentations in the nineteenth century, but in the twentieth century they did not have to skirt the law. Although they used the courts and legal protection tactically, they probably did not think of the law in their daily lives until the time came to use it. Nor is it likely that when they brought suits, they thought they were exercising their independence and performing acts of citizenship. Rather, they used the courts as a last resort, when all other avenues had failed them in their quest for marriage or at least for child support and paternal responsibility.

Although in the twentieth century, women's sexual activity outside of marriage may not have seemed as reprehensible as it had in the past, they went to court for many of the same reasons as in the nineteenth century. Recuperating their honor and that of their families remained important. They had to show that they were virtuous and had had only one man as a partner. Honor and reputation were crucial to women's lives. Women also wanted their children to live respectable lives, not as illegitimate but with the honor of a name and a paternal inheritance. Furthermore, it was always difficult for single mothers to raise their children and also work. Women's financial need was so great that any shame from going to court and publicizing their extranuptial children paled in comparison. Not all single mothers went to court, however. They had to have a network of information, to have read newspapers or magazines, and to have known how to contact charitable agencies that were established to help mothers.

Charitable organizations supplied lawyers as well as practical information. Mothers could receive information and access to free legal aid at the organization Sauvons les mères et les bébés (Let Us Save Mothers and Babies) and L'Union féminine française (French Women's Union). The larger Ligue pour la protection des mères abandonnées (League for the Protection of Abandoned Mothers) opened its doors for the first time in February 1925. Designed as an agency where abandoned mothers could leave their babies for adoption, it also facilitated marriages and paternity searches. The League reported that poor mothers, or future mothers, arrived on its doorstep "timid" and "fearful." During its first year of operation, it "facilitated six marriages, and twelve recherches de paternité." The League had a lawyer available who met with the women to initiate paternity searches, and in 1926, he wrote to the director of the organization, "Madame, I am happy to inform you that the tribunal of Versailles rendered its judgment yesterday concerning Mlle M. The child... obtained a *pension alimentaire* of 150 francs per month." The charitable organizers of the League considered the abandoned mothers who came to them as their "protégées" or wards. Mothers found out about this and other agencies by individual word of mouth, from newspapers, and from hospitals and other institutions where they gave birth. Lawyers also advertised their services in handling paternity suits.[12]

Despite the efforts of these charitable organizations, in all of France, on the average only about 800 women each year launched recherche de paternité suits from 1920 through 1922. Of these, about a third were rejected. Between 1930 and 1932, only 737 women took action for recherche de paternité and about half were rejected.[13] To maximize their chances, lawyers and their clients filed their cases under a multiplicity of rubrics: recognition of the child (*reconnaissance*), recherche de paternité with filiation, *pension alimentaire*, and/or dommages-intérêts. Judges could rule that a mother had no legal grounds in one type of case but allow another. There is no way to estimate how many cases settled out of court.

The judicial process could last several years. At an initial inquiry to determine if a mother had sufficient evidence to bring a paternity suit, a judge could find insufficient proof to hear a case and order the woman and her lawyer to come up with more or different evidence. Sometimes a judge specified the types of witnesses a woman needed to attest to concubinage or told her to find letters with a written indication of paternity. Accusing women of immorality remained part of the accepted male discourse after 1912, as it had been before, and judges allowed putative fathers to bring counterevidence to demonstrate a woman's sexual misconduct, thereby throwing doubt on his paternity. The accused man would blame the mother for having had other sexual partners besides him. During the proceedings, judges could further call a woman's morality into question, casting aspersions on her if she were older than the putative father, if she had a past history that might raise doubts about her honesty and sexual morality, or if her occupation, such as that of a waitress or actress, marked her as a woman possibly of "loose morals." Unlike prior to 1912, however, some judges focused less on a woman's alleged immorality and more on evidence of a man's unequivocal written avowal of paternity, of his promise of marriage, on witnesses attesting to *concubinage notoire* and the couple's intimate life together, and of his paternal interest in rearing the child.[14] Judges and lawyers, especially those involved with *Assistance judiciaire*, functioned as legal gatekeepers, screening cases and refusing to handle those that were either brought in bad faith or did not stand a chance, thus keeping some women out of the courts, without redress, and opening the gate to allow others to plead their cases.

If women did not have evidence for judicially declared paternity, they would often just ask for a *pension alimentaire*. If they had other evidence, they could also ask for damages. Of the 128 cases in a sample of women who went to court in Paris using *Assistance judiciaire* between 1913 and 1939 to try to obtain filiation, damages, or child support, two-thirds (85) filed under the rubric of recherche de paternité. Of these, 28 cases simply involved an initial presentation before the judge, who would decide if the woman had a case at all. If he found she had enough evidence for her suit, he would hear the case, or ask her to bring further evidence. The judge also asked the defendant to bring counterproof that the plaintiff had had other lovers besides him. Of those who filed paternity suits for filiation, approximately 28 percent lost their cases because of insufficient proof. Only one-fifth of the women in the sample asked only for a *pension alimentaire*. They had to bring the same proof as mothers seeking filiation, but judges held them to somewhat looser standards. A mere 9 percent of them only requested reparations for damages done to them personally.[15] The paternity suits also included a request for child support, except when the mother asked only for her child's filiation with the family of the deceased putative father or if the children brought claims after they reached adulthood. During the two decades of the interwar period, the *pension alimentaire* almost always literally covered just food. Judges did not award generously, and it was difficult for men or women to obtain cost-of-living adjustments when the local economy, or their economic circumstances, changed.

By bringing paternity suits, women disrupted the status quo and disturbed those who did not want to be disturbed, such as the putative fathers and their families.[16] To avoid scandal for the men and to preserve their honor and the sanctity of their legal families, the law prohibited an audience at these proceedings. Journalists could attend but could not reproduce the courtroom debates. They could print the final judgments, but without revealing names, although they sometimes violated that injunction. Substantial press coverage, especially in the numerous *faits divers* (brief human interest news items) of the newspapers, regaled readers with stories of sex and broken promises, playing to the public preoccupation with sexual dramas in the courtroom.

The Impact of the War

The devastating loss of life among French men during World War I led to consideration of paternity as part of a greater effort to protect children.[17] The pronatalism and fear of depopulation that had led legislators to change the law in 1912 intensified during the war and became more strident in subsequent decades. Public policy increasingly defended and supported motherhood, including unwed motherhood, as a social function, with unwed fathers occupying a secondary, yet material, place in the pro-family discourse of the war and postwar years.[18] Moreover, populationists exhorted men to do their unselfish patriotic and paternal duty by producing more children, preferably within a legal marriage, but if outside such a marriage, they were to help support their children financially to enable women to be better mothers and raise healthier children.

The war did not stop women from filing paternity suits. Soldiers' letters back to their lovers and families produced in court by new mothers constituted critical evidence in ascribing paternity. During the war, letter writing in France took on new dimensions, with letters sustaining bonds of affection even outside of marriage.[19] Sometimes, men admitted their paternity. Pascal Vidal wrote heartfelt letters to Antonia Morelle indicating that he was the father of Eliane Pascaline, born in July 1917. Morelle, who had legally recognized her daughter, went to court in 1919 within two years of Eliane's birth, asking for a *pension alimentaire*, dommages-intérêts, legitimation of her daughter, and recherche de paternité, basing her case on Vidal's written avowal of paternity. Passionate letters said he never wanted to leave "my parents, you, my little girl—you are my France." He not only referred to Eliane as "his" little girl, but also asked Morelle to gather the papers necessary for marriage. By 1919, however, Vidal had married another woman. This case took the relatively short time of one year to go through the court system. In weighing the evidence, the judge declared Morelle ineligible for damages, since a marriage promise did not precede intimate relations and there was insufficient evidence that he had broken an engagement. The child could not be declared legitimate, but paternity was judicially declared and Pascal Vidal named as the father on Eliane's birth certificate. Moreover, he had to pay a *pension alimentaire* of 40 francs a month until Eliane reached her eighteenth birthday.[20] In another instance, a judge found no unequivocal avowal of paternity. In 1918, Mlle Richer claimed she "lived maritally" in a "free union" with Marcel Ficher and they had had a son in November 1915. She claimed a *pension alimentaire* that she said he had promised. He denied such a promise, and since his letters did not support her, she lost her case.[21]

In a few cases that came to court between 1914 and 1918, the putative father had died during the war. For example, Adèle Grécourt, a seamstress, asked that Gaston Jacquet be declared the legal father of her daughter, named France Germanie Grécourt, born in Paris in March 1916. Grécourt legally recognized her daughter, but Jacquet had been "killed by the enemy in September 1915." However, while on military duty, he had written two letters in which he acknowledged the pregnancy and promised to marry Grécourt during his next leave. Therefore, the judge ordered that his paternity be duly noted on the child's birth certificate, despite his parents' objections. The court decision allowed the daughter to inherit a portion of the property and gave her a family affiliation, albeit to a family that did not want her.[22]

In another case typical of those ending in a father's wartime death, Yvonne Roule brought a suit for recherche de paternité against the family of Auguste Molet, who she alleged was the father of her daughter, Augustine. Roule and Molet had had a sexual relationship before he was mobilized, and he had died of wounds in 1914. Since Molet could neither read nor write, Roule produced no letters from him. She did, however, provide evidence that prior to Molet's death, he had paid the wet nurse for their daughter and "acted in the capacity of a father." Moreover, Roule produced letters from Molet's sister in which she referred to Augustine as her niece. The judge took this as proof and ordered Molet's legal paternity established and noted on their daughter's birth certificate. She did not seek a *pension alimentaire*.[23]

A new law of 1917 enabled the mother of a natural child fathered by a man killed in the war to claim that child as his legitimate offspring, thus simultaneously providing those "who had died for France" with heirs and valorizing their paternity. This legislation was in the interests of the children, even if legitimating the child materially or emotionally hurt the father's family.[24] It echoed a 1792 decree, promulgated during another war, that had likewise tried to obliterate distinctions between legitimate and illegitimate fatherless children. In 1792, however, legislators had sought to make the state the "father" of both legitimate and illegitimate orphans. In 1917, in contrast, the political, social, and cultural climate favored rearing war orphans in families (perhaps also reflecting the realities of the national budget).

In 1920, Suzanne Cornicard tested this law when she asked that her daughter, Suzette, born in October 1914, be legitimated. Cornicard had legally recognized her daughter just before she took her case to the civil tribunal of the department of the Seine and declared that by application of the law of 7 April 1917, Suzette was also the legitimate daughter of Gabriel Winckel, "killed by the enemy" in 1914. Winckel's widowed mother would not give her approval to the legitimization, because she had never known of the child. However, in a letter of September 1914, just before his death and the birth of the baby, Winckel had written to Suzanne: "I've received your letter in which you ask for my authorization for [recognition of the child]. You need to go to the mayor's office and ask for a provisional declaration . . . which I will sign with joy." In the same letter, he wrote: "If you see the possibility of marrying, take all the necessary steps as soon as possible, and tell my mother to do the same." After the baby was born, he wrote: "I tell you that it breaks my heart not to be able to fulfill my duty as father and not to be able to recognize my dear little Suzette whom I so love." Cornicard's lawyer said that these letters showed Winckel's intention to recognize and legitimize his daughter by subsequent marriage with the mother. The judge agreed and ordered that Suzette's legitimation be inscribed in the margin of her birth certificate.[25]

Courtroom dramas to legitimize children of men who had "died under the flag of France" appeared among families of all social circumstances, and an unwed mother could bring a suit against the widow of a man killed during the war claiming that the widow's now-deceased husband had fathered a child with someone else before he married her. When Jean-Louis Bordin's mother recognized him when he was born in 1911 in the countryside of Brittany, she listed his father as "unknown." A guardian named for Jean-Louis brought the case for legitimation against the parents of the putative father, who had been killed "fighting for France." In letters planning for marriage just before war broke out, the father even referred to Jean-Louis by his own patronymic. Jean-Louis Bordin became officially legitimate in 1924 at the age of thirteen.

Pierre Sache's mother took action in 1921 against the widow of a military captain who had died in 1916. Pierre's mother did not claim child support; she only wanted Pierre to have his now-deceased father's name on the birth certificate for the honor of being legitimate and perhaps for later inheritance claims.[26] Not all parents and widows of soldiers who had died in the war objected to the legitimation of the soldiers' out-of-wedlock children. In 1920, George Angot's mother approved the legitimation of the two daughters he and Aline Risser had had, whom they had legally recognized before he died.[27]

In the occupied zones of northeast France, a number of women became pregnant as the result of rape by German soldiers as armies trooped through. An unknown number of these women had abortions, despite their illegality. Although some politicians approved "aborting the child of the barbarian" to save the "purity of the blood" of the French "race," others insisted that France needed the children, who were, after all, half French, and also that the "murder of innocents," even in the womb, was wrong. In the minds of many politicians, women did not have the right to refuse France children the country needed. For the French families, however, it was not that simple. If they regarded their own sons' illegitimate offspring as intruders in their families, how much worse the children of the Boches! One proposed political solution was for the French state to assume *puissance paternelle*, and for Assistance publique to pay the women's childbirth expenses and place the babies with wet nurses and foster parents, whom they would pay. Blood ties were replaced by the politics of repopulation; paternal responsibility was not an issue, since the genitor was German. These children, "born of a French mother, nourished with French milk, and raised in France, would be French."[28]

Although some husbands may have stood by their wives, others took legal action to deny paternity of children born to their wives in an occupied zone during the war.[29] Tensions and contradictions appeared between men's masculine duty to become fathers for the nation and their equally strong masculine prerogatives to preserve their family lines. "While I served the flag of France, and did my duty at peril to my life, a miserable little being has brought disorder, shame and dishonor to my family," one man protested.[30]

In the intensely pro-natalist patriotic culture that was widespread in the immediate postwar era, having children and behaving responsibly toward them became a mark of manhood, or male virility, in addition to fulfilling one's responsibility to the nation. Writers lauded paternity as a national duty and as a symbol of a regenerative postwar France, linked to the pervasive and ever-present crisis of masculinity and concern with manliness, honor, courage, and sexual prowess in an unstable modern world.[31] Men faced new insecurities when they recognized that women had managed without them while they had been away at war. In 1915, a law had even "authorized mothers to exercise parental authority and to take legal action without the authorization of their husbands, provided that a court ruled the affair was urgent and that the mobilized spouse was unable to assume his responsibilities."[32] Paternity gave men a key role in the new social order, one they may not always have willingly accepted. Society had always valued paternity within marriage, but with the increasing intensity of the discourse on depopulation, paternity within and outside of marriage received increased valorization. Paternity made men more masculine—especially if they did not have to change diapers. To be a man may have meant placing the interest of the country on a par with one's own. One wonders how Mussolini's 1927 dictum that "He who is not a father is not a man" played in Provence, Pas-de-Calais, or Paris. Politicians were less obsessed with the alleged immorality of single mothers and increasingly objectified the sexual conduct of men and women as targets of government intervention to increase the birth and survival rate of the nation's children.

Masculine honor and reproductive duties intertwined, with courts aiding in constructing the boundaries of sexual and parental behavior for men and women. Furthermore, judicially declaring paternity was one way to support the many deprived children, in whose interests judges constructed paternity to ensure that legally ascertained genitors materially supported them, often requiring some filiation even from the father's family if he had died in the war. Paternity was at the nexus of discourse on sexuality and population, bringing honor to men, although many men resisted this type of honor, especially if their paternity was in doubt. To be a man not only involved paternity; it might also involve denying paternity as a mark of material self-preservation and honor. To maintain their honor as well as control over their name and property, men had to accuse women of behaving dishonorably by having other lovers. If women behaved dishonorably in forming sexual liaisons, men could behave dishonorably in not acknowledging their liaisons or the resulting children. The judges in postwar Paris were seeking to reestablish paternal authority and fatherhood as a patriotic honor. They, and some elements of the popular press, also sought to establish motherhood as an honor.

In 1925, the popular daily newspaper *Le Matin* launched a campaign to protect mothers, especially the unwed, and also to extend male forms of honor, such as serving their country, to women. With headlines such as "Let us protect and honor mothers, all mothers," writers argued that the "decrease in births is a national catastrophe," and that it was society's fault for dishonoring the unwed mother, obliging her to live in poverty and social misery. *Le Matin* compared France with Germany and Austria, which supposedly behaved more honorably toward unwed mothers, concluding that "the impoverishment of our race lies in the situation of the unwed mother and natural child." In neither Germany nor Austria, according to *Le Matin*, did the birth of a natural child constitute a "material hardship, dishonor, or the loss of social position for the mother."[33] Director of Assistance publique Louis Mourier, writing in *Le Matin*, praised his program of "aid to prevent child abandonment" as a means of protecting and honoring the unwed mothers, but did not mention the role of the fathers who abandoned mothers and children. Mourier also lauded the establishment of *pouponnières*, institutions where unwed mothers were lodged and fed free of charge to breast-feed their own babies and also babies of others who had to work and could not keep their infants with them. Mourier declared that Assistance publique would adopt the material role of the absent father. Other public officials, doctors, and feminists declared that recherche de paternité and protection to unwed mothers did not go far enough. Some appealed to humanity, declaring that just as the child was natural, so the mother was natural, entitled to rights of motherhood that she had purchased with her pain and her blood. They called for the legal assimilation of the natural child into the legal family to ensure that child's physical and moral development, taking recherche de paternité further than the existing law and court decisions.[34]

In keeping with a new respect for single mothers, even the language changed. People disparagingly referred to unwed mothers as *filles-mères* (literally, "girl mothers"), leading the feminist Jane Misme to complain that "everything is unfair toward the women, even grammar." Newspapers should forbid the use of the term *fille-mère* and substitute *mère célibataire*, Misme said.[35] Leading male doctors were of the same opinion and called for a change in terminology. As the head obstetrician at the Lariboisière Hospital wrote: "Let's not speak of *filles-mères*, because all these unfortunates are mothers who have given a child to a country, which has so great a need for children. Almost always these *filles-mères* are abandoned, so let us call them abandoned mothers [*mères abandonnées*]. One should search for the father whenever possible, but the collectivity should not abandon the poor mother. It is not a question of charity.... Instead of deriding her, we should give her respect."[36]

Such respect was slow in coming, but often occurred in the courts when women filed paternity suits or claims for damages during the two decades between the wars.

Damages and Reparations

Recherche de paternité and dommages-intérêts rested on different principles. A successful suit for recherche de paternité gave the child a monthly pension and possible filiation, with nothing specifically for the mother; a successful suit for damages provided a woman with reparations and nothing specifically for the child. In the 1920s and 1930s, judges ruled that a woman could collect damages under the same terms as in the nineteenth century.

Women continued to take men to court for breaking marriage promises as they had during the nineteenth century, for familiar reasons. If everyone knew of a couple's engagement, she would likely win her case. A child was not always involved. For example, Mlle Dabrot, from a "very honorable family," was engaged to marry Joseph Spanol, a metalworker. The wedding date, fixed for September 1914, was postponed because of the outbreak of war. Spanol was mobilized and taken prisoner; during his captivity, Dabrot sent him letters and packages. When he returned at the end of 1917, the wedding date was again fixed for civil and religious ceremonies in February 1918. He then failed to show up. Dabrot's family searched for him and found him nonchalantly eating lunch; he responded simply that he had changed his mind about marrying her and had sent her a note that morning. Dabrot had to endure the indignity of telling all the wedding guests to leave. Moreover, Spanol later had the gall to go to Dabrot's mother's house to take several items, including the engagement ring. In this clear-cut case, the judge decided that Spanol had to pay Dabrot all charges associated with the cost of the wedding and also two thousand francs in damages.[37]

In another instance, in 1920, Mme Broshe sued M. Maurevin for child support and damages representing the cost of raising her son for fifteen years. A priest testified on Broshe's behalf that she had taken care of her son and had also sent him to a religious school. Maurevin never denied his paternity but declared that he had only modest resources and could not give Broshe the damages she demanded. Furthermore, the boy had died in 1917. The judge declared that Maurevin did not have to make back payments in child support, but he did have to pay reparations, reducing the amount from the 5,000 requested to 2,000 francs.[38]

Women might request damages, child support, and filiation in the same suit. Throughout the 1920s and 1930s, women could succeed in one respect but not the others, according to their evidence. Although judges tried to keep suits for damages and those for paternity separate, they required written evidence for both. In 1924, Zélie Augnac, a domestic servant, asked for 20,000 francs in damages and a monthly pension for her child, claiming that she was a victim of abuse of authority and a false marriage promise from her master. The judges rejected her case for damages and for child support, declaring that its object was an "implicit recognition of paternity" and that seduction by abuse of authority or a marriage promise would be considered only if there were also written statements by the putative father as proof of paternity, thereby confounding reparations and paternity suits.[39]

Mlle Genin asked M. Derache for 2,000 francs in reparations for breaking an engagement to marry; in addition, she wanted child support for the baby and for the courts to declare Derache the father. The judge found numerous letters from 1923 in which Derache formally promised marriage. Then, in 1928, without any stated motive, according to the judge, "he acted with imprudence and pure caprice" and broke his engagement with Genin and married someone else. Just before Derache broke the marriage promise, Genin gave birth to a baby boy, whom she legally recognized. In 1930, the judge decided that 2,000 francs was a modest amount for Derache to pay in reparations for the "moral injury" Genin had suffered. However, the judge found neither letters in which Derache avowed paternity nor any evidence that he had ever acted "like a father" in materially supporting the baby. The judge said that "marriage promises cannot authorize a judicial recognition of paternity." Therefore, she lost her request to ascribe legal paternity to Derache, but the broken marriage promise was sufficient to condemn him to pay reparations and child support.[40] Judges maintained the letter and spirit of the law in demanding the man's unequivocal affirmation of paternity, but continued in their judgments that an engagement for marriage had the force of a contract and breaking it without cause resulted in damages to the wronged party. They also kept child support separate from filiation. In 1933, the Cour de cassation reiterated the necessity of written proof of paternity to supplement claims of fraudulent seduction before awarding damages.[41]

In the 1930s, judges acknowledged *concubinage notoire* as similar to a marriage promise, insisting, however, that such an arrangement had to have been disrupted without cause in order for damages to be awarded. In 1938, Mlle Jussieu sued M. Lebrun for 20,000 francs in damages for a broken marriage promise and fraudulent seduction. She insisted that he had promised to marry her and had renewed that promise several times, thereby seducing her. She had gone to live with him and his mother. Lebrun insisted that he had never made a formal marriage promise; he had thought of marriage, he said, but had "abandoned the idea for reasons of which he is the sole judge." This judge ruled that a broken marriage promise is not in and of itself a cause to award damages, but having had relations during a long period of time and breaking off this relationship without due cause constituted moral and material prejudice, sufficient to award Jussieu 3,000 francs in damages, far below what she had requested. The judge declared that there was no evidence that a promise of marriage or fraudulent seduction had led to the woman's loss of innocence; she had already been thirty-four years old, presumably old enough to know better.[42]

Throughout the two decades, judges repeated their view that the rupture of intimate relations would not constitute a civil fault, even if it resulted in pregnancy and childbirth. Likewise, a rupture of concubinage would not entitle either party to sue for damages. If the woman insisted the man had forced her into such a relationship by illicit means, then the courts took into consideration "intelligence," social position, age differences, physical force, and written evidence. Feminists complained that the new law permitting recherche de paternité led to less humane outcomes for the mothers than had been the case in suits for dommages-intérêts during the nineteenth century; after 1912, it was harder for women to obtain reparations for themselves for fraudulent seduction or a broken marriage promise.[43] Nevertheless, some women used tort law to their advantage, much as they had in the nineteenth century.

Obtaining reparations and child support from married men was possible under article 1382 of the Civil Code. Although married men were exempt from paternity suits, women used article 1382 to claim damages and child support from married men much the same way as they had before 1912. Judges continued to divide paternity between biological and behavioral ties and between filiation and child support, never giving married men filiation with a child of their adultery. In 1923, Mlle Dodat, a telephone operator in Paris, sought the huge sum of 200,000 francs in damages for herself and 8,000 francs in a *pension alimentaire* for the children she had with M. Vielabus, a married engineer where she had worked. Fraudulent seduction or a broken marriage promise was not at issue; Vielabus's copious correspondence provided sufficient evidence of his responsibility. In 1912, when she was nineteen and he was forty-eight, they had begun a sexual relationship, which had resulted in three children over a period of seven years. The birth certificates of each child listed Dodat and Vielabus as parents, but since he was married, he could not legally recognize them. Because she could not file a paternity suit against a married man, she sought reparations from Vielabus as well as child support. The judge declared that Vielabus had provided Dodat with an apartment in Paris and therefore had already repaired the damage he had done to her. He also left her with some money to take care of her needs, and had left each of the children 20,000 francs, which they could obtain only when they reached adulthood. As a result of successive pregnancies, including miscarriages, Dodat had suffered serious damage to her health, but despite her large pharmacy bills, the judge ruled that she could not demand more reparations from Vielabus. Nevertheless, the children needed financial help while growing up, so the judge ordered Vielabus to pay Dodat 3,600 francs every three months until the oldest child turned eighteen, reducing his payments by 1,200 francs when each child turned eighteen or if any died before that age.[44]

A decade later, Mlle Gachet asked the court to repair an injustice that M. Monin had caused her as a result of their long-term sexual relationship while he was married to another. He had ended their relationship but promised to provide for his natural daughter. Although the law prohibited him from recognizing a child of his adultery, no law prohibited him from fulfilling his natural obligation in helping feed her. But his promise resembled a will, with provisions for his daughter only after his death. The judge declared that at the time of Monin's death, his natural daughter would be an adult, able to earn a living and in no need of his support. Based on Monin's correspondence, this judge found sufficient proof that Monin had freely and voluntarily taken upon himself to provide for the child, "as a duty of his conscience," and that he had the "sentiments of a father." Therefore he ordered Monin to pay Gachet 500 francs per month as a pension for their daughter and also awarded her damages because the seduction had been based on a false marriage promise. Monin appealed the part of the suit for damages and won; moreover the appeals court reduced child support by more than half. The Cour de cassation then heard the case and ruled that she could not collect damages because she had voluntarily entered into concubinage with Monin for fourteen years. The judges at the Cour de cassation declared that concubinage was "essentially precarious and unstable, susceptible to be changed according to the will of one of the [parties]"; if one person broke it, the other could not collect damages. The judges recognized the natural obligation to provide for a child born of adultery, however, so Gachet could not collect damages for a broken relationship but the child could receive support. Most judges ruled that concubinage resembled marriage, but the judges in this case saw it as a "precarious and unstable" relationship, not entitling the abandoned partner to receive damages.[45]

Making a clear separation between recherche de paternité, which included filiation, and providing just a *pension alimentaire*, some judges would bend the law and order adulterous fathers to provide food for their children, insisting that such action was not recognition of paternity. On 23 December 1935, the Cour de cassation gave a Christmas present to the children of an adulterous man in deciding that he had to provide for them. The judges declared: "The commitment of the father to provide food for the children of his adultery does not indicate recognition or a tie of filiation . . . but a natural obligation, derived from a duty of conscience, which is neither illicit nor contrary to good morality." A mother could not take a married man to court for damages resulting from a ruptured relationship or for recherche de paternité, but she could take him to court to get him to fulfill his "natural duty of conscience . . . and civil obligation" to contribute to the child's needs for nourishment.[46] This would not disturb the public order, and a man would not have two families. Judges wanted to keep the issues of damages separate from paternity searches, but that was not always possible.

Paternity Outside of Marriage

What constituted paternity outside marriage became a major question during the interwar period. The answer lay with the judges. After deciding that the law was retroactive to include children born before 1912, judges then tackled the matter of the family's responsibility when the putative father had died. Jurisprudence pushed wartime laws further and stipulated in a series of controversial decisions that mothers could take the parents, widows, and other legitimate heirs of deceased putative fathers to court in the name of their minor children. If the judge declared paternity, the child would belong to that father's family and be entitled to his family name and a portion of the inheritance.[47]

It was not a question of bringing a paternity suit against a married man; the man had to have been unwed at the time of conception. Of paramount importance was maintaining public order and avoiding scandal for the putative father, the woman he had legally married, and his family. All proceedings took place within the strict time limits set by the law, so men could be free from worry that their extranuptial children might pursue them throughout their lives. Nevertheless, twenty-one years after the child's birth, that young adult could still show up on the doorstep of the alleged father and his family or bring a paternity suit against them. In determining the amount of monthly child support payments, judges considered the needs of the child and the material circumstances of the father; in most cases, the support would cover just food, and there would be no monetary adjustment without another court appearance, and no means of enforcement.

What legally constituted paternity outside of marriage was open to debate, since the law did not explicitly define an unequivocal avowal of paternity or what it meant to have acted as a father. Legislators likewise left the definition of concubinage vague, with the result that judges had difficulty deciding what constituted "drinking, eating, and sleeping together" and whether a couple's intimate relationship resembled a legal conjugal marriage. In 1922, the Cour de cassation ruled that regardless of whether a man and woman had actually shared housing, it was necessary for them to have given the appearance of being a conjugal couple, and for their intimate relations at the time of conception to have been continuous, stable, and known to their community. Neighbors were frequent and regular witnesses.[48] Nevertheless, having supplementary evidence, such as letters indicating paternity or that a man had behaved as a father was usually de rigueur.

In 1922, Madeleine Biron went to court against M. Herzenstein asking that he provide for their son, Maurice, born in November 1919. She brought witnesses attesting that she and Herzenstein had rented a room together, but after the baby's birth, they had no longer lived there. Evidence for *concubinage notoire* was slim, so Biron also brought evidence that Herzenstein had acted as a father. She summoned three witnesses who testified that Herzenstein had found and paid the wet nurse with whom he and Biron placed their infant. When Biron took Maurice back from the wet nurse, Herzenstein visited them every Saturday for several months. Witnesses for Biron attested that during these visits "Herzenstein comported himself as a father, seeming to show a great affection for the baby." Witnesses for Herzenstein said that he had indeed paid the wet nurse, but that he had done so from "fear of scandal." He claimed that he had always doubted that he was the father, because he had been in hospital for part of the legal period of conception, and that Biron had rented a room of her own ten months before the baby was born. This was the trope to indicate that she was a woman of loose morals who had a room to meet with lovers. He also contended that she had threatened him in order to get him to pay for the wet nurse. The judge disregarded his objections, especially because no witness attested to any "violence" or "menacing behavior" that Biron might have committed against him. The judge decided that "paternity entails the duties and obligations toward a child" that Herzenstein had already shown, which he must continue to provide. Therefore, he decided Herzenstein was the "natural father" of Maurice, and ordered Maurice's birth certificate changed accordingly. Furthermore, Herzenstein had to pay a *pension alimentaire* of 120 francs a month for Maurice until he turned nineteen.[49]

If a woman could prove that a man had once fulfilled his duties as a father, and then stopped, it was likely that the judge would demand further payments of child support until the child's majority or at least until the child was sixteen or eighteen. Although Biron produced no letters from Herzenstein avowing paternity, the judge found witnesses' statements that Biron and Herzenstein had shared a room and that he had participated in rearing the child as a father convincing. What constituted "acting as a father" was open to interpretation, and could include paying another person, such as a wet nurse, to care for the child, as well as having directly participated in rearing the child.

Other judges ruled differently, arguing that having intimate relations and renting rooms for short periods of time, even many times during the legal period of conception, did not constitute *concubinage notoire*—especially if some of the meetings were clandestine. In the spirit of the law, these judges maintained that the couple had to have lived together, sharing meals and a bed during the entire legal period of conception, and that their relationship had to have seemed like "regular" and "stable conjugal fidelity," a "life in common" under the same roof, in the eyes of the community.[50] In 1924, a judge ruled that despite six different witnesses establishing that Laville and Boussac had had intimate relations during the entire period of conception, their relationship was not one of concubinage. Laville lived with her sister and had just come to visit Boussac. They spent many nights together and from time to time went away for weekends in the country. In the absence of any other proof, he declared Laville's suit unfounded.[51]

By the 1930s, judges appeared to rule that living together was not required if other evidence of a stable relationship existed, and family or neighborhood members bore witness to that relationship. Such an intimate life could have been on weekends if the couple were domestic servants who had to lodge with employers.[52] Mlle Gaurel filed a paternity suit against Dobeuf in 1931 for judicial recognition of his paternity, child support, and reparations for a broken engagement, summoning five friends and neighbors to confirm their intimate relationship. Gaurel was a domestic servant and these witnesses said that she had spent every Sunday with Dobeuf, who they believed was her fiancé. Another witness reported that four or five times during the legal period of conception, Dobeuf had rented a room to be with Gaurel. Upon further inquiry, Gaurel brought evidence that Dobeuf had made preparations for marriage, but he broke off the relationship. The judge did not believe that their intimate relations had begun only after the marriage promise. Furthermore, Dobeuf had had grounds for breaking the marriage agreement because Gaurel had lied about her age, claiming that she was ten years younger. Therefore, the judge ruled against her demand for reparations for a broken engagement. Yet he accepted witnesses' testimony for *concubinage notoire* and declared Dobeuf the father, fixing child support at 150 francs a month until the child's majority.[53]

There was no consistency in judges' determinations of when a couple's life together resembled marriage. Some judges declared that two servants working in the same hotel could not be considered to have lived in concubinage.[54] Finally, in 1935, the Cour de cassation ruled that paternity outside of marriage could be judicially declared when the mother and putative father had lived in a state of concubinage, even for a short term, during the legal period of conception. It was not necessary for the couple to have shared common housing in a manner resembling marriage. It was sufficient that their relations had been continuous and stable, with a character of intimacy, in a manner such that the community would presume her fidelity as they would presume that of a legally married woman.[55]

A mother's case was strengthened by evidence to supplement that of concubinage. Mlle Ory went to court on behalf of her son, Michel, to get judicial recognition of M. Laurent's paternity. At the inquiry in 1936, a judge ordered Ory to establish concubinage between her and Laurent in 1934 during the legal period of conception. Laurent in turn brought evidence of her "commerce with another man." The judge heard the case a year later. Seven witnesses testified to her good conduct and fidelity to Laurent; some noted that Ory went to stay with Laurent every weekend, and each supplied different details. One witness remarked that he had picked her up and returned her to her place of domestic service. Another added that she kept her clothes at his place, noting that after the baby was born and their relations ruptured, she had to go get them. The judge decided that this constituted *concubinage notoire*, even though they did not live together all the time. Laurent's witnesses testified to the contrary, but the flirtatious activity they attributed to Ory was not during the legal period of conception. In addition, she produced two letters from Laurent. On the eve of the childbirth, he inquired about her health and wrote that he thought of her often, sending her his "thousand kisses." The judge decided these letters, combined with witnesses' testimony, were sufficient proof of paternity. Laurent's name was recorded on Michel's birth certificate, and he had to pay a *pension alimentaire* of 200 francs a month until Michel turned eighteen.[56]

Mlle Roche was less successful when she brought a case against M. Forte in 1935 for recherche de paternité and dommages-intérêts. The judge decided that their relationship did not satisfy the definition of *concubinage notoire*, and she had no letters demonstrating paternity. They only spent a week together during the possible time of conception; she remained a stenographer in Dijon, and he took a job with the Postal Service in Dax, about 800 kilometers away. He maintained an affectionate correspondence with Roche, but his attitude suddenly changed when he learned of her pregnancy. He refused to marry her, writing "I will send you money when you wish.... Pardon me for the harm that I've done to you." All information on her character was good, and no one condemned her sexual relations with Forte. She lost her paternity suit, but the judge asked him to pay a *pension alimentaire* of 125 francs a month until the child turned sixteen.[57]

Drinking, eating, and sleeping together did not always constitute sufficient proof for establishing paternity outside of marriage. Unequivocal written avowal of paternity was usually required, but there was little agreement on what that constituted. Individual judges had great leeway in their decisions, with few guidelines from the Cour de cassation. In 1925, that court ruled that starting the paperwork necessary for marriage could constitute an unequivocal avowal of paternity. Some lower-court judges ruled that there had to have been a letter in the father's own handwriting addressed to the mother, and unless she obtained those letters legitimately and legally, she could not produce them as evidence; others seemed not to care if the written proof were typed or dictated to another person. By the 1930s, judges relaxed their standards of proof. If a man made a statement to the police or in a formal document indicating his paternity, some judges would accept that as proof. By 1935, written avowal of paternity could be implicit or explicit.[58]

Marcel Combes unwittingly wrote an ideal letter to Hélène Mory, which she produced in her 1920 paternity suit: "Dear little one, don't worry; I am the father of the infant who just came into the world and I am there to recognize [the baby] and to get married to you and we will raise our *bambin* [*sic*] as best as possible so that he [*sic*] does not find harm, because, *chère petite*, I am a father and I hold my child dear." Despite these words, either grammatically incorrect or because he really did not know that his child was a girl, four years later, the author of the letter, and of the baby, did not carry out his duties, and the mother won her paternity suit against him. In 1924, Marie Doger produced a letter from M. Broudas, who had been mobilized to the Ruhr, in which he acknowledged the pregnancy, writing that he understood that she wanted to remain pregnant, although he did not see himself with "a kid." When the case settled in 1927, he was judicially declared the father and had to pay monthly child support of 150 francs.[59]

Judges became more insistent by the 1930s, not only that the man had written letters strongly indicative of paternity, but that he had also demonstrated affectionate ties as a father before condemning him to pay child support or judicially declaring him the father. A lump sum payment of 100 francs to the wet nurse could have been prompted by fear of scandal, as in the Herzenstein case cited above, and would not by itself qualify as contributing to the education and rearing of the child.[60] Letters expressing love for his child continued to be a major criterion, and military service again offered opportunity for letter-writing. Mlle Mathieu met M. Verlain in 1929, and they lived together from March 1930 to May 1931, when he left for military service in Algeria. Eight months after he left, she had a daughter. He contributed to childcare until September 1933. Women would have longed for letters with unequivocal avowals of paternity like his. His letters from Algeria included phrases such as: "It would give me the greatest pleasure if you care well for the little one . . . and hug her for me . . . you will see that we three will be happy." Those letters bore other signs of his paternity, such as signing them with an embrace from "her papa" and always signing them "your little husband who loves you for life." In a letter of 8 June 1932, he goes so far as to say, "do not be afraid, our little one will have a name." Subsequent letters repeat the phrase, "I love our little one"—referring to her as "our" little one and not just "the" little one, thus indicating his paternity. By 1935, however, Verlain had had a change of heart, claiming that he had not lived with her during the legal period of conception, because he had been in Algeria. Besides she was of "notoriously bad conduct." Despite his protestations, the judge announced that his letters convincingly showed fatherly affection and unequivocal avowal of paternity, and he declared Verlain the "natural father," stipulating that he pay 500 francs a month in child support.[61]

When a woman had neither letters giving unequivocal affirmation of paternity, nor proof that the man had contributed to the rearing of the child, nor witnesses to testify that she had lived in *concubinage notoire* with him, she lost her paternity suit. For example, when Mlle Thorin, a maid, sued M. Leroy, a painter, she based her case on all possible grounds. Using a nineteenth-century trope of innocence, Thorin insisted that she had given in to his sexual entreaties only after he had promised marriage. He countered that sexual relations had begun right away, and he had never promised marriage. In his decision against Thorin, the judge declared that fraudulent seduction usually involves a woman's naïveté and inexperience, but since Thorin already had one child before she met Leroy, she was not inexperienced. This judge also decided that a material and moral "community of life" had never existed between them. Indeed, the judge opined that their relationship had been clandestine and furtive, without any sign of stability. Even though in 1935, the year of this decision, the highest court allowed *concubinage notoire* when the man and woman had different residences, it insisted that such a relationship have the appearance of stability. Moreover, Leroy's letters from the very beginning expressed doubt about his paternity. After she told him of her pregnancy, he wrote, "I'm not at all sure the child is mine, because you know that I always paid attention." Whether this means coitus interruptus or use of a condom is not certain. Use of condoms became more widespread after 1918. He had paid a wet nurse 100 francs, but the judge did not regard this as acting as a father. The judge decided Thorin's case was unfounded, but not that she had acted in bad faith.[62]

According to the 1912 revision of paternity law, despite the objections of leading feminists, mothers could face criminal prosecution and a prison sentence of one to five years if they were convicted of bringing charges in fad faith.[63] Judges in civil tribunals could decide whether the woman should go to a criminal court on such misdemeanor charges. A sampling of the civil tribunals of Paris revealed no such instances, but the lawyers may have filtered such cases, and many women operating in bad faith may never have reached the courts. The one known case appeared in Sens (in the Yonne department, southeast of Paris), where the judge ruled that bad faith had not been sufficiently established. As the noted jurist René Savatier declared, "The long and difficult discussions [about bad faith (*mauvaise foi*) in the legislative debates] remain almost academic, almost never applied."[64]

Rather than filing a paternity suit, women without written proof could seek just a *pension alimentaire*. Their lawyers continued to operate on the principle that paternity was divisible; a man who had helped create a child must help nourish that child, but he did not have to provide the child with his name or inheritance, disassociating property and paternity. Providing child support did not have as great an impact on the family as did judicially attributing paternity. In some cases where the mother asked the judges to declare paternity and also award child support, the judges opted for only the latter. Mothers seeking only a *pension alimentaire* had to offer the same proof as those seeking filiation, but judges were less strict in interpreting the evidence. Nevertheless, judges ruled against a quarter of the mothers in the sample.

None of the mothers requesting just a *pension alimentaire* had letters from the presumed father in which he wrote anything that a judge might construe as an admission of paternity. All of the couples had lived together maritally, some only for a short period of time during the probable time of conception; most women claimed a marriage promise. In an emblematic case, Mlle Sollieu claimed that she had become M. Corbeau's mistress only after he had promised her marriage, bringing several witnesses who attested to this marriage promise. He had kept delaying the wedding date because, he said, he could not find a suitable apartment in Paris for them. Although he never wrote a letter even implying his paternity, the judge found sufficient evidence to insist he pay a *pension alimentaire*.[65]

Women's situations were in some cases quite complicated, involving the local and appeals courts as well as the Cour de cassation. Simone Roulet's story shows the effects of a paternity suit on a young woman; it also indicates what life was like for those with family money; it reveals that a woman of the upper classes did not have to hide her sexual freedom and might travel around with her lover in the provinces even as a teenager; and it alludes to abortion. Simone Roulet, from a prominent family, with an estate in southwestern France, met Lieutenant Georges Louis when she was a seventeen-year-old living in Toulouse. Both Louis and Roulet agreed on most of the circumstances of their relationship, except that she said he had seduced her, whereas Louis countered that Simone had instigated the relationship. At first, Roulet based her paternity suit on "seduction by surprise"—a euphemism for rape. She soon changed her story, however, and said that she had been seduced after Louis promised her marriage. Not being able to produce evidence of a marriage promise, Simone again changed the basis of her case and submitted a letter Louis wrote to her as proof of paternity. Fraudulent seduction was not the issue, and Roulet did not bring charges for damages. Regardless of who initiated the sexual relationship, they agreed they had been together in the summer of 1924, when they had traveled and stayed overnight together at hotels. They were together in Toulouse during the month of September, until he departed for a military academy in the Loire valley. When she realized she was pregnant, she wrote to him, and his replies constituted her major evidence in the paternity suit she filed after her daughter, Josette, was born on 3 May 1925.[66]

In Louis's letter to her of 10 October 1924, he gave her "a million kisses" and used the following key phrase: "I wish that *ton bobo* would disappear as soon as possible. . . . Keep me informed." The appeals court judge, Gisbert, who ruled in Roulet's favor, decided that these sentences constituted written admission of paternity, despite referring to the pregnancy as "her boo-boo," or injury, and not their future baby whom he will love like a father, as in letters by other men. Louis knew of Roulet's pregnancy, wanted it to disappear, and also wanted to be kept informed about the pregnancy and its possible end, whether in an abortion or a baby. As both Roulet's and Louis's lawyers pointed out, this letter does not indicate an agreement between the two parties to terminate the pregnancy or Louis's assistance to achieve this goal, both criminal offenses. But according to the judge, Louis's language demonstrated his "complicity in the *enterprise*," and a tacit, but very clear recognition that he would have been ready to collaborate with Roulet on the termination of the pregnancy.

In trying to establish a paternal connection between Louis and the baby, one of Roulet's lawyers asserted that Louis had paid the costs of childbirth. Another of her team of lawyers, in trying to establish that she was a good mother, declared that she had paid for the childbirth at the clinic herself, from her inheritance. Her mother, Mme de Salviac, claimed that she had paid the clinic for the costs of Roulet's delivery, to show what a good mother she was. In keeping with the established fashioning of the women as good mothers, even accepting their situation as single mothers, Roulet's lawyers continued to show that she had assiduously cared for Josette while living with her own mother. A sum of money that Louis sent to Roulet became a subject of controversy; her lawyer argued it was for child support and demonstrated that Louis had acted like a father. Louis's lawyer argued that it was to repay a loan Roulet had advanced him when he was out of funds. The judge, however, declared that this interpretation was "unreasonable."

As an indication of the changing times and the greater sexual freedom for women in the 1920s, no one apparently cast a negative view of Roulet and Louis going off together on holidays, where they shared a room. Judges reserved their moral condemnation for her mother, Mme de Salviac, for her failure to manage Roulet properly, leaving her unsupervised, with freedom to live an independent life at the young age of seventeen when she was inexperienced and not entirely capable of defending herself against seduction. Louis, in an effort to disprove his paternity, however, alleged that Roulet had loose morals and had enjoyed sexual relations with a medical student at the probable time of conception. The appeals court found the evidence Louis offered too imprecise to constitute proof of her bad conduct. Moreover, the legal period of conception coincided with the time she was with Louis during those three months in the summer of 1924. Judge Gisbert of the appeals court might have been inclined to favor Roulet, who had kept the baby, despite the availability and affordability of abortion to a young woman of her family background. Abortion was illegal, but possible to obtain. Since the principle proof of paternity was only the implicit suggestion of abortion, the Cour de cassation on 17 February 1930 annulled the appeals court decision, and Roulet collected neither child support nor damages; nor could Josette bear the name of Louis or receive an inheritance from him. The Cour de cassation found neither unequivocal avowal of paternity nor evidence of *concubinage notoire* or any other terms of proof as stipulated by article 340. During the stress of the legal proceedings, Simone had a nervous breakdown and entered a clinic, leaving Josette with her grandmother, Mme de Salviac.[67]

One major issue was whether advice to have an abortion constituted an admission of paternity. In the highly charged pro-natalist and anti-abortion atmosphere of the mid 1920s, it is likely judges would not be well disposed to Louis's advice to abort, and therefore it is surprising that the Cour de cassation ruled as it did. In September 1925, at the time the Roulet case was in the courts, *Le Matin* quoted doctors who called for legislation treating men who urged their wives and lovers to have abortions as criminal accomplices. Furthermore, the top legal scholar at the time maintained that advising abortion could constitute an avowal of paternity.[68]

When Mlle Hugues brought M. Ducoin before the civil tribunal of Lille to declare him the father of her baby boy in March 1926, she brought Ducoin's letters written upon hearing of her pregnancy, in which he advised her to get something from the pharmacist and to see a doctor. Based on this evidence, the Lille court declared Ducoin the father, and the appeals court of Douai upheld this decision in 1930. Ducoin then brought the case before the Cour de cassation, contending that advice to abort a pregnancy did not constitute an unequivocal avowal of paternity. The Cour de cassation disagreed, declaring that his two letters of August 1925 demonstrating his distress constituted his acknowledgment of responsibility for the pregnancy. The court ruled that although his avowal of paternity was implicit, it was unequivocal. Those who lost their suits, like Roulet, lacked convincing written admission of paternity or other evidence besides advice to have an abortion.[69]

Paternity searches were not limited to mothers acting in the names of their minor children. Adult children could seek legal recognition from their fathers, and in some cases from both parents, although these instances were rare. In 1925, the same year that Simone Roulet took her case before the civil tribunal of Toulouse, Jean-Louis Bernard was in court against his putative father, Anselme Patureau-Mirand in Châteauroux, in north-central France. Bernard claimed he was the legitimate son of M. and Mme Patureau-Mirand.[70] When Jean-Louis Bernard was born in June 1902, the doctor had immediately turned him over to a midwife, Mme Trotignon, who registered his birth, declaring his mother and father unknown. She reared Bernard until her death when her daughter, Mme Bataille, took over. Bataille alleged that both she and her mother had received subsidies from Patureau-Mirand for rearing the boy. None of this was unusual when parents wished to hide their child. When Jean Bernard celebrated his eighteenth birthday in 1920, Mme Bataille told him that his true parents were Mme and M. Patureau-Mirand. Bernard wrote to Patureau-Mirand, who was then serving as a legislative deputy, introducing himself as his son and asking to be part of the family. A short time later, he wrote again, telling Patureau-Mirand that he was going to go to court for a legal recognition of paternity and maternity if he persisted in ignoring him. Later that week, a priest at Châteauroux visited Bernard and presented him with 50,000 francs, a rather hefty sum, on behalf of Patureau-Mirand, who promised him an equal sum in 1925. This may have been money to keep Bernard quiet, but he used it to wage his legal battle for recognition from his putative parents.

It took almost three years of investigation before the judge decided that sufficient legal evidence existed to bring the case to court. In a confrontation between the parties in April 1924, Patureau-Mirand argued that Bernard was being manipulated by the political Left, which wanted to launch a scandal in order to unseat him as a deputy for the Indre. The newspaper *Le Matin*, clearly siding with Bernard, reported that "honest Jean Bernard only wants his name; he is not in the midst of any political adventure"; he was indifferent to politics, it said, dividing his time between his soccer team and his work in a department store. Whether the publicity led Patureau-Mirand to lose his seat is uncertain, but the candidate from the Cartel des Gauches defeated him in the victory of the Left that swept France that year.

In a rare and early instance of the use of physical features to determine paternity, the first meeting between Bernard and his alleged father and mother was to ascertain if there was a physical resemblance. Bernard's lawyer declared that Bernard "carries on his face the signature of nature in looking like Patureau-Mirand—with the eyes and nose of his mother and the forehead and chin of his father." Furthermore, although Bernard was athletic, he was slightly stooped, as was Patureau-Mirand. Patureau-Mirand's lawyer retorted, "if nature had signed, that day she had illegible handwriting." The judge decided that Bernard resembled the couple he said were his parents. Additional evidence convinced the judge to allow an inquiry for Bernard to prove that Mme Patureau-Mirand had given birth to a child on 5 June 1902, and that he was that child.[71] *Le Matin* began an inquiry of its own, publishing details of this case and destroying any hope for privacy the parties may have had. If Bernard's story were true, he would have been born about two months after the marriage of his mother and father. The reporter for *Le Matin* interviewed members of the community, including domestic servants of Mme Patureau-Mirand's mother, asking if anyone had noticed if Mme Patureau-Mirand was pregnant. They would only say that it was "not a happy wedding."

Patureau-Mirand told a tale in his defense that *Le Matin* described as a "lamentable story for a bad movie." Patureau-Mirand alleged that a friend who had fallen on the field of battle had confessed on his deathbed that he had a child and related the details that corresponded to Bernard's life. Patureau-Mirand gave money to support this boy out of loyalty to the dead comrade. However, he could not remember the fallen soldier's name, or whether his friend had told his story on the battlefield or in an ambulance. Despite Patureau-Mirand's defense, the judge ruled in March 1927 that M.

and Mme Patureau-Mirand were the parents of Bernard, who henceforth bore the name of Jean-Louis Bernard Patureau-Mirand. Bernard was not asking for money, but as the legitimate son of Patureau-Mirand, he would have been entitled not only to the name but to a portion of the inheritance.[72] The Patureau-Mirands sought to protect their honor and avoid scandal, perhaps believing that they were safe because so much time had elapsed since Bernard's birth.

As the Patureau-Mirands learned, children could disrupt parents' lives more than two decades after their birth. When Gustave Martin reached adulthood, he initiated a paternity suit against Lebrun, winning on appeal in Toulouse in 1936, when he was twenty-five. He based his case on letters that Lebrun had written to his mother when he first learned of her pregnancy. Those letters focused on his wish to deny any scandal and contained implicit advice to abort. As Lebrun wrote: "How the devil is it possible? We took all precautions. . . . It is terrible for me, after having worked so long to arrive at this good position, to see the result of my efforts collapse in one blow at the moment when I have arrived at my goal. You understand that this will be a scandal, an indelible stain for me in the position I now hold. What will my bosses and my subordinates think? And my mother if she hears about this? Surely the *mauvais gens* [malicious people] will not fail to inform her. I don't want this to happen for the entire world. I assure you, I am sorry and I don't know what I can do. Oh, what a calamity, what a calamity," adding in this and other letters: "I don't want anyone to know about this and will make all efforts to that end. If you have the will, I do also." The judges decided that this vague allusion to ending the pregnancy was sufficient avowal of paternity and declared Lebrun the natural father of Gustave Martin.[73]

Judges also based their decisions on stereotypes and discrimination. In 1924, an eighteen-year-old young woman filed a suit against her brother-in-law, a sculptor "of Algerian origin," accusing him of sexual violence against her, and named her sister as an accomplice. She alleged that as a result she had had a child, and attributed paternity to her brother-in-law. In criminal court, the judge brought in experts who said that the baby had "Arab characteristics." Based on this preliminary visual investigation, the judge sent the brother-in-law to prison to await trial for violence and an offense against decency. Her sister remained free on her own recognizance.[74]

Experts began exploring the use of blood groups to ascribe paternity in 1928. This method was limited, however, and could not prove paternity, but only affirm if a child could *not* be the offspring of a particular man or woman. Use of blood groups gained momentum in the 1930s, when doctors and scientists investigated the inheritability of blood types. The primary goal was to prove a wife's adultery, and by 1934, blood groupings were usually used to prove that a child was not that of the mother's legal husband. Marriage did not always indicate paternity, and now husbands had a scientific tool, if they wished to use it. Blood grouping said nothing about acting like a father; they only indicated if two people were not related by blood.[75] Consequently, French law and jurisprudence was slow to accept proof of paternity (or nonpaternity) by blood groupings, since doing so was not mandated by article 340 of the Code.

M. Mouffek, the defendant in a case of recherche de paternité in 1935, tried to establish the impossibility of his paternity by means of biology. Although Mouffek and Yvonne Hebert had lived together during the legal period of conception, he alleged that Hebert was sexually unfaithful during this time and proposed to establish the impossibility of his paternity by a comparison of his blood, Hebert's, and the child's. The judge refused, and ordered both parties to come back with circumstantial proof of paternity, as stipulated by article 340. Although the judge maintained he could base his decision in part on physical resemblance, such as skin and hair color, he could not base it on blood type. Some legal commentators, such as René Savatier, favored admitting blood groupings in 1936, at least for eliminating individual men as genitors. Savatier asked: "Isn't the essential goal in the process the discovery of the truth? And to achieve this goal shouldn't the judge put as his disposal all the new resources?" On the other hand, he noted the tension between biological paternity and affective fatherhood: accepting an analysis of blood in paternity suits would change the idea of paternity from a "paternal duty" on the part of a "real father to something determined by biological processes."[76]

Not all men resisted paternity, and some insisted on it. M. Jouannet sought custody of his daughter Pierrette before he died on 2 August 1930. In her subsequent paternity suit against the representatives of Jouannet's estate, Pierrette's mother brought sufficient written evidence to convince the judge that Jouannet had always concerned himself with his little daughter, who had been born in September 1928, and that he had acted as a father to her, preoccupied with her care and contributing the relatively large sum of 1,000 francs per month to it. In a letter of 5 June 1930, he wrote: "It is most essential to entrust me with the child. I would be able to raise her honestly and appropriately." Without other written proof of paternity or evidence of *concubinage notoire*, the court declared Pierrette the daughter of Jouannet, entitled to his name and to an inheritance from his estate.[77]

In another instance, Jean Robert insisted on his paternity in 1937 when his sister and brother-in-law went to court seeking to annul Robert's recognition and legitimation of Colette, apparently coveting the portion of inheritance due to Colette from her paternal grandfather. When Colette was born in 1923, her mother, Germaine Moret and Robert had legally recognized her, and soon thereafter, Robert married Moret and legitimized Colette. About a decade later, however, Robert's sister, Mme Chaunu, argued that Robert could not have been the father, since he had been in the Foreign Legion during the possible time of conception. But Robert brought evidence that he had been on leave and was with Moret for several days during that time. Undeterred, the Chaunus argued that Moret had also had intimate relations with other men during that time. The judge, however, affirmed: "The recognition of a child cannot be annulled as a lie unless it is established that no relations could have existed between the child's mother and the supposed father during the legal period of conception." Furthermore, it was in "the moral interest of the young girl to preserve her father's recognition and legitimation of her, which at this time does not appear as a deceit; consequently, the public order is not in jeopardy."[78] Here the judge articulated one of the guiding principles of the court cases involving paternity: his decision preserved public order. When judges based their decisions on preserving moral order, no one could take exception, even when they stretched the law.

A child could not have two legal fathers, and two men could not legally recognize a child, yet the genitor could be deprived of paternity and the man who cared for the child could be declared the father, even in 1906. Adolphe Durand first voluntarily legally recognized Joseph Eugène in 1875, shortly after the boy was born. Then Claude Launié did the same in 1884. In 1905, when Joseph was over thirty, Launié wanted to annul Durand's recognition. In ruling in Launié's favor, the judge did not give preference to the first man who had recognized the boy, as the law suggested, but argued that Durand, the genitor, who was homeless, had never provided paternal care. Furthermore, Joseph had not known of Durand's recognition until he was drafted into the army in 1892. Joseph had always lived with Launié, with whom he had a father-son relationship. The judge still allowed a connection with the genitor, however, and henceforth Joseph bore the surname of Durand-Launié. Biology could not be detached, even when paternity was given to someone else.[79]

Paternity was sometimes defined by emotions and by providing for the child. M. Chantemesse insisted on having legal paternity of a child not biologically his. Mlle Pétrini lived with M. Chantemesse, but she also was having a sexual relationship with M. Finochi when she became pregnant. After her daughter, Jeanne-Marie, was born, she and Finochi recognized the child. Yet Chantemesse continued to live maritally with Pétrini and provided both materially and emotionally for Jeanne-Marie from birth. He also recognized her, but after Finochi did. Chantemesse went to court seeking to have Finochi's recognition annulled, but Finochi objected. The appeals court of Aix-en-Provence declared that regardless of who recognized the child first, the major consideration was the interest of the child, and Finochi's recognition, rather than Chantemesse's would not be good for Jeanne-Marie. Moreover, Finochi had never acted like a father or even provided for her; furthermore, he was now married to another woman, and they had their own legitimate child. Chantemesse's recognition stood; Finochi's was annulled.[80]

By law, the person who recognized the child first had paternal authority, but in this case, jurisprudence opted for the interests of the child over a strict interpretation of the law; this judge privileged acting as a father over blood ties and protected Finochi's marital family. Annulling recognition of a child was not difficult. If a married man had recognized his out-of-wedlock child, someone, usually an heir, could have that recognition annulled. An ex-wife either out of spite, or out of interest in the inheritance, could bring her ex-husband to court to annul the recognition of the child he had sired while still married to her.[81]

Judges may have decided that a man should pay a *pension alimentaire*, but collecting child support was extremely difficult. The law and judicial decisions may not have had the desired impact; real power in family matters often resided outside of the courts and law. Divorced and separated mothers have always had trouble collecting from absent fathers; this was no different for judicially declared paternity. To encourage child support, a law of 1924 addressed men who failed to provide financially for their families, making abandoning one's family a misdemeanor if a man failed to support his family for three months or more. As Louis Marin, the author of the bill declared, "abandonment of families was one of the most odious acts in all classes of society, creating both material and moral damage."[82] Although the law focused on material responsibility, it implied that abandoning one's family constituted a moral crime against the family. The law also applied to fathers who disappeared, to divorced fathers, and to the few whom the courts had declared fathers of their extranuptial children. During the depression of the 1930s, less than a decade later, collecting child support became more of an illusion, regardless of the law. Unemployment "aggravated even further the impecuniosities of the fathers, and by ricochet that of the mothers."[83]

⁂

There is no way to know how accurate judges were in attributing paternity to reluctant men in the first half of the twentieth century. Anthropological studies of 2006, with genetic testing as proof of paternity, demonstrate that men who believe children are biologically their own are correct 96 to 98 percent of the time. Those who refuse their paternity, however, are often in denial, and are indeed the biological fathers 70 percent of the time.[84] It is entirely possible that judges and the mothers, relying on circumstantial and behavioral evidence, were correct more than two-thirds of the time in the first three decades of the twentieth century.

Jurisprudence was governed by considerations of public order, the tranquility of families, and respect for marriage, while also allowing consensual unions. Without specifying what they meant, other than stability and support of the family and of the nation, judges frequently and interchangeably used the catchphrases "public order" and "moral order" as rallying cries to preserve what they wanted. Judges especially invoked the concept of public order to justify their decisions that bent the law. If they acted to preserve public order, they appeared conservative, although in effect they could be considered activist judges. Few politicians would object to their decision, however, because to do so marked one as a radical or revolutionary who cared little for public order—either moral or social. In the invocation of public order, judges of the twentieth century differed little from those of the nineteenth. In stretching the law, judges demonstrated understanding and perhaps empathy with the men or women who came before them. The judges own social stature, their reliance on men's written word, as well as their stated desire to preserve the moral or political order might mark them as conservative; their recognition of women's sexuality and their willingness to recognize concubinage, however, denoted a certain open-mindedness. Empathy with people in a legal, social, or economic predicament is a psychological foundation of a democracy and human rights. If the judges empathized with the people brought before them, they exhibited some of the Third Republic's tendencies toward solidarism, a political philosophy founded on the notion of a nation as an organic unit, where the good of the nation rested on the welfare of all its citizens.

Mothers appropriated and exercised some rights of citizenship in filing paternity suits, but full citizenship still belonged to men. The laws of the putative father's nationality applied; in the few cases when he was not French, the laws of his nation applied, and were often more restrictive. However, by the 1930s, the laws of France applied even if the father was foreign. In Alsace and Lorraine, German law prevailed until January 1925. In German law, as in French, a man could escape paternity charges if he could prove that the mother had had other lovers. Like French law, it held that the man who lived with the mother for the 181–302 days before childbirth was the father of a natural child. Court-declared paternity meant the man had to help pay for the childbirth and furnish food for the child for sixteen years following birth. Unlike French law, but similar to French jurisprudence, German law did not exempt married men from paternity searches, but they could only be liable for child support of their extranuptial children and not filiation.[85]

French law greatly disadvantaged indigenous women in the colonies, leaving power to the colonial governor. If he so decided, the children of a white French father and an indigenous mother would be outside the law and forbidden to file a paternity suit. French feminists tried to change this, but in 1928 they were still campaigning to protect indigenous women from the "fleeting loves" (*amours passagères*) of white Frenchmen. In this they had the support of senators, notably Paul Strauss, who expressed the noble sentiment, "France owes it to itself to proclaim that before the law there are no inferior races."[86]

How people lived their intimate lives was too important to be dominated by the political discourse, the law, and the courts. The rhetoric of the ideal conjugal family did not resonate with behavior, as men and women formed families through concubinage, had short-term love and sexual relationships, and sought legal redress for relationships gone awry. The courts, as agents of the state, were crucial elements in the social construction of paternity and the family. Paternity mattered as a cultural and social reflection of what people thought of themselves—their names, their family heritage, their property, their careers, their sexuality, and their roles as parents—and as a consequence, paternity suits reflected the interaction of individuals and communities with the state. They helped define identities, rights and duties, as judges increasingly found ways to make men materially responsible for their children born outside of marriage, basing their decisions in part on how men and women fashioned their stories and lived their lives. As during the nineteenth century, distinctions between the social and the legal did not always obtain; judges interpreted the law, generally broadening the grounds of admissible evidence, which by 1940 included concubinage, implicit and explicit written expressions of paternity, and behavior as a father. Jurisprudence even allowed women to collect damages and child support from married men, using tort law as a way around limitations of paternity searches. Paternity took different forms, both in lived experiences and judicial decisions. It could consist of a biological genitor who was also a nurturing father, without a dichotomy; or biological paternity could differ from affective fatherhood. Starting with the Old Regime, sanguinity or purity of blood can be seen in men's denial of filiation of an extranuptial child who the family thought was not of their blood and by the attempts to use blood groups in determining paternity. Nevertheless, if men acted as fathers, that behavior could replace a blood connection in defining paternity.

Basing his analysis on Michel Foucault's statement that "the bourgeoisie's 'blood' was its sex," Robert Nye convincingly demonstrates that "[b]ecause their fortunes were dependent not simply on inheritance, but on viable and talented *inheritors*, there was much more at stake in marriage and reproduction for bourgeois families than there had been for Old Regime nobles."[87] Although Foucault did not specifically address issues of paternity and the family in his analysis of the discourse of blood and power, his statement that "the blood relation long remained an important element in the mechanisms of power, its manifestations, and its rituals" applies. The courts customarily assigned or denied paternity basically in terms of blood, but without biological proof. Moreover, the distinction between blood kinship and emotional kinship was not clear-cut. In the absence of blood and genetic tests, court-determined paternity was complex, involving language about past behavior and public perceptions. Sex became a public issue encompassing the mother, father, the community, and the courts. Foucault argues that "power's hold on sex is maintained through language."[88] In cases of paternity, power resided in the civil courts, with the reliance on the language of written proof, the testimony of family and neighbors, and behavioral evidence of emotional ties. By the end of the 1930s, more than ever before, paternity was both biologically and socially constructed.

Biology still made women mothers, according to the essentialist view of women current at the time. If they gave birth, whether married or not, they were empowered to rear, educate, and morally provide for the child. If they were unmarried, they had sole power in rearing the child, possibly with some financial help from the men—if they could collect. Article 341 of the Civil Code authorizing *maternity* searches had remained unchanged since 1804, indicating that a woman who bore a child had responsibility for that child as the social and biological mother.

Since paternity derives from sex, when issues of paternity go to court, sexual power is formulated and contested in a public space. Discourse in the civil tribunals, on the most apparent level, focused on children's survival and on protecting the property of the father and his family; but it was also about sexual power. Women and men used their power in court, in a complex interplay between law and gender as they navigated and made use of the courts, of the law, and of the shifting concepts of seduction, abandonment, single motherhood, fatherhood, and the family in order to exercise their citizenship and improve their situations and those of their children. Women did not lose power over their children when they sought and received child support; they continued to have *puissance paternelle*. Relationships among blood ties, sexuality, and power played out in how the courts dealt with paternity.

Throughout judicial proceedings, sexual conduct remained paramount, with gender imbalance in acceptable codes of behavior. What went on in the courts, however, was a type of gendered and often formulaic discourse. Men and women performed their roles in court using a culturally approved script, just as they had in the nineteenth century. Proof of a woman's sexual fidelity was a key issue in determining paternity; a man's sexual fidelity rarely mattered. Nevertheless, judges were more accepting of women's sexuality and more open to various living styles than they had been in the previous century, neither consistently rewarding women for their young innocence nor condemning them for their open sexuality. Just as the mother could exercise power over the man by going to court to get him to pay for his sexual behavior, he could exercise power by attributing sexual immorality to her. Because the courts held some men financially responsible for child support, sexual power was redistributed, allowing more for the mothers—within the parameters of approved sexual behavior. Female sex workers and women with many partners could not successfully sue a man for child support.[89] Women bringing suit still tended to define themselves in court above all as good mothers.

By the twentieth century, concern for the child's well-being overrode sympathy for the destitute mother, representing a shift in moral priorities.

As a result, court decisions requiring men to bear some financial responsibility for their out-of-wedlock children, and ascribing filiation made paternity less of a decision for men than it had been. In the nineteenth-century era of individual rights for men, one of the key components was the freedom of choice—including whether to act as a father to an extranuptial child. In the twentieth century, women and the courts limited that choice. Many men, however, fulfilled their responsibilities to the mothers and children quite willingly without any external pressure. They were a presence in their children's lives, both materially and emotionally, and therefore not a presence in the court.

Marriage likewise differed from the nineteenth century. Increasingly, but inconsistently, society considered that men and women who shared a bed and took their meals in common could be regarded as being in a state of concubinage resembling marriage. The community did not always openly disparage women's sexuality when she entered freely into concubinage. Nevertheless, she could not always obtain support for the resulting child from the man involved, unless he explicitly or implicitly acknowledged his paternity. The "new woman" or "modern woman" of the 1920s and 1930s did not live apart from the "new man." Women were increasingly economically independent, sexual, and accustomed to spending time in public places. But those public spaces could be dangerous for them. The new men enjoyed the new women, but they were also supposed to be responsible fathers—at least materially—within and outside of marriage. Women, especially single mothers, had always faced a double responsibility in acting as good mothers and also in providing for their children. Men now faced a similar double responsibility. Not only were they to help support their children, but they were also supposed to act as good fathers. Moreover, it was the community that attested to the behavior of men and women; private life played out in public spaces, and not just for the urban poor. Women's expectations of responsible male sexuality may have raised the standards of men's behavior toward their extranuptial children, but not without resistance from some men. By going to court, women reconfigured gender relations and male responsibility.

CHAPTER FIVE

Families Dismantled and Reconstituted, 1880–1940

When women went to court to obtain child support or judicially declared paternity for their children, reconstituting a family with the father was not their stated goal, and the men brought to court did not seek to form a family with the mother and child. Judges, therefore, did not reconstitute families when ascribing paternity; moreover, to have done so would have been against the law. Men and women could choose how to compose their families, either by dismantling or reconstituting them. A man could break apart a family by denying paternity of a child his wife bore. The state could also dismantle and reconstitute families by depriving fathers or mothers of their parental authority and moving those children to a related family member, to a state institution, or to foster parentage. Starting in 1923, the legalization of child adoption reconstituted families in a new and significant way, endowing the child with partial or full family membership and an inheritance. This chapter breaks from the path of paternity searches hewn in the previous chapters and uses concepts of fatherhood to treat related aspects of paternity and a variety of family formation strategies, showing how individuals had agency, not only in cases of recherche de paternité, but also in dismantling and forming family bonds more generally. The history of paternity denial, of deprivation of paternity, and of adoption complements that of recherche de paternité and provides a further glimpse into contested paternity, the evolution of the French family, the roles of the state and kinship systems, and the relationship of nonconformist families with society. This chapter continues to demonstrate how the notion of paternity was more than the relationship between a father and child; it was linked to a range of beliefs, customs, and laws concerning what did or did not constitute a family.

The French cultural kinship system, one that did not usually include outsiders, functioned to preserve the family property and name. An idealized view of the family as an organic unit related to the conception of a nation as an organic unit, dependant on the family and its purity. Daily lives, even representations and constructions of the family, however, involved a type of practicality whereby families reconstituted themselves for their own immediate and long-term goals, with family purity not always requisite. Families had long included members not related by blood or marriage; in the twentieth century, through adoption and other family forms, families more freely admitted those outside the blood kinship groups. Even French nationalists came to accept some dismantling and reconstitution of families with a view to saving the children and hence the future of the nation, although the desire to preserve the idealized legal conjugal families and their lineage remained.

Disavowal of Paternity

Previous chapters have shown how a man might not accept responsibility for a child born to a woman with whom he had a sexual relationship outside of marriage. That refusal could also apply to children born within a legal marriage. If a married man's wife bore a child whom he strongly suspected was not his, his honor, as well as the moral and material economy of his family, might require that he deny paternity of that child in order to preserve his lineage, property, and name. According to the Civil Code, the man married to the child's mother at the time of conception was the father, responsible for contributing materially and morally to rearing and educating the child, acting as a father, and providing the child with a civil status and inheritance. Since the law of 6 December 1850, however, if during the legal time of conception they had been geographically far apart, if he was physically unable to have children, if she had hidden her pregnancy and the birth of the child from him, or if she had left their marital household and their community knew about it, a married man could deny paternity of a child born to his wife.

In both the nineteenth and twentieth centuries, a married man went to court to disavow paternity when he could prove his wife's adultery, usually with the help of a community of witnesses. A married man had the right to reject a child of his wife's adultery, although he was free to commit adultery himself without having to bear responsibility. The sexual double standard gave almost unlimited sexual freedom to married men—unless a woman had good lawyers and found a judge willing to bend the law when she sued a married man for damages and child support, as some successfully did in the 1930s. A woman's adultery was a criminal offense, punishable by a prison term ranging from three months to two years; however, judges were lax in enforcing this penalty. A better strategy for a man faced with his wife's adultery was separation, divorce, and disavowal of paternity.

A man's reproductive and marriage strategy was directed toward ensuring an inheritance for his heirs and maintaining his family honor and bloodline, as Robert Nye has eloquently explained. By disavowing paternity, a man protected his honor and preserved his family property for his legitimate progeny. Honor was linked to property, and denial of paternity gave the man an element of power—blood relations being an aspect of the mechanism of power, according to Michel Foucault—and saved his inheritance for transmission by his bloodline.[1] As a point of honor and power, these fathers were also insisting on being the progenitors. A husband could deny paternity of any child that might impede his reproductive strategy, including his extranuptial children and any children his wife might have by another man. Realizing his goals depended on his wife's sexual fidelity, not on his own. A married woman's sexual fidelity was the key element in maintaining family integrity and public moral order. A husband's denial of a child born to his wife when he did not think the offspring was of his blood was to keep order in his family. However, denial of paternity created disorder to maintain order.

To deny paternity, a husband had to bring proof of his wife's adultery, which he most frequently did by showing that she had left their marital home to live with her lover. A man rarely invoked other proofs of her adultery, such as an accident to him rendering sexual relations impossible; his incarceration in a prison or hospital; or his having been away on military service during the legal time of conception. Sometimes a man claimed ignorance of his wife's pregnancy and childbirth as evidence that he was not the father of her child. The key was the wife's *public* infidelity; if friends, family and community knew about it, the husband's pride and sense of honor would dictate that he divorce his wife and deny paternity of the child she had conceived. For a married man, biological paternity and social fatherhood were linked; in denying biological paternity of a child born of his wife's adultery, he also denied his emotional fatherhood of that child. His successful legal action disavowing paternity required altering the child's birth certificate, thereby notifying the world that he was not the father; the child could not carry his family name and was not entitled to inherit from him. It also meant he would have nothing to do with the child. This was not usually a problem, since his wife had already left his home before she gave birth; sometimes the child was already several years old.[2]

At first glance, it would appear that if a man went to court to deny paternity of his wife's child, that very public action would dishonor him and show the world he was a cuckold. But, in most cases his family and community already knew, so he lost nothing by going to court. Moreover, by taking action against her, he could regain his honor and pride. Avoiding ridicule resulting from a wife's adultery was paramount. After divorce became legal in 1884, it was likely that the couple were separated, divorcing, or divorced at the time of court action. Divorce and denial of paternity were preferable to prison for stabbing one's rival in the back, as Henri Gaveau did. Gaveau, a 40-year old roofer, had married a "charming woman," who left him and went to live with one of Gaveau's friends. In an effort to avenge his honor, Gaveau invited his rival to his house, where he was very cordial, but as he was seeing the man to the door, he stabbed him seven times in the back. His rival collapsed, but was not gravely wounded, and Gaveau was arrested.[3]

The key in determining if a husband won his case, which he almost always did, was that his wife had "abandoned the marital home." Men commonly used this phrase in formulaic fashion. The testimony of witnesses—family, friends, and neighbors—supplied the proof; they might also specify that she had committed adultery, or had numerous sexual partners (*une conduite irrégulière*). Sometimes both the husband and wife brought witnesses; her friends testified that her husband still had sexual relations with her and that no evidence of her adultery existed.[4] In a typical case of disavowal, Oscar Caron went to court in June 1898 disavowing his wife's son, Raymond, born the previous month, on the grounds of her adultery and "the physical impossibility of cohabitation" during the legal period of conception. He brought witnesses indicating that his wife had "abandoned him," had left their "marital home" during that time and was guilty of "irregular conduct." Furthermore, she had hidden her pregnancy from him, and he only found out about the child from the list of recent births published in the newspaper. He may have had suspicions in order to have looked in that list in the first place. Unlike other instances of repudiation of paternity, however, he brought the charges as soon as he knew about the baby's birth. The judge, however, took two years to hear the case and evaluate all documents and witnesses' testimony. This delay was not unusual in paternity cases, including disavowal, because of the need to gather evidence and the sluggishness of legal proceedings.[5]

One emblematic case, based on witnesses and letters, that characteristically demonstrates that the wife asserted her own agency dates from 1907, when August Roux, an employee in the administration of Postes et Télégraphes, sought to deny the paternity of a child born to his wife while she was still legally married to him. One witness said, "At the time when Roux told me about his wife's childbirth, I knew only that she had left him eight or nine months before." Two other witnesses put the departure of Mme Roux from her husband "well before the birth of the child." They added that Roux had been surprised by the child's birth and had not even known that his wife was pregnant. Her estrangement from her husband was borne out by her own testimony that after she left her husband, she did not have any relations with him. In a letter to her husband at the time of the divorce proceedings, but prior to the court case he brought denying paternity, she wrote: "What do you want to do with my child?... It shows that you really have no honor and are nothing but a coward to have as your instrument of vengeance a little being who is not yours. My child is cherished, lacks for nothing, and does not need the protection of a stranger. I do not think it surprises you to learn that my daughter is not yours!" The judge allowed him to disown the girl. The mother's admission that the child was not her husband's was not unusual. Cases in which the husband denied paternity of his wife's child were generally uncontested, but still required legal proceedings.[6] A man's honor was a complicated matter. If his wife committed adultery and his community knew about it, he had to defend his honor by divorcing her and disavowing the child. But honor also required that he not harm the child.

Court cases involving a married man's repudiation of paternity did not change significantly after the war. Masculine virility, demonstrated by being the father of many children, lost its status when his wife committed adultery and not all those children were his. His concept of honor and preserving the bloodline for transmission of his property prevailed. In the early 1920s, in dozens of cases, fathers disowned children born during the war. The husbands said that they had been absent during the legal time of conception, usually away at the war, and that their wives had hidden the pregnancy and childbirth from them. Furthermore, in many cases, witnesses testified that a man's wife had had a lover while he was away, and that she had left her marital home and had never returned or communicated with her husband. The public nature of her behavior sullied his honor.

Maternity may have been a patriotic duty, and single motherhood was becoming more acceptable, but a woman's adultery and resultant child were perceived as a grave dishonor to a man, especially one who had fought in the war. In the 1930s, the public nature of a married woman's infidelity, pregnancy, and childbirth became more important than before. Witnesses from the family and neighborhood appeared by the score, bearing tales of her infidelity and spousal abandonment. Moreover, judges frequently mentioned the importance of the husband's family name, making clear that the child could no longer carry the husband's name nor "belong to his family."[7]

A man had to do the honorable thing by denying paternity; this was more honorable than charging his wife with the crime of adultery. Furthermore, if she went to prison for adultery and he had not disowned those children who were not his prior to her sentencing, he would have sole responsibility for them. To some, denying paternity preserved a man's honor more, and hurt him and his children less, than sending their mother to jail for adultery. Honor was also more important for a man than assuming responsibility for children who might not be his.

Men who disavowed paternity, however, had to be careful; it was irreversible. A night watchman divorced his wife in 1896 and disavowed the child she had given birth to in 1895. However, a short time after the divorce, he and his wife resumed a life in common, and he said that he had always considered her his wife and the child, whom he helped raise both materially and as a father, as his own. His wife died in 1921, and in 1928, he sought to adopt this child, François, now a 33-year-old man. The court rejected his request because he had once disavowed him.[8] As a result, François was legally illegitimate.

Rejection by someone regarded as a father could be quite traumatic to a child. Although both the Code and the magistrates urged disavowal shortly after the child's birth, it often occurred years later. In the sample of cases after 1884, when divorce became legal, about a third of the time the mother was divorced from her first husband and her new husband was listed as the child's father.[9] The birth certificates of the remainder cited the child's mother's name, but in the space for the father's name, the words "unknown" or "not named" (*père non dénommé*) appeared. Since the mother's husband at the time of conception was legally the father of her children, regardless of the name on the birth certificate, he could disavow them, and those children became illegitimate. No one could legitimize these children, because article 331 of the Code stipulated: "Legitimation or recognition of children born of an adulterous or incestuous relationship is forbidden." As part of a series of laws pertaining to inheritance and the family, legislation of November 1907 modified this article and allowed the legitimation of children born of a mother's adultery by her subsequent marriage to the child's biological father—but only if that child was born more than 300 days after the mother's legal separation from her first husband. This law meant little to some mothers and children. A child conceived during a marriage but born later still had to be disavowed. If a mother married the biological father, he could claim paternal authority only if her prior husband disavowed the child. Having two fathers meant something different a century ago than it does now, and it was not permitted.

A law of 1924 allowed children born of a mother's or father's adultery to be legitimized by the remarriage of their mother or father, but the children still had to have been born more than 300 days after the separation, and both the newly married parents had to take action to recognize the children and legitimize them at the time of their marriage. These children were then entitled to the same legal rights as legitimate children. The issue in disavowal, and in society in general, was the adultery of the mother. It may have become honorable to protect the child, but the father's honor and blood ties with his children had precedence over the well-being of the child, despite a child-centered rhetoric.[10] A man still found it more honorable to deny paternity of his wife's child and thus deprive the child of a legitimate status and family ties than it was to live with the idea that marriage indicates paternity when the child was not biologically his.

Marriage served both emotional and material functions. In addition to procreation, raising a family, and transmission of property, it was also a bond of mutual affection and a source of pleasure.[11] When men and women took their affection and pleasure elsewhere, that aspect of conjugal family life faded. Law and customs tolerated male adultery without imposing consequences, but for women, any form of adultery was fraught with dishonor, because bringing a child who was not the husband's into the household would weaken patriarchal property lines and power. Moreover, it indicated her sexuality outside the social and moral order, beyond the control of her husband. Repudiation of one's wife's misbegotten children was inextricable from male honor. Disavowal proceedings indicate a communal definition of manhood in which the community might censure a husband if he did not act honorably by repudiating his wife's child when the community knew she had left him for another. Cases of disavowal of paternity are indicative of the public nature of intimate lives. Witnesses had to attest to a woman's adultery, which they knew from the "noise on the street." On warm days in urban neighborhoods, people conducted their private lives in squares, parks, and on street corners and terraces. In cooler weather, they could have romantic preludes to sexual affairs in the numerous cafés or in the stairwells and courtyards of their apartment buildings. Only a small proportion of men denied paternity, however, and many did so as a by-product of divorce. The untold majority, whose life stories never appear in the court records, were responsible fathers, whether or not legally married to the mothers or biologically related to their children.

Deprivation of Paternal Authority

Toward the end of the nineteenth century, the French state became increasingly involved in family affairs and in defining proper parental behavior, sometimes dismantling families prior to reconstructing them, and distributing children in the process. The law of 24 July 1889 on the deprivation of paternal authority (*déchéance de la puissance paternelle*) to protect morally endangered children (*enfants moralement abandonnés*) allowed for the deprivation of paternal authority in cases where state officials judged one or both parents unfit.[12] Based on the dominant cultural concept that men had the governing parental authority, public authorities, the law, and parents referred to this as paternal authority (*puissance paternelle*) even when it applied to mothers. In language, if not in lived experiences, the patriarchy prevailed. This law was one of the most important legislative decisions of the century, because it deprived fathers of a right that they considered their natural right confirmed by the Civil Code of 1804. The Code had entrusted fathers with paternal authority as a means of having them ensure the moral and social order of their families, and by extension of the body politic. With the law of 1889, the state could decide that certain fathers were not ensuring moral order, and indeed were detrimental to it; therefore, state officials could take action to disempower those fathers and take their children away from them. Mothers as well as fathers could be deprived of paternal authority and have their children removed, but their behavior had to have been egregious in the eyes of neighbors and the police. Moreover, if the mother was married, she did not have paternal authority, only the father did. Mothers could hold *puissance paternelle* only when unmarried. Endangerment of children leading to deprivation of paternal rights included leaving the children in extreme filth, habitual drunkenness, sexually or physically abusing the children, beating the children beyond what was considered normal paternal correction, being arrested for begging or theft, leaving children alone, a mother engaging in prostitution or leading her children into prostitution, or anything neighbors and police defined as "scandalous misconduct."

This 1889 law was part of a larger assemblage of laws and regulations pertaining to maternal and child welfare, redefining parenthood to include social responsibility, or at least responsibility to one's children, both inside and outside of marriage.[13] These welfare laws, enacted from the 1870s through the 1920s, were based on the premise that state authorities, exercising a type of paternalism, knew best what constituted an acceptable family and how to protect children, even from their parents. Laws included state and medical regulation of wet nurses and foster parentage (1874); the regulation of women's work so that they could be better mothers (1892); the recognition of a mother-child family by providing subsidies for breastfeeding (1885 and 1904); increased welfare for abandoned children (1904), and the 1912 law permitting recherche de paternité. The morally healthy conjugal family remained the fundamental building block of a healthy nation, but state authorities now thought they knew best what a healthy family looked like and could do a better job at protecting children than some biological parents could. With an important class differential, especially if the biological parents were living in poverty or if the head of household was the mother, officials like judges, police, and doctors exercised parental authority.[14]

Initiative in passing this 1889 law began in 1881 with Théophile Roussel and René Bérenger, two senators associated with many of the measures for the protection of children. Conservatives opposed the measure because it restrained a father's "natural right" to paternal authority and diminished patriarchal power.[15] Government officials complained that it would cost the state money to care for the children removed from their parents. The law's supporters placed it within the revolutionary plans for state assistance to children and families. It finally passed as part of a republican agenda for state action to regulate the social and moral order.[16] The 1889 law embodied a reconceptualization and restructuring of paternal authority, of gender relations, and relations between the family and the state, removing paternal authority from the realm of natural law and making it social and regulated by civil law. State authorities could decide what was best for protecting children; they could take legal authority away from parents who were deemed to have abused their children and give it to other family members or state agencies. Taking paternal authority away from biological fathers reversed a centuries' old right of fathers to educate and provide for their children. By making the rights of children preeminent, this law set limits on the father's power in his home.

The procedure for depriving a parent of paternal authority required men and women to formulate their identities as good mothers and fathers. It also allowed the public prosecutor (*procureur de la République*) to position himself as the officer responsible for saving the children and preserving the moral order. The prosecution depicted the parents as neglecting or morally corrupting the children, whom the state would then protect. The mothers and fathers represented themselves as good parents, doing whatever they could to raise moral and obedient children. Occasionally, a case began when a parent or child was arrested for begging or theft, but more often the process began when a family member or neighbor denounced a parent to the local police superintendent for morally abandoning his or her children. An investigation followed in which detectives from the Criminal Investigation Department (*police de sûreté*) visited the family and interrogated neighbors.[17]

Mutual surveillance was part of urban society. Community and family members' testimony, often so crucial in paternity cases, was even more critical in depriving parents of their paternal authority. Social webs functioned to protect children, even if that necessitated taking them away from their biological parents. Public officials relied on local information. In nineteenth- and twentieth-century Paris, middle-class families sought to protect their names and honor by safeguarding their privacy. Working-class families made less distinction between the private nature of the household and the public nature of the neighborhood.[18] Apartments were tiny, walls were thin, and sound reverberated in the courtyards; and the apartment building, its stairwells and courtyards, the streets, markets, and local public squares made up a village community. In the very public nature of family life among the poor in Paris, neighborhood networks functioned to exclude others, reporting certain parents to the police in the avowed interest of saving the children. Neighborhoods enforced their own community values and helped to reinforce the state's concepts of good parenting, either by reporting allegedly bad parents or by responding to interrogation. In informing on and ostracizing particular parents, community members established themselves as the moral police and judge, and reflected members' desires to protect their own interests and reputations. Testimony and denunciations often appeared formulaic, not always to be taken as truth; they often came from a self-appointed protector of the community's social order. Statements from family and neighbors included tales of the unfit parent committing some transgression, with distinct gender differences: women were bad mothers by reason of sexual immorality, slovenliness, and neglect of their children, whereas men were bad fathers because of violent behavior, usually when drunk, beating their children, or sexually abusing them. Destitution was not always a cause for deprivation of paternal authority unless there was abuse. Most parents fought to keep their children.

"I do not want to abandon the exercise of *puissance paternelle* to Assistance publique," cried 42-year-old Jean L. in 1902, in refusing to give up his legitimate children. An investigation into his family had begun when his wife was arrested for complicity in theft with a man neighbors accused of being her lover. The police commissioner reported that the couple lived in three furnished rooms in an area of inexpensive lodging houses in Belleville, one of the poorest working-class areas of Paris. Jean L. worked regularly, earning wages of 8 francs a day; his wife did not work outside the home. Her mother, who also lived with them, contributed her 5 francs a month she obtained in welfare to the household economy. The couple had nine children. The oldest child at eighteen was already married and out of the house. Mme L., her mother, and the four youngest children lived in one room. The two teenaged girls, Julienne and Charlotte, slept in a tiny room with only one bed. The father and the ten-year-old son slept in another room. The 8-year-old boy, Charles, slept just a few houses down the street with relatives.[19] The inspector reported that he found only the four youngest children, dirty and dressed in tatters, at home. The other children were at work or at school; no one reported bad conduct from any of them.

This family's living quarters made privacy in their daily lives impossible. All reports indicated the desperately deprived condition of the family, and critics alleged that the parents were raising their children "on the path of vice." Less critical reports indicated the real economic destitution of a family with so many children, but declared that the family received some public assistance and did not want their children taken away from them. Mme L.'s morality came into question when neighbors accused her of having a lover outside the neighborhood. Moreover, she used vile language. Several neighbors had nothing bad to say about the couple's conduct, but others mentioned that they quarreled a lot and that Mme L. and the two older daughters left and returned at all hours, while the younger children were left to themselves, in the most "immoral conditions." L. had five complaints of theft against him, with four in 1898. Apparently, times were bad for the family, because the same year the couple started to receive aid from their local welfare bureau, including rent vouchers. The police inspector wanted the children taken from their parents, but the outcome is unknown. Many cases for deprivation of paternal authority ended inconclusively, reflecting the prosecutor's tendency not to go to court or seek a judicial decision unless he had a strong case.

When the courts deprived a father of his paternal authority, that authority often devolved on Assistance publique. This action doubly reinforced the influence of the public sphere over intimate family lives. The recognized natural son of René A., twelve-year-old Henri, a sickly and difficult child, whom some described as "vicious" or a bit deranged, was taken away from his alcoholic father, who reportedly had beaten him. His mother had recently died, and his father, who had been detained numerous times for begging, remarried. The allegedly wicked stepmother, according to neighbors' reports, deprived Henri of food, and slapped him when he brought her a small bouquet of flowers. Other witnesses reported that Henri's parents wanted to get rid of him. Assistance publique of Paris removed the right of paternal authority from René, and then transferred it to the French Union for the Rescue of Children (Union française pour le sauvetage de l'enfance), a state-supported private agency that placed children with foster families or in a school it ran for abandoned teenaged children. A doctor diagnosed Henri with tuberculosis and placed him in the Union's temporary shelter.[20] This case was emblematic of several in which a child protection agency and Assistance publique asserted paternal authority and sent the children to foster parentage or a special school where they would learn a trade, if no other family members could take them.

When police removed children from abusive parents, the courts could divide child custody and paternal authority among state agencies, private welfare, and the family. In 1908, a couple lost custody of their eight children. These parents reportedly drank alcohol to excess and failed to provide the children with food or clothes. This was not so much a question of morality as of poverty aggravated by alcohol abuse. Residents of the same tenement testified that the children would be better off if they were placed in an institution for the "protection of children." Of the eight children, the oldest one went to an uncle and the youngest stayed with his parents; Assistance publique took the others and sent them outside of Paris to foster parents or placed them in highly regulated special schools where they could learn a trade. Neighbors voiced confidence in agencies for the protection of children, regarding them as a refuge from drunken fathers who beat their children.[21]

In some instances, one parent used the law to try to deprive the other of paternal authority, and community members backed one or other. Families members also used the law to help resolve disputes or to support them in their quarrels with other family members. Cases of child abuse often defied proof. In 1907, Jeanne Claude accused her estranged husband of committing "obscene acts" on their three children. The police investigated and heard testimony from the neighbors that Jeanne Claude's husband, contrary to her complaint, was a hard worker and good father. No one knew what went on behind closed doors.[22]

Grandparents sometimes demanded that a grandchild be taken from the parent, but the grandparent did not always accept custody. One grandfather complained that his own daughter, the child's mother, "lived by the most shameful debauchery" and was leaving his 8-year-old granddaughter to fend for herself in the streets. The 70-year-old grandfather claimed he was unable to care for the child, however, and wanted the girl put with Assistance publique. Upon police investigation, some neighbors testified that the mother drank and that the child was "vicious," while others attested that she was "a good mother." The courts let her keep her daughter.[23]

A grandmother initiated a classic Cinderella case in which the children of a first marriage were mistreated by an evil stepmother. Family and neighbors interceded to protect the children. Victor L., a traveling salesman, married Rosine R. and they had three children: Fanny, Andrée, and Robert, aged 15, 14, and 9, respectively, at the time of the investigation in 1898. Rosine died in January 1892, and Victor married Jeannette K. in August of that same year. Early in 1898, Rosine's mother filed a suit to deprive Victor of paternal authority, charging that he and Jeannette beat her grandchildren and mistreated them by leaving them alone and depriving them of food. Deprivation of food was a refrain in describing bad parenting. Without reservation, neighbors depicted Jeannette as a wicked stepmother. Mme Marthe V., a 21-year-old dressmaker living down the street, took Andrée as an apprentice; she had no complaints about Andrée's morality but indicated that she was not a good worker, was somber and uncommunicative, left to her own devices too much, and was without direction. Marthe V. blamed the stepmother, calling her a "wicked woman" who detested both Andrée and her sister; she beat them both and too easily influenced the father, who, in the fashion of Cinderella stories, was depicted as spineless. The concierge also called the stepmother "very wicked," adding that she often hit the girls and locked them in their rooms, giving them only potatoes to eat. The concierge and other neighbors confirmed that the girls were "kind and intelligent," and that their conduct was good, but they testified that Victor and Jeannette beat them and on occasion left them alone in the apartment for a few months at a time.

Victor's statement to the prosecutor insisted it was the girls' own fault if they were not treated well. He said that he frequently traveled for his work and was away from home when the problems between the girls and his wife escalated; she punished them by allowing them only soup and bread to eat. He also admitted that she beat them during his absence. When he told his wife to be less severe, he declared, she became angry, so he reprimanded his daughters and asked them to show more respect to their stepmother. He alleged that his daughters had asked him to choose between them and his wife. He admitted that when Fanny talked to him and used "vulgarities," he had given "her a smack in the face, as is my right and my duty. She then opened the window and yelled: 'Help! Murderer! This monster wants to kill us!' This monster was me, their father!" In December, he found their conduct so bad that he wanted to put them in a house of correction. At the judicial hearing necessary before such incarceration, his neighbors and their grandmother spoke well of the girls. When the girls were called before the judge, Victor was astonished that "they had [undergone] a complete transformation," becoming very polite. They admitted that they had done him wrong and asked for pardon. He forgave them, took them home, and asked them to bring their wages home at the end of each month, saying he would then furnish all that they needed. He portrayed himself as a good, disciplining father trying to raise moral daughters and blamed his daughters, Rosine's mother, and his neighbors who attacked Jeannette.

The court found that Victor had beaten his two daughters "in a manner exceeding the rights of paternal correction, and frequently abandoned them, denying them food, lighting and heat. He had thus compromised the [children's] morality and security." Victor was accordingly deprived of paternal authority, and the family council gave Rosine's mother, a 74-year-old widow, temporary guardianship of the children. Victor had to pay her 86 francs a months in child support. His appeal was denied.[24] Biological paternity was insufficient when the man did not act as a father—as neighbors, police inspectors, and the law defined such actions.

Courts did not always award custody or paternal authority to the grandparents, even if they sought it, either because the grandparent was too old or too physically incapacitated.²⁵ The children went to other relatives or to Assistance publique. They would remain in the system, sometimes circulating among relatives, foster families, and the institutions of Assistance publique until their majority. Even when a grandparent did receive custody, fathers could sometimes retain paternal authority. Sixteen-year-old Marthe T. wanted to deprive her father of his paternal authority over her so that she could live with her grandmother, which she had been doing for several years. After an investigation, the court gave guardianship to her grandmother but allowed the father to retain paternal authority until she turned twenty-one, unless he attempted to violate the terms of guardianship.²⁶ Deprivation of paternal authority affected the middle classes as it did the poor, with middle-class families usually having relatives able and willing to take the children.

Fathers who had legally recognized their natural children often fought to retain them and their paternal authority. Paul B. had lived in concubinage with Marie R. from 1890 to 1893. They had two children, Paul Jr., born in 1890, and Jean, born in 1893. Marie died following the birth of Jean, and five years later, B. married Marie's sister, Marguerite. B., a journalist who had been a lawyer but had left the profession, had once had a "certain fortune," but by 1902, his financial situation was precarious. The case began in September 1901, when 11-year-old Paul Jr., who was living in Paris with his father, wrote to his uncle and aunt, who lived in Nancy (in eastern France), complaining that his father beat him with a stick. Furthermore, he went days without eating and was often beaten on the ears and nose until he bled. A month later, he wrote to his grandparents saying that he had worn his shirt for more than a month and had not had new bedsheets or a pillowcase in many months, adding that when he asked for clean shirts, socks, or bed linen, his father said that what he had was good enough and that he didn't need anything else. His letters were full of complaints about his father not giving him good food. He sent and received his letters through the grocer next door, who wrote to the grandparents and uncle, René J., saying that Paul had the marks of a beating on his leg and had a bruised eye; he was rarely clean. Moreover, he found it strange that a child of Paul's age did not go to school. René arrived and absconded with young Paul to Nancy. B. accused his brother of "surreptitiously kidnapping" the boy. B. admitted that "during the few months my son lived with me, I had to correct him several different times because he was rude and disobedient, but I never did the things that my in-laws accuse me of and I protest their malevolent insinuations."

The Commissariat of Police reported that B. was honorable and of regular conduct and should not be forced to forfeit his paternal authority. It is just that Paul, "who has a difficult character" preferred his grandparents to his father and stepmother. Paul's uncle refused to send him back to his father, arguing that the grandparents had raised the boy from the ages of three to ten, and that during the past year, when Paul had lived with his father and stepmother, his father had mistreated him. Medical certificates revealed that Paul had three raised welts on his left leg, seemingly produced by a stick and dating from about ten days prior to the examination, when Paul would have been in Paris. In addition, doctors reported another welt on the right leg. Investigators found no indication of moral or material abandonment and reported that B. "is a good *père de famille*, endowed with an excellent heart." The prosecutor dropped the case, evidently considering those bruises insufficient to deprive B. of his paternal authority; besides Paul was already living with his uncle and grandparents—where he could stay.[27]

Some men who lived in concubinage did not contest their paternity, but rather claimed that they did all they could to be good fathers and fulfill their duties to their biological children. Alain C. accused Alice G., his former *concubine* of immorality and sought to deprive her of her authority over their natural children and assume authority and guardianship himself. She defended herself by invoking tropes of good morality, saying she no longer wanted to live a life of concubinage and Alain did not want to marry her; furthermore, she was proud of having breast-fed the children, as befitted a good mother.[28]

Cases abound attempting to deprive mothers of their *puissance paternelle*. These women were usually widows or unmarried women allegedly living by sex work and accused of leading their daughters into a life of prostitution.[29] Some women committed other moral offenses, such as gambling. Charles L., a 46-year-old draftsman, filed a suit against his wife, Elisabeth L., a chambermaid, to deprive her of any legal authority over their child, Juliette L., born in 1891. Charles L. accused his wife of excessive gambling at the horse races and morally abandoning their daughter. Elizabeth accumulated gambling debts and had to borrow money, going to England and threatening Amelie L., Charles's sister, with a scandal if she refused the loan. Charles declared that his wife had made his life a "veritable hell." By 1901, she had left their marital home. By then Juliette was living in England with her paternal aunt, Amelie L., who the inspectors declared was an honorable schoolteacher, able to take care of the material, intellectual, and moral needs of her niece. Charles L. mentioned his serious bronchitis, which prohibited him from working, and asked the *procureur* to proceed rapidly with his case for the *déchéance maternelle* [*sic*] of his wife, with guardianship going to his sister. Charles died on 18 November 1901 before the case was closed; the outcome is unknown.[30] It is likely that the status quo was preserved, with Juliette continuing to live with her aunt in England.

Sometimes, mothers accused their own daughters of morally abandoning their granddaughters. In the midst of her paternity suit and appeals that went on for four years, at age twenty-one, Simone Roulet had a nervous breakdown and entered a clinic in Toulouse, during which time her mother, Mme de Salviac, took care of her daughter, Josette.[31] Upon leaving the clinic, Roulet was placed as an intern in a convent in Pau, where she took care of little girls, although her mother accused her of neglecting her own. According to Roulet's lawyer, Mme de Salviac's behavior became increasingly bizarre. She exhibited "a ferocious hostility toward her own daughter," seeking to detach Josette from her mother, even giving her own patronymic, Salviac, to the little girl. She wanted young Josette to regard Simone as an older sister whose job kept her far from home. Each time that Simone came to Toulouse to see her daughter, Mme Salviac sent her away on the pretext of her nervousness and the desire to avoid the revelation of Josette's true filiation. Mme de Salviac's lawyer insisted that Simone "persisted in an absolute indifference to her daughter, always abandoning her to the care of her mother." Simone's lawyer argued that Simone had no income of her own, no job, and did what she thought was in the best interests of the child, saying that as distressing as it was for Simone, she went along with her "imperious" mother. Meanwhile, Louis, the putative father, was free from any paternal obligations.

In 1930, after Simone made her final legal appeal and the Cour de cassation ruled against her paternity suit, when she was twenty-three, she received a scholarship to study nursing in Paris. Soon thereafter, Assistance publique of Paris employed her as a nurse in charge of children then labeled as "abnormal," and at the outbreak of the war, she was mobilized, going to the front with an ambulance corps that performed light surgery. In June 1940, she was sent back to Paris and served in a hospital; her personal and professional conduct received high praise, and in 1943, she was with the Red Cross. During all this time, Josette remained in the care of her grandmother. In 1943, Mme de Salviac instigated legal action to win paternal authority so that she could place Josette in a religious home for wayward girls. Mme de

Salviac tried to prove that Simone had abandoned Josette and was too dangerous, neglectful, and immoral to be allowed to raise Josette. Simone fought to retain parental authority, and in 1943, the case was settled out of court. Simone retained legal custody of her daughter, now eighteen, the same age that Simone had been when Josette was born. No father wielded *puissance paternelle* in this case; two women fought over it.

Adoption

It is unlikely, but not impossible, that some of the children taken from their abusive parents were informally adopted by foster parents. As with deprivation and disavowal of paternity, adoption also involved the transfer of *puissance paternelle* and the circulation of children.

Adoption, more than the deprivation and disavowal of paternity, may be considered as a type of gift exchange with different dimensions essential to the maintenance and reproduction of society. Gift giving and receiving involves voluntary sharing. It creates a set of obligations on the part of the giver and receiver and brings the two closer together. In giving and receiving, especially in the circulation of children, the gift is not completely alienated from the donor after it is given. Something of the donor remains in the gift, and sometimes the donor has the right of use; this is especially true of sacred objects.[32] Although many families did not consider children as sacred, to some they were, and children were objects of reciprocity arrangements. When the paternity of one man was annulled and the paternity of the child given to another man, that child might retain a part of the first father, not only in the effects of his child rearing, but also by bearing his name along with that of the second father. In societies with a market economy, the objects of the exchange take on a moral or spiritual value where the receiver is obligated to make a return gift; this need not be a gift in kind, but could be service or gratitude, as a social exchange.[33] Based on Marcel Mauss's theories of the moral nature of markets, of obligations and of human transactions and of a gift economy, the twentieth-century exchange of children among neighbors, kin, and the state may illustrate a new kind of family based on the moral and material value of children and other family members. The market exchange of children, a set of relations based on a gift economy, part of Mauss's "archaic" societies, may have been part of the moral economy of modern France, especially when family formation was the issue. When children were commodities of exchange in a French society that had the lowest fertility rate in Europe and where government officials were preoccupied with depopulation, children were scarce commodities, requiring collective intervention for their preservation. The exchange of children, was not just the giving and receiving of a gift, but also depended on their value in the family's moral and material economy. In some respects, parent-child relationships such as recherche de paternité, disavowal and deprivation of paternity, and especially adoption, were part of this larger system.

During the nineteenth century, adoption was not intended for children; only adults over the age of fifty could adopt other consenting adults. Adoption was usually based on bonds of affection and kinship ties for the purposes of transmitting an inheritance, consolidating family ties and property for those without heirs, soothing a guilty conscience, having someone to care for one in one's old age, or even gaining a title of nobility. That the adoptee reside with the adopter was not always part of the agreement, although adoptees had usually lived with the adopting parents for a minimum of six years prior to adoption, as stipulated by articles of the Civil Code that had remained unchanged from 1804 until 1923. Adoption could be considered as an exchange of goods, in this case, people, and as a moral transaction to maintain human personal relationships among individuals and groups, based on calculations in which the gain outweighed the costs. It involved notions of parenting not based on blood. Like marriage, adoption was a means of establishing alliances, creating families and frequently solidifying kinship groups. Family and kinship networks were more complicated, however, than reciprocal gift giving. They were legal, economic, or moral communities, and sometimes residential ones. Kinship mattered when it involved keeping an inheritance within the family, providing for children, and in a reciprocity arrangement, with the children helping the adopters in their old age.[34]

Throughout the nineteenth century, adoption was a popular theme among novelists. In George Sand's novel *Indiana*, first published in 1832, Monsieur Hubert, a nouveau-riche bourgeois, adopts the orphaned Laure de Nangy, who at the time of the adoption is no longer a child. Her grandfather's château has been nationalized during the Revolution, and Hubert has purchased it, leaving her family impoverished but with a title. She takes care of him in his old age and as a result of the adoption inherits his fortune—and her family's former château. Hubert has no family or other heirs.[35] In Honoré de Balzac's novel, *Ursule Mirouët*, published a decade after *Indiana*, the eponymous heroine is orphaned and raised by an old guardian, Doctor Denis Minoret who dotes on her. As the daughter of the doctor's deceased wife's illegitimate brother and a young German woman he married for love, Ursule remotely belongs to Minoret's kinship group but is not in direct line for an inheritance. Balzac often refers to her as Minoret's *fille adoptive* (adoptive daughter). Although he is her godfather, there is no formal adoption, and there are therefore no legal grounds for her to be his heir. Minoret does not legally adopt Ursule, because Balzac has him die before she turns twenty-one, the minimum legal age for adoption. Upon Minoret's death, Ursule becomes the victim of his nephews' machinations in the battle for his inheritance.[36] Minoret and Ursule constitute a family, in which he acts as a father; although not a legal family, it is what sociologists call a "reconstituted family" (*famille recomposée*), or a family by choice.

Jurisprudence on adoption during the nineteenth century closely followed the Civil Code. In contrast to paternity searches, there was little political or social activity to change the law or get around it. Furthermore, unlike paternity searches, adoption was legal in many instances. According to more than a dozen articles of the Code, single men or women and legally married couples could adopt for purposes of property transmission if there were no other heirs, especially no children. Neither husband nor wife could adopt without the consent of his or her spouse. The person adopting had to have furnished assistance or given uninterrupted care to the adoptee for at least six years during the adoptee's minority, or have saved the life of the adoptee from fire, flood, or the ravages of war. One could not adopt a natural child without both the permission of the parent(s) who had legally recognized that child and the consent of the adopted adult. Nullification of adoption was difficult. If a single man were to adopt and then marry, and he and his wife then had a biological child, the adoption was still not nullified, despite the requirement that the adopting parent have no biological children. In an effort to ensure that the adopter would not have children, he or she had to be at least fifty years old. Many cases came before the courts during the first half of the nineteenth century, with judges ruling in favor of adoption rather than against by a ratio of about 2 to 1. Adoption, in effect, had been a financial operation limited to the transmission of name and property among consenting adults throughout the nineteenth century and into the twentieth. As such, it was a civil act, requiring witnesses and formal legal approval.[37]

The adoption of natural children by biological parents was a legally gray area, even when those children were adults and adoption improved their civil status and their inheritance rights. In the early nineteenth century, the courts had misgivings about parental adoption of natural children and appeared to rule equally for and against, but by the mid nineteenth century, jurisprudence began to accept the adoption of natural adult children by their mothers.[38] In 1834, the tribunal of Toulouse had refused Catherine Girard the right to adopt her natural son, but the appeals court consented to the adoption. In the same year, the Rennes tribunal allowed the adoption of Pauline-Julie by her unwed mother, who had legally recognized her. Adoptions of extranuptial children by their fathers were rare, but in 1835, the court of Paris, which in the past had refused to allow these adoptions, ratified François-André Trenchant's adoption of his natural son, Auguste-Camille Logeais, born in 1802 or 1803, whom he had legally recognized in 1821.[39] In 1842, the Cour de cassation ruled that mothers or fathers could adopt legally recognized illegitimate children, since adoption "transformed the blemished illegitimate filiation" into the more favorable adoptive one.[40]

Between 1840 and 1870, the courts regularized 3,275 acts of adoption in all of France. Many of these adoptions included more than one adoptee, averaging about 106 acts of adoption per year and 3,609 people adopted.[41] Thirty percent of those adopted were legally recognized natural children, and 20 percent of the total were unrecognized. These data do not indicate the age of the adoptee or whether parents were adopting their own natural children. This was probably the case in only a few instances, because more complete data from the 1920s and 1930s indicate that aunts and uncles or total strangers unknown to or unrelated to the birth mother were usually the adopters. For the entire period from 1840 to 1886, 13 percent of adoptions were by aunts and uncles and the remainder by persons whose relationship to the adoptee is unknown. During this period, most adoptions in France were legalized in Paris, although after mid-century, increasing numbers of adoptions occurred in other large cities, such as Lyon and Bordeaux. A roughly equal number of single men and single women constituted the vast majority of those adopting; married couples comprised only between 20 and 25 percent of the total. Of over 8,000 adoptees between 1840 and 1886, roughly half were women. If adopting parents had a gender preference, the data do not reflect it. Between 1872 and 1886 (the last year with available data), there were an average of 109 adoptions per year (roughly the same as in the period from 1840 to 1870), with 138 adoptions of 151 children in 1872, after the Franco-Prussian War and the Paris Commune. This was the highest number for any one year, indicative of a postwar need also seen almost a century earlier, in 1792. During these fifteen years of the Third Republic, however, the proportion of natural children adopted decreased by 10 percent; 25 percent of adoptions were of legally recognized natural children and 15 percent were unrecognized. Only 10 percent of the adoptions were by aunts and uncles, and 5 percent by other family members, leaving half of the adoptions by others. This slight change in adoption patterns indicates a few more adoptions of orphans and abandoned children by non-family members, extending adoption beyond known kinship.

Some adoption occurred outside of official laws and court proceedings. Unofficial adoption included the integration of abandoned children into the families of wet nurses or foster parents. It was not unusual for mothers to have one or more of their children reared outside the home by wet nurses or foster parents, either through abandonment or just by giving them away, purportedly on a temporary basis, with the numbers varying by time and place.[42] In nineteenth-century France, thousands of babies abandoned in the cities were sent to wet nurses and foster parents in the countryside. Abandoned children who survived infancy—and only about a third of them did until the last quarter of the century—stayed with foster parents for the rest of their childhood, up to about the age of twelve, receiving a *pension alimentaire* from Assistance publique. It was a relationship that usually required the children to contribute their labor or wages to the foster family. Although reportedly about half of the foster parents were fond of the children, they did not leave them an inheritance; usually, foster parents were poor and took in the children for their labor and the money from Assistance publique.[43] This major form of the "circulation of children"—fosterage and informal adoption—was marked by a fluidity of relationships; children circulated among their mothers, state institutions, and foster parents. The fosterage system may be seen as an alternative to legal adoption that at the same time preserved the blood ties between biological mother and child so important in nineteenth-century ideology, but kept natural fathers out of the picture. Adoption and fosterage were complementary acts; one did not negate the other. Both provided homes for children, but fosterage did not usually involve a name or inheritance.[44]

As the mortality rate of abandoned children decreased after 1874 with the regulation of wet-nursing and foster parentage, it is possible that foster parents, after they reached the age of fifty, would adopt abandoned children when they turned twenty-one, assuming the foster parents had cared for those adoptees for at least six years, as specified by the Code. All parties, including the adoptee, the adoptee's relatives, if known, and the authorities of

Assistance publique, which possessed *puissance paternelle*, had to consent to the adoption and transference of that authority to the adopting parents. In unusual circumstances, a person or couple could request to adopt a particular abandoned child. In 1861, the director of Assistance publique in Paris wrote to one of his administrators in an area where thousands of abandoned babies had been sent to wet nurses, asking for detailed information on the "constitution, health, physique, degree of intelligence and character" of a particular girl born in 1859, abandoned in 1860, and sent to Saint-Calais (Sarthe), as well as the color of her eyes and hair, stating that there was someone in Paris who wished to adopt a child, but no reason is given for that particular child being wanted. It is possible that this was the natural child of one of those seeking to adopt. A decade later, in 1872, the assistant head of the Paris Bureau des Enfants assistés, wrote to the administrator in Saint-Calais asking, "Do you have in your area two orphans, one aged 2 or 3 years and the second of 15–16 months, blond, who can be presented for adoption to people "in affluent circumstances and without children?"[45] It is likely that the couple would then care for these children, and when both the children and the parents were old enough, according to the law, they would legally adopt them.

The many thousands of abandoned illegitimate babies whose tiny bodies filled the foundling homes before they were sent out of the city to wet nurses during the nineteenth century, usually to die, did not engender an outpouring of sentiment for formal child adoption. Moralists shunned adoption of these babies because they wanted to avoid rewarding the sexual activity and alleged immorality of poor women who bore children outside of marriage. Infertile married couples with sufficient resources to adopt were reluctant to adopt abandoned and illegitimate children, because the so-called stained birth of those children threatened their all-important lineage and blood ties; they also thought that such children would inherit the vices and immorality, if not also the biological diseases, of their mothers. Furthermore, politicians feared that allowing the adoption of children might be a way for men to bring their illegitimate children covertly or illegally into the family fold, thereby dispersing the inheritance due the legitimate heirs. There was little initiative to save these babies through adoption until science and culture freed them of the taint of disease and immorality. Around the turn of the twentieth century, save-the-children movements flourished, and with the intensified interest in protecting children, educating them as good republican citizens, rearing them in worthy families, and providing parental support, a new interest in permitting child adoption surfaced.

Forms of child adoption involving family members and kin, outsiders, and occupational endogamy had existed for centuries. Kin solidarity manifested itself in the institution of legal guardianship, in which households would raise their orphaned relatives and look after their property until their majority. Artisans informally adopted the orphaned children of fellow artisans, and members of craft corporations contributed funds to the orphaned children of their deceased members.[46] This type of adoption did not confer a name or inheritance or involve full paternal filiation. Families and guardians protected their own and their children's property, and also provided those children with material, and perhaps emotional, support. Orphans without the benefits of kin and community were housed by religious charities, which sometimes gave them to families who took them as much for their labor as out of love.[47]

Legislative debates on adoption at the beginning of the twentieth century echoed those of a century earlier, with discussions about whether adoption was in the cultural roots of French society and in harmony with public sentiment. Proponents argued that adoptions were becoming more frequent in society, and people were not deterred in their desire to adopt by the restrictive articles in the Civil Code. Custom and jurisprudence permitting the adoption of consenting adults and the informal adoption of kin and community children had paved the way, as did a cultural shift in attitudes away from the cherished bloodline of family constructions to families created by choice. Adults could always choose other adults to adopt, but now the shift led to the adoption of abandoned children. That transformation of attitudes was in part based on a change from neo-Lamarckian concepts of the transmission of acquired characteristics, such as an unwed mother's alleged immorality, toward more of an emphasis on medicine and on the role of nurture and education in creating republican citizens for the nation. The adoption of abandoned children therefore became acceptable, especially when it meant saving children's lives to prevent national depopulation, an obsession among policy makers. Arguments against adoption in the formulation of the Civil Code at the end of the eighteenth century were based on the notion that adoption would destroy the family. More than a full century later, few claimed that adoption would destroy the conjugal family, rather, most viewed adoption as creating foundational families, much as the few proponents of adoption had done at the end of the eighteenth century. During the 1914–18 war, some legislators tried to extend the 1804 laws on adoption to include children whose fathers had "died for France" and other orphans, much as legislators had done in 1792; this time they had success over the longer term.

The social devastation and loss of life of World War I and the subsequent influenza pandemic left a large number of legitimate orphans and childless families without heirs. To many, adoption was still more palatable when legitimate orphans lacked parents. Those who retained their suspicion of adopting natural children lost their hearts to orphans whose fathers had died in wartime. Legislators called the orphans of the war *pupilles de la Nation*, echoing analogous phrases during the wars of the Revolution. As wards of the state, these children were entitled to pensions until they reached the age of eighteen. In effect, the state, acting again in a paternal capacity, adopted these children to provide them with the "material and moral" protection of a father, but was happy to divest itself of that paternal authority, and expense, by allowing families to adopt them. Adoption also provided "replacement children" for couples who had lost sons during the war and allowed bereaved parents to create new families. In the twentieth century, formal family adoption became an accepted charitable institution for minor children whose biological parents were dead or could not provide. It was also a way to support the family as the bedrock of the French nation, albeit a different family form.

On 19 June 1923, the French legislature enacted a law permitting child adoption, almost without discussion. Article 343 simply stated: "Adoption can take place if there are legitimate motives [*justes motifs*] and if it presents advantages for the adoptee."[48] The motivation to broaden the grounds for adoption arose from a concern for children's welfare and from an emotional need on the part of men and women without children to rear them, even if they had not biologically created them. The significance of biology and emotion in constructing paternity and the family was becoming more ambiguous, with biological ties remaining important, unless renounced, but emotional ties and bonds of affection becoming indicative of good parenting, at least as grounds for adoption. The 1923 law, modified in 1930, allowed the person adopting to exercise paternal authority over a minor child, thus redefining an acceptable family as one by choice and not just by blood. To reduce the probability of the adopting parents having biological children, the minimum age of the adopting parent had to be forty. Adopters could have no biological children alive who might inherit, and the parent had to be at least fifteen years older than the adoptee. Furthermore, an adopting parent or parents had to have demonstrated an attachment to the adoptee by having taken care of the child they adopted for a sufficient amount of time to demonstrate that they had raised the adoptee as their own, and that the adoptee would materially and morally benefit from the adoption. Single men and women as well as conjugal couples could adopt, but the number of adoptions in France remained low, between 1,000 and 1,700 each year from 1924 to 1942.[49] In Paris, records exist only for between 135 and 155 adoptions per year coming before the civil tribunals of that city from 1928 through 1936, with no significant changes during that period, even during the years of the depression. About one-third of all adoptees had been with the adopting parents for ten years or more. Adoptions included child adoptions where the adopting parents had had the baby since infancy and adopted the child after two or three years, or even after many more, as well as adoptions of adults, one of whom had been with the adopting person as long as fifty-four years.[50] The terms of the 1804 Civil Code still obtained, and many adoptions were of consenting adults.

With the interwar emphasis on the virtues of motherhood and on men acting as good fathers, adoption afforded childless men and women, within and outside of marriage, an opportunity to become parents. Conservatives may have considered that allowing single women to adopt children would be a means to control the sexuality and independence of the new women of the 1920s, making these women resemble the ideal mother in the home (*mère au foyer*). Some feminists approved of single women adopting, within the context of advancing women's independence. Many women could not find husbands, because of the great number of young men who had died in the war, and many men had lost their "virility" because of the effects of war, including the permanent effects of poison gas. Women were therefore deprived of the "joys of maternity" and men of the "joys of paternity." Adoption offered a solution to childlessness, as well as contributing to a "sentiment of social solidarity."[51] Advocates of adoption encouraged the adoption of very young children who looked like the adoptive parents and might thus be better integrated into the adopting family. Men's concerns about their property may have inhibited adoption in the nineteenth century, but with the increase of feminism and women's agency in the twentieth century, women's voices played a role in the legalization and encouragement of child adoption. Furthermore, single motherhood gave women certain rights, at least that of *puissance paternelle*. Adopting fathers also played an important role, both materially and emotionally in providing for the children and "acting as a father." In the postwar culture, a family based on emotions coexisted with a family based on blood, and the law now sanctioned the concept of mutual obligations and reciprocity among individuals within a community that included the circulation of children.[52]

Adoptions in France did not primarily function to rescue orphans of unknown parentage, even after the 1923 law, so facilitating the adoption of abandoned children and overcoming the reluctance to adopt them remained a worry. Some writers appealed to couples and single women to adopt. Their main concerns were the interests and well-being of the children and enabling more women to be mothers. It was up to the collectivity to aid these children through adoption, but adoption should not be made too easy, because it might then compromise the children's future. The socialist feminist argument, however, disagreed with private adoption of these abandoned children and called for the "state to raise these wards and give them a happy and healthy life by establishing institutions that would assure their solid education and a trade according to the aptitudes that would guarantee them work for life."[53] Both groups had their goals partially addressed but perhaps not satisfied. Assistance publique provided minimum education for most of the abandoned children; a few joined new families through adoption.

Adoption agencies soon proliferated to help single mothers give up their children for adoption and to facilitate the adoption of those children by others. The adoption agencies primarily focused on the adoption of abandoned babies of unknown parents by married couples. Mothers could abandon their babies at foundling homes, often anonymously, and after 1923, they could officially leave their babies with Assistance publique for eventual adoption. Assistance publique obtained paternal authority over the abandoned children, which it could then confer on a private, but state-supported, adoption agency. Mothers also had the option of going directly to a representative of an adoption agency. If and when the child was adopted, paternal authority was transferred to the adopting parents.

The main adoption agency in Paris, the section on adoption of the Society for the Mutual Aid of French Women (L'Entr'aide des femmes françaises), looked for orphans and abandoned children under the age of six who could be incorporated into new families. Based on the idea that adopting families might want their communities to believe that the child was their own biological offspring, the adoption agencies advertised that they maintained secrecy for the families and had only the children's best interests in mind. They did not provide a subsidy to the parents, because adoption should be "only out of love and in a spirit of absolute material disinterest." The

League for the Protection of Abandoned Mothers and Childhood in Distress (Ligue pour la protection des mères abandonnées et l'enfance en détresse) also facilitated many adoptions.[54]

A family or individual seeking to adopt needed to make a formal request to one of these agencies, supplying as much detail as possible about their age and qualifications, including two written references from professional people, such as members of the clergy, teachers, mayors, or police commissioners, attesting to the honorability and "worthiness" of the potential adopter. Adoption agencies and Assistance publique insisted that the adopter be French and required evidence of the moral and material advantages the adopter could provide for the child.[55] For example, in 1930, Robert D. and his wife, both over forty years old, wanted to adopt a girl born in the free public maternity hospital and abandoned at birth whom they had received from the adoption department of L'Entr'aide des femmes françaises almost immediately after birth and had raised for three years. After investigation, this agency received reliable information that the couple was raising the child with the "utmost affection" and contributed to her "well-being materially and morally." The couple adopted her.[56]

Adoption agencies and Assistance publique facilitated adoption by single men and women as well as by married couples. For example, L'Entr'aide des femmes françaises in 1934 helped a single woman, a florist living in Paris, adopt a natural child whose mother had abandoned her and whom the florist, now over forty years old, had reared for eight years.[57] In 1933, Justin M., a 51-year-old never-married accountant, adopted 2-year-old Gilbert S., whom he had taken in at the time of Gilbert's birth. Young Gilbert's parents were unknown. It is also unknown why Assistance publique, through the League for the Protection of Abandoned Mothers, gave Gilbert to a single man at the time of the baby's birth and abandonment, or how Justin M. took care of him. Justin M. officially adopted Gilbert after having him only two years, an unusually short time to have formed "profound ties of affection." The adoption agency noted that Justin M. enjoyed "considerable public esteem, and his conduct has always been irreproachable"; apparently, he could also be a good father.[58] It is not known whether these single men and women were living in consensual unions. They are described as single and neither divorced nor widowed.

Few of the adoption cases in Paris between 1928 and 1936 for which records remain were of abandoned children who had been deposited with an institution of Assistance publique or with a private adoption agency. Only after 1933 did those children comprise as many as one-third of all adoptions in Paris. Assistance publique officials were willing to give infants to adopting, and perhaps adoring, parents but acted with great caution, especially soon after the promulgation of the law. In the mid 1920s, approximately 35,000 children were abandoned annually to Assistance publique throughout France, but only about 100 were adopted in 1926. Assistance publique had asked for 5,000 francs from the adopting parents, ostensibly to repay its costs and as a sign that the parents could afford to raise a child. Not finding much response, however, in 1926, it eliminated all payment for adopting an abandoned child. Henceforth anyone could adopt if they could show that they were "honest" and good parents.[59]

The adopting parents had to demonstrate how adoption would benefit the adoptee, and they had to have a good salary or some property; moreover, they had to have "already contributed to rearing the child as their own." The phrase that adoption would "confirm the ties of affection that had already existed between" the parent and child appeared like a mantra in all adoption cases. With adoption in the 1920s and 1930s, parental affection, including from a father, took precedence over biology. All of the adopted children who had been left with Assistance publique or with adoption agencies took the last name of the adopting parents, and the adoption was noted on the adoptee's birth certificate. The birth mother was stripped of her *puissance paternelle*.

The clearest, albeit formulaic, statements about the bonds of affection that Assistance publique and the adoption agencies required are apparent from the following situations. Marthe, a wealthy 45-year-old widow, had married Marius D. in 1919; he died in 1929. Neither she nor her husband had any legitimate, legitimated, or adopted children. When Jacqueline was born on 28 December 1921, her mother immediately abandoned her to Assistance publique who placed her with Marthe and Marius D. The couple D. raised Jacqueline from the age of one month. According to the records, Mme D. had "a great affection [for Jacqueline] and the greatest desire to be attached to her by a legal tie. For more than six years during the minority of the child, Mme D. gave the most assiduous and uninterrupted care to her and provided for her education, her needs, and her rearing as if she were her own daughter." The adoption became final in 1933.[60]

In a similar situation, Marc R., an aviation mechanic, and his wife adopted a boy born in the free maternity hospital in 1927 and legally recognized by his mother. Eleven months after his birth, the mother abandoned her baby to Assistance publique. L'Entr'aide des femmes françaises received the boy and immediately gave him to the couple R., who "raised the child materially and morally, with great ties of affection." The birth mother relinquished her authority over the child, and the adoption became legal. This boy, who was nine at the time of adoption, had been raised by the adopting parents from the age of one.[61]

Some adoptions of abandoned children followed a more circuitous route. Jeanne F., born in November 1924 and abandoned by her mother to Assistance publique, was sent to a wet nurse outside of Paris less than two weeks later, as was customary for abandoned children. The wet nurse's neighbors took an extraordinary interest in young Jeanne. The couple D., who owned a house nearby, provided gifts, clothes, and financial aid to the wet nurse to help her feed the infant. The couple essentially cared for Jeanne, treating her as their own, and after five years, they adopted her.[62]

Assistance publique presented prospective adopting parents with a choice of "a little girl or boy of your secret wishes." Adopting parents could choose a child physically resembling them in terms of hair and eye color. "We have wards—very beautiful, very gifted, and very qualified to fulfill the pride of their adoptive parents," the director of Assistance publique declared. Adopting parents preferred a baby whose father and mother were both unknown. In part, this was to avoid problems of inheritance. If the child had living relatives who were known, the property that child would inherit from adoptive parents might go to the child's relatives.[63]

Adopting a baby of unknown parentage would also allow the adopting parents to rear the child as their own, without fear that the birth mother would try to claim the child and that the courts would honor blood ties. It is not clear, however, how judges would have decided if the birth mother had wanted her child. According to the Code, a child always had the right to claim ties with the mother, but those cases were extremely rare, and with adoption, if the mother were known, she had to sign away her *puissance paternelle.*

Adoption in the interwar period realized some of the goals of revolutionary legislators such as Michel Azema and Jean-Jacques Cambacérès, who argued during the Convention in 1793 that adoption would create greater equality between the classes. In the desire to have children and heirs, people of property accepted children of unknown parentage into their families. In 1926, the marquis de P.-C., a property owner, and his wife, married for twenty-two years and childless, adopted seven-year-old Marguerite, born in 1919, not legally recognized by either her mother or father, and abandoned immediately to Assistance publique. The marquis and his wife had had young Marguerite since she was only a few months old, having taken her from the hospital before the adoption law passed.[64]

In 1931, a 61-year-old general, an officer of the Legion of Honor, and his 54-year-old wife adopted their maid's daughter. The couple had been married for twenty-six years and had no children. As the formula went, since the natural mother was in domestic service "and had no personal fortune, this adoption would present considerable advantages to the adoptee."[65] There is no reason to think that this was an adoption arising from guilt, and that this officer was the natural father, although he may have been. The biological father's identity, as in all of these adoptions, is shrouded in secrecy. When the parents of the abandoned child were unknown, there was no certainty that they were poor, but evidence indicates that women who went to a free maternity hospital and later abandoned their babies, as did the mothers of most of these adopted children, were among the poor and pregnant of Paris.

In addition to the adoption of abandoned children, many other adoption patterns existed in which neighbors, grandparents, aunts, uncles, and siblings had vital roles in child rearing and constructing a family. The passing around of children in the children's and the biological and adoptive parents' interests suggests trusting ties of kinship. Child-custody situations leading to adoption also provided reciprocity arrangements and a moral exchange of goods. Roughly two-thirds of the adoptions between 1925 and 1936 resulted from kinship or marriage ties, equally divided between close kinship (usually siblings) and marriage relationships. The word "child" to signify the adoptee was still inappropriate, because the adoptees ranged in age from three to fifty-six at the time of adoption. The average age of close kinship adoptees was twenty-one, and that of adoptees by marriage (when a husband or wife adopted the children of the other by a previous marriage) was twenty-seven. Adopted adults still had to approve of the adoption. Showing little change from the pre-1923 adoption patterns, people adopted adults as a means of designating an heir and building in guarantees of reciprocity and care-giving at both ends of life, where the adopting parent would first support the child and the adoptee would later support the parent in his or her dotage. Adult adoptees customarily added the name of the adopting parent to their own, resulting in a hyphenated name.

Kinship adoptions indicated the desirability of finding a good home for the adoptee as well as of finding an heir and providing an inheritance. Relatives who had no biological children often adopted legitimate as well as natural children from within the family when the birth parents had died or could not provide sufficiently for the child.[66] Although an adult at the time of adoption, the adoptee was usually a young child when the relative first assumed custodial care. In the 1920s, the adoption of nieces or nephews after the father had died in the war and the mother had also died was a common arrangement. In several instances, the father went to war leaving his child, or children, with his sibling because the mother had died or was unable to raise them, and the custodial sibling later adopted the children. When Marie B.'s brother was killed in 1916, she and her husband took care of his son "as their own," and they eventually adopted him as a 43-year-old in 1934.[67]

Usually, upon the death of a parent, or both parents, the family council awarded the orphaned child to an aunt or uncle, who regularized the situation by adopting after that child had lived with her or him for many years. In November 1925, Léon P., a single, 48-year-old clerk of the civil court, adopted his nephew Roger P., aged twenty-one. Roger was the son of Louise P., who had died on 20 September 1925. There is no mention of young Roger's father, and since he bore his mother's name, he was probably a natural child, and his mother had not won a paternity suit. Searching for the father and the strain of filing a paternity suit may not have seemed necessary when her brother was willing to be a father to her son. The reports from neighbors and friends attested that Léon had always treated his nephew in a fatherly manner, and that there were "ties of the most profound affection uniting them."[68]

A father or mother would sometimes give up their youngest child to a financially better off relative, who might eventually adopt the child. This might be either the ultimate parental emotional sacrifice or a self-interested exchange in which the parent relinquishing the child received money or labor in return. In 1928, for example, a wealthy delicatessen merchant and his wife adopted her ten-year-old nephew. At the death of the child's father three years earlier, the child's mother had given the boy to her sister and brother-in-law who had "raised him as their own."[69]

If a mother died shortly after giving birth, a father might keep the older children, whom he could care for and who could work, while the youngest would go to a childless aunt or uncle for adoption. Rebecca L. was born in March 1928, the youngest of six children. Her mother died in childbirth, however, and Rebecca's childless, relatively affluent aunt and uncle, both aged forty-four, immediately took charge of Rebecca, whom they raised in Paris and in their country home, just outside the city. Rebecca's father consented to the adoption in 1931, three years after Rebecca's birth. Given that this family was Jewish, with the adopting uncle having been born in Russia in 1887, it is disheartening to think of what may have happened to Rebecca and her family before she reached adulthood.[70]

Single men adopted nieces and nephews under a variety of circumstances. In 1931, Charles L., an inspector of mines and a commander in the Legion of Honor, adopted his 11-year-old niece, Alice, the daughter of his brother Louis, who had died in 1929. Alice was the youngest of four children. As the obligatory phrase went, Charles L. had "treated her as his own" and had helped rear her since her birth. Moreover, Louis had left his family a very meager inheritance, and Charles could better provide for her. With the agreement of Louis's widow, Charles had already been taking responsibility for Alice's education.[71]

A man did not have to be a rich landowner or a commander in the Legion of Honor to adopt a niece or nephew. In 1934, a taxi driver who had been a widower since 1931, adopted his niece, the natural child of his deceased wife's sister, whom he and his wife had raised since 1929, when the girl was ten and her own mother had died. L'Entr'aide des femmes françaises stated that the taxi driver had the most "benevolent affection" toward his niece, whom he had raised materially and morally.[72] One man adopted his wife's niece after both his wife and their only son had died. At the time of the adoption, his niece had been living with him for ten years; he was seventy-seven and she was thirty-nine. They had been attentively caring for each other, although not biologically related.[73]

Women, whether single or married, frequently adopted the natural child of a sister whom they had cared for since early childhood. In 1928, Alphonsine P., who was divorced and without children of her own, adopted Renée P., the natural daughter of her sister, who had died twenty-one years earlier when Renée was four years old. Since then, Alphonsine had taken care of Renée's needs.[74] In effect, Alphonsine had acted as an adoptive parent long before the law passed. Other women adopted children of their sisters after raising them for from ten to as long as twenty-five years prior to adoption.[75] In 1931, a 71-year-old, never-married woman, a wealthy property owner living in Paris, adopted her deceased sister's son, now a 56-year-old lawyer, whom she had raised since the age of two when he left the wet nurse.[76]

Some adopting parents, including single men or women, had no known kinship with the adoptee but were thought to be the ones best able to rear and educate the children and leave them an inheritance. If they had raised the adoptee as their own since early childhood, they might have hoped for solace from them in their declining years, or just have wanted to formalize their relationship based on love. In November 1928, a childless couple in their late fifties adopted their 14-year-old goddaughter, Georgette, the natural child of Augustine F. Since Augustine had no family and had always been in delicate health, the godparents had taken care of Georgette since she was born. When Augustine died in March 1928, the godparents immediately filed for adoption.[77]

Single men sometimes adopted apparently unrelated adults whom they had raised. In 1928, Eugène C., an unmarried masseur, adopted Raymond, a natural child legally recognized by both his mother and father at his birth in 1913. Raymond's father had been killed in the war when the little boy was four, and when his mother died a year after that, a maternal aunt and uncle took him in for a year. Then, in 1919, the family council named Raymond's paternal aunt as legal guardian, but allowed Raymond to live with Eugène C., who eventually adopted him, because he had "always acted toward the child as a true father, affectionately giving Raymond all the care necessary."[78] Georges D., at the age of seventy, adopted Mlle M., a seamstress, who was fifty. Both her parents had died, and for the preceding forty-five years, he had provided her with uninterrupted care and affection, "always considering her as his daughter."[79]

Single women also sometimes adopted unrelated adults. Eugénie B., a widowed property owner, adopted a married Army captain in 1930, when she was seventy-four and he was forty-five. She had cared for the adoptee since he was five years old, "surrounding him with tenderness and affection and taking care of all his needs and his education." She had given him more than his parents could, since they were not only in a "modest situation" but divorced, and his mother was ill. Eugenie's only child had died in infancy when she was twenty-six; her husband had died just before she began adoption proceedings. It was said of single women who adopted that "all the public knows that she lives a good life and is of good morality and has the general respect of all."[80]

Stepchild adoption occurred with the same frequency as other kin adoptions. The stories follow similar patterns: a childless widow or widower adopted his or her stepchild after both the adoptee's birth parents had died, or if only one had died but the other had relinquished parental authority. Stepparents could not adopt if they had biological children of their own. This form of adoption was not usually to rear children, since the adoptees were on average in their late twenties, but more out of kindness and for transmission of inheritance. These adoptions demonstrate the closeness of families, spousal attachments, and people's attempts to choose an heir with built-in guarantees of support at both ends. A married man might adopt his wife's children by her first marriage, accepting them into his family because he had no biological children himself and because no adultery was involved—the children were legitimate but lacked a father because of divorce or death.

In March 1925, Henri B., a 49-year-old bank director, adopted his two teenaged stepchildren, a boy and a girl. His wife's first husband had died in the war, and Henri B. had taken care of the children as his own for the six years since his marriage in 1919.[81] There were also cases of stepparent adoptions when the biological parent was not dead but had been divorced. In October 1925, Dr. Jacques L., aged forty-six, adopted his wife's daughter, then aged nineteen. His wife, Jeanne, and her first husband had divorced in 1911, and she had retained custody. Since Dr. L.'s marriage to Jeanne in 1912 when her daughter was three, he had taken care of the girl "as if she were his own." Furthermore, Dr. L.'s mother had acted as an affectionate grandmother to the child. The child's father relinquished his right of *puissance paternelle* and approved the adoption. The girl, it was said, had a "filial regard" for Dr. L. and his mother.[82] A husband, such as Dr. L., could have no legal authority over his wife's children by a former marriage unless he adopted them and the biological father had either died or disowned them, regardless of whether the mother were alive or had died. Jeanne had not died.

Sometimes, after her husband had died, a woman would adopt a child of his first marriage, even though that child was not related to her by blood. In 1932, a 51-year-old widow adopted her husband's child, whom she and her husband had reared and educated since their marriage in 1915, at which time his daughter was twelve; at the time of adoption, the adoptee was twenty-nine, suggesting that its purpose could still have been the transmission of name and property and care in old age.[83]

The relationship of the adopting parent to the stepchild could be quite remote. In June 1928, a 51-year-old widow, Mme J., adopted her late husband's sister's illegitimate daughter, who was then twenty-two. When that sister-in-law had died in 1914, leaving her 7-year-old daughter, Mme J. and her husband had taken in the girl and "raised her as their own."[84] A man's legal wife might also adopt his illegitimate child. Although nineteenth-century moralists had decried this practice, since it would bring a "stranger" into the family bloodline, by 1928, it was not so shocking. In December 1928, Elise M., the widow of Jean, whom she had married in 1918, adopted his 21-year-old illegitimate daughter, Jeanne Marie, who had been born in Hanoi in 1907, nine years before his marriage to Elise. After Jean's death in 1925, Elise "continued to care for his illegitimate daughter as if she were her own."[85] Relationships by adoption could become very complex when grandparents and step-grandparents adopted, as in a case in which a step-grandfather adopted his wife's two grandsons, aged twenty-four and twenty-two, whom they had raised since birth, and assured their future by bringing them into his insurance agency as partners.[86]

Kinship adoption demonstrated the strength of family ties and the desire for an heir. Since the adopting parents had no other children, the adoptees could inherit and also serve as reciprocal caregivers. Affection and love were not out of the picture. Adoption played a social as well as a familial role; it functioned to integrate orphans and abandoned children both into a new family and into society. The key in adoption was the determination that the adoption was in the best interests of the child, that ties of affection existed between child and adopting parent, and that there had been evidence that the adopters had provided the adoptee with relatively long-term care, and had raised him or her as their own. The adoptee may have been expected to repay this care in the old age of the adopting parent. Formal legal adoption did not signal the beginning of a family but usually occurred many years after the family had been formed de facto.

Changes in adoption laws were slow and incrementally small. In 1958, a law lowered the minimum age of the adopting parent from forty to thirty-five, and in 1966, the minimum age was lowered to thirty if the adoption was jointly by a couple who had been married at least five years. Authorities were still worried about protecting the conjugal family and still prohibited adoption when the conjugal family contained biologically legitimate children. New legislation on adoption in 1966 in effect provided terminology for the two types of adoption that had existed since 1923: adoption of a parentless child (*adoption plénière*) and adoption of an adult (*adoption simple*). The law, however, made clear distinctions between the two. With *adoption plénière*, the patronymic of the adopting parents replaced the birth name of the child, and the adopted child was integrated into the adoptive family, thereby rupturing ties with the birth family, which in many cases was unknown anyway. This was most common with the adoption of young children. With *adoption simple,* usually of older adoptees, the adopted person retained the name and attachment to the blood parents, adding the adoptive name to his or her own.[87] If the adoptee was over fifteen, she or he had to consent to the adoption, and the adopting parent's name was added to that of the adoptee; if the adopted child was younger than fifteen, then the birth parents, if known, still had to consent to adoption, unless the police and courts took those children from their parents in a case of deprivation of paternal authority. Birth parents' consent to adoption equaled a declaration of child abandonment. However, birth parents could retract their consent within three months, unless by changing their minds they would compromise the health or morals of the child. Finally, a July 1996 change in the law lowered the age of the adopting parent by two years, to twenty-eight at the time of adoption; if married, the adopter had to have the consent of his or her spouse. That law also opened conjugal adoption to couples without requirements of age, but if one of the married partners was not yet twenty-eight, the marriage had to have been in effect for at least two years. This is based on the rather faulty assumption that if a couple were legally married for two years without children, the relationship was stable and also sterile.

Adoption facilitated mutual obligations and gratifications based on the emotional and material aspects of paternity and the family and on the strength of affective ties often greater than blood or biological ties. De facto adoption existed long before legal adoption and demonstrates how common it was for children to be reared by persons other than their biological mother and father. Families had flexible survival strategies. The main reasons for adoption were to find parents for and save orphans and abandoned children, to provide children for sterile couples who wanted them, to assure the transmission of an inheritance, business, or property to chosen heirs, and to fulfill an emotional need for mutual love and affection between adoptee and adopting parent.

There were, however, subsidiary aspects of adoption that encompassed the myriad types of adoptions in France. Adoption was possible even if the children were not true orphans with both parents dead or unknown. Some were unwanted children of an unwed mother. In other instances, the nuclear family had too many children for its household resources and the parents gave one child away. Or the adopted children had been taken away from abusive parents. Families disrupted by death, illness, or divorce might allow their children to be adopted by others in newly reconstituted families. This was often accomplished upon the remarriage of the parents, with the new spouse adopting the children of a partner's prior marriage, or by outsiders, either kin or friends, adopting them. Sometimes, however, that remarriage led to abuse of the children of the first marriage, making adoption by yet another family member an option.

"Cinderella" situations, where the new stepparent had mistreated the children, appear in cases for deprivation of paternal authority. The relative or foster parent taking in a morally abandoned child might eventually adopt that child. Transferring children within a family or kinship group occurred when the adopting parent bore a responsibility or debt toward another member of the family or to an outsider, or simply had a desire for children and sympathy or love for a child, or had no heirs. Adoption reinforced the family and provided a stable home when the birth home was no longer viable, such as when uncles and aunts adopted and educated a niece or nephew, with the promise of an inheritance, and the adoptee, who might also have a better position in life than would have been the case with his or her birth family, cared for the aging adopting parent(s) in return. Adoption enabled a range of domestic configurations, created resilient and adaptable households and reconstituted families.[88] There was one exception, however. Although conjugal couples and single individuals could legally adopt, couples in concubinage could not.

~~~

Paternity and power were the motivating forces behind the dismantling and reconstitution of families, but family constructions also involved women and maternity. When a married man took action to deny paternity of a child resulting from his wife's adultery, he strengthened his power and control within his family and community, reasserting his masculinity after being publicly cuckolded. Disavowal of paternity usually accompanied or followed divorce, and in rejecting this paternal authority, the man was also abdicating responsibility for his wife's actions. A man may have thought *puissance paternelle* was his natural right, but it was also part of civil law and at the heart of the construction of the conjugal family.[89] By disavowing a child, the man limited his paternal authority, but he did this of his own free will. In contrast, if the court deprived a man of this authority, it was quite another matter. By taking children away from an abusive father, the state appropriated his *puissance paternelle*, thus diminishing his masculine honor as head of the family.

Adoption helped reconstitute families. It involved both men and women adopting and forming legal and emotional families, with mothers often relinquishing their children. By involving mutual obligations between the adopter and adoptee, adoption relationships also involved power exchanges. Families by adoption included fathers (except in cases in which single women adopted) and required that the men act with affection toward the children, *en qualité de père*. Men who adopted could be single, married, or widowed, but they had to provide both materially and emotionally. These men were fathers by choice, unlike men whose paternity was judicially declared and who had no emotional sense of responsibility toward their children.

The creation of new families through adoption did not negate the notion that legal conjugal families with legitimate children were still sacrosanct. Despite a formulaic line in the adoption records declaring that an adoption created a "veritable family that demonstrates all kinds of affection," others regarded adoptive families as more "fictive" than "veritable."[90] Jean Carbonnier, a leading legal scholar, declared as late as 1999, "Filiation by adoption is a purely juridical filiation, resting on the presumption of an affective but not biological reality.... It is a filiation of imitation."[91] Biological bonds and affective ties continued in uneasy coexistence in reconstituting families.

Adoption was to encourage families and protect children. At the same time, protection of the legitimate family from the intrusion of unrelated children, with the resultant biological discontinuity, remained important. The conjugal family remained the ideal, while adoption was tainted with the specter of illegitimacy, and the adoption of unwanted children was perceived as a threat to the "veritable" family formed by marriage. Although the state sought to protect children, acting through adoption agencies, the Assistance publique, police, and judges, and helped create new families through deprivation of paternal authority and adoption, it also sought to protect the conjugal family. The protection of the legally married family rested on a woman's sexual fidelity and the purity of bloodlines. Yet adoption allowed a child not of the father's bloodline into a family. Adoption was recognized because the sexuality or adultery of a man's wife was not in question, and society had become more accepting of the extramarital sexuality of single women. While still critical of female sexuality outside of marriage, organizations sought to provide good homes for those natural children; adoption was the solution.

Denial of paternity rested on the importance of biological paternity within a conjugal family, preserving the patriarchal family and men's rights. On the other hand, laws and practice involving paternity searches, deprivation of paternity, and adoption eroded the supremacy of that biological family in French society. During the first half of the twentieth century, with greater acceptance of previously marginal family forms, the *pater potestas* and paterfamilias family model weakened. Recognition of concubinage as an alternative family form had begun at the end of the nineteenth century and achieved greater acceptance at the end of the twentieth. In the later half of the twentieth century, as the next chapter shows, biology and emotion as constitutive elements of paternity and the family continued to coexist in tension, and concepts of concubinage as a family further expanded.

CHAPTER SIX

Paternity and the Family, 1940 to the Present

Women who filed paternity suits represented themselves as good mothers, even outside of legal marriage, regardless of the nature of the sexual relationships that had led to their pregnancy. Most men fashioned themselves as good fathers, but primarily within a conjugal family where they were material providers and where they helped rear and educate their children. Others saw themselves as fathers outside of marriage, either as adoptive parents or in concubinage. Men and women played these roles daily, exercising a good deal of agency in their private lives and in the public theater of the courtrooms. In those same public theaters, magistrates and lawyers played many roles, sometimes serving as casting directors, deciding who was allowed to appear on the stage, who received the parts of good parents, who led appropriate intimate lives and warranted a stage appearance, whom they would cast as an immoral person, and whom they would not allow on stage at all because of failure to audition properly. Magistrates and lawyers would then work along with the state authorities, who functioned as producers, directing the behavior of men and women who played their parts as lovers, mothers, and fathers. They would decide on the script that described good parenting and appropriate intimate life, one that supported the moral and social public order. In arrogating to themselves the authority of writers and directors, they limited the authority of the actors, who had once had greater individual freedom. Magistrates, also working as assistant playwrights, could modify the script the legislators, as authors, handed to them, taking into account the needs, behaviors, wishes, and self-fashioning of the actors in family dramas. Magistrates also represented the state and public policy and tried to influence individual and family intimate behavior.

The heterosexual reproductive conjugal family was initially directly in the limelight on center stage, since it had served as the core of French society, but during the twentieth century, it moved off to side stage on the right, making way for other, previously marginal but now socially acceptable family forms that emerged from the wings in the interwar period and took positions front and left. Families on the public stage could be conjugal, blended, fictive, monoparental, or consist of heterosexual domestic partnerships, as long as parents provided for their children, did not neglect or abuse them, and did not engage in scandalous or publicly immoral behavior. Perceptions of such immoral behavior differed according to the gender of the actors. For women, but not for men, it consisted of having several lovers. From 1940 through the end of the century, the scenery, props, and sometimes the script changed. Scenery changes first included the wartime occupation and Vichy regime, and later the acceptance of concubinage for heterosexual and homosexual couples. Antoine Loysel's aphorism "Boire, manger, coucher ensemble, c'est mariage ce me semble," used by authors of legislation to justify heterosexual concubinage as grounds for paternity suits at the beginning of the twentieth century, was later written into the script at the very end of the century when groups argued for the legalization of homosexual as well as heterosexual unions. Moreover, advances in biology provided new and significant props, changing the nature of paternity searches from a complicated system that had based biological paternity on social behavior, to the use of blood and genetic tests in a determination of biological paternity. Divisibility of paternity remained in the script, however, differentiating a father's responsibility for child support from his responsibility to provide his name and family identification to the child. A division also obtained between biological ties of paternity and behavioral aspects of social fatherhood.

The desire for the protection of the patriarchal family, which had dominated much of the official discussion involving paternity, remained an important component of the rhetoric during the period from 1938 through 1945. In the post-1945 period, especially starting in the 1960s, however, the social order anchored in the patriarchal family began to erode with a sudden and rapid evolution in French society away from family structures of the past and toward a social and moral order more rooted in individual choice for both women and men, and with greater emphasis on emotional relationships. By the last quarter of the century, the social and moral order became more centered on the ungendered individual.

Family Code and Vichy Rhetoric

The conjugal family appeared on center stage at least in law and politics from 1939 to 1945.[1] The Family Code (Code de la famille) of 29 July 1939 incorporated ideas of pronatalism and fears of depopulation that had marked the political discourse during the entire Third Republic, but which had been largely absent from the public stage on which people played out their lives. Intimate lives were too important to be dominated by public ideologies. Designed by the Haut Comité de la population under the Édouard Daladier ministry (1937–March 1940), this Family Code had a two-pronged approach to family welfare and relief of the perceived demographic crisis and its consequences. It authorized family allowances (*allocations familiales*) for those in need, and also allowed for subsidies (*primes de naissance*) for second and subsequent children born to a married couple. The Vichy government's modification of this code and attempts at implementation in the 1940s demonstrated the continuity of Center-Right familialist policies from the Third Republic through the Vichy regime. As a populationist policy to protect future generations, family welfare constituted the core of this legislation. The goal, however, was not just to have the national and municipal governments provide financial assistance for needy families; it was also to enforce the responsibility of family members to help manage their own welfare by strengthening patriarchal power. By 1939, paternity searches that required fathers and genitors to help support their children had been so accepted and ingrained in society and in political philosophy that formulators of this Family Code did not even address recherche de paternité, which had been such a thorny issue a mere half century earlier.

The Family Code built upon child-support legislation of the previous half century, following the arguments of those who maintained that ensuring paternal responsibility would help save children's lives and the state money and also help increase and regenerate the population of France. It also tried to change the guidelines for adoption by permitting tribunals to rupture the ties between the child and his or her "family by blood," so that an adopted child would more closely resemble a legitimate child in a conjugal family. This went further than having the family of origin consent to the adoption. Moreover, the adopting parents had to be a couple united by a legal marriage.[2] The Family Code, designed to support legal conjugal families, went into effect on 1 January 1940, after war had broken out, but before the German invasion of France.

Family allocations and birth bonuses, which Vichy rhetoric approved but implemented only sporadically, idealized a father who worked for the good of the fatherland and a mother who stayed home and raised healthy, hardworking children—also for the good of the fatherland, and the fathers. Pronatalist views during Vichy, based on the idea that the nation was a moral unit and that having children was a man's and a woman's patriotic duty, resembled views of the Third Republic's social Catholics and of the right-wing National Alliance for Population Growth (Alliance nationale pour l'accroissement de la population). The idea that a man must not only have children but also materially support them carried over from the Third Republic. Under Vichy and the Family Code, however, men were to have those children within a legally established conjugal family, eschewing concubinage. In a Christian society, the idea of which Vichy rhetoric incorporated along with the pronatalist nationalism, the father was in command of the conjugal family. If the father was performing his patriarchal duties, the mother could stay home and raise the children. The state was to support and defend the family. A series of regulations and decrees, especially between 1940 and 1942, completed the legislation pertaining to the Family Code and set guidelines for implementation.

Family allowances were central to the Code as measures to prevent degeneration and depopulation and to reinforce the material contributions of fathers. Supporting the patriarchal family, as crucial as it was to policy makers, was less critical than supporting the children. Preferences in allocating family assistance went to conjugal French families with two or more children who were in need. Ideally, the father was to claim the allocation, but a mother was also allowed to seek it, especially if she was the primary provider for the children. If neither the mother nor father were part of the working population because of problems such as illness, unemployment, or mobilization, they were entitled to assistance for the first child. Normally, however, according to the 1939 Family Code and subsequent decrees of April and October 1940, the family allowance started with the second child, and that child had to be legitimate and French.

In the absence of direct parents, the allowance could go to brothers, sisters, aunts, or uncles—whoever assumed responsibility for the care and feeding of the children. The Family Code acknowledged families by adoption as real and not fictive; the allowance for adopted children went to the adopting parent. Generally, a child had to be seventeen years or younger, but the allocation could continue until the age of twenty for those children in school, in apprenticeship, or unable to earn a living because of a chronic illness or infirmity. If the parents were not married, it was more difficult for them to obtain assistance, but not impossible. To support children, even if it meant a tacit acknowledgment of consensual unions, article 11 of the Family Code stipulated that the parents of natural children could only qualify for a family allowance if both mother and father had legally recognized them and provided mutually for their care. In the absence of a mother and father, assistance went to those having permanent custody of recognized natural children. This article was enacted as part of the Family Code in 1939 before the war and the Vichy regime; subsequent revisions tended to ignore it.[3]

In the face of the appalling dearth and hardships of war and occupation, the guidelines made the requirements for family allocations more restrictive, despite parents' increased need and the strong pronatalist rhetoric from government officials. Instructions of 9 June 1941 lowered the maximum age for children receiving assistance to fifteen. Only if the child was infirm or in an apprenticeship could assistance continue until the child was seventeen; however, if the child was pursuing an education, family assistance could be obtained until that child was twenty years old. For a second child, the family could receive 10 percent of the average salary in the department; the family could obtain 20 percent for the third child. For the fourth and subsequent children, they could receive for each 30 percent of the average salary of the department. Family allocations were clearly intended as a supplement to the father's pay if he had several children within a conjugal family, and not as welfare for the unemployed. For family allowances, 1940s rhetoric and policy no longer accepted *concubinage notoire* as resembling marriage. A mother could, however, receive an allowance for a natural child whom she had legally recognized, provided that she alone was raising the child out of her own earnings, but not if she was living in concubinage.[4] However, the government would have needed an army of inspectors or called upon entire neighborhoods to look for concubinage, and a woman might have received assistance if she successfully concealed cohabitation.

Bonuses for the birth of children differed from family assistance and were not accorded to single mothers or to those living in concubinage. Vichy policies echoed the views of conservative Catholics at the end of the nineteenth century who claimed that any assistance to single mothers, even aid designed to reduce infant mortality, was a "bonus for debauchery." To encourage legal marriage and to entice couples to have more children, these birth bonuses applied only to conjugal families.

Even before the war and Vichy regime, a pronatalist and repopulationist decree of 12 November 1938 called for paying a bonus to mothers who stayed home with their children. Based on the premise that her husband and children suffer when a mother leaves home to go to work, providing a bonus for her to stay home would help prevent two social scourges: infant mortality and divorce. The bonus, however, was a meager 5 percent of the average departmental salary for the first child, increasing to 15 percent for the third and subsequent children. A mother and her children could not live on this; she had to depend on a gainfully employed husband. The July 1939 Family Code incorporated this measure, and five months later, a decree of 30 December 1939 called for a subsidy for the birth of a first child if born to a French family within two years following a legal marriage. The government paid the birth bonus first to the mother, but if she had died, the father, guardian, or person responsible for the child could receive this bonus. The recipient had to use the money solely in the child's interest. Implementation would demand even more inspectors and neighborhood vigilance to ensure that the parent used the money exclusively for the child. There was no subsidy for the cost of childbirth. Children legitimated by marriage received no mention. In 1940, implementation instructions repeated that children had to be legitimate, born within two years after the parents' marriage, and also born subsequent to 1 January 1940. In 1942, reflecting the strongly patriarchal attitude of the Vichy administration, the government gave a stay-at-home mother's bonus to the father rather than to her directly.

Vichy rhetoric insisted that strong families make strong countries; marriage created morality and reinforced the patriarchy. To many at the time, the dominant political beliefs about families and the romantic mystique of legally married conjugal families glorifying fatherhood and motherhood represented security, calm, and national renewal in a world terribly disrupted by war and occupation. "Liberté, Egalité, Fraternité" gave way to "Travail, Famille, Patrie" (Work, Family, Fatherland), and men were obligated to work and support their nation and their families. In Vichy's pronatalist and familialist rhetoric, creating two or more children to replenish the race was good, but not sufficient; it was also necessary to provide for their well-being.[5] If a father did his job properly by working as a material provider, then the mother should stay home and nurture the children. Vichy propaganda and legislation reinforced the male-breadwinner model, which had not previously been strong in France.[6] What the rhetoric left unclear was a man's obligation to his children if he was not married. In one respect, official Vichy attitudes toward paternity and the family deviated from those of the Third Republic: concubinage was no longer an acceptable substitute for a legal conjugal family. A man's performance of his duties as a father comprised a key aspect of paternity, but it had to be within marriage.[7]

Tensions and contradictions suffused official policy and people's lives. On the one hand, the ideal family under a strong patriarch was the policy goal; on the other hand, society acknowledged the single-mother family and limited the genitor's role in the family after a successful paternity suit to mere material support. Vichy did not outlaw divorce or change the terms of paternity searches, but the procedures were slower, and fewer women brought cases to court. The Vichy regime could not eliminate either, because they were both so entrenched in society, but in 1941, the government "forbade any divorce during the first three years of marriage" and limited the possible grounds for divorce after three years to physical spousal abuse; adultery was no longer sufficient.[8] The regime did, however, add another article to the Family Code in 1941, stating that a woman could give birth anonymously by just signing an X in place of her name (*accouchement sous X*). This article, designed to prevent abortion and infanticide, also restricted paternity searches, since mothers who made use of it could not file a suit.[9]

Legitimacy was a reflection of moral order—in the Third Republic as in Vichy—but that moral order could be open to interpretation. The Vichy chief of state, Marshal Philippe Pétain, himself demonstrated the loose relationship between official policy and private lives by proposing the so-called *loi du jardinier* ("gardener's law"), which originated with Pétain's wife, who sought to regularize the situation of their private gardener and legitimate the children born of his adultery. To allow him to do so would have contravened all the laws on adultery and legitimation, which the Third Republic observed ostensibly to keep the legally married family sacrosanct— something Vichy idiom also held dear. By decree on 3 September 1941, however, a man was allowed to legitimate his children born of adultery if he divorced his wife who was not the mother of the children and married the woman who was.

There was much uproar at the time that this would mean the end of the family. Opponents, even members of Pétain's own cabinet, thought it would "legalize polygamy" and actually "encourage adultery. The protection of the innocent illegitimate child, desirable as it might be, should not run counter to the protection of the marriage, the spouse, and legitimate children."[10] It allowed the appearance of a man having two families, something impossible during the Third Republic. This decree violated the moral imperatives of Vichy and official pronouncements on the family. Supporters disagreed that it violated Vichy directives on the family and justified this decree on the grounds that it was pro-family because it legitimized innocent children. It also helped Pétain's gardener, and presumably Mme Pétain. By a stretch of social logic, the *loi du jardinier* could be presented as a wartime measure, legitimating children not born within legal wedlock. During the revolutionary and Napoleonic wars and again in 1917, the French governments had also taken action to legitimate extranuptial children, but not quite this way. The *loi du jardinier* was short-lived, ending with the fall of Vichy.

Paternity and Private Lives, 1940–1945

The disjuncture between discourse and practice was not limited to Pétain's *loi du jardinier*. The private lives of Parisians continued as they had before, but with extraordinarily greater hardships. They faced unimaginable fear, constant food and fuel shortages, and severe travel restrictions. If they were Jewish, their situation was even more deplorable, and included the prospect of exile, denial of citizenship, incarceration, deportation, and death. Nevertheless, Parisians continued to commit adultery, get divorced, and file paternity suits during the Occupation. They also continued to use the civil courts to settle family matters and assign paternal responsibility, just as they had done under the Third Republic. There was little to distinguish these court cases from many of those brought before the civil tribunals during the interwar period, unless a participant was Jewish.[11]

The paternity suit that Jeanne Victoire and her son Henri brought against Henri Roget illustrates the interdependence of families, the critical importance of letters and written avowals of paternity, and the general acceptance of a sexual relationship that was not quite *concubinage notoire* but more a wartime sexual encounter. This drama had begun during another war, in the winter of 1916–17, when Jeanne Victoire was working as a waitress in a hotel near her family home in the department of the Vosges in eastern France, a reasonably safe distance from the war front. During that winter, she had a sexual relationship with a young soldier, Henri Roget, who was stationed there.[12] By April 1917, when he was deployed elsewhere, Jeanne realized that she was pregnant. He wrote fourteen letters to her between March 1917 and May 1918, all of which she saved and turned over to her lawyer when she began a paternity suit in 1939. In one of Roget's first letters of March 1917, he wrote tenderly of the nights they had spent together "in your little room where we were so happy.... Each day I loved you more." In April, after learning that she was pregnant, he was solicitous of her welfare: "You know well, my little Jeannette, that I will do all that is possible for you. I would really be a heartless lout, my little treasure, to let you suffer after all that you have done for me. I am astonished that no one... perceives anything. Can you hide... [the pregnancy] from them?" In July, he wrote: "you know that there was never a question of a future between us and you know that we would never marry, but bear in mind that I'm not heartless and I will never forget my little Jeannette. I have not ceased to love you and you are always *la petite amie*. When you... need something write to me." Calling her *la petite amie* indicates that he thought of her as a girlfriend and nothing more. His letters did not change significantly after she had a 9-pound boy on 4 November 1918. Jeanne legally recognized her baby son and named him Henri, after his father. Until the end of May 1919, Roget continued to write to her, and he worried about her well-being. He promised to help her out materially if she asked, but there is no evidence whether he provided child support. Jeanne paid her sister and brother-in-law a monthly stipend to raise Henri until he was fourteen. For the first year after young Henri was born, Jeanne underwent several surgeries, and the following year she was very weak. Therefore, she could not file a paternity suit within the two-year limit stipulated by the 1912 law.

Contact between Roget and either Jeanne or Henri Victoire is not evident until 1939, the year in which Henri reached his majority and had his last chance to file a paternity suit. Although de jure he filed the suit, as the law required, de facto he was not a legal presence, and Jeanne Victoire was more actively involved in the legal proceedings. The procedure for recherche de paternité lasted from 1939 through January 1943, taking about a year longer than similar suits before the war. Their lawyer based his argument on an implicit avowal of paternity contained in the letters, which acknowledged sexual relations during the possible time of conception and promised material support. In 1943, the judge in occupied Paris ruled that implicit written indications of paternity were acceptable proof, but Henri Roget appealed. In his appeal, Roget brought his evidence of Victoire's immorality with testimony of her having had several lovers; she brought her witnesses who attested to her moral behavior. On 3 March 1944, an appeals court judge agreed with the civil tribunal judge that Henri Roget was the father of Henri Victoire. It would henceforth entitle Henri to carry Roget's name and to inherit from Roget when he died. Immediately after this decision, on 21 April 1944, Jeanne Victoire sued for damages to cover the 50,000 francs she had paid to her sister and brother-in-law for rearing her son. The legal grounds for this type of suit, unchanged since the early nineteenth century, were abuse of authority or fraudulent seduction based on false promises of marriage. The letters, however, divulged that he had never promised marriage and that she had voluntarily engaged in sexual relations with Roget. Therefore, her lawyer thought her case was weak, and they dropped it in February 1945.

This case resembles many in the interwar period and indicates that the government of Vichy and the Occupation was not an aberration in terms of jurisprudence and recherche de paternité but was on a continuum with the Third Republic.[13] Lawyers in 1942 and 1943 even invoked jurisprudence of the 1920s and 1930s as a type of precedent. Jurisprudence during the Occupation and under Vichy did not condemn Jeanne Victoire for her sexual liaison; she had tried to support her child as a good mother and was fortunate to be able to rely on her sister and brother-in-law, a railroad employee, for material assistance and social networks. Her actions were characteristic of the culture of expediencies that had typified single women's lives since the early nineteenth century.

The family drama of the Kahan and Ponelle families involved a custody battle after divorce, and reveals some of the problems of blended or reconstituted families and the criteria for good fatherhood. It also poignantly demonstrates the impact of the Occupation and of official anti-Semitism.[14] In 1927, Léon Kahan, who was Jewish, married Arlette Ponelle, who was Catholic; they had two boys. Arlette's brother, Jean-Pierre Ponelle, a *couturier*, married Renée Chavet in 1929, and a year later they had a daughter, Doris. The Kahan and Ponelle households were closely tied in terms of marriage, friendship, and residential proximity, so closely tied that Renée Chavet Ponelle and Léon Kahan had intimate relations. The Kahan couple divorced in 1937; Arlette Ponelle Kahan was granted custody of their two boys, and Léon Kahan was required to pay a sizeable *pension alimentaire*. Two years later, Renée and Jean-Pierre Ponelle divorced. The judge left guardianship of Doris to Renée's mother, Mme LeBois, with both parents having visitation rights. This was not an unusual arrangement among urban families in easy economic circumstances and with close family ties and where the mother had committed adultery. At the beginning of 1940, Renée Ponelle married her ex-brother-in-law, Léon Kahan. Since the Ponelles' divorce in 1939, Doris had lived with her grandmother, three blocks away from her mother and not far from her father.[15] She walked back and forth between her mother's home and her grandmother's. Her father saw her on Sundays. In July 1940, he discovered that Mme LeBois and Doris had fled Paris, as did so many hundreds of thousands of other Parisians during the mass exodus when the German army rolled in.[16] They managed to get to the seaside resort of Arcachon in the Gironde, and Jean-Pierre received written word that they were safe.

In September 1940, the authorities in occupied France ordered a census of all Jews, and Vichy statutes of October 1940 excluded Jews from positions of responsibility in government, teaching, and cultural life. From 1940 to the winter of 1942, some Jews who had the financial means could pay for exit visas and passports, although these were difficult to obtain. Léon Kahan, who had been one of the directors of a large petrol company, had the resources and became one of the countless Jews who fled the Occupied Zone. By spring 1941, Kahan was in the southeast of France, intending to flee to Algeria, when he wrote to his ex-wife, Arlette, asking for custody of his boys so that he could take them to Algiers.

Kahan's request provided the motivation for this custody battle. Arlette refused Léon's offer and warned Jean-Pierre that his ex-wife, Renée, would soon take his daughter to Algeria, alleging that they had already left for the "Free Zone" and were headed for Algeria, and then the United States, with Doris. A few weeks later, Jean-Pierre Ponelle brought his suit to obtain legal custody of his daughter, Doris, who was then twelve years old. He argued that "because of certain questions of religion, Mr. Kahan left the Occupied Zone to go to the Free Zone with the goal of going to Africa if not America."

Doris's mother (now Renée Kahan) did not want the custody case to go court, so her lawyer proposed that guardianship rest with Doris's maternal grandmother, with a *pension alimentaire* from Jean-Pierre fixed at 1,500 francs per month until Doris was eighteen. Showing a lack of understanding of the reality of the situation in France, Renée Kahan's lawyer further stipulated that if she were to leave for Algeria, Doris should remain in Paris with her father for six months of the year and in Algeria with her mother for the other six months. Ponelle rejected this, and in August 1941, Renée Kahan brought a countersuit demanding guardianship and custody of Doris. In a letter to Ponelle, in August 1941, she said "Doris and maman under the orders of Dr. D. [the Paris doctor] left for Mégève (in the Haute-Savoie) for two months and we no longer think they will arrive the beginning of the week since they've lost a lot of time trying to pass [from the Occupied to the

Free Zone]. They will send their address when they arrive and will return to Paris at the beginning of October, where I will wait for them, having renounced my trip to Algeria in order to pursue the legal proceedings you have begun."[17] This is the only news we have of Renée Kahan.

Doris and her grandmother managed to cross the Demarcation Line from occupied to non-occupied France despite the severe restrictions on travel across the frontier that the Germans imposed during the first two years. Ponelle alleged that their departure had been clandestine and sudden, and that there was no actual medical need, but the only way they could get across the line of demarcation was with a doctor's certificate for a "serious illness." Even for a temporary pass, the very few who were able to cross had to wait in lines for hours, if not days, to get the authorization to cross the boundary.[18] Jean-Pierre Ponelle complained that he could not get permission to visit them. Doris's first postcard to her father from Mégève indicates that her doctor in Paris said that she was getting thinner and had a fever, and that he recommended mountain air for a cure. Aside from a diagnosis of mild scoliosis (curvature of the spine), not generally considered an acute "serious illness," it is unclear what her ailment was. In October 1941, they returned to Paris. Although they had the money to go to Algeria, they stayed in France.

None of the letters contains a word about the war or shortages or the situation for Jews. On the contrary, this upper bourgeois family continued their lives more or less as before—except for Léon Kahan. Part of the reason for the silence about wartime problems may have been censorship of the mail, although none of the letters bear the bold black lines indicative of expurgation. Most letters and postcards were from Doris, discussing her health or her new dress, or were requests from Mme LeBois for more money for the doctors' bills. The banality of each postcard and letter is not surprising, given the severe censorship, as well as Doris's probable youthful reluctance to write. Throughout the war, Ponelle continued to contribute a minimum of 1,000 francs per month to Mme LeBois for taking care of Doris. In June 1942, Mme LeBois and Doris went to a thermal spa in the Nièvre, on the border within occupied France, for a "cure"—Doris for her scoliosis and Mme LeBois for rheumatism.

Ponelle might have expected to win his custody case; he was Catholic and his ex-wife was now married to a Jew. This was not the case, although Ponelle's lawyer based his argument on Renée Kahan's immorality, on the welfare of young Doris, and on Ponelle's excellence as a father. Ponelle's lawyer alleged that Kahan had "sacrificed" his two sons when he divorced, although he materially supported them in relative affluence until he left for Algiers in 1941. However, in a tense argument, Jean-Pierre's lawyer acknowledged that Kahan and Renée Ponelle had "sacrificed two homes, but it had a moral dénouement; they married." If there was anti-Semitism in the case, it was veiled. Ponelle said that he had not contested the divorce because Kahan had "more money in this battle," and that "he was beaten by the money of his brother-in-law." Ponelle's lawyer based his argument on the same criteria that lawyers had used in family cases before 1940—good fatherhood. Ponelle had acted *en qualité de père* and had participated "materially and emotionally" in rearing Doris. He not only paid a monthly pension for Doris's care but also paid for medicine and vacations, sent her presents, and spent Sundays with her when they were both in Paris. So why did he not get custody? In a turnaround from a focus on a woman's immorality, the Kahan-LeBois countersuit focused on Ponelle's immorality and on Doris's best interests. Ponelle was living with a "mistress" who was one of his models, although he married her in 1942, just before the case went to court. The judge denied both the mother's and father's arguments for custody. Instead, he ruled that it was in Doris's best interest to remain with her grandmother, since she had raised Doris for nine years. Questions of the child's best interest and of morality trumped a Jewish connection. Moreover, Doris's grandmother was raising her Catholic, ensuring she made her first Holy Communion.

The Occupation and Vichy regimes did not put an end to cases of disavowal of paternity and discussions of adultery. According to Miranda Pollard, "Adultery loomed large in Vichy's discourse on sexuality"; it had also pervaded much literature during the Third Republic.[19] The story of the Duprès shows the complications of adultery, divorce, and paternity during the war and reveals some of the problems of wartime shortages, perhaps because the letters of the Duprès did not go through the post, but were rather hand-delivered and slipped under apartment doors. Pierre and Suzanne Duprès married in 1934. He was a 29-year-old government employee working in the Paris region. A year after they married, they had a son, Alain. Early in 1939, Duprès became the assistant head of a department in the Ministry of Finance, but he was mobilized to Tours until June, when his unit left for the Charente. He was demobilized at the end of July 1940. During this time, Suzanne remained in their suburban Paris house near her parents.[20]

On 24 December 1940, Suzanne had a son, Daniel, whose paternity was questioned because Duprès had been geographically separated from her during the possible time of conception; her family, moreover, knew that she had engaged in adultery. Between August 1940 and December 1941, Pierre Duprès took a separate residence, and Louis LePont, Suzanne's lover, moved in with her. On 1 January 1942, Suzanne visited Pierre, and not finding him home, slipped a note under the door. She was annoyed because he had promised to give her something each month for the care of their son. She wrote: "I know that I have acted badly, but what you have done is not much better.... If you don't want to see me, or if you want nothing more to do with me, I prefer that you take revenge on me rather than make my little one suffer.... You are wicked to wish to humiliate me. I have given you pain and sorrow; it is not your fault.... I think of my little Alain ... Nevertheless, I affectionately embrace you."

Almost three weeks later, they renewed their correspondence by putting notes under each other's doors, which reveal the effects of wartime deprivations and hardship. He wrote to her saying that he would not be responsible for paying for the electricity for everyone living in her house. He added: "your place is next to me and you should take it for your sake and that of the little ones. Believe me, it's your duty and it's in their interest.... Don't continue in your error.... Think of your little Alain. If you return, Suzette, be assured that I will forget all. But you must break completely with the past. I want you to understand that it is your duty and also your happiness to return and take your place near me." In each letter, she mentions her need for coal to heat the house and to cook. "I thank you a thousand times for the coal. You do us a great service because we no longer have any fire in the house.... Would it be possible to have a little more?" She adds that she is still in turmoil. "I do not want to be separated from my little Alain. I love him as much as Danny and I don't see life without either one. This is too serious a decision for me to make right away. I need more time." She ends by asking him not to judge her too badly. "I am not as guilty as you believe. It is only death that will separate me from either one of my children. I love you always with affection."

On 26 and 30 January, she implored him for more coal. This lack of coal was a universal and serious problem under the Occupation; supplies were inadequate, and it was severely rationed. She was also tortured about her decision not to return to her husband:

> Sometimes I would like to go back to the past and erase all that has happened.... My heart refuses that, however. Pierre, do not make me miserable.

Do not take Alain, I beg you. I am so unhappy.... I am not as sinful as you think. I cannot find my place next to you. I often miss your sweet words. You have asked me to return to you. Have you thought carefully of what would happen if I returned? Would you love me as before? I would like to make you happy, but for the moment it is not possible.... Please have a little patience and if my health gets better I will tell you frankly what I will do. Pierrot, if I become even sicker, you will come to see me won't you? I would not like to die without having seen you.

This is her last letter—but she did not die then.

In March 1942, Pierre Duprès began divorce proceedings, charging Suzanne and Louis LePont with adultery. They acknowledged that they were living together maritally and had had a child together, Daniel, born in December 1940. A judgment of nonconciliation issued in July of 1942 was followed by the birth of a daughter to Suzanne, on 11 January 1943. Suzanne's father filed the birth certificate reporting Duprès as the father, since she was still technically married to him. The divorce was final on 7 July 1943, in favor of Pierre. Proceedings for disavowal of paternity began immediately. LePont said the girl born in January 1943 was his, but his saying so was not enough. Since Suzanne and Pierre were legally separated at the time of conception, the child could lawfully be LePont's if Pierre filed an action to disavow.

Daniel was another story. Pierre had to bring witnesses attesting that he had been away from home during the legal period of conception, and that his wife had never visited him. This he did. She did not contest the divorce or the disavowal of paternity. The disavowal was effective as of 24 May 1945, by which point, Suzanne was no longer Suzanne Duprès but Suzanne LePont. Nothing distinguishes these proceedings from similar ones before the war. In the files of Pierre's lawyer, there is no language condemning Suzanne for immorality or for her failure to fulfill her role as a "good mother." Only Duprès called on her to do her duty as a mother and wife, using language the Vichy authorities would have approved of.

Paternity searches, denials of paternity, and family formations during Vichy and the Occupation differed little from those under the Third Republic, except for the additional horrible hardships of the time. Jeanne and Henri Victoire's paternity suit could have taken place at any time after 1912. Although people's daily concerns during the Occupation centered on fear and on food and fuel (for which one either stood in line or turned to the black market), the problems of provisions do not emerge as crucial from these letters, in part, perhaps, because of censorship, and in part because the correspondence only affords a snapshot of family life relevant to paternity, custody, adultery, and divorce. Only Suzanne Duprès, who hand-delivered her notes, wrote of the ever-present need for coal. No one mentioned food packages. Suzanne Duprès may have grown some of what she needed in her garden; the Ponelles were well-to-do, and Jeanne Victoire lived in a relatively rural part of the Vosges. Negotiating precarious marriages and paternity was critical, at least from the evidence in the lawyer's files. Léon Kahan's being Jewish gravely disrupted his life, however, and his eventual fate is unknown.[21] His two sons and his ex-wife no longer received their pension after 1941, and the legal proceedings for custody evolved only because Kahan was Jewish.

Likewise, on a most basic level, there is little to distinguish family strategies during the war years from those during the Third Republic. Family lives are driven by an interaction of social forces as well as people's emotional bonds. Women relied on their families for help in rearing their children. Suzanne Duprès's father lived upstairs in the same house. Furthermore, during the divorce, the court declared him the guardian of her children. Renée Ponelle Kahan had her mother to care for her daughter, and Jeanne Victoire paid her sister and brother-in-law to raise her son. In these middle-class families, relatives stepped in to help, just as they did among all classes during the nineteenth and early twentieth centuries. The extent to which Vichy policies influenced family strategies varied more by religion than by gender. Suzanne Duprès and Renée Ponelle were not rhetorically stoned for their adultery, nor was Jeanne Victoire for having an extranuptial child. Surprisingly, even though he was a good father, Jean-Pierre Ponelle was denied custody, but he nevertheless retained his legal *puissance paternelle*.

Vichy ideology sought to regulate women's sexual behavior and viewed their adultery as a "social danger."[22] According to rhetoric and policy, women were above all to be good mothers, to love their children and rear them well; as symbols of the National Revolution, they were also to be pious and run a good household. But dramatic differences appeared between the roles that Vichy assigned women and how they lived their lives. Suzanne Duprès committed adultery, but in all her correspondence, she expressed love for all her children, and she struggled to maintain a home for them. However, she refused her legally married husband's enjoinders to fulfill her duty and be by his side. Vichy rhetoric appears only in his letters—unless his efforts to persuade her to return represent his own private feelings. Moreover, she had contributed three children to repopulating France, and she married her lover, the father of two of her children, eventually legitimizing them. She may have been one of many women who escaped the surveillance that Vichy designed to control illicit female activity. If the law punished those who deserted their families, it did not punish Renée Kahan or Suzanne Duprès, perhaps because they did not desert their children, just their legal husbands. Or, in these instances, Vichy official ideology did not accomplish its goals.

Under Vichy, and to some extent during the Third Republic, the ideal family was conjugal and reproductive—strong, secure and calm, glorifying both fatherhood and motherhood. The creation and protection of children for the future of France was the guiding principle. A father's performance of his duties remained a key aspect of paternity, as Ponelle's lawyer argued and as Henri Roget's letters implied. The ideal family under a strong, patriarchal father was the ideological goal, although not always realized in practice. Private lives and public policy ran along different roads, if not at cross purposes. Except insofar as they forced Jews out, made travel exceedingly difficult, and created terrible shortages of food and fuel, the Vichy and Occupation authorities were absent from the lives of those who engaged lawyers and filed legal suits for recherche de paternité, child custody, disavowal of paternity, or divorce. Personal life appears to have continued for some as in prior decades.

For millions of others, however, these years were ones of families broken, not by individual choice, but by governmental decisions—by war, imprisonment, deportation, and death. Fathers were torn from their families to fight in the war, and many remained as prisoners of war for almost five years. Vichy and Occupation authorities removed others to serve as laborers in Germany, and many died even further east. Mothers had to manage without the fathers of their children. Untold numbers of Jews were rounded up, deported, and sent to internment and extermination camps, where they died of malnutrition and disease or were simply murdered. These included practicing Catholics who had a Jewish parent or grandparent who had immigrated to France. Entire villages were obliterated.[23] The horrors are endless; what is surprising is that none of the families whose lives appear in this chapter seem to have been influenced by Vichy rhetoric or enormously disrupted by the five years of war and occupation, except the Kahan family. In postwar France, however, private lives and public policy more often intersected; if they ran along the same road, it was one of the superhighways, with many exits and entrances, lots of construction, and occasional closed roads.

Postwar Paternity

In 1989, Anne-Gilberte Drossard and her daughter, Aurore Drossard, then twenty-two years old, filed a paternity suit in a Paris court against the estate of the actor Yves Montand. As Aurore bemoaned when looking at her birth certificate, "in place of the name of the father, I see only an x. I have the impression that I'm only half alive." She insisted that she did not want money, only recognition of paternity so that she could bear Montand's name. Montand had admitted his liaison with Anne Drossard, but had denied paternity of Aurore and refused to submit to paternity tests while he was alive. In 1994, five years after Drossard initiated the paternity suit, and three years after Montand's death, the judge ruled in her favor, declaring that Aurore Drossard was indeed Montand's daughter and entitled to a portion of his estate. Montand's family and heirs appealed the decision. In March 1998, a judge ordered an exhumation of Montand's body and a DNA test on his remains; the results, announced in June 1998, indicated that Drossard was probably not his daughter.[24]

In some respects, this story resembles the many hundreds of paternity cases brought to court in Paris since 1912, without exhumation and genetic tests. Although the extant records of paternity suits do not readily reveal the mothers' motives in taking the men to court, the Drossards may be illustrative of other women—except for the fame and fortune of the putative father. Despite the wealth of Montand's estate, Aurore Drossard said that she wanted to know her father for her own emotional reasons. She indicated that she felt "incomplete" with the "x" in the space on her birth certificate where her father's name should have been. In her case, paternity would be a liaison conferring an inheritance and lineage based on biology. No matter what Aurore claimed, the question of property and inheritance seemed central. If the judge could legally rule that Drossard was Montand's daughter born of an adulterous relationship, she could claim an inheritance equal to one half of what one of Montand's legal children obtained.[25]

There are distinct differences, however, between the paternity cases of the early twentieth century and that of Drossard v. Montand, indicating the rapid evolution of laws and society. Earlier in the twentieth century, Aurore and Anne-Gilberte Drossard's case would not have been heard. Not only had

Montand been married at the time of conception, but Anne-Gilberte Drossard waited more than two years to file suit; and according to newspaper reports Montand never lived with her, never wrote letters saying the child was his, and no neighbors or friends attested that they had lived together maritally. More significantly, only after the passage of the 1972 law on filiation and paternity could a man who had a child as a result of his adultery be brought to court on paternity charges, although judges could have ordered him to pay a *pension alimentaire*. Aurore Drossard, who filed suit after she reached adulthood, did not deny that she was the child of an adulterous relationship between her mother, who was single, and Montand, who had been married to the actress Simone Signoret at the time of Drossard's conception and birth. After 1972, French law allowed for the use of blood-type testing, although consanguinity had been discussed and used in courts since 1935 to prove non-paternity. DNA tests as the legal base for determining paternity date from 1993, making determination of paternity biological, although fatherhood remained behavioral and emotional.[26] The issue of proof of paternity has always been paramount, with reliance on social behavior as an indication of biological paternity before 1972. Since the end of the twentieth century, the biological sciences have enabled more certain proof, but the issue was, and is still, how to characterize paternity outside of marriage.

Between 1912 and the major legal revisions of 1972 and 1993, jurisprudence reflected social and cultural changes related to the development of scientific proof of paternity and the increasing recognition of the equality of all children, whether born within or outside marriage. Most significantly, an acceptable French family came to include many who were not legally married but who would "eat, drink, and sleep together," marking a significant change from the conjugal patriarchy of the eighteenth century. As in the late nineteenth and early twentieth centuries, when widespread customs and attitudes were not in tune with the law, judges had the options of enforcing the law or circumventing it. Gradually, they circumvented the 1912 law by responding to women who turned to the courts.

In 1955, the law caught up with jurisprudence and allowed children of adultery to demand and receive material support, but not filiation, from married men. Until that year, men who committed adultery bore no legal responsibility for resultant children, either as material providers or as fathers providing them with a legal identity. Jurisprudence as early as the 1930s, however, had begun to use tort law to obligate adulterous men to pay damages to mothers and help support the children born of that adultery.

Paternity with full filiation still could not be legally established for children of adultery, in part because they were an exhibit of their parents' infidelity, and in part owing to the still-present desire to protect adulterous men. Moreover, legislators contended that if the law allowed a man to recognize children of his adultery, he would have two families, a concept they abhorred.[27]

For all natural children, including those not born of adultery, this 1955 law broadened the grounds for paternity searches. In the past, a broken engagement had allowed a mother to request damages, but it was not always sufficient proof in recherche de paternité; it had been up to the judge to decide. Now, it qualified as proof of paternity, at least for child support, as well as for damages under the still-important article 1382 of the Civil Code. Although written proof still had greater evidentiary weight than verbal statements, by this law, such proof could be implicit, as judges had been ruling for decades, and did not have to be explicit, as the 1912 law had specified. Finally, this law permitted the use of blood groupings in paternity suits, but only if the man requested it as proof of non-paternity.[28]

The normative model of conjugality as the dominant family construction crumbled under the weight of radical social change during the 1960s and the increased individualism of women and men in the post-1968 period. Although official family policies of the last decade of the Third Republic continued through the Vichy era into the first decade of the postwar period, the 1960s diverged significantly from that past. The events of 1968 and the emergent women's movement galvanized members of society to mobilize for equal rights for women and independence for young adults, creating a generational rupture reminiscent of the young male individualism that marked the revolutionary cohort at the end of the eighteenth century.[29]

In the 1960s and 1970s, women were part of that cohort, having gained full legal citizenship in 1944. Furthermore, women's political pressure groups from the late 1950s on sought to modify family laws to provide greater equality within marriage and also give women the means to prevent unwanted pregnancies. Their relative success started with the Neuwirth law of 1967 to legalize contraception, which had been illegal since 1920. A series of laws followed, such as a new divorce law, the decriminalization of adultery in 1975, and the Veil law of the same year that allowed abortion as a matter of a woman's choice, which provided some greater equality within marriage and some erosion of the husband's *puissance maritale*. These legal reforms reflected the vast cultural and social transformations of the family, most notably an increase in the number of cohabiting couples. As couples across a broader spectrum of the population, including middle-class professionals, increasingly practiced and accepted concubinage as a premarital relationship or as an alternative family form to marriage, distinctions between legitimate and natural children contradicted how those couples thought about their relationships and rights.[30] Finally, medical science involving blood-type groups gained in reliability and usage. These phenomena demanded amendments to the law.

The legislation of 3 January 1972 on filiation and child support revised existing laws and enlarged the scope of recherche de paternité, making legitimate and natural children equal. It reflected the rapid social and cultural changes since 1960 and jurisprudence of over more than a half-century. The 1972 law completely changed article 342 of the Civil Code, which had previously exempted married men from paternity suits, and made those men accountable. Debates leading up to the 1972 changes were primarily concerned with adultery and a child's right to parental support, but the result was a major legislative reform on child support and the filiation of natural children. More than any act since 1912, it changed the way the law defined contested paternity outside of marriage. Referring to the natural rights and equality of all children in language reminiscent of the late eighteenth century, the law permitted children of adulterous relationships to sue for financial sustenance from their putative fathers on the same terms as all natural children. However, the law maintained the divisibility between food subsidies and filiation. Both parents, including adulterous fathers, were obliged to provide food, clothing, shelter, and education for their children until the children reached adulthood and achieved independent lives, it stated, but that obligation did not entail filiation and legal paternity. Furthermore, children born of adultery could be legitimated by the subsequent marriage of their parents and could inherit from their parents and grandparents, just like natural children not born of adultery. Before the law of 1972, if paternity was proven, the children could have inherited only from their mothers and fathers, but not from paternal grandparents or paternal collaterals; and when there were legitimate children, the judicially recognized child could only inherit half of what each of the legitimate children inherited. As a result of the 1972 law, however, recognized natural children and those whose paternity was judicially declared could now inherit from their grandparents as well as from collaterals on the same terms as legitimate children, creating greater equality of all children.[31]

The procedure to file a paternity suit barely changed from 1912, but the 1972 act made significant modifications in the categories of accepted proof by incorporating the five decades of jurisprudence and social changes. Recherche de paternité, with full filiation along with child support and damages to the mother, was now permitted in situations of sexual mistreatment or fraudulent seduction. This included abuse of authority, use of force, exploitation of a woman's weakness or inexperience, or the breach of a marriage promise or engagement; precise indication of these acts was still up to the judges. *Concubinage notoire* remained an important category of proof, but it was not necessary for the couple to have lived together as long as they had had a stable and continuous relationship during at least part of the legal period of conception, as judges had been ruling since the 1930s. In part, however, proof of paternity was still founded on the assumption of a relationship between the mother and putative father that resembled a conjugal family. As during the first half of the twentieth century, this rested on a series of presumptions about what constituted legitimate relations between a mother and father, and left that determination up to the judges. Written proof from the father in which he had made an avowal of paternity remained important, but reflecting jurisprudence, after 1972, the proof did not have to be "unequivocal." It could be implicit. As the leading legal scholar Jean Carbonnier acknowledged, a man "did not have to declare that the child was his own, as he had to do with a formal recognition. An expression of paternal affection was sufficient, but not indispensable. It was not even necessary that the putative father make an allusion to the baby. It was sufficient that he knew about the pregnancy and had never demonstrated the least suspicion about the mother's fidelity."[32] It left unchanged proof based on kidnapping and rape during the legal period of conception, still estimated at 180–300 days before childbirth. Finally, as the 1912 law stipulated, and the 1972 law repeated, the mother could demonstrate that the alleged father had contributed to the care and feeding of the child or had otherwise participated in the child rearing. This law allowed the use of blood tests in paternity cases, but a mother might not have wanted to use them, because they could not prove that a specific man was the genitor, only that he was not.

After a mother's or child's presentation of the case, the presumptive father had the opportunity to prove his innocence, which he usually did by trying to establish the woman's infidelity and untrustworthy nature, just as in previous decades. But, after 1972, social and circumstantial evidence of a woman's immorality was no longer as important as before; blood tests were used to prove the same thing. A man's legal ability to present blood tests demonstrating that he was not the father, which privileged the biological basis for paternity over the emotional, at least in terms of defining paternity outside of marriage, became critical after 1972. The other categories of his defense remained virtually unchanged. As proof of non-paternity, a man could still use any means to show that the woman had had sexual relations with several men in a manner approaching debauchery, or he could show that she had had intercourse with just one other individual, whom he could then name as the putative father. Finally, adopting the same circumstantial evidence as in disavowal of paternity, he could show that it was physically impossible for him to have been the genitor, either because he was far away or was impotent.

The law modified the grounds for disavowal of paternity of a wife's child. Many legislators sought to restrain actions to disavow paternity, pointing out that it was one thing to establish true biological filiation and quite another to destroy filiation established by a civil act—that of marriage.[33] Although by law the man married to the mother was still the father of her child, blood tests minimized the need to for him to produce public evidence of her adultery in order to disavow a child conceived or born during marriage. The 1972 law allowed a child to be integrated into the mother's family with her second husband. Furthermore, after 1972, both a mother and her husband, or ex-husband, could now file a suit contesting the paternity of a child conceived within that marriage. This granted a woman equal power to disavow a man's paternity of her child.

Judges retained considerable power in interpreting both the law and the evidence, but because the criteria for judicially declaring paternity were broader than before 1972, mothers now had more power to decide if they simply sought child support or if they wanted paternity legally established by the state through the courts—or if they wanted both. The overarching concern in judicial decisions was to assure the quality of children's lives. Judges still ordered child support according to the financial resources of the man and the needs of the child up to that child's adulthood and ability to live independently; they could pronounce that the child bear the father's name and receive a portion of the inheritance—if that was what the mother requested and the evidence warranted. In addition, the law permitted judges to order the judicially declared father to contribute to the cost of childbirth and to the pre-and postnatal care of the mother for three months prior to and three months after childbirth—again if that was what the mother requested. Suits to repair damages to the mother could now be combined with paternity searches, so judges could also order the judicially declared father to pay the mother for the material and moral prejudice he had caused her.

The 1972 law continued the evolution from male legal sexual irresponsibility in the nineteenth century to more legal sexual responsibility in the twentieth. Culture and the law agreed that fathers had a duty to provide for their children, whether paternity was legitimate, natural, or adulterous. The law allowed judges to reject the paternity claim for filiation but still order the man to pay child support when paternity was probable but not certain, as judges had been doing for decades, extending some aspect of paternal responsibility to a possible father. Proof for requiring child support rested on the same criteria as proof in paternity searches, but it now also applied to children born of adultery, making all men responsible for some of the consequences of their sexual activity—if there was sufficient evidence. However, the man was not necessarily responsible to the mother, but rather to the child to whom he had given life. With the 1972 law, and in accord with the culture of increased emotional and material responsibility of all fathers, if the judge ordered a specific man to pay child support, or subsidies, and found that he (the *père subsidant*) was emotionally attached to the child, the judge could also award him visitation rights.[34] No longer was the object of a paternity suit only a material provider. Since they could not positively prove paternity, only non-paternity, blood tests left open the assignment of paternity. Therefore, blood tests, and the judges, allowed a man brought to court for paternity or child support who *might* have been the father to maintain emotional ties to the child if he wished. Judges might also require him to pay child support and not maintain personal contact with the child.

In another new feature, but one that still distinguished paternal child support from filiation, the law of 1972 allowed a mother to seek child support from several men if she had had more than one lover during the legal period of conception. This action would not be recherche de paternité, but was a legal action for "an indemnity destined to assure the rearing and education of the child."[35] If all evidence, including blood tests, was inconclusive, judges could order two men who had had sexual relations with the mother to provide subsidies to the child, considering this as debt payment and as requiring men to take responsibility for their sexual actions. This debt payment established no legal bonds with the mother or child, not even visitation rights. It was sufficient that the man had had sexual relations with the woman during the period of conception, or any of the following: that he had promised marriage, that he had provided gifts to the mother or child, that he participated in choosing a name for the child, that the community knew of his cohabitation with the mother, that both had received mail at the same address, that anyone had produced photographs of the two being intimate, or if there were a physical resemblance between the possible father and child. Collecting was still another matter, because unknown numbers of fathers still sought to avoid responsibility. In the late twentieth century, alimony and child support payments from divorced fathers and from men found liable in paternity suits were sometimes irregular or nonexistent; they claimed to be without resources, or they simply moved and left no forwarding address.[36]

The question of what constituted paternity was still multifaceted, with several possible answers. It included both biological paternity and paternity established by acting like a father, either within or outside of marriage. The father was still the man married to the mother, but other men could also be fathers. Although the 1972 law proclaimed the equality of natural and legitimate children, as with all family laws, it left implementation vague. If a woman, but not the judge, asked the man to submit to blood typing, the man could legally refuse to be tested, as Yves Montand had done. The woman then had to bring a suit and have a judge order the test. This maintained some sexual liberty for men to the detriment of women and their children, and contributed to the continued tolerance of male irresponsibility, despite judges' ability to order a man (the *père subsidant*) to financially support the child, at least partially, or pay reparations to the mother. With sufficient biological proof based on blood groupings, and upon the request of a mother or father, a judge could destroy family lines that had been established by a civil act of marriage or by a birth certificate, if biology did not conform. The law of 1972 was one of a series of further rapid social and legal changes defining who was a father and what comprised a family.

The law on recherche de paternité of 8 January 1993 built upon the legislation of 1972 and reflected the two decades of social change, including wider acceptance of gender equality, an increase in state welfare to mothers, and the advent and acceptability of genetic or DNA testing. Amazingly vague even for French family law, article 340 now simply stated, "Paternity outside of marriage may be judicially declared. Only serious presumptions or circumstantial evidence can be admitted as evidence."[37] As with all previous versions of article 340, the child was the one legally initiating the suit. However, the revised article had not changed the time delay for instituting a paternity suit and it still had to begin within two years after the child's birth, or within two years after the end of concubinage or after the father ceased supporting the child; therefore mothers brought the suit in the child's name, as they had been doing since 1912.

New in 1972, and rearticulated in 1993, the judge could order the father to reimburse the mother for all or part of her delivery and support for three months prior to childbirth and three months afterward. The judge was not to deduct this amount from the damages a mother could still claim under article 1382. Furthermore, continuing the changes made in 1972, the law acknowledged the divisibility of paternity by allowing judges to dismiss the paternity suit but still order the man to pay subsidies to the child, as *père subsidant*. "Qui fait l'enfant doit le nourrir" (Who makes the child must feed it) had applied to a married couple at least since the eighteenth century; during the nineteenth century, some judges applied it to single putative fathers as a duty of conscience, but the legislation of 1972 and 1993 extended it yet further as a civil obligation to the child, even if paternity were uncertain and if the putative father were married to someone other than the child's mother. However, collecting from recalcitrant fathers was still difficult, and more mothers sought assistance from welfare.[38]

The law of 1993 allowed a man to deny his paternity with evidence from genetic testing, and permitted a woman to seek a judge's order for DNA tests from the man and the child. DNA testing provided the predominant and sure proof of paternity, biologically identifying every child's father. By 1993, circumstantial evidence of paternity or non-paternity was secondary to biological proof. Understood as part of circumstantial evidence, however, this 1993 law still permitted implicit as well as explicit evidence of *concubinage notoire* and written avowals of paternity; a mother and her lawyer could still summon witnesses to testify about a man's prior behavior toward the child and whether he had acted as a father. A combination of circumstantial evidence would enable the judge to decide if the judicially declared father should have visitation rights or other parental authority over the child. The judge and putative father could still call witnesses to testify about the woman's immorality. Nevertheless, the ability to use DNA testing as proof of a biological connection meant that the 1993 law minimized the five legal conditions specified in the 1912 version of article 340 for initiating a legal procedure. Written admissions of paternity, for example, had a lesser importance than a DNA test, but could still attest to an emotional attachment to the child. Biological paternity determined by genetics still differed from behavioral and emotional fatherhood, so the question of defining paternity outside of marriage was still open. However, with more certainty about biological paternity, some men may have used that evidence to exercise social fatherhood and become involved in their children's care, fueling the father's rights movements that have developed in France and elsewhere.

Change of the law in 1993 did not lead to an increase in paternity suits, with only 598 legal actions taken under the rubric of recherche de paternité for 1994, although that was almost triple the number from 1990, when there were only 212 cases. These data are, moreover, open to a variety of interpretations. An examination of paternity suits for the year immediately following passage of the law did not allow sufficient time for women to have filed their cases under the new law and have had the judges hear them to indicate a cause and effect between the law and behavior. Furthermore, women were having fewer unwanted pregnancies as a result of the development and dissemination of the birth control pill and the concomitant development of the French family planning movement. Of the approximately 200,000 children born in 1994 to unmarried parents, a vast proportion of them were no doubt born to couples in permanent relationships who chose to have children; the fathers may have recognized their children and provided for them without other legal action. Carbonnier maintains, however, that the law had an indirect importance belied by the small number of court cases. Because of the "fear of being brought to justice, a number of natural fathers [*pères naturels*] are motivated to voluntarily recognize their children.... One can no longer blame the narrowness of the legal grounds for initiating a case, but it is still necessary to take into account the ignorance and poverty of the natural mothers [*mères naturelles*]. Probably, many abandoned mothers find it repugnant to engage in a procedure that would give the deserting father some power over rearing the child."[39] Finally, as had been the case for at least two centuries, a mother first had to track down the putative father to initiate the legal procedure in his home area. Filing a suit for recherche de paternité remained a long, delicate, and costly process, not only requiring lawyers and depositions, just as in the 1920s and 1930s, but now also including costly genetic testing. The procedure could constitute an emotional and financial drain on women. With sufficient welfare and child support from her family and from the state, or earning sufficient income on her own to support herself and her child, a woman might find it hardly worth the effort to take the putative father to court to claim child support that she might never collect. But she might still go to court to claim a name and inheritance for the child, or the child might seek that identity as an adult, as Aurore Drossard did.

Despite the changes in 1993 allowing DNA evidence, the other requirements for a legal case were not so different from earlier in the twentieth century. The cumbersome legal conditions for initiating a paternity suit inherent in the 1912 and 1972 laws remained even after the passage of the 1993 law, although that law was intended to make the legal procedures easier. If the mother did not bring a suit for recherche de paternité in the name of her child within two years after childbirth, or after the end of concubinage or after child support ceased, the child might do so within two years of turning eighteen. If the putative father had died, legal action could be taken against his heirs. If the mother had died, or could not take legal action on behalf of the child, then the guardian authorized by the family council could bring the suit. If the father could prove the impossibility of paternity by reason of blood type, DNA, sterility, or distance from the mother during the probable time of conception, then the case was closed. If DNA or circumstantial evidence proved his paternity, then the judge could order him to pay child support until the child could live independently and to reimburse the mother for the cost of childbirth and for the six months comprising her pre- and postnatal care.

Since 1993, judges have continued to separate emotional and legal fatherhood from merely providing subsistence when they decide whether a child should bear the father's name and be entitled to inherit from him, or whether the father is merely a *père subsidant*. Lacking absolute proof of the man's paternity, but with sufficient indication of it, a judge could order the man to provide only child support. If the mother did not wish the courts to declare the man the father of the child, she could ask for only a monetary contribution to repair damages. Furthermore, a judge could judicially declare a man's paternity or he might deny the suit completely. This had not changed much from the earlier jurisprudence but was now authorized by law. The 1993 law differed from earlier legislation and jurisprudence in allowing a judicially declared father to obtain parental authority over a child he had once denied, and after he had failed to perform any fatherly duties. Fathers, whether they are or are not the mothers' husbands, have gained more power in rearing the children. When judges awarded such men paternal authority, it severely limited the authority of mothers, who had previously had sole parental authority over their natural children. As throughout the past, judges had a large amount of latitude in their decisions.[40]

A man could still contest paternity of a child born to his wife. The procedure for disavowal of paternity was not much different from earlier jurisprudence, except for the profound effect of DNA testing. Action had to be taken within six months of the child's birth, or of the husband's discovery of the birth (if the birth had been hidden from him) or within six months of his return if he had been away. A husband might also deny paternity of a child born before the 180th day of the marriage if he had not known of his wife's prior pregnancy or if he did not comport himself "as a father" after the birth. If his legal action to deny paternity were successful, the child would officially become a natural child, but if the mother remarried and her next husband was the biological father, the child then could become relegitimated. The intent of the law was to enable the biological father to be the true legal and affective father, eliminating one way in which paternity had been divisible between biology and emotion.

In twentieth-century culture, the courts and society continued to hold paternity divisible between full filiation with the father (based on firm proof, such as genetics) and just material support (when there were circumstantial indications of paternity but no absolute proof), if that was what the mother and child wanted. The divisibility of paternity between the purely biological and the more emotional became ever more unclear, especially in light of the new reproductive technologies. A sperm or egg donor is a biological parent, but those donors are often anonymous, and those directly rearing the resulting children wish that the donors remain unknown. The man who raises the child becomes the father, acting as a father, regardless of what the genetic tests reveal. Contemporary culture is trying to cope with the concept that a biological genitor may not be the father in terms of emotion and behavior, and that the man who has taken charge of rearing a child and his or her education can be a father even if he is not the genitor. Adoption procedures set the stage for accepting that the man who acts as a father may not, and need not, be the genitor. After 1972, and especially since 1993, French courts have used biology to determine the genitor, but they also have attributed paternity based on sentiment and behavior. Filiation rests not on natural ties or natural law, but has become an institution to create legal ties between individuals. In determining filiation and fatherhood, culture and courts recognized family constructions that differed from the heterosexual reproductive model.

Determining paternity has been complicated, and modern technology has not always made it easier. In one case from 1987, the male partner (*concubin*), who was sterile, wanted to have a child with his *concubine*, who already had three children by a former marriage. Fifteen months after the birth of the child by artificial insemination with donor sperm, the couple separated, and the woman returned to live with her former husband, taking her three older children with her, plus the little girl whom her *concubin* had wanted. Her former husband, who remarried her, legally recognized and legitimized the little girl, who was not genetically his. The *concubin*, who also was not the genetic father, brought an action to annul the recognition, and won his case, but he had to pay 100,000 francs to the girl and 20,000 francs to the mother, presumably for child support and the girl's education.[41] A donor sperm did not make the donor the father, nor did it make the sterile *concubin* the biological father. However, the *concubin* had wanted the child and had helped raise her for fifteen months, so the court recognized his emotional attachment. And, since he was declared the father, he had to contribute to supporting his daughter. On the other hand, the mother's husband, who was not the biological genitor of the child either, but who presumably would henceforth contribute to raising the child, was not the legal father. Thus new reproductive technologies have further transformed the relationship between biology and fatherhood; wanting the child and acting as a father plays an important role, similar to adoption. A new type of paternity belongs to a man who legally recognizes a child whom he knows is not his biological child. This interpretation of paternity privileges the more uncertain emotional connection over the proven biological one, but it is only one of many interpretations; others, and other magistrates, still privilege the biological.

The right to carry a father's name dominated paternity searches throughout the nineteenth and twentieth centuries, both reflecting and reinforcing the patriarchal nature of the family. The man controlled his name as the key to his honor, his property, and power. That right eventually extended to a man who was emotionally or legally attached to the child but was not the genitor. Women also gained control of their patronymics, demonstrating greater equality within a legal family. Starting with the law of 11 July 1975, a married woman could keep her own family name in marriage, especially if she had been known by that name professionally. This law also affected divorce reform by allowing a woman to maintain her ex-husband's name after divorce if she had been known by that name professionally and if she wished to have the same name as her children. The choice of whether to take her husband's name or keep her own increasingly belonged to the woman.[42]

Parents also had greater choice in naming their children. The law of 23 December 1985 relative to the equality of men and women in marriage let children hold the name of both their parents, with the mother's name added to the father's, if the parents wished. Naming, however, still had limitations. The hyphenated name was one a person could use but not transmit; only the father's name could be transmitted to the children. Natural children bore the mother's name if she was the first or only person to recognize the child legally. If the father later recognized the child, then both parents needed to make a joint declaration to an officer of the court to enable the child to bear the father's name as well as the mother's. If the child was over thirteen, he or she must consent. If both parents legally recognize the child at the same time, the child could have the name of the father, or of both parents, as in the case of legitimate children.[43] Naming rights followed social practice of the late twentieth century where both parents, in principle, shared in child rearing and child support. Adopted children, under adoption *plénière*, took the name of the person who adopted them, or that of the husband if a married couple adopted. With adoption *simple*, adoptees could keep their name and ties with their family of origin, but add the name of the adopting parent, which they had been doing since 1923. The law did not change the situation in names for adopted children.

Puissance paternelle underwent enormous changes from the late nineteenth century onward.[44] With the 1889 law permitting state authorities to deprive a father of his *puissance paternelle*, the paterfamilias model of the family gradually weakened, and parental authority became more shared. Language and law changed from *puissance paternelle* to *autorité parentale* (parental authority) by legislation of 4 June 1970. *Puissance*, literally translated as "power," is a stronger term than *autorité*, and *parentale* applies to both parents, whereas *puissance paternelle* was strictly a father's power, although single mothers who had legally recognized their natural children almost always had *puissance paternelle*, and in some circumstances married mothers could wield it, starting in 1889. A woman's right to carry her own patronymic or a child's rights to a mother's surname may have limited a man's marital and paternal authority, but a law of 22 July 1987 on the division of powers between mothers and fathers gave a man greater power than before regarding his extranuptial children. Prior to this law, mothers of natural children had sole legal parental authority if they had legally recognized those children before the fathers, which they likely did. This law of 1987, however, allowed for a division of parental authority over these children and reflected the increasing tendency for couples to live together in long-term consensual unions without a legal marriage, and the possibility that the father was also involved in child rearing. These children were not in the same category as the natural children of decades past, when they and their mothers, without the fathers, comprised their family. In 1987, as well as in 1887, children born of consensual unions could have lived with both parents in families that resembled conjugal families, or if they did not live with both parents, both parents might have been involved in their upbringing. Prior to 1987, however, even if a father had legally recognized his natural child, his legal authority had been limited to consent to the child's marriage. With the passage of the law of 1987, a divorced or separated father, or one from a union that was no longer consensual, could demand visitation rights, which jurisprudence had already awarded him in specific court cases. The law acknowledged that many divorced men wanted to help rear their children, and to avoid a lengthy judicial procedure, divorcing parents could simply declare in court that they would exercise joint parental authority. In practice, however, as in much of private family life, it all depended on agreements between fathers and mothers.

Legislative proposals and laws evolved rapidly, reflecting the social changes of the late twentieth century and the increased attention to children's rights. These rights changed from the "right to life," whereby each child once born had the right to sustenance and care that marked the depopulationist language so strong at the end of the nineteenth century, to a right of equality of citizenship for natural and legitimate children at the end of the twentieth century that echoed the language of the late eighteenth century and resonated with the failed socialist proposals for recherche de paternité at the end of the nineteenth century. Neither the law nor society focused on women who had been seduced and abandoned, but late twentieth-century legislative proposals recognized the vast number of children who were living with unmarried parents in a consensual union, estimating that one child in three was born of unmarried parents, and more than half of all children did not live with both their biological parents.[45] Mentioning the need to maintain social order, and acknowledging new reproductive technologies, deputies in the legislature introduced a measure that called for the inadmissibility of paternity or maternity searches in cases of medically assisted procreation with a donor.[46] Legislators have been thinking about families, paternity, and legitimacy in new ways for decades, if not centuries, but in the late twentieth century, legislation rapidly reflected new angles of vision and diverse family forms.

Many of the judicial and legislative changes resulted not from reproductive technologies and the surety of genetic testing, but from the movement for sexual equality and the prevalence of consensual unions without marriage. The law of 16 December 1997 removed distinctions between children born of a legally married couple and those born outside a legal marriage, and a law of 2005 eliminated the distinction between, and reference to, "natural" and "legitimate" children in the civil law.

The Pacte civil de solidarité (PACS)

The French family has evolved from a patriarchal heterosexual reproductive model to the recognition of single-parent families, usually consisting of a mother and child, to fictive families through adoption, and finally to legal recognition of domestic partnerships of same-sex or different-sex couples, recognizing the volition of individual women and men. Legislation of 15 November 1999 established the Pacte civil de solidarité (PACS) recognizing same-sex and different-sex domestic partnerships as a civil contract between two people who have reached their age of legal majority and are not tied by legal marriage to someone else. The campaign for the PACS was to legitimize and legalize heterosexual and homosexual consensual unions and centered on whether gay and lesbian couples could be families with rights to lineation. Loysel's aphorism "Boire, manger, coucher ensemble, c'est mariage ce me semble" became a rallying cry to legitimize both heterosexual and homosexual unions outside civil marriage. The law passed, with the support of the socialists, after almost a decade of debate on legal protection for homosexuals and recognition of gay and lesbian partnerships.[47] Sounding not dissimilar from judicial decisions during the twentieth century except for including same-sex couples, it acknowledged the legality and not just the social acceptance of concubinage among same-sex or different-sex couples, defining concubinage as "a union of fact, characterized by a life in common presenting the character of stability and continuity between two people of different or the same sex, who live as a couple." By the terms of the PACS, domestic partners can register their relationship before a representative of a lower court (*tribunal d'instance*), but not at the city hall as is done in marriage, and declare mutual material support. Couples declaring a PACS, who are sometimes known as *pacsés* or *pactisants*, cannot be related through the third degree and must have a common residence.[48] *Pacsés* have joint taxation and welfare benefits after three years together. Several articles of the Civil Code pertaining to taxes were amended, inserting after the reference to "spouse" the phrase "and the partners united by a civil pact of solidarity." The PACS also added significant phrases to the social security code, entitling the PACS partner to survivor's social security if no one else, such as a surviving spouse from whom the deceased PACS partner had not legally separated, or their children, invokes their priority within a determined time.[49] If the couple united by the PACS separates, they have to do so by an official declaration at the court where they registered their initial pact. If one partner ruptures the PACS unilaterally, the injured party can claim dommages-intérêts.

Although the PACS recognizes different family forms, it has significant limitations. In recognizing domestic partnerships, it stops short of recognizing them as equal to marriages conducted in local city halls; moreover, it denies lineation and filiation to these couples and may have delayed the consideration and acceptance of legal marriage among same-sex couples. The PACS allows for unions that are distinct from, and definitely far from equal to, what the Code considers legal marriage and legal families. Same-sex couples and other *pacsés* do not have the same rights as legally married couples in terms of inheritance and adoption. If they have children, there can be no joint custody if they separate, and they cannot jointly adopt unrelated children together; nor can one partner adopt the other's children. Rights to inheritance are another limitation. People united by the PACS may not inherit from each other like married spouses if one predeceases the other. Under French law, everyone can bequeath a portion of their property as they please, but its size depends on how many relatives they have and the nature of those relations. Although not referring to families formed by the PACS as "fictive," the law distinguishes PACS families from those united by legal marriage. The PACS (like laws pertaining to adoption and recherche de paternité) was intended to not impinge on the legal family's bloodline for inheritance; the legally married family is still protected, and the PACS partner is still an outsider to the inheritance lines.[50] Legal recognition of same-sex couples has *au fond* a relationship to filiation, which by denying filiation to homosexual couples, the law fails to address. Despite the enormous flaws in the PACS regarding filiation and adoption, and the fact that it is not a legal marriage, it legalized concubinage, both homosexual and heterosexual. French culture has come to accept differently constructed families in addition to the legally married heterosexual reproductive couple.

Marriage, paternity, and family structure are primarily determined by private intimate behavior, but are still legislated by the Civil Code and interpreted by the magistrates. Article 212, the first one the mayor reads at a marriage ceremony, states: "Spouses [*les époux*] owe each other mutual fidelity, aid, and assistance." The Code attempts to recognize modern society, and the terms *mari* (husband) and *femme* (wife) have been replaced by *époux/épouse* (spouse). Articles 214 and 215, which had stipulated that the wife must live with her husband, that she needs his authorization to deal with property and business, and that he is obliged to furnish her with the necessities of life, now read, "spouses are mutually obligated toward each other in a life in common. The family residence is where they have agreed." Legally married couples no longer have to live together and may have separate residences for professional reasons (article 108). Furthermore, children are the responsibility of both parents.[51]

The PACS may have temporarily closed the door to gay and lesbian marriages, but that door soon opened a crack, only to be rapidly slammed shut, but not locked and able to be reopened. Noël Mamère, the mayor of the small town of Bègles (Gironde), conducted a marriage for a same-sex couple on 5 June 2004. He, other members of the Green political party, the gay couple, and members of the gay community with their lawyers sought to redefine marriage and the family. They argued in universalist terms, much as did the advocates of the PACS, referring to universal marriage and not "gay" marriage. Two hours after the ceremony, however, opponents of "gay" marriage made a request to nullify the marriage, and less than a year later, in April 2005, the appeals court in Bordeaux annulled it.

The couple, the mayor, and their team of lawyers took their case to the European Court for the Rights of Man. In part, they based their case on the universality of marriage and on the grounds that the Civil Code did not specify the difference in sex as a condition for marriage, and on the adage "that which the Code does not forbid, it permits." Their opponents defined a legal marriage in terms of the specific union between a man and a woman to found a family. The European court determined that marriage is defined by each nation's laws. In 2006, 61 percent of the French population, according to one survey of 1,016 people over the age of fifteen, supported same-sex marriage, although only 35 percent of the French population approved of adoption by same-sex couples. On 21 June 2006, Ségolène Royal, a leading member of the Socialist party and its 2007 presidential candidate, herself at the time living in a domestic partnership without a civil marriage and the mother of four children, publicly took a stand supporting same-sex marriages, viewing it as an equal rights issue.[52]

⁂

At the beginning of the twenty-first century, a mother could decide if her husband was the father of her children. A mother outside a legal marriage could decide if she wanted the father to help support the child and how much. With DNA testing, she and the putative father would have greater certainty about biological paternity. A mother of natural children lost some power, however. Prior to 1985, if she legally recognized her child, she would have sole parental authority. The father who later legally recognized the child or who had paternity attributed to him by the courts did not have paternal authority, because, as the argument went, he had denied his parentage and had not provided for the child. At the end of the twentieth century, there was a presumption that the couple had shared an interest in the child, and if the father legally recognized the child, even subsequently to the mother, or even if she took him to court on paternity charges, he could still have paternal authority over that child; it became an authority that both mother and father could share.

Late twentieth-century laws, culture, and genetic testing made paternity less of a choice for a man than it had been previously; he could no longer so easily escape a paternity suit. Once the courts ascribed paternity to him, however, he had greater choice and opportunity to act as a father involved with the child both materially and emotionally. Roman, canon and Napoleonic law defined fatherhood as existing within conjugal marriage: "Pater is est quem nuptiae demonstrant." At the beginning of the twenty-first century, Gustave Rivet's 1910 modification of that maxim, "Pater est quem concubitus demonstrant," could also apply to men in heterosexual concubinage. In neither case does the law require the father to be the genitor, but it does require that the relationship be heterosexual.

Prior to the twenty-first century, three basic forms of parental attachment existed. The exemplar for most of the preceding centuries was "legitimate filiation," in which the mother and father of the child were married to each other and the father was defined as the mother's husband. A second form of filiation, "natural filiation," occurred when the parents were not married to each other at the time of conception. A child of such a couple could still be legitimized by subsequent marriage, or have filiation determined by a judicial declaration of paternity. The third form, filiation by adoption, formerly called fictive filiation, results purely from choice. Since

2005, however, all distinctions have been obliterated in France, and legitimate, natural, and adoptive children have the same rights; even the terms "legitimate" and "natural" are no longer part of civil law. After more than 200 years, the radical revolutionary goal for each child to have the same rights, whether of married or single parents, has finally been realized.

The nature of the family has changed, demonstrating the extreme elasticity of the institution as well as the concept. The base for more than half of all family constructions is no longer the legally married heterosexual reproductive couple. In 1965, only 6 percent of all births were to people in concubinage. Not all data are comparable, but in 1997, the proportion of births outside of marriage mushroomed. In urban areas, out-of-wedlock births exceeded 60 percent of the total, but it is not known how many were to parents living in concubinage.[53] Data for 2006 reveal that almost 60 percent of first children are born outside of marriage, and an estimated 50 percent of all births in France occur outside of marriage. Only Sweden, Norway, and Denmark have as high a percentage of children born outside of marriage.

Although legal marriage has remained a choice for many, by 2007, living as domestic partners was not just *faute de mieux*, with the implication that a legal marriage was better; it was their preferred choice. Because of the rapidity of changes in the last quarter of the twentieth century, in many ways there has been a silent revolution in marriage, paternity, and the family. But taken over the *longue durée*, and for all classes, it is an evolution that has been going on for more than a century. Concubinage, or a type of domestic partnership, has long been a way of life for many, especially the poor, but by the twenty-first century, it had become a way of life for some of all classes and sexual orientations, not just the poor and not just those of the political far Left who opposed legal marriage as a capitalist construction.

A century ago, concubinage was a failed marriage strategy for the poor. Women entered such relationships in the hope that when they had sufficient income, they would marry. At the beginning of the twenty-first century, for many couples, domestic partnerships are not pre-marriage arrangements but ends in themselves. As a result of this evolution of the family, the distinction between natural and legitimate children, so strongly ingrained in the Civil Code has been erased from French civil law. The PACS is an accepted and legal mode of conjugal life for heterosexual and homosexual couples. More than 40,000 PACS were signed in 2004, including both heterosexual and homosexual couples, and between 1999 and 2006, more than 500,000 people chose this type of union.[54]

What does that say about paternal responsibility and recherche de paternité? Recherche de paternité still exists, but often when the biological identity of the father is in doubt. When a woman now brings paternity charges, those suits resemble going to court against a former husband from a legal marriage to try to obtain child support. However, if the domestic partner has not recognized the child, a mother might first ask for recognition, and based on genetic testing, the judge may declare the man the father of the child and then order him to pay child support. But if the man wishes, and the judge agrees, he can also have some paternal authority over the child, which prior legislation denied him.

It is not surprising that the number of paternity suits has not increased: it is more likely that women would take their former domestic partner to court for child support, and not recherche de paternité, since he would have recognized children of a consensual union. Concubinage changed from being a marginal family form to one legally recognized. Recherche de paternité became less necessary with the greater acceptance of domestic partnerships, implying recognition of paternity, with increased available welfare, and with contraception allowing women some control over the results of their sexuality activity.

Epilogue

The concept of paternity varies by time, place, and culture, and it remains problematic, complex, and personal in the Western world. Since the eighteenth century, sometimes gradually and sometimes in giant leaps and bounds, the legal, social, and cultural acceptance of a variety of family arrangements has successfully challenged the patriarchal heterosexual reproductive family that had tended to dominate society, culture, and the law. Consensual unions without a legal marriage, and families consisting of only a mother and children—along with a variety of other family arrangements—have become widely accepted in France as well as elsewhere in Europe and in the United States. Despite this reconceptualization of fatherhood and families, early in the twenty-first century, paternity still remains very much contested, and we are still considering the question of what constitutes paternity and fatherhood, especially outside of marriage. With genetic testing available since the end of the twentieth century, the debate has added dimensions, raising new questions about the biological and social aspects of paternity. Is paternity still based on acting as a father, even if the man is not genetically tied to the child? If a man has the same DNA as the child, does that make him a father if he does not take part in the child's life?

Lawyers in modern France appear to remain sanguine about biology as the fundamental basis of filiation; they presume that the mother's husband is the biological father of the child, just as they have been doing for the past 200 years. Seeing no apparent contradiction, they also admit that affection and acting as a father is another foundation of paternity, as they had been doing for about as long. The situation is less complicated because of genetic testing, but also more complex because of medical interventions with sperm donors, and the desire of men to be fathers, whether biological or not. There is still a great yearning on the part of women and children to know the biological progenitor and perhaps make him financially responsible, and for men to know if they are the biological fathers. With adoption and the use of sperm banks, paternity belongs to the men who rear the children, but some adopted children still want to know their biological progenitor, and fathers and children still desire some emotional relationship. Moreover, in custody battles some genitors seek recognition as the father, resulting in a social father sometimes losing custody of a child because of a legal challenge from the biological father based on a court-ordered genetic paternity test. Movements for fathers' rights have developed in which men seek more connections with their children, whether genetic or not. In battles over biological paternity and affectionate fatherhood, biology tends to be dominant in France, although magistrates still interpret the law in individual cases.[1]

Recherche de paternité remains a contemporary issue, not only in France, but also in the United States, where television programs feature contested paternity. Talk shows bring young people on stage asking, "Who's the father?" and these paternity searches contain all the elements of popular television: mystery, medicine, power, trauma, honor, sex, and love. Daytime television talk shows devoted to finding fathers have a large audience. On these programs, the host announces the results of genetic paternity testing; if the tests exonerate a man, he often jumps with joy and the young woman leaves the stage in tears. Or a different man may quietly, and even happily, accept his paternity. Why would people appear on such a show, making their intimate lives so public? Their reasons are similar to those of many women who have been going to court in France for over two centuries. Women who participate on these television shows looking for the genitor of their children risk humiliation, but they do it for their fifteen minutes of fame, the free DNA tests that the shows provide, and to seek child support and an identity for their children. These are not courts, however, and no judge can obligate the man to pay or provide a name. It is up to him to honor his responsibility. Many women who filed paternity suits in France may have resembled "Jenny, a 24-year-old single mother ... [who] said she had two children and wanted to know which of two former boyfriends was the father of the youngest. Unemployed, evicted from her apartment, Jenny said she had no place else to turn. 'I have nothing to hide,' she said when asked if she had any qualms about appearing on national television. 'But I wouldn't want people to look down on me as some kind of slut. I was just too trusting and too lonely.'"[2] In nineteenth- and twentieth-century France, men and women probably entered into sexual relations for much the same reasons they do in the twenty-first century—trust, loneliness, love, security, hope, fun, and a myriad of other reasons. Unlike Jenny, however, women of the past two centuries did not directly leave historians their own words about their relationships, except through the prism of the court records.

Newspapers in the United States frequently report on court cases involving paternity and genetic testing. When DNA testing demonstrated that the children of a man's wife were not genetically his, courts in states as diverse as Texas and Massachusetts have ordered those men to continue paying child support for those children.[3] These courts determined that in the interest of the children, fatherhood was social and not biological; the men had been acting as fathers and should continue their support. In the past, although paternity was contested, maternity was not. Genetics and reproductive technologies can now redefine motherhood as well as fatherhood. The Maryland court of appeals ruled that if a gestational carrier using donated eggs does not want to rear the children she delivers, the court cannot require her to have a legal, material, or emotional relationship to those children. The chief judge declared that if a man can refuse to be a father, a woman can refuse to be a mother.[4] Laws to define paternity could now apply to maternity. There could be an *x* on the birth certificate in place of the mother's name, as has been permitted in France for over half a century. The public's fascination with stories of private lives involving sexual activity is not unique to the early twenty-first century in the United States.

For at least the past two hundred years, French journalists and their readers have also been fascinated with the private lives of individuals, revealing salient, if not salacious, details of people's innermost private family lives, pushing the boundaries of the rights to privacy. Not only did the *Gazette des tribunaux* report almost daily on civil proceedings, but other newspapers, such as *Le Matin*, carried similar sensational stories intriguing readers with sex, seduction, paternity, morality, power, honor, and the rights of individuals. With the topic of recherche de paternité, the broadest range of the French public—the courts, the press, the community, and the laws—embraced the innermost private sphere of the family. Moreover, the private sphere of the family spread out into the broad range of the French community, demonstrating the ill-defined and permeable borders between public and private and revealing changing ideas about paternity and the family throughout modern France.

The differences in France between the nineteenth century and the late twentieth century are significant. First, the law of 1912 permitting recherche de paternité did more than end the age of paternal irresponsibility begun by the Civil Code in 1804. It ushered in a new stage in the history of the family by recognizing a consensual union as a family form resembling marriage. The heterosexual reproductive family remained the ideal, but behavior, culture, and the law recognized new family forms. Second, the fertility rate continued to decline, suggesting that men and women were consciously trying to avoid births. Starting in the 1960s, oral contraception and then other means of contraception became available to women, resulting in fewer unwanted pregnancies; and when contraception fails or is not used, abortion is now legal as backup. Third, welfare provides partial support for a mother and child, requiring less frequent recourse to paternity suits out of dire economic need, but not eliminating them for providing a biological identity, a name, and some emotional and material support. Fourth, proving paternity, or, more correctly, the progenitor, has become less difficult with the advent of genetic testing. Fifth, consensual unions are more widespread and acceptable among all social and economic classes; in cases of domestic separation, women are more likely to file for child support and less likely to initiate a paternity search, although both men and women frequently resort to DNA testing to prove or disprove paternity and resulting responsibility. Because of the expense of genetic testing and associated court costs, however, paternity suits are a socially differential option, usually more available to the rich than to the poor, just as was the case in previous centuries. Finally, there has been a revalorization of paternity, which may make men more inclined to accept paternal responsibilities, within and outside a legal marriage, either out love, of a sense of honor, or as demonstration of their masculinity.

Associating paternity with masculinity and honor is not new. Masculinity, like paternity, is a shifting concept, depending on time, place and culture, and is manifested in many ways.[5] In 1804, virility was an identifier of masculinity, at least according to some writers and politicians, but virility did not equal paternity unless the man was married to the mother; a man did not have to behave as a father to his children. Starting with the aftermath of World War I, virility was again strongly associated with masculinity, but was also increasingly associated with paternity; "being a man" could involve providing for children. Toward the end of the twentieth century, some men may have more readily accepted responsibility for their children outside of marriage—evidence of a new, more sensitive masculinity. Although paternity may have limited men's individual freedoms and created financial burdens, it extended their spheres of authority. Men had long held power in public arenas and in conjugal families, but acting as fathers provided them with more authority in different family forms, sometimes to the chagrin of women who lost sole authority over their children in single-parent or nonconjugal families. Men's concepts of their rights and duties were changing, with more emphasis on emotional engagement with their children, as well as on being good providers. As a result, legislative changes of the 1980s allowed divorced and separated fathers to have greater visitation rights and authority over their children's everyday lives and education. Men now can receive parental leave in France and the United States, as well as in Germany, Italy, Britain, Spain, Portugal, Denmark, Finland, and Sweden—and they do not have to be legally married. Moreover, fathers in some of the European Union member nations and the United States can have parental leave when adopting.[6] Adoption by women or men in same-sex couples is not generally possible, but gay and lesbian couples find new ways to construct extended families when lesbians have children authored by gay men and those men continue some involvement in the children's lives.[7] Countless other men, however, often called "deadbeat dads" evade any financial or emotional responsibility for their children, abandoning both mother and child. Such men leave no trace for their families, or for historians. We see these men by their absence, in the hardships divorced and abandoned women face in what is called "the feminization of poverty."

An epilogue affords some room for speculation. A brief glance at religion, public policy, feminism, property, and class provides a sweeping backdrop for placing changes in paternity and the family in a very broad context.

Inasmuch as marriage is a Catholic sacrament, and living together without the blessing of clergy is a sin in Catholic dogma, the fewer people who avidly follow the Catholic Church's teachings, the fewer who are likely to believe in the sanctity of marriage as prescribed by the Church, and the more who are likely to accept a variety of other family forms. It is thus of some significance that the Church has declined in power in France since the Revolution, both politically and as a force in people's lives, although this decline has been neither universal nor consistent, affecting urban more than rural populations. Three hundred years earlier, Loysel may have found it necessary to add "mais il faut que l'Église y passe" to his aphorism, "Boire, manger, coucher ensemble, c'est mariage ce me semble," but by the twentieth century, Church approval of private life and loves was becoming irrelevant for many.

Since the Revolution, the state has required a civil marriage; a Church wedding has become optional. From 1815 through the 1870s, the power of the Church and clergy waxed and waned, with their principles of sexual morality influencing behavior and court decisions in varying degrees during this time. The Third Republic became outwardly secular and anticlerical, leading to a decline in the power of the Church. The influence of the Catholic Church rebounded under Vichy, and then went into another decline. People may consider themselves Catholic, but Church teachings about sexuality and reproduction do not always affect their daily lives. With a change in religiosity and an increase in secularism in France, moral judgments of the community and family also shifted. It is risky to speculate about whether behavior set the tone for transformations of moral judgments, or if changing moral judgments allowed for behavioral alterations. It is possible that the increasing acceptance of consensual unions reflects the declining power of organized religion in people's lives.

Family formation and paternity in some respects have reverted back to a version of premodern rural marriages, sometimes called broomstick marriages, in which a couple established a marital relationship by jumping over a broomstick, sometimes just a symbolic one, a type of wedding ritual without benefit of clergy or the courts, but with full community knowledge. In Beaumarchais's play and the Mozart opera *The Marriage of Figaro*, Susanna and Figaro are married when the count places a wreath on Susanna's head with local peasants and nobility as witnesses. In the twenty-first century, as in earlier times, couples may live together in a consensual union for many years without a legal marriage. People in the English-speaking world sometimes refer to these relationships as common-law marriages, which in some jurisdictions are legally binding. This relationship could become problematic, however, in terms of paternity, inheritance, and property settlements when the relationship ends, either by separation or by death.

Some goals of the French Revolution took a long time to achieve. At the turn of the twenty-first century, few of the old stigmas of illegitimacy apply, with legal differences obliterated between children that had formerly been designated as legitimate or illegitimate. Government officials in Europe see "very little difference between being married and cohabiting, and very little difference between children born out of wedlock and those that are born within marriage." In Norway, 49 percent of all births at the turn of the twenty-first century took place outside of marriage. In France, the figure was 41 percent, in Britain 38 percent, and in Ireland about 31 percent. Demographers estimate that these are children born to couples in consensual unions.[8]

Raisons d'état also contributed to social change. With the development of a secular state at the end of the nineteenth century came a heightened sense of nationalism and increased interest in the quantity and quality of the French population. In the state's efforts to increase the number and well-being of the nation's children, the place of paternity became paramount in propaganda and laws. If fathers bore more responsibility for their children, both financially and emotionally, many government officials argued, those children would live longer and healthier lives. For men, having children and supporting them not only became a sign of virility, but also a means to defend their nation. Although elements of the state's apparatus affected the intimate affairs of French families throughout the nineteenth and twentieth centuries, this does not imply social control by a hegemonic state. As this book has shown, women as well as men displayed independence and agency. Moreover, state involvement in private lives was exceedingly nuanced, accomplished by broad laws, a powerful judiciary, and community pressure. In the final analysis, private matters depended on the will of individuals; only when those relationships went awry did they resort to the public spaces of the courts. Judges and legislators may have had the preservation of their vision of moral and social order on their agenda, but they also constructed their decisions and redesigned laws according to some behavioral norms. Power rested with the judges, but also with individuals who "escaped the rules of jurisprudence."[9]

Both the "first wave" of feminism at the end of the nineteenth century and the "second wave" in the late 1960s and 1970s contributed to changes in state policy, society, and culture in France by furthering the rights of women in speech and actions. Perhaps emboldened by feminism, women exercised some rights of autonomy (albeit often initially either as victims or as mothers and not generally as empowered individuals without reference to gender) by filing paternity suits and demanding reparations. At the end of the twentieth century, feminists argued for equality in the law, the workplace, and the family. Since French women were citizens, universal concepts of being French applied. Recognizing a French universalism, however, involved dealing with a contradiction involving sexual differences, as Joan Scott has argued.[10] Gender relations and their destabilization were fundamental to achieving greater equality for women and for French citizens regardless of gender or sexual orientation. In the pursuit of equality, single mothers had to give up their right to have the sole *puissance parentale*, now referred to as *autorité parentale*, sharing it with the fathers, in return for child support and paternal filiation.

This book opened with an insistence that protection of family property had been a mainstay of men's rights, status, and honor; the paterfamilias had to preserve the legacy for his bloodline, and fathers feared dispersal of their property to those they considered outside their bloodline.[11] Family alliances by marriage established that lineage. Michel Foucault aptly observed that the "deployment of alliance" as a "system of marriage, of fixation and development of kinship ties, of transmission of names and possessions . . . lost some of its importance as economic processes and political structures could no longer rely on it as an adequate instrument or sufficient support."[12] With the decline of marriage as a sacrament, and with the transformations in capitalism, the role of family property in paternity diminished. As the agrarian economy developed into an urban and service economy, family property became less symbolic as a signifier of status. On a more practical level, men no longer sought to avoid dividing that property among many children; lineal blood inheritance became less critical and the rules of marriage and family formation less stringently based on blood.[13] With the transmission of both land and moveable property assuming less importance in family formation and alliances, men came to insist less on the purity of their families. By the twentieth century, the practice of living in a consensual union, which had long been a staple born of economic necessity for urban working-class families, had become socially acceptable to members of the French middle and upper classes.

In the postindustrial world of the late twentieth century, comportment became important in determining a man's status, and comportment came to include acknowledging and fulfilling paternal responsibilities. This shift did not happen overnight, but resulted in part from state propaganda urging men to do their duty to the nation to produce more and healthier children. It also may have resulted from the women's movement fostering equality within families. Men, too, may have come to realize some of the pleasures of child rearing. In an increasingly child-centered environment, providing for children assumed a major place in people's lives, as well as in the popular press and government pronouncements. Sensitivities of the late twentieth century, starting with the feminist and civil rights movements of the 1960s, also included attention to child rearing and child support, both within and outside of legal marriage. Advances in biology and medicine, including genetic testing and contraception also made the bloodline more certain and the determination less dependent on a woman's behavior. It is ironic that as blood relationships have become more determinable, their significance with regard to the meaning of fatherhood has declined in some cases.

The designers of the 1804 French Civil Code highly valued paternity within marriage and excoriated women who had children outside of marriage. Basing their argument on the premise that conjugal families were the moral and institutional building blocks of the state, and that marriage alone determined paternity, they opposed paternity searches. During the nineteenth century, judges obeyed the letter of the law, finding ways to protect marriage by dividing paternity between filiation and child support. Almost a century after the promulgation of the Civil Code, a different notion of the relationship between the state and the family had developed, in part taking into account the years of judicial decisions. Conjugality was still the cornerstone of the nation, but legislators, as part of the new state paternalism, attempted to balance the protection of married men and their families with a new commitment to protecting children, even if that meant reducing paternal authority and men's independence. Women succeeded in using the 1912 law to their advantage throughout the twentieth century, continuing to stretch the law as they had been doing during the nineteenth century. People's relationships, families, sexuality and independence were too important to submit to the written law. When the law did not accord with morality and with how people lived their lives, they ignored or transgressed the letter of the law.

Two centuries after the promulgation of the Civil Code, the heterosexual reproductive family is no longer the cornerstone of the state edifice. As this book was going to press, Nicholas Sarkozy, the president of France, and his wife, Cécilia, divorced. Elaine Sciolino, the *New York Times*'s principal reporter in France explained that the "sang-froid" of the French regarding the issue is "partly that the French no longer treat marriage as a particularly sacred institution." The marriage rate in France has declined more than 30 percent in the past generation, she noted, and nearly one out of two marriages now ends in divorce.[14] New family types (consensual unions, single parent, and reconstituted) are providing the foundation in the other three corners. This book has ended on a note indicating a decline in the patriarchal conjugal family, a greater acceptance of alternative family forms, an increased paternal responsibility to children, a society more tolerant of differences, and definitions of paternity still in flux. These changes have not come without a struggle on the part of men and women, on both the private and public levels, and there is no reason to believe that they are universal or permanent or that the struggles are over.

NOTES

Abbreviations

AAP	Archives de l'Assistance publique
AJ	Assistance judiciaire
AN	Archives nationales de France
Arch. Paris	Archives de la Ville de Paris et Département de la Seine
BHVP	Bibliothèque historique de la Ville de Paris
BMD	Bibliothèque Marguerite Durand
GT	*Gazette des tribunaux*
JO	*Journal officiel de la République française*

Introduction

1. The Civil Code as well as the revisions in 1912 referred to paternity searches as *recherche de la paternité*. I have throughout used the modern term *recherche de paternité*. Some others may refer to it as *recherche en paternité*. It is a matter of style. All translations in this book are mine unless otherwise indicated.

2. Henri-Edmond-Pierre Dufaure de Gavardie, *Journal officiel: Débats parlementaires, Débats du Sénat*, special session, 11 December 1883, 1447.

3. Ariès and Duby, general eds., *A History of Private Life*, vol. 4, ed. Perrot, and vol. 5, ed. Prost and Vincent; Kertzer and Barbagli, eds., *Family Life in the Long Nineteenth Century*. In addition to these edited volumes on the history of the family, French historians have contributed to our understanding of the private life of women of the bourgeoisie. Martin-Fugier, *La Bourgeoise*; id., *La Vie élégante*; Sohn, *Chrysalides*.

4. Delumeau and Roche, eds., *Histoire des pères et de la paternité* is the most complete. See esp. chap. 11, "La Volonté d'un homme," by Jacques Mulliez, devoted to recherche de paternité, particularly during the Revolution. See also Knibiehler, *Les Pères aussi ont une histoire*. For new work on fathers and paternity, see Childers, *Fathers, Families and the State in France, 1914–1945*, and Judith Surkis's original book, *Sexing the Citizen*, which problematizes men and masculinity within the framework of the conjugal couple.

5. Lucey, *The Misfit of the Family*, 4.

6. In discussions of the law, the works of André-Jean Arnaud have greatly influenced me. See esp. *Essai d'analyse structurale du Code civil français* and *Les Origines doctrinales du Code civil français*.

7. Certeau, *The Practice of Everyday Life*, xi–xiv, 125. Italics in the original.

8. Bourdieu, *The Logic of Practice*, 132.

9. Foucault, *The History of Sexuality*, 1: 58, 63–67, 86, 93–95, 106.

10. Surkis, *Sexing the Citizen*, 2–3. For an important vision of judicial archives, see Natalie Zemon Davis's now classic *Fiction in the Archives*.

11. Judith Butler's work, esp. her books *Gender Trouble* and *Undoing Gender*, opened my eyes to the complicated issue of gender performance. Although my book is scarcely a biography or even a prosopography, theoretical concepts inherent in the "new biography" are relevant. See Accampo, *Blessed Motherhood, Bitter Fruit*; Berlanstein, *Daughters of Eve*; Margadant, ed., *The New Biography*.

12. Roberts, *Disruptive Acts*, 3, 5.

13. The classic and exemplary study of masculinity in France is Nye, *Masculinity and Male Codes of Honor in Modern France*. See esp. chap. 4. Other important works include Forth, *The Dreyfus Affair*; Maugue, *L'Identité masculine en crise*, and Rauch, *Crise de l'identité masculine, 1789–1914*.

14. Foucault, *The History of Sexuality*, 1: 120.

One • Families and the Social Order from the Old Regime to the Civil Code

1. France was not unique in this view of women's chastity. As Samuel Johnson said, "Consider, of what importance to society the chastity of women is. Upon that all the property in the world depends. We hang a thief for stealing a sheep; but the unchastity of a woman transfers sheep, and the farm and all, from the right owner. I have much more reverence for a common prostitute than for a woman who conceals her guilt. The prostitute is known. She cannot deceive: she cannot bring a strumpet into the arms of an honest man, without his knowledge." James Boswell, *The Journal of a Tour to the Hebrides with Samuel Johnson, LL.D.* (1785), www.gutenberg.org/etext/6018 (accessed 1 September 2007).

2. Fournel, *Traité de la séduction*, 5–7; Vigarello, *A History of Rape*.

3. Fournel, *Traité de la séduction*, 305, 336.

4. Hanley, "The Jurisprudence of the Arrêts," 1–40. *Rapt de séduction* disappeared from the legal categories during the Revolution and was replaced by *enlèvement*, or abduction.

5. Robert-Joseph Pothier (1699–1772), a prominent legal scholar whose treatises helped form the opinions of those writing the Civil Code, argued that *rapt de séduction* was an impediment to marriage, especially when the woman was seduced by fraud, bad faith, or violence. Pothier, *Traité du contrat de mariage*.

6. Ibid., 1: 187, 241, 247, 249, 258, 268. From 1556 to 1792, the age of majority was thirty for men and twenty-five for women.

7. Farr, "Parlementaires and the Paradox of Power," 326–27, 343 (slightly modified). See also Haase-Dubosc, *Ravie et enlevée*.

8. Dabert, *De la responsabilité civile du séducteur;* Pothier, *Traité du contrat de mariage,* 187; Pothier, *Œuvres complètes,* 10: 185, on *rapt,* and 41–44, on dommages-intérêts for breaking a marriage promise.

9. Fournel, *Traité de la séduction,* 61

10. Phan, "La Séduction impunie," 53–55; Millet, *La Séduction,* iii–22; I am variously translating *dommages-intérêts* as "compensation," "damages," or "reparations."

11. Pothier, *Œuvres complètes,* 10: 25, 42–44, 73; Garaud and Szramkiewicz, *La Révolution française et la famille,* 44–47.

12. Fournel, *Traité de la séduction,* 61, 118.

13. For the *déclarations de grossesse,* see Fairchilds, "Female Sexual Attitudes and the Rise of Illegitimacy," 627–67; Phan, *Les Amours illégitimes;* Demars-Sion, *Femmes séduites,* 111–70; Grimmer, *La Femme et le bâtard,* 200–207.

14. Phan, *Les Amours illégitimes,* chap. 1; Demars-Sion, *Femmes séduites,* 50–55.

15. Fillon, *Les Trois bagues aux doigts* contains fascinating tales of seduction, love, and marriage.

16. Farge, *Fragile Lives,* chap. 3, esp. 31–33.

17. Garaud and Szramkiewicz, *La Révolution française et la famille,* 63.

18. Fournel, *Traité de la séduction,* 12, 27.

19. Pothier, *Traité du contrat de mariage,* 322; Phan, *Les Amours illégitimes,* 80.

20. Fournel, *Traité de la séduction,* 91. Legislators two centuries later echoed these sentiments. See Chapter 6.

21. Ibid., 28.

22. Demars-Sion, *Femmes séduites,* 67, 85.

23. Phan, *Les Amours illégitimes,* 44, 47; Demars-Sion, *Femmes séduites,* 187–89, 286–96, 413.

24. Fournel, *Traité de la séduction,* 119; Demars-Sion, *Femmes séduites,* 334–35.

25. Phan, *Les Amours illégitimes,* 55.

26. Fournel, *Traité de la séduction,* 31, 32, 36, 48, 50.

27. Farr, "Parlementaires and the Paradox of Power," 343; Phan, *Les Amours illégitimes,* 80.

28. Lynn Hunt discusses the "band of brothers" during the Revolution in her *The Family Romance of the French Revolution;* Nye, *Masculinity and Male Codes of Honor,* 45–54; quotation from Desan, *The Family on Trial,* 211; Demars-Sion, *Femmes séduites,* 396–402.

29. These data pertain only to the town of Cambrai and might reflect the personalities of the local magistrates. Demars-Sion, *Femmes séduites,* 381. The analysis of gift giving derives from Godelier, *L'Énigme du don.*

30. Berthe and Langre, eds., *Maximilien Robespierre,* 39, 68–70, 80–83.

31. Brinton, *French Revolutionary Legislation,* 8.

32. Garaud and Szramkiewicz, *La Révolution française et la famille,* 48–50.

33. Grimmer, *La Femme et le bâtard,* 161–63.

34. A "recognized" illegitimate child refers to someone whose father took legal action to claim the child as his child, and who acknowledged paternity on the child's birth certificate, either shortly after birth or at a later date. Mothers also could, and often did, legally recognize their natural children.

35. Kelley, *Historians and the Law in Postrevolutionary France*, 127–28.

36. Boudouard and Bellivier, "Des droits pour les bâtards," 122–44; Foriers and Perelman, "Natural Law and Natural Rights," 13–17; Tuck, "The 'Modern' Theory of Natural Law," 99–119. Jean-Jacques-Régis de Cambacérès, a lawyer from Montpellier, was the most influential person in framing family legislation during the entire period from 1791 to 1804. Oudot was the Jacobin deputy from the Côte d'Or.

37. Brinton, *French Revolutionary Legislation*, 31, citing *Archives parlementaires*, Cambacérès's speech of 4 June 1793, 66: 34–36, and Berlier's speech of 9 August 1793, 70: 654.

38. Brinton, *French Revolutionary Legislation*, 23, citing *Archives parlementaires*, 24: 497–98 (1 April 1791).

39. For more on the law of 1791 see Desan, *The Family on Trial*, 181–85.

40. Gouges, *Écrits politiques*, 1: 208. Article XI of the *Déclaration des droits de la femme et de la citoyenne*, September 1791. "*Je suis mère d'un enfant qui vous appartient*, sans qu'un préjugé barbare la force à dissimuler la verité; sauf à répondre de l'abus de cette liberté dans les cas déterminés par la loi" (italics in original). Second quotation from p. 211. Last quotation from p. 212.

41. They invoked Roman law, which stated "Pater is est quem nuptiae demonstrant." The legal historian André-Jean Arnaud has demonstrated that the editors of the Civil Code, especially Cambacérès, were familiar with the principles of Grotius, Pufendorf, and their successors in the modern school of natural law. Arnaud, "La Référence à l'école du droit naturel moderne," 3–10.

42. Cambacérès, *Rapport sur le Code civil, fait au nom du Comité de législation*, 2–3. This was his second draft of the Civil Code. Murat, "La Puissance paternelle et la Révolution française," 93. For more on Cambacérès's ideas of natural law and how they related to individualism and property, see Jean Bart, "L'Individu et ses droits," 352–53; Boudouard and Bellivier, "Des droits pour les bâtards," 125–27.

43. Boudouard and Bellivier, "Des droits pour les bâtards," 123.

44. Cambacérès, *Projet de décret sur les enfants naturels*, 1–7; id., *Nouveau rapport…concernant les enfants nés hors le mariage*, 1–5; id., *Rapport sur le Code civil, fait au nom du Comité de législation*. For the opposition, see *Opinion du citoyen Berlier…à la Convention nationale sur les droits à restituer aux enfants nés hors du mariage*, 19, 29–34.

45. Cambacérès quoted in BMD, DOS 347 PAT, document 14. Chambre des Députés, No. 796, session of 1911, report by Maurice Viollette, appendix to the proceedings of the meeting of 27 February 1911; Nicoleau, "De la preuve judiciaire," 70.

46. Cambacérès, *Projet de décret sur les enfants naturels*, 1–7; id., *Nouveau rapport sur les articles…concernant les enfants nés hors le mariage*, quotation from p. 4. See also his *Rapport sur le Code civil, fait au nom du Comité de législation*. Desan, *The Family on Trial*, 205–12, and chap. 5, has the most detailed and clear analysis of this law.

47. Dalloz, *Recueil périodique et critique*, Quatrième partie, Lois et décrets, rapports et discussions législatives, 113. Emphasis added.

48. Berlier quoted in Desan, *The Family on Trial*, 209.

49. Emphasis added. Cambacérès was not alone in 1792 and 1793 in arguing for equality between legitimate and illegitimate children. He was supported by petitions and by arguments from several others, most notably from Charles-François Oudot. See Ronsin, *Le Contrat*

sentimental, 143–45; Garaud and Szramkiewicz, *La Révolution française et la famille*, 116–30; Oudot, *Essai sur les principes de la législation des mariages privés et solennels*, 13–15; Traer, *Marriage and the Family in Eighteenth-Century France*, 154–56.

50. Dalloz, *Les Codes annotés... nouveau Code civil*, 639. Fewer than six months before this 12 brumaire decree, a decree of 28 June 1793 called for a hospital in each major city that would allow mothers secretly to leave their natural children, considered *enfants naturel de la patrie*, to a foundling home. The decree also promised aid to the mothers if they needed it, but they were not allowed to name the putative father. Hospitals accepted foundlings, but no aid was provided to the mothers for almost a hundred years.

51. *Adresse à la Convention nationale, au nom d'une infinité de pères & mères chargés de familles* (Newberry pamphlet series Case FRC 131), 3–4, 6, 8, 12, 14–15. Of the fifty names listed, many had the same surname and seem to have been members of the same family.

52. Ibid.

53. They reversed Rousseau's assertion that "instead of saying that civil society is derived from paternal authority, we ought to say rather that the latter derives its principal force from the former." Rousseau, "A Discourse on a Subject Proposed by the Academy of Dijon: What Is the Origin of Inequality Among Men, and Is It Authorized by Natural Law?" 103; Boudouard and Bellivier, "Des droits pour les bâtards," 137. In part, protection of alleged fathers of natural children was to protect young unmarried men who might themselves have been victims of paternal pressure. See Desan, *The Family on Trial*, chap. 7.

54. Cambacérès, *Rapport sur le Code civil, fait au nom du Comité de législation*, 2, 5, 6.

55. Ibid.

56. Cambacérès, *Projet de Code civil présenté au Conseil des Cinq-Cents au nom de la commission de la classification des lois*, 4–7. He had struggled with these tensions since the year II. Cambacérès, *Rapport sur le Code civil fait au nom du Comité de législation*; Mulliez, "'Pater is est...': La Source juridique de la puissance paternelle," 412–31. His source for this is Fenet, *Recueil complet des travaux préparatoires du Code civil*, vol. 5, session of 29 fructidor an X, 81, 113–15.

57. Cambacérès, *Projet de Code civil présenté au Conseil des Cinq-Cents*, 10; Desan, *The Family on Trial*, chap. 7.

58. Brinton, *French Revolutionary Legislation*, 52, quoting Antoine Bergier, *Opinion sur la question... des enfans naturels*, Conseil des Cinq-Cents (Paris, 1798), 6.

59. Cases come from Douarche, *Les Tribunaux civils de Paris pendant la Révolution (1791–1800)*, 1: clxiii–clxv. I thank Suzanne Desan for telling me about this reference.

60. Ibid., 1: clxiv–clxix, 669–71. For their part, the Dantonists evidently objected to being associated with this *fripon*. Chabot is quoted as exclaiming: "What is my law? You ask? I answer: the natural law, the one that says: Poor people, go after the rich; girls, go after the boys. Obey all your instincts [Quelle est ma loi? demanderez-vous? Je réponds, la loi naturelle, celle qui dit: pauvres, allez chez les riches, filles, allez avec les garçons. Obéissez à tous vos instincts]," www.royet.org/nea1789-1794/notes/acteurs/chabot.htm (accessed 17 October 2007). My many thanks to Peter Dreyer for discovering this quotation.

61. Gager, *Blood Ties and Fictive Ties*.

62. Gutton, *Histoire de l'adoption*, 45–50, 72, 80–84. I address the concept of adoption as a gift exchange more fully in Chapter 5.

63. Berthe and Langre, *Maximilien Robespierre*, 23, 40, 46, 48–49; quotation from p. 40.

64. Azema, *Rapport et projet de loi sur l'adoption*; Berlier, *De l'adoption*; Gutton, *Histoire de l'adoption*, 108–9.

65. For a discussion of the metaphor of the nation as father, see Heuer, *The Family and the Nation*, 90–98.

66. Oudot, *Essai sur les principes de la législation des mariages privés... et de l'adoption*, 7, 13, 16, 17.

67. Mulliez, "'*Pater is est...*': La Source juridique de la puissance paternelle," 418–23.

68. Cambacérès, *Rapport sur le Code civil fait au nom du Comité de législation*; id., *Rapport fait à la Convention nationale sur le premier projet du Code civil*, 9 August 1793. He wrote that adoption "corrects the errors of nature." Also quoted in Ewald, ed., *Naissance du Code civil*, 241–42. Ewald and his collaborators edited and wrote introductions to a selection of documents. They thematically extracted the documents from Pierre-Antoine Fenet's multivolume compilation of debates and proposals leading to the Civil Code. I have maintained the pronoun "his" and references to fathers and sons because the legislators always used the male pronoun and referred to men and boys, not to mothers and girls. Relations between a mother and child escape mention because the natural attachment of mother and child did not interfere with men's liberty.

69. Cambacérès, *Rapport sur le Code civil fait au nom du Comité de législation*, 3–4.

70. Desan, *The Family on Trial*, chaps. 5–9.

71. The redactors of the Civil Code included Cambacérès, who had become less radical than he had been in 1793 and 1794, and Napoleon who intervened on certain family issues. Others were Jean-Étienne Marie Portalis, François-Denis Tronchet, and Alexandre-Étienne Bigot de Préameneu. As Bigot de Préameneu declared, "the blood ties that unite and constitute families are formed by the sentiments of affection that nature has placed in the hearts of relatives for each other. The energy of these sentiments increases with the closeness of the kin relation, and finds its highest point between fathers and mothers and their children. There is no wise legislator who has failed to consider that these different degrees of affection provide him with the best order for the transmission of property." Quoted by Lucey, *The Misfit of the Family*, 2.

72. Fenet, *Recueil complet*, vol. 11, bk. 2, *Des biens et des différentes modifications de la propriété*, title 2, *De la propriété, présentation au Corps législatif et exposé des motifs par M. Portalis, 26 nivôse an XII* (17 January 1804), cited by Ewald, *Naissance du Code civil*, 286–87.

73. Adam Smith, *The Theory of the Moral Sentiments* (1759), pt. 6, § 2, chap. 1, paras. 2 and 3 (Edinburgh: Hay, 1813).

74. Fenet, *Recueil complet*, vol. 10, bk. 1, *Des personnes*, title 8, *De l'adoption et de la tutelle officieuse*, discussion du Conseil d'État, séances du 6 frimaire an X (27 November 1801); 14 frimaire an X (5 December 1801); 16 frimaire an X (7 December 1801); 24 brumaire an XI (18 November 1802), in Ewald, *Naissance du Code civil*, 241–62.

75. Ibid., 244–47, 249. Napoleon quotation from 246–47.

76. Ibid., 246–51. Cambacérès quotation from 246; Thibaudeau quotation from 249.

77. Ibid., 243–44 (Tronchet's argument).

78. Ibid., 244–47 (Bonaparte's arguments).

79. Dalloz, *Répertoire de législation de doctrine et de jurisprudence en matière de droit civil*, 275–84.

80. Although the revolutionaries lowered the age of majority for men and women to twenty-one, partially to limit paternal authority over adult sons, the Civil Code raised it to twenty-five for men and twenty-one for women.

81. The Civil Code provided for other forms of adoption, rarely exercised. These allowed for the adoption of an individual who had saved the adopter's life. It also provided a form of legal guardianship without the automatic transmission of inheritance.

82. Brinton, 52 quoting Bergier, *Opinion sur la question... des enfans naturels. Conseil des Cinq-Cents* (Paris, 1798), 6.

83. Fenet, *Recueil complet*, vol. 12, bk. 3, *Des différentes manières dont on acquiert la propriété*, title 2, *Des donations entre vifs et des testaments*, présentation au Corps législatif et exposé des motifs par M. Bigot-Préameneu, 13 floréal an XI (3 May 1803), in Ewald, *Naissance du Code civil*, 301–6.

84. Ewald, *Naissance du Code civil*, 223.

85. Louis, *Le Droit de cuissage*, 8–9. Robert Nye discusses how the masculine concept of honor was linked to the production of heirs and transmission of family property through bloodlines in *Masculinity and Male Codes of Honor*, vii, 9, 62. See also Reddy, *The Invisible Code*, xi, xii, 111, 121.

86. Women continued to make *déclarations de grossesse* during the nineteenth century. Although such declarations had no force in law, and were infrequent, the custom remained evident in the 1830s in the departments south and west of Paris. In an area of the Morvan, southeast of Paris, and in Paris as well, women made *déclarations de grossesse* in the 1880s, and these declarations existed in some rural areas into the turn of the twentieth century. Even in Paris, some women sought out the mayor of their *arrondissement* to make these declarations. See Paul Viollet, *Histoire du droit civil français*, 3d rev. ed. (Paris: L. Larose & L. Tenin, 1905), 511-12n2, in Phan, "Les Déclarations de grossesse," 62; Fuchs, *Poor and Pregnant in Paris*, 203.

87. For a compelling analysis of the Civil Code, see Arnaud, *Essai d'analyse structurale du Code civil français*. The Code may also represent a triumph of Rousseau's philosophy. In *Émile*, Rousseau maintained that the "law of nature" leaves "men uncertain of the paternity of the children they are expected to maintain"; women, therefore, should be subject to men's judgment and laws. Okin, *Justice, Gender, and the Family*, 33.

88. Fenet, *Recueil complet*, vol. 8, bk. 1, *Des personnes*, title 2, *Des actes de l'État civil*, communication officielle au Tribunat, opinion du tribun Benjamin Constant contre le projet, 4 nivôse an X (25 December 1801), 8: 130–40, quoted in Ewald, *Naissance du Code civil*, 232–40.

89. Quoted by Louis, *Le Droit de cuissage*, 28.

90. Fenet, *Recueil complet*, vol. 10, bk. 1, *Des personnes*, title 7, *De la paternité et de la filiation*, présentation au Corps législatif et exposé des motifs par M. Bigot-Préameneu, 2 germinal an XI (24 March 1803), 135–41, quoted in Ewald, *Naissance du Code civil*, 223–28.

91. Boswell, *The Kindness of Strangers*, 345. According to the 1579 and 1639 laws in France, any child born of a nonmarital union was disinherited. However, if a woman could determine paternity, then she could bring suit to try to force the father to pay financial damages. Paternal responsibility was a matter for adjudication. Farr, *Authority and Sexuality*, chap. 4.

92. Arnaud, *Les Origines doctrinales du Code civil français*, pt. 2, 187, 220; and Arnaud, *Essai d'analyse structurale du Code civil*, i–iii, 11, 45, 49, 63–67, 128. For a general discussion, see Halpérin, *L'Impossible Code civil.*

93. Kent, *Gender and Power in Britain, 1640–1991*, 143.

94. Allen, *Feminism and Motherhood in Germany*, 19; Dickinson, *The Politics of German Child Welfare*, 18–19.

95. Heuer, *The Family and the Nation*, 45, 76, 90, 155.

Two • Seduction and Courtroom Encounters in the Nineteenth Century

1. Hanley, "The Jurisprudence of the Arrêts," 1–40.

2. The legal publishing house of Dalloz regularly printed and distributed collections of court decisions. Furthermore, the popular newspapers such as the *Gazette des tribunaux* and the *Gazette du Palais* published judges' decisions, paying more attention to the higher courts. It is likely that judges read the press and lawyers' treatises and knew how other judges had decided. Publication of the *Gazette des tribunaux* began in the late eighteenth century but stopped during the Revolution. It resumed publication in 1825 and continued until 1955, reporting on selected judicial proceedings in Paris, with sparse attention to provincial court proceedings. The amount of space devoted to each case depended on the presumed public interest, the salient features of the case, the human dramas inherent in the proceedings, as well as on the juridical importance of the case. Intended for lawyers and magistrates, it also had a large nonprofessional audience interested in the daily melodramas of private lives as well as in judicial proceedings.

3. I use the terms "magistrates" and "judges" interchangeably.

4. Rousselet, *Histoire de la magistrature française*; Sharp, *The French Civil Service*, 180–86, 340–54; id., *The Government of the French Republic*, 183–205; Royer, Martinage, and Lecocq, *Juges et notables au XIXè siècle*, 58–65.

5. Kalifa, *L'Encre et le sang*, 107; Maza, *Private Lives and Public Affairs.*

6. Article 312 stated, "L'enfant conçu pendant le mariage a pour père le mari."

7. Pierre Larousse, *Grand dictionnaire universel du XIXe siècle* (Paris: Administration de Grand dictionnaire universel, 1874), 391–92, 594. The word "filiation," is an English and a French term that most concisely indicates these aspects of family relationships and lineage. The phrase "author of the pregnancy" was the popular term for "genitor" during the nineteenth century. I use the two interchangeably.

8. Dalloz, *Recueil périodique et critique de jurisprudence, de législation et de doctrine*, 1855, pt. 5, p. 230; pt. 2, p. 177; 1862, pt. 1, p. 208; 1848, pt. 2, p. 98; 1864, pt. 2, p. 197. Paul Coulet and Albert Vanois, lawyers at the appeals court in Paris, insisted that paternity was indivisible and that recherche de paternité should remain forbidden. See their *Étude sur la recherche de la paternité* (Paris: Marescq, 1880), 121, 128–29.

9. Thompson, *The Virtuous Marketplace*, 40–41, 144; Bardet, ed., *La Première fois.*

10. Dumas *fils*, *Les Femmes qui tuent et les femmes qui votent*, 27.

11. Coulet and Vanois, *Étude sur la recherche de la paternité*, 114–28; Millet, *La Séduction*, 117, 179–81 117.

12. Segalen, "Le XIXe siècle: Le Manteau des jeunes filles," 133.

13. Quotation from Millet, *La Séduction*, 61; Coulet and Vaunois, *Étude sur la recherche de la paternité*, 142.

14. Mossuz-Lavau, *Les Lois de l'amour*, 189–90; Vigarello, *A History of Rape*, 106–45.

15. Articles 330 to 340 of the Penal Code concern *attentats aux mœurs*, including rape and adultery; articles 354 to 356 deal with the kidnapping of minors.

16. Millet, *La Séduction*, 22–23, 33; Vigarello, *A History of Rape*, 128–37.

17. Steinhard, *Des conséquences civiles de la séduction*.

18. Coulet and Vaunois, *Étude sur la recherche de la paternité*, 103.

19. Nye, *Masculinity and Male Codes of Honor*, 10.

20. It is impossible to know the social class or numbers of women who went to court to try to get child support or collect damages from the published collections of jurisprudence, extant judgments of civil tribunals, or newspapers.

21. Nicoleau, "De la preuve judiciaire," 119.

22. Schnapper, *Voies nouvelles en histoire du droit*, 563–64. Poughon, *De la séduction*, 62. Although the Code protected male liberty, it appealed to conservative Catholics because it upheld the sacrosanct married family.

23. Article 1382 reads: "Tout fait quelconque de l'homme, qui cause à l'autrui un dommage, oblige celui par la faute duquel il est arrivé à le réparer."

24. Foriers and Perelman, "Natural Law and Natural Rights," 21.

25. Courts of Riom in 1818, Liège in 1822, and Toulouse in 1833 later echoed this decision. See Steinhard, *Des conséquences civiles de la séduction*, 26–27.

26. Dubois, *Les Fiançailles et promesses de mariage*, 132–33, 141–42, 159–60; Halpérin, *Histoire du droit privé français*, 86. See also Millet, *La Séduction*, 12, 159–60; Nicoleau, "De la preuve judiciaire," 119.

27. Dalloz, *Table alphabétique des dix années (1867–1877)*, 487–91.

28. Dalloz, *Recueil general des lois et arrêts: Table alphabétique, 1791 à 1850*, 1: 657.

29. Millet, *La Séduction*, 166–69.

30. Nicoleau, "De la preuve judiciaire," 144.

31. Coulet and Vanois, *Étude sur la recherche de la paternité*, 48–53. The language of seduction is reminiscent of Pothier's language discussing dommages-intérêts in eighteenth-century law and custom. For information on Zangiacomi, see Debré, *La Justice au XIXe siècle*, 44; *GT*, 26 March 1845, 496, provides his name as "sieur Labia." Coissac, *De l'interprétation par la jurisprudence*, 2–4. Sources differ on whether the decision was on the 21 or 24 March 1845. Article 1142 stated: "Toute obligation de faire ou de ne pas faire se résout en dommages et intérêts, en cas d'inexécution de la part du débiteur."

32. It is quite likely that women also broke engagements, but reports of men going to court for damages do not appear in the records.

33. Scott, *Only Paradoxes to Offer*, 64.

34. Millet, *La Séduction*, 64.

35. The numbers of abandoned children in Paris during these decades averaged 4,500 per year, comprising between 10 and 18 percent of total births in the city. Neither the number nor proportion of abandoned children increased in the early 1840s, but the rhetoric did. See my books *Abandoned Children*, 67–78 and *Poor and Pregnant in Paris*, chap. 2; Nicoleau, "De la preuve judiciaire," 147–70.

36. Legouvé, *Histoire morale des femmes*, 7–12.

37. Ibid., 72–73.

38. Schnapper, *Voies nouvelles*, 566.

39. Considérant, *Exposition abrégée du système phalanstérien de Fourier*, 95–96.

40. Offen, *European Feminisms*, 106.

41. Scott, *Only Paradoxes to Offer*, 71, for the quotation; Grogan, *French Socialism*, 134–50; Moses, *French Feminism*, 73, 74, 80, 98.

42. According to one of their spokesmen, Frédéric Le Play, fathers should be able to dispose of their property and inheritance as they wished. *La Réforme sociale* 1 (1864): 199, as cited in Schnapper, *Voies nouvelles*, 568–69.

43. Simon, *L'Ouvrière*, 300–301.

44. Steinhard, *Des conséquences civiles de la séduction*, 14–15, 66–67. A sample of *Gazette des tribunaux* from 1852 through 1854 revealed no stories of seduction, broken marriage promises, or damages. It is all conjecture, but an improvement in the economy in the 1850s and fewer publicized decisions in the mother's favor may have led to a decrease in mothers seeking child support in the courts; the ratio of illegitimate births relative to legitimate births remained fairly stable.

45. Nicoleau, "De la preuve judiciaire," studied 95 court decisions between 1804 and 1912 and demonstrated that dommages-intérêts or *aliments* were refused in only six cases.

46. Coulet and Vanois, *Étude sur la recherche de la paternité*, 57–60. See also Steinhard, *Des conséquences civiles de la séduction*, 26–27, 111.

47. In two other cases for 1850, appeals court judges upheld the lower courts decisions in favor of the women but insisted they were not permitting recherche de paternité. For Caen and the other cases, see Dalloz, *Recueil périodique*, 1855, 2: 177–78.

48. Giraud, *Des promesses de mariage*, 46–48.

49. Coulet and Vaunois, *Étude sur la recherche de la paternité*, 78–79.

50. Ibid., 78–82.

51. Giraud, *Des promesses de mariage*, 46–48.

52. *GT*, 2 December 1860, 1–2. Case from the civil tribunal of the Department of the Seine, 3rd chamber, audiences of 17 and 24 November 1860.

53. If she could have collected, this could have amounted to about double what she would have earned per year.

54. *GT*, 28 December 1860, 1–2. Case from the civil tribunal of the Department of the Seine, 1st chamber, audience of 26 December 1860. The sexual relationship was in southwestern France, but the court was in Paris because M. had moved there. Parts are loosely translated.

55. Coulet and Vanois, *Étude sur la recherche de la paternité*, 62–64. Louis, *Le Droit de cuissage*, 200–209, mentions several court cases where the judge awarded in favor of the young woman who accused a man of *l'abus de situation sociale et d'autorité*. Seduction by abuse of authority is the legal terminology for *le droit de cuissage*. It could range from sexual harassment to unwanted sexual advances, and rape. For additional court decisions, see Steinhard, *Des conséquences civiles de la séduction*, 23; Coulet and Vanois, *Étude sur la recherche de la paternité*, 71.

56. Sources for this case, proceeding from the civil tribunal to the Cour de cassation come from the *GT*, 10 September 1864, 885–86; Millet, *La Séduction*, 69–72. Millet and the *GT*

differ on some details; Millet says she was sixteen at the time relations began and the first time she went to court for dommages-intérêts was 1862.

57. To place children *en pension* usually indicated that a parent paid a small sum of money to someone to lodge or board a child while the child worked. It could also mean the children boarded at a workshop.

58. "A man's ability to control his daughter's sexuality counted heavily in his perception of his own honor" (Nye, *Masculinity and Male Codes of Honor*, 30).

59. Coulet and Vanois, *Étude sur la recherche de la paternité*, 66–69, 194. See also Giraud, *Des promesses de mariage*, 45.

60. Steinhard, *Des conséquences civiles de la séduction*, 27–28, 37; Millet, *La Séduction*, 185–88; Coulet and Vanois, *Étude sur la recherche de la paternité*, 57–89.

61. Millet, *La Séduction*, 95–97.

62. Ibid., 98–105; quotation from 98–100.

63. Bernard, *Histoire de l'autorité paternelle*, xi–xx, 221, 364.

64. Nord, *The Republican Moment*, 8–13, 115, 120, 220.

65. Acollas, *Droit et liberté*, 47, 55, 67–70, 86–97. From 1866 to 1869, the number of abandoned children in Paris increased to almost 4,500 per year, as against an average of 3,600 per year from the 1850s through 1865. The proportion of illegitimate to live births remained stable in the 1850s and 1860s at 26 percent. See Fuchs, *Abandoned Children*, 68–74.

66. Verdict of the Tribunal civil de la Seine, 24 February 1876, in Coulet and Vanois, *Étude sur la recherche de la paternité*, 71–75.

67. Steinhard, *Des conséquences civiles de la séduction*, 14–15, citing *GT*, 16 June 1900, 4 July 1905, 27 December 1905, 1 February 1906, and 8 April 1906.

68. The legal historian Jean-Louis Halpérin regards Magnaud as an example of the boldness of jurisprudence. Others regard Magnaud as emblematic of activist judges, not an exception. Elected to the Chamber of Deputies from Paris in 1906 as a *radicale-socialiste* member of the Gauche radicale, he denounced legal arbitrariness. See Halpérin, *Histoire de droit privé*, 180 and Kalifa, *L'Encre et le sang*, 177. Château-Thierry is a small town 100 kilometers north-east of Paris. Rossel, *Le Bon Juge*, 29–38, 191–200.

69. Magnaud, *Les Nouveaux Jugements*, ed. Leyret, 42–44, 79, 241; id., *Les Jugements*, 93–112; Royer, Martinage, Lecocq, *Juges et notables*, 359–369.

70. Magnaud, *Les Jugements*, 93–112; Rossel, *Le Bon Juge*, 29–38, 191–200.

71. Rossel, *Le Bon Juge*, 9–14; quotation from p. 13 is a loose translation.

72. *GT*, 24 March 1892 and 12 October 1992. See Louis, *Le Droit de cuissage*, 179–79.

73. Giraud, *La Vérité sur la recherche de la paternité*, 31; Dubois, *Les Fiançailles*, 142, 168.

74. In 1891, a 14-year-old girl shot and wounded a man in a public square in a town in the Charente. She declared that he had seduced her, and that when she became pregnant he abandoned her. He insisted that he ended the relationship because of rumors of her immorality. The tribunal acquitted her because she was under sixteen and had acted without discernment. *Événement*, 16 December 1891, in BMD, DOS 364.CRI.

75. Butler, *Precarious Life*, 45.

76. Butler, *Excitable Speech*, 5, chap. 1.

77. Foucault, *History of Sexuality*, 1: 179.

78. Malaurie and Aynès, *Cours de droit civil*, 360.

79. Scott, *Only Paradoxes to Offer*, 63–64, 67.
80. Butler, *Undoing Gender*, 117.
81. Halpérin, *Histoire du droit privé*, 84, 179.

Three • Find the Fathers, Save the Children, 1870–1912

1. Steinhard, *Des conséquences civiles de la séduction*, 52. The first quotation comes from the court in Dijon, 10 February 1892. Subsequent quotations are from *GT*, 1 February 1906, tribunal of Bar-sur-Aube, 10 November 1905, and 30 September 1905, 6th chamber, tribunal of Paris, 10 June 1905.

2. Arch. Paris, D1U5, Tribunal civil, AJ, 100, 1–20 January 1906, #3748 of 1905, judgment of 11 January 1906.

3. Arch. Paris, D1U5, AJ, 100, 1–20 January 1906, #2955 of 1905, judgment of 18 January 1906. For a similar argument, see Arch. Paris, D1U5, AJ 150, 11–30 November 1909, #3609 of 1909, judgment of 16 November 1909.

4. Arch. Paris, D1U5, AJ 150, 11–30 November 1909, #5158 of 1909, judgment of 19 November 1909. The 50 francs a month was slightly less than equivalent to the wages she might have received if she could have worked. In 2006, it equaled about €6 a day in purchasing power.

5. Arch. Paris, D1U5, AJ 180, 2–20 October 1911, #4040 of 1910, judgment of 12 October 1911.

6. Arch. Paris, D1U5, AJ 180, 2–20 October 1911, #942 of 1911, judgment of 9 October 1911. This is what Bataisse might have expected to earn as a laundress. For a similar case, see Bonzon, *La Recherche de la paternité*, 32.

7. E.g., Gaillard, *Recherches administratives, statistiques*, 296–300.

8. Desloges, *Des enfans trouvés, des femmes publiques...*, 27–32. In the 1840s, Alphonse Esquiros asked: "Is it fair that the man who is the most culpable, often the only one culpable, be the only one also to escape any punishment?" Esquiros, *Paris*, 2: 387.

9. Rousseau and his followers decreed, "Women, their bodies and bodily passions, represent the 'nature' that must be controlled and transcended if social order is to be created and sustained. Unlimited feminine desire must always be contained by patriarchal right. Women's relations to the social world must always be mediated through men's reason; women's bodies must always be subject to men's reason and judgments if order is not to be threatened." Pateman, *The Sexual Contract*, 98–100.

10. Coulon, *De la condition des enfants naturels reconnus*, 3; Cinquin, *Étude sur la déclaration judiciaire de paternité naturelle*, 41; Viollette, *La Recherche de la paternité*, 17. The following articles of the 1804 Civil Code detail the restrictions on recognition of children and their rights to inheritance.

> 331. Legitimation or recognition of children born of an adulterous or incestuous relationship is forbidden.
>
> 338. The natural child, even though acknowledged by the father, cannot have the rights of a legitimate child.

756. Only children legally recognized by their father or mother can inherit from that parent.

757. Illegitimate children have no rights to inherit the property of their grandparents or other relatives.

11. Fuchs, *Poor and Pregnant in Paris*, 101–2.

12. Dumas *fils, Le Fils naturel*, 6, 51, 115. This play was presented for the first time in Paris on 16 January 1858. The quotation comes from the preface, published in 1868. The Comédie-Française revived the play in 1878, just when the first legislative proposal to permit paternity searches entered the legislature, and the Odéon theater revived it again in 1898. The play was performed throughout the first decade of the twentieth century, receiving praise for its social morality. Pedersen, *Legislating the French Family*, 140–41.

13. Dumas *fils, La Dame aux Camélias*, 47–50. This play first appeared as a novel in 1848 and became a hit stage play in 1852. It influenced magistrates at the time and legislators two decades later. Dumas wrote the preface in 1867.

14. Paul and Victor Margueritte, "Questions féministes: La Recherche de la paternité," *Echo*, 11 November 1898, BMD, DOS 347. PAT, document 4. The Committee on the Reform of Marriage in 1905 included writers such as Paul Adam, Henry Bataille, Octave Mirabeau, Marcel Prévost, Jules Renard, Paul and Victor Margueritte, and Ghénia (Eugénie) Avril de Sainte-Croix. See Dupâquier and Fauve-Chamoux, "La Famille," 33.

15. Millet, *La Séduction*, 168–69, 161, 61, 80–81, 94, 185–88.

16. Ibid., 179–81, 160–61, 176, 203.

17. Ibid., 142–43.

18. For a careful analysis of the parliamentary debate on recherche de paternité since 1878, see Pedersen's dissertation, "Legislating the Family," chap. 4. See also Schnapper, *Voies nouvelles*, 353–73.

19. *JO, Débats parlementaires, Débats du Sénat*, ordinary session, 11 December 1883, 1441, 1447. Senator Alfred Naquet charged his colleagues that if they do not want to use the term *recherche de la paternité*, they should call it *recherche de la filiation*. Legislators used the phrase *recherche de la paternité*; I have adopted the more modern phrasing recherche de paternité unless quoting directly.

20. *JO, Débats parlementaires, Débats du Sénat*, ordinary session, 7 December 1883, 1420–24; Cazot quotations from ordinary session, 8 December 1883, 1425, 1427, 1433, and 1429. Cazot was a republican who nevertheless sought to support legal marriage as the bulwark of social order. In 1883, he opposed recherche de paternité. His use of the word "bastard" is a rare occurrence. See also Pedersen, *Legislating the French Family*, 131–33.

21. Steinhard, *Des conséquences civiles de la séduction*, 36; *JO, Débats parlementaires, Débats du Sénat*, ordinary session, 9 December 1883, 1434.

22. *JO, Débats du Sénat*, 11 December 1883, 1429, 1442.

23. René Bérenger, *JO, Documents du Sénat*, 16 February 1878, Annexe 71 *bis*, 4718–4719; Nicoleau, "De la preuve judiciaire," 223. Between 1878 and 1912, there were roughly fifty law theses devoted to the question of recherche de paternité. Almost all were in favor of its legalization, indicating the sentiment of the academic legal community.

24. Coulet and Vanois. *Étude sur la recherche de la paternité,* 187, 191, 97–98, 205. See also Giraud, *La Vérité sur la recherche de la paternité,* 22. Giraud was a jurist and friend of the feminists Léon Richer and Maria Deraismes.

25. BMD, DOS 347 PAT, document 2; *JO, Documents parlementaires, Chambre,* Annexe No. 1484 ordinary session, 9 July 1895, 868, and Annexe No. 1639, special session, 28 November 1895, 1516; Annexe No. 2524, ordinary session, 17 June 1897, 1407–14. This proposal had similar provisions to the measure that finally passed in 1912.

26. For Catholic support, see Lambrechts, *Six projets de loi,* esp. pp. 26–52, where he specifically supports the motives of Rivet and Bérenger.

27. Socialist sponsors of the bill included Jean Jaurès, Alexandre Millerand, Marcel Sembat, Édouard Vaillant, and René Viviani. *JO, Chambre, Documents parlementaires,* Annexe No. 1147, 28 January 1895, 141. See also Pedersen, "Legislating the Family," 294; Nicoleau, "De la preuve judiciaire," 217–19.

28. For a social Catholic view, see Haussonville, *Salaires et misères de femmes,* xviii–xix. For reference to canon law, see Génestal, *Histoire de la légitimation des enfants naturels.* For the leading Catholic opposition to the paternity searches based on a woman's abuse of men and morality, see Brunetière, "La Recherche de la paternité," 349–80.

29. See *JO, Débats du Sénat,* 7 June 1910, 1466–69 (Rivet's proposals); 14 June 1910, 1508; 16 June 1910, 1514–16; 8 November 1912, 1381; 9 November 1912, 1333–46; Wahl, *La Recherche de la paternité,* 9.

30. The five cases in which paternity suits were henceforth permitted were:

1. Abduction or rape when the period of abduction or rape coincided with that of conception.
2. Seduction by fraud, abuse of authority, promise of marriage or engagement, and if there was the beginning of written proof.
3. When there were letters or other private writings of the putative father that resulted in an unequivocal admission of paternity.
4. When the putative father and mother had lived in *concubinage notoire* during the legal period of conception.
5. When the putative father contributed to the rearing and education of the child *en qualité de père.*

Paternity suits would not be permitted:

1. If the mother's notorious loose living [*inconduite notoire*] during the legal period of conception were established, or if she had relations [*commerce*] with another individual.
2. If the putative father was absent during the same period, or if as a result of some accident, it was physically impossible for him to be the father of that child.

31. Julien Gojon, *JO, Documents de la Chambre,* 19 October 1897, Annexe, 2715, 2.

32. Pedersen, *Legislating the French Family,* 158. Women accused of bringing paternity charges in bad faith would be tried under the Penal Code. Article 400 of the Penal Code would be completed by the following: "L'interdiction de séjour pendant cinq ans au moins et dix ans au plus, dans un rayon déterminé, pourra en outre être prononcée dans ce dernier

cas." Dalloz, *Recueil périodique et critique, Quatrième partie, Lois et Décrets, Rapports et discussions législatives* (1912), 113–28.

33. Halpérin, *Histoire de droit privé*, 224–25.

34. *L'Assiette au Beurre*, a generally anti-establishment journal of social protest not overtly aligned with any political party, excoriated a broad range of individuals and social issues. The change in attitudes toward recherche de paternité from 1902 to 1910 could reflect the viewpoint of the artists or that of the editors, as well as just a desire to mock current legislative debates. Applebaum, *French Satirical Drawings*, vi–vii.

35. Rivet, *La recherche de la paternité*, 198–203. Although incest and adultery are vastly different, legislators sometimes collapsed the two as forms of sexual deviance, and failed to recognize the damages done to victims of incest.

36. Nye, *Masculinity and Male Codes of Honor*, 37–38.

37. Rivet, *La Recherche de la paternité*, 31, 265; Rivet, *JO*, Débats du Sénat, 1 June 1910, 1466–67.

38. Acollas, *L'Enfant né hors mariage*, 91–96; Rivet, *JO*, Débats du Sénat, 7 June 1910, 1466–67; Louis Martin, *JO*, Débats du Sénat, 9 June 1910, 1482; Wahl, *La Recherche de la paternité*, 39.

39. Coissac, *De l'interprétation par la jurisprudence*, 84–99, 119. Legislators debated the issue of cohabitation and decided that cohabitation and concubinage were not identical. A domestic servant lived in the same house as her master. Legislators wanted to diminish the possibility of a domestic servant bringing charges against her master.

40. Rivet, *La Recherche de la paternité*, 28–29. The length and animosity of the senators' vituperative pronouncements against women who might bring paternity charges in bad faith as the men debated on 8 November 1912, when most of the bill had already passed both houses, was especially gratuitous. See *JO*, 9 November 1912, Senate, 8 November 1912, 1333–46. See also Cinquin, *Étude sur la déclaration judiciaire*, 76; *La Recherche de la paternité*, Conférence faite à la loge "La Fraternité vosgienne," 12–13.

41. Savatier, *La Recherche de la paternité*, 34–37.

42. Poittevin, *Les Théories de M. Alexandre Dumas fils*, 31; Richer, "La Recherche de la paternité," 207; Dumas fils, *La Dame aux Camélias*, preface, 48.

43. Fatoux, *La Juridiction correctionnelle*, 18; Baudin, *La Recherche judiciaire*, 159. After passage of the law in 1912, feminists and socialists still objected to the "bad faith" clause because it violated women's civil rights.

44. BMD, Fonds Roussel, Coupures de Journaux, 1909–10, Recueil no. 4. Extract from *Le Radical*, 1 February 1910 and *Le Siècle*, 12 February 1910; BMD, DOS 347 PAT, press clippings. See also René Viviani and others in *Congrès international de la condition et des droits des femmes*, 193, 391–93.

45. Reddy, "Marriage, Honor, and the Public Sphere," 437–72.

46. *JO*, 9 November 1912, Senate, 8 November 1912, 1333–46.

47. Allen, *Feminism and Motherhood in Germany*, 19, 142–48. It is impossible to determine why France resisted change. In part, it was legislative inertia and an active jurisprudence that compensated; in part, a desire of legislators to protect themselves and their sons from paternity suits; in part, the heritage of the Revolution, protecting men's individual rights and privacy.

48. For a Catholic emphasis on the legal family and the preservation of family property Dupanloup, *Le Mariage chrétien*, 66, 295, 327.

49. Nicoleau, "De la preuve judiciaire," 182; Crémieu, *Les Preuves de la filiation naturelle*. Natural children had a higher infant mortality rate than legitimate children. Fuchs, *Poor and Pregnant in Paris*, chap. 3.

50. Millet, *La Séduction*, 134–35.

51. See, e.g., *JO, Débats parlementaires, Débats du Sénat*, special session, 8 December 1883, 1435–36, 1437.

52. Variot, "Conférence sur l'allaitement," 130. Variot was a leading advocate for infant and maternal health. This argument was not limited to doctors or repopulationist radicals in the government. Social Catholics in the Senate shared this concern. See d'Haussonville, *Salaires et misères de femmes*, xvi–xx.

53. Rivet, *La Recherche de la paternité*, 75–77, 89–90, 294.

54. Pouzol, *La Recherche de la paternité*, 169. See also Dumas, A., *L'interdiction de la recherche de la paternité*. Data on infanticide and abortion are notoriously inaccurate. Although England permitted paternity searches and London had an illegitimacy rate of only 4 percent, compared with a rate four times as high for Paris, this can not be taken as cause and effect; there were many other factors influencing illegitimacy rates.

55. Quoted in Millet, *La Séduction*, 138.

56. Strauss, *L'Enfance malheureuse*, 34; Strauss, Commission de la dépopulation. *Rapport général sur les causes de la mortalité*, 9; *JO*, 9 November 1912, Senate, 8 November 1912, 1339. According to one reformer if the law permitted recherche de paternité then "the debauched man, the supervisor or patron, whether married or single, who can today play with the honor of young girls placed under their authority, would be more respectful.... The fear of incurring responsibility [for the child] will exercise a salutary break of the Don Juans." See Ponsolle, *La Dépopulation*, 29–30.

57. Quotation from *JO*, Sénat, 14 June, 1508; Amiable, *De la preuve de la paternité hors mariage*, 8–9, citing the *Statistique de la France*, vol. 11 (1881), 33. Amiable called upon his fraternal Freemasons to support recherche de paternité as a moral duty and juridical obligation incumbent on fathers.

58. BMD, DOS 347 PAT, document 15. See also *Congrès international de la condition et des droits des femmes*, 193, 391–93. On the floor of the Senate, Paul Strauss, a leading proponent of a child's right to life after birth, uttered these sentiments to shouts of "Très bien" and loud applause. *JO*, 9 November 1912, Senate, 8 November, p. 1337. See also Cinquin, *Étude sur la déclaration judiciaire*, 112–14. It did not matter, some declared, whether the woman entered into the relationship freely, or she was seduced with false promises; the innocent child did not ask to be born. Giraud, *La Vérité sur la recherche de la paternité*, 5. "Right to life" sometimes appears as *droit de vivre*.

59. *JO, Débats parlementaires, Débats du Sénat*, special session, 8 December 1883, 1436, and 11 December 1883, 1441; Amiable, *De la preuve de la paternité*, 9; Cinquin, *Étude sur la déclaration judiciaire*, 113–14; Rivet, *La Recherche de la paternité*, 4, 120–23, 170; Poughon, *De la séduction*, 5; BMD, DOS 347 PAT, document 3, Chambre des Députés, session de 1897. Annexe au procès-verbal de la séance du 17 juin 1897, Rapport fait au nom de la commission relative à la recherche de la paternité, 8. R. Davenne, was less sanguine about the state assuming

charge of the children. Davenne, "Enfants naturels," *Le Droit des femmes*, no. 365 (2 March 1890): 51–53, and no. 368 (20 April 1890): 86. For a discussion of the press emphasis on crime at the turn of the century, see Kalifa, *L'Encre et le sang*, 235, 238, 253.

60. Rivet, *La Recherche de la paternité*, 180–83, 203. Quotation from Millet, *La Séduction*, 198. Radical republicans, such as Rivet and his co-supporters of this measure, often invoked the Declaration of the Rights of Man. As heirs to the First Republic's ideology, they also used phrases reminiscent of natural law espoused by Cambacérès and others in the 1789–93 period. The social Catholic Othenin d'Haussonville referred to article 340 as an "absolute and brutal" law in terms of what it did to the children, emphasizing that the state had a right to perform its duties to prevent moral outrage. Haussonville, "Socialisme d'état et socialisme chrétien," 18.

61. Coulon, *De la condition des enfants naturels reconnus*, 15, 19–20, 51, 212; quotation from 172.

62. See, e.g., Daubié, *La Femme pauvre au dix-neuvième siècle*, 51, 123; Acollas, *L'Enfant né hors mariage*, 5–7, 47–54, 78–80, 106–7. *JO*, 9 November 1912, Senate, 8 November 1912, 1333–46.

63. Some regarded the 1884 divorce bill as a gain for women's rights. In 1893, single and separated women were accorded legal status; in 1897, women could be witnesses in law courts, and in 1907, married women gained control over their own wages.

64. Rivet, *La Recherche de la paternité*, 50–53, 58–59, 118. Italics in the original.

65. Gouges, *Écrits politiques*, 1: 208–212. Quotations are from *Les Droits de la femme*, article XI and conclusion. See also Scott, *Only Paradoxes to Offer*, 42–44, 71–73; Klejman and Rochefort, *L'Égalité en marche*; Offen, *European Feminisms*.

66. Scott, *Only Paradoxes to Offer*, 3.

67. R. Davenne, "Enfants naturels," *Le Droit des femmes*, no. 368 (20 April 1890): 86, and no. 371 (1 June 1890): 124.

68. *Le Journal des femmes*, no. 8 (July 1892); Léon Richer, *Le Droit des femmes*, no. 377 (7 September 1890): 193–94.

69. *Le Temps*, 17 May 1892.

70. From August through October 1899, articles in *La Fronde* condemned article 340. Cova, "Droits des femmes et protection de la maternité," 145.

71. Chauvin wanted the father to pay an indemnity to the mother for her loss of time at work. The mother, she argued, should have the right to obtain damages from the child's father to pay the cost of her delivery and to provide supplementary income that would enable her and her baby to survive during the first six months after birth, when she could not work much because she was obliged to stay home and nurse her infant. Mme d'Abbadie d'Arrast added that although this proposal was in advance of public opinion, she hoped it would have a practical result—to maintain order and morality. See *Deuxième Congrès international des œuvres et institutions féminines*, 1: 124, 269–70.

72. Marie LaCécilia, Dame déléguée aux enfants assistés de la Seine, *Congrès international de la condition et des droits des femmes*, 391–93 (first quotation), and 193, 269 quotations of Durand (emphasis in original).

73. *Congrès international de la condition et des droits des femmes*, 262; *La Fronde*, 4 May 1899. Not only did feminists disagree on recherche de paternité, but some, such as Ghénia

Avril de Sainte-Croix, appear to have changed their minds. Thanks to Karen Offen for providing me with relevant pages of *La Fronde* for April 1898 and May 1899.

74. *Deuxième Congrès international des œuvres et institutions féminines*, 1: 276–77.

75. Roussel, *Quelques lances rompues pour nos libertés*, 92–93; see also id., "La Recherche de la paternité," *L'Action*, 19 February 1905, in BMD, DOS 347 PAT.

76. Roussel, *L'Almanach féministe*, 1907, reprinted in *Quelques lances rompues pour nos libertés*, 44, 93. For a biography of Roussel, see Accampo, *Blessed Motherhood, Bitter Fruit*.

77. *Congrès international de la condition et des droits des femmes*, 264, 269–73; *La Fronde*, 4 May 1899.

78. *JO*, *Débats parlementaires, Débats du Sénat*, ordinary session, 7 June 1910, 1469; Coirard, *La Famille dans le Code civil*, 213. Feminists advocated recherche de paternité and marriage reforms in several public venues.

79. Stora-Lamarre, *La République des faibles*, 7; Nicoleau, "De la preuve judiciaire," 223; Pedersen, "Legislating the Family," 300; Rivet, *La Recherche de la paternité*, 26–7, 117–19. For similar views, see Coulon, *De la condition des enfants naturels reconnus*, 27, who told fathers that natural law applied both to them and their children.

80. *Le Droit des femmes* (1890) in BMD, DRO 396 Bul.

81. Dumas *fils*, *Le fils naturel*, 6, 52. See also his preface to *La Dame aux Camélias*, 47–50; Poittevin, *Les Théories de M. Alexandre Dumas fils*, 31–36; Richer, "La recherche de la paternité par Alexandre Dumas fils," 207. In a speech in 1900, Jacques Bonzon spoke against recherche de paternité. See *Deuxième Congrès international des œuvres et institutions féminines, 1:* 263, 271, 274. By 1905, his argument had changed and he supported paternity searches, provided they limited the father to *une pension alimentaire*. This would be the price a man had to pay for his "fault" of seduction and breaking the marriage promise. But, more important, it represented his obligation to provide bread for the child he helped create. Bonzon, *La Recherche de la paternité*, 27–28, 38–39.

82. Lambrechts, *Six projets*, 29, 32.

83. *La Recherche de la paternité*, Conférence faite à la loge "La Fraternité vosgienne," 6; Rivet, *La Recherche de la paternité*, 26–7, 117–19.

84. Rivet, *La Recherche de la paternité*, 26–7, 117–19. See also Commission de la depopulation, *Rapport général sur les causes de la mortalité*, 9; Report of the Senate debate on the proposal of Bérenger in *GT*, 5–7 December 1883; Report of the Chamber of Deputies, 6th Legislature, ordinary session, 1897, "Rapport fait au nom de la Commission relative à la recherche de la paternité," in BMD, DOS 347 ENF; *Deuxième Congrès international des œuvres et institutions féminines*, 1: 270–87. Haussonville, *Socialisme et charité*, 82–87.

85. Fleury, *Des causes de la dépopulation*, 22–23; Haussonville, *Socialisme d'état et socialisme chrétien*, 22–25; id., *Salaires et misères de femmes*, xx, xxxii; id., *Socialisme et charité*, 86–87; Marie Georges-Martin, "Le Conseil national des femmes françaises," *La Revue philanthropique* 13 (1903): 695–701; *Deuxième Congrès international des œuvres et institutions féminines*, 1: 485–86, 289; Ronsin, *La Grève des ventres*, 161–62.

86. Davenne, "Enfants naturels," *Le Droit des femmes*, no. 365 (2 March 1890): 51–53, and no. 368 (20 April 1890): 86; Fuchs, *Poor and Pregnant in Paris*, chap. 5.

87. Coulon, *De la condition des enfants naturels reconnus;* Halpérin, *Histoire de droit privé*, 224, 233. Articles 756–66, 773, and 908 of the Civil Code enabled extranuptial children to in-

herit from their mother and father, but not from their grandparents. The portion of the inheritance allotted to them was less than accorded to legitimate children, however, and in proportion to the number of legitimate children in the family. In instances in which there were legitimate children, the out-of-wedlock child could inherit only half of the portion to which she or he would have been entitled if legitimate. Only if there were no other relatives (whether ascendants, descendants, or collaterals) who could inherit (brothers, sisters, cousins, aunts, uncles, nieces, nephews, grandparents) could the out-of-wedlock child receive the entire estate.

88. Nicoleau, "De la preuve judiciaire," 47–54; Giraud, *La Vérité sur la recherche de la paternité*, 22; Salzes, *La Recherche judiciaire de la paternité*, 6–7, 79.

89. Halpérin, *Histoire du droit privé*, 225–26. Articles 762–66 detail inheritance rights for children of adultery. The feminist press, in particular, insisted that these children have the same rights to food as others, and should not be excluded from inheritance. See *Le Droit des femmes*, articles by R. Davenne and Léon Richer, no. 375 (3 August 1890): 171.

90. *JO, Débats parlementaires, Débats du Sénat*, ordinary session, 7 June 1910, 1473; 16 June 1910, 1514. Antoine Loysel (1536–1617) a prominent judge of the *parlement* of Paris assembled a series of customs, proverbs, and court decisions in his *Institutes coutumières*, republished thirteen times between 1607 and the 1780s. Rivet either did not know of Loysel's ironic qualifier stipulating the Church's approval or chose to ignore it since it was counter to his own argument.

91. Coulon, *De la condition des enfants naturels reconnus*, 28; id., *De la réforme du mariage*, 67; Toulouse, *La Question sexuelle et la femme*, 75–76.

92. There were several high-profile cases of natural children seeking inheritance from their adulterous fathers earlier in the century. See Mainardi, *Husbands, Wives, and Lovers*.

93. Millet, *La Séduction*, 50–51, 53, 61; Mossuz-Lavau, *Les Lois de l'amour*, 201; Dupâquier and Fauve-Chamoux, "La Famille," 33; Louis, *Le Droit de cuissage*, 20, 28.

94. Maugue, *L'Identité masculine*, 74, 136; Nye, *Masculinity and Male Codes of Honor*.

95. Alexandre Dumas *fils*, *Les Femmes qui tuent et les femmes qui votent*, 135. "The law, in effect, is not an absolute thing," Bérenger declared (*JO, Débats parlementaires, Débats du Sénat*, special session, 7 December 1883, 1420).

Four • Courts Attribute Paternity, 1912–1940

1. Arch. Paris, D1U5, Tribunal civil, AJ, 230, 1–9 April 1914, #7719 of 1913, judgment of 7 April 1914.

Note on Sources: The summary judgments of cases brought before the civil tribunals of Paris (no dossiers exist) allow a glimpse of the women who filed paternity suits, the men's responses, and the judge's decisions. I examined a random sample of forty-five bound volumes of judgments from the *tribunal civil* of Paris brought to the courts by *l'Assistance judiciaire* (what might be considered legal aid) from the years 1900 through 1939 (one in twenty) from over 800 volumes of civil suits of all varieties. This source provides an unprecedented glimpse into working-class Parisian family life. I discovered 128 instances in which a woman brought suit against a putative father for child support and/or judicially declared paternity under the law of 1912. These volumes of judgments are held by the Archives de la Ville de Paris, D1U5 Tribunal civil de Paris. The numbering system of each volume changed between 1993, when

I began the research, and 2002, when I finished. I did not change the numbers to correspond to the new system. Just how many woman filed paternity suits or sued for child support is impossible to determine, because these suits are buried among multitudinous other civil judgments and arranged by date and court. In order to broaden the base of my research to include those of the middle classes who could afford to pay their own lawyer, I consulted the *Roles et répertoires* of the *tribunal civil*, which pointed to a sparse number of cases of *pension alimentaire, désaveu de paternité*, and recherche de paternité that came before court chambers in Paris without Assistance judiciaire, primarily in the *1ère chambre* of the *tribunal civil.*. The year 1920 yielded only six cases of recherche de paternité, while the volumes for *l'Assistance judiciaire* for the same year revealed forty-one cases. No significant differences existed between the small group who paid for their own lawyer and the larger group who needed *Assistance judiciaire* to supply one, except for their socioeconomic level.

To obtain further information about people from diverse geographical areas and socioeconomic situations, I consulted various newspapers, such as *Le Matin* (which had the second largest circulation in Paris), *Le Temps* (the newspaper of record), and the *Gazette des tribunaux* (which reported on civil and criminal court cases). René Savatier's book, *La Recherche de la paternité. Étude pratique de législation et de jurisprudence* (Paris: Dalloz, 1927) provides a legal summation of some of the decisions of the civil tribunals, of the appeals courts, and of the Chambre civil de la Cour de cassation for the first decade after the promulgation of the law. Savatier was a professor in the law faculty at Poitiers and a leading legal authority on recherche de paternité. Additional cases that permit a glimpse of lives of men and women from different areas of France and from a variety of social classes appear in the collection of legal decisions printed in Dalloz, Jurisprudence générale, *Recueil périodique et critique*. These volumes were published throughout the nineteenth and twentieth centuries, and I sampled volumes for selected years.

I am aware of the risks and limitations in relying on judicial records; they do not represent the normality of everyday life, but rather relationships gone awry. In the cases of paternity searches, however, they reflect the interaction of individuals and communities with the state, as represented by the courts.

Because of French privacy rules, I have changed names of plaintiffs and defendants in all cases from the court records, but not from the press or printed sources that had published names. When newspapers printed names, I have used the published names.

The best approximation of the amount of damages and child support (*pension alimentaire*) that judges awarded to mothers and children is to compare each award with the equivalent purchasing power of the euro in 2006. Judges were relatively consistent in the purchasing power of their awards, generally allowing for minimally sufficient amounts in *pension alimentaire* to feed the children—if the mothers could collect. The awards were insufficient to completely support the mother and child; she had to work. See www.insee.fr/en/indicateur/achatfranc.htm (accessed 19 October 2007) for comparisons with 2006.

2. Judges, legal commentators, and the popular press tended to use the phrase recherche de paternité (or *recherche de la paternité*) to describe a civil suit that involved different quests for paternity, child support, or an indemnity to the mother, as during the nineteenth century, and not just those brought to court for filiation. To be precise, the 16 November 1912 law permitting paternity searches was a revision of article 340 of the Civil Code, and not a law unto itself,

however referring to those legislative revisions as the 1912 law is useful shorthand and represents how people mentioned article 340 after 1912.

3. Rousselet, *Histoire de la magistrature française*.

4. Savatier, *La Recherche de la paternité*, 177, 181–86, 213.

5. Language evolved, like jurisprudence, and by the 1930s some commentators referred to a mother's legal authority over her children as *puissance maternelle*.

6. Dalloz, *Recueil périodique et critique*, 93. Judges referred to article 62 of the Civil Code, which said: "The act of recognizing a child will be inscribed on the registers on that date; and it will be mentioned in the margin of the birth certificate." The legal age of majority was twenty-one, but child support rarely went beyond the child's eighteenth birthday.

7. Archives départementales de la Sarthe, 2U598, 1924, quoted by Sohn, "Les Rôles féminins dans la vie privée," 586.

8. Arch. Paris, AJ 400, 1–15 July 1924, #2338 of 1924. Judicial and newspaper accounts refer to young single mothers as "Dlle" or "Delle" for *demoiselle*. That term meant an unmarried young woman, but *mademoiselle* has replaced it; therefore I have changed that designation to "Mlle." If the records provide women's first names, I have used them instead of the title of "Mlle." I chose not to provide fictional first names.

9. Dalloz, *Recueil périodique et critique*, 1925, 34, 90, and 1920, 89–93; Carbon, *Le Désaveu de paternité*, 35–36.

10. Battagliola, "Mariage, concubinage, et relations entre les sexes," 68–96; Frey, "Du mariage et du concubinage," 803–29; and my own work, *Poor and Pregnant in Paris;* Roberts, *Civilization Without Sexes*, 81, 93–102, 181–82.

11. Scott, *Only Paradoxes to Offer*, Introduction.

12. BHVP, Fonds Bouglé, Fonds Mme Léo Wanner. On 21 March 1937, Albert Gruber wrote a column of juridical advice in the women's journal *Minerva*, BMD, DOS 347 PAT, document 35.

13. Cova, "Droits des femmes et protection de la maternité," 704. Sources do not specify if the judge decided against the plaintiff, if he just refused to hear her case, if she specifically sought recherche de paternité with full filiation, or if the case was one seeking only a *pension alimentaire*.

14. Arch. Paris, D1U5, AJ 370, 18–31 January 1923, #1940 of 1921, judgment of 18 January 1923. See also AJ 530, 1–10 July 1930, January 1928, judgment of 1 July 1930; AJ 550, 1–14 May 1931, #5112 of 1928, judgment of 12 May 1931; and AJ 710, 9–17 March 1937, #2495 of 1934, judgment of 12 March 1937.

15. The organization of the archives made it impossible to discover how these inquiries were resolved.

16. Roberts, *Disruptive Acts*, Introduction.

17. Audoin-Rouzeau, *La Guerre des enfants*, 16–17.

18. Rhoades, "Renegotiating French Masculinity," 293–327.

19. Hanna, "A Republic of Letters," 1338–61; id., "*Your Death Would be Mine*."

20. Arch. Paris, D1U5, AJ 287, 1–8 January 1920. This would be less than €34 a month in purchasing power in 2006, probably insufficient even for food.

21. Arch. Paris, D1U5, AJ 270, 1–30 June 1918, #2903 for Richer and Ficher. See also D1U5, AJ 250, 1–31 July 1916, #676. Letters did not reveal paternity, yet she still had the chance to show that they had lived together in concubinage until the outbreak of war.

22. Arch. Paris, D1U5, AJ 250, #1544 of 1916, judgment of 25 July 1916. It is unlikely that in naming her daughter France Germanie, Grécourt was hedging her bets on the outcome of the war; in French, needless to say, "Germany" is not "Germanie" but "Allemagne." Most likely, it was an anagram of the more common French woman's name "Germaine."

23. Arch. Paris D1U5, AJ 287, judgment of 5 January 1920. The significance of her naming her daughter Augustine when the putative father was Auguste must have been noticed.

24. Sohn, "Between the Wars in France and England," 105; Hanna, *"Your Death Will be Mine,"* 130.

25. Arch. Paris, D1U5, AJ 301, 1–16 July 1920, #27,895 of 1919, resolved 1920.

26. Arch. Paris, Tribunal civil, first chamber, DU5 (2191), #2008 of 1924 (not AJ) for Bordin; AJ 390, 1–15 February 1924, #7191, judgment of 11 February 1924 for Sache. The date of the judgment was three years after the mother first filed her suit.

27. Arch. Paris, D1U5, AJ 291, 1–10 March 1920, judgment of 3 March 1920. See also D1U5, AJ 370, 18–31 January, 1923, #5517.

28. Women raped by Germans were frequently acquitted of abortion and infanticide. Wishnia, "Natalisme et nationalisme," 32, quotation from 39; Audoin-Rouzeau, *L'Enfant de l'ennemi*; Rhoades, "Renegotiating French Masculinity," 297.

29. Arch. Paris, AJ 370, 18–31 January 1923, #1213 of 1921. AN, BB18/6170, for abortion in the area of Amiens in 1918.

30. Sohn, "Les Rôles féminins dans la vie privée," 892.

31. Nye, *Masculinity and Male Codes of Honor*; Forth, *The Dreyfus Affair*.

32. Thébaud, "The Great War and the Triumph of Sexual Division," 50.

33. *Le Matin*, 15 July 1925, 1A. In Germany, recherche de paternité was allowed unless the mother wanted to keep the father's name a secret. As in France, the father had to provide subsistence to his legally declared child. The amount of child support in Germany was according to the "social situation" of the mother; in France, it depended on the father's situation. In Austria, the mother could declare the identity of father under oath; this could be done during pregnancy, as with *déclarations de grossesse* under the Old Regime. If the putative father admitted to having had relations with the mother, he was required to pay child support. There was no obvious means of enforcement. If he denied paternity, he had to do it under oath, with redoubtable penalties for perjury.

34. *Le Matin*, 30 July 1925, 1A.

35. Jane Misme, "Carnet d'une féministe—Il n'y a pas des filles mères," *L'Œuvre*, 16 March 1922, in BHVP, Fonds Bouglé, Articles de presse, boîte 5, thèmes.

36. *Le Matin*, 4 September 1925, 1G, and 9 September 1925, 1G, 2A.

37. Arch. Paris, D1U5, AJ 330, August–October 1921. In 1920, 2,000 francs had the purchasing power of €1,695 in 2006.

38. Arch. Paris, D1U5, AJ 287, 1–8 January 1920. Of the ten women in the sample from the civil tribunal of Paris who filed for damages, the judges ruled three cases *mal fondé* (unfounded), with a fourth not even receiving a hearing and rejected immediately for lack of evidence.

39. Dalloz, *Recueil périodique et critique*, 1924, 1: 38. In 1920, courts declared that seduction without fraudulent maneuvers could not serve as proof in a court action to declare a man's paternity, and in 1925 many cases appeared before the judges the Cour de cassation who

insisted on written proof of marriage promises or paternity even for dommages-intérêts. Dalloz, *Recueil périodique* (1921), 26, and Dalloz, *Recueil hebdomadaire de jurisprudence en matière civile* (1925), 41, 250, 305.

40. Arch. Paris, D1U5, AJ 530, 1–10 July 1930, #510 of 1929, judgment of 8 July 1930. In 1930, the franc was valued about half of what it had been from 1920 through 1926, and mothers receiving a *pension alimentaire* for a fixed amount in the early 1920s would have had about half the support they had been awarded in terms of purchasing power.

41. Dalloz, *Table alphabétique (sixième) de cinq années du Recueil Dalloz (1932 à 1936)*, 439.

42. Arch. Paris, D1U5, AJ 4295, 1–16 June 1938, #4356. For an earlier similar case, see D1U5, AJ 550, 1–14 May 1931, #5152, and for a rejection of a suit for damages and child support, see D1U5, AJ 4215, 20–31 December 1935, #2241.

43. *La Française*, 24–31 December 1932, discussing the law proposed in the Chambre des Deputés on 11 July 1932 titled "Proposition de Loi tendant à une organization plus efficace de la responsabilité civile pour dommages de maternité en cas de séduction," in BMD, DOS 347 PAT, document 29; *La Mode de demain*, June 1936, in BMD, DOS 347 PAT, document 32.

44. Arch. Paris, D1U5, AJ 410, 1–14 February 1925, #1938. This would amount to 14,400 francs in a year, equivalent in 2006 terms to €11,000 a year for the three children, almost double other judges' awards per child, but consistent with the father's income.

45. *Gazette du Palais* (1935), 555, in BMD, DOS 347 PAT, document 26. The sum of 6,000 francs per year in child support, the equivalent to €4,146 in 2006 was almost double what most judges in the civil tribunal AJ records were awarding. This case, however, did not come through *Assistance judiciaire*, and may well have been within the father's ability to pay.

46. Dalloz, *Table alphabétique (sixième) de cinq années du Recueil Dalloz (1932 à 1936)*, 436–41; See also Arch. Paris, D1U5, AJ 287, 1–8 January 1920, judgment of 8 January 1920; AJ 301, 1–16 July 1920, #3083, judgment of 10 July 1920.

47. BMD, DOS 347 PAT, document 32, unidentified press clipping.

48. For the 1920s, see Savatier, *La Recherche de la paternité*; Dalloz, *Recueil périodique et critique* from 1920 to 1939; Coissac, *De l'interprétation pour la jurisprudence*, 21–24, 28–29, 62–68; and BMD, DOS 347 PAT, documents 35 and 41, unidentified press clipping, apparently from the *Gazette du Palais* in 1922.

49. Arch. Paris, D1U5, AJ 410, 1–14 February 1925, #5682 of 1922, judgment of 3 February 1925. This case took three years in court, from the initial hearing, to summoning witnesses, to the final decision. See also AJ 410, #1938 of 1923, judgment of 14 February 1925.

50. Arch. Paris, D1U5, AJ 550, 1–14 May 1931, #885 of 1930, judgment of 11 May 1931. For opinions on the necessity of "regular" and "stable" concubinage and "conjugal fidelity" over a period of time, see AJ 550, #5152 of 1929, judgment of 12 May 1931; AJ 650, 12–20 March 1935, #896 of 1932, hearing on 12 March 1935; and AJ 710, 9–17 March 1937, #4599, hearing of 12 March 1937.

51. Arch. Paris, D1U5 2191, first chamber, 1 January–15 February 1924, #8625 (not AJ), initial inquiry in 1919 and decision in 1924.

52. Courtroom tales rarely reveal a domestic servant seduced by her master or his son; only one such instance appeared. Eighteen-year-old Mlle Michel entered domestic service with the Leblanc couple in 1916. Leblanc was fifty-five. Michel alleged that Leblanc took advantage of

her age and inexperience and they had relations between 1917 and November 1921. When he discovered she was pregnant, Leblanc settled her in a clinic, where she gave birth five months later to a son, whom she legally recognized. Leblanc paid all costs at this private clinic and visited her there, saying that he and his wife thought of themselves as parents to the young girl because they did not have children of their own. His avowal of parental affection for Michel was convincing; she lost her case. Arch. Paris, D1U5, AJ 4014, 16–31 December 1927.

53. Arch. Paris, D1U5, AJ 550, 1–14 May 1931, #885 of 1930, judgment of 11 May 1931.

54. Arch. Paris, D1U5, AJ 4155, 1–9 November 1933, #4074. For another instance, see BMD, DOS 347 PAT, document 34.

55. Dalloz, *Table alphabétique (sixième) de cinq années du Recueil Dalloz (1932 à 1936)*, 33;id., *Recueil hebdomadaire de jurisprudence*, 1935, 473–474.

56. Arch. Paris D1U5, AJ 4275, 25–30 November 1937, #6160 of 1936, heard on 26 November 1937. If she received the funds, she probably could have fed her child on that, but not much more.

57. BMD, DOS 347 PAT, document 34, probably clipped from the *Gazette du Palais* of 6 April 1935. Driving time in 2006 between Dijon and Dax is estimated at more than eight hours.

58. Savatier, *La Recherche de la paternité*, 43, citing cases from 1920 to 1925 from Rennes, Riom and Nancy. See also Dalloz, *Recueil hebdomadaire de jurisprudence*, 1925, 41, 250. For the 1935 Cour de cassation, see Dalloz, *Table alphabétique (sixième) de cinq années du Recueil Dalloz (1932 à 1936)*, 439.

59. Arch. Paris, D1U5, AJ 301, 1–16 July 1920, #3160, judgment of 2 July 1920 (Mory); AJ 4014, 16–31 December 1927, #179 of 1927 (Doger).

60. Arch. Paris, D1U5, AJ 650, #896 of 1932, judgment of 12 March 1935.

61. Arch. Paris, D1U5, AJ 650, 12–20 March 1935, #5778 of 1933. This is double most awards in purchasing power.

62. Arch. Paris, D1U5, AJ 650, 12–20 March 1935, #896 of 1932. For other examples, see D1U5, AJ 287, 1–8 January 1920, judgment of 3 January 1920; D1U5, AJ 510, 1 August–22 October 1919, #3018 of 1928, judgment of 22 October 1929; Perruchot, *Résultats de la loi du 16 novembre 1912*, 70.

63. Vérone, *La Situation juridique des enfants naturels*; id., "La Recherche de la paternité," *Jus suffragii*, 25 January 1913, in BMD, DOS 347 PAT.

64. Savatier, *La Recherche de la paternité*, 162–163; Fatoux, *La Juridiction correctionnelle du Tribunal civil*, 25.

65. Arch. Paris, D1U5, AJ 550, 1–14 May 1931, #5112 of 1928. For additional cases, see AJ 350, 1–7 May, 1923, #5243 of 1921; AJ 390, 1–15 February 1924, #2772 of 1923; AJ 400, 1–15 July 1924, #5533 of 1923; AJ 410, 1–14 February 1925, #5061 of 1924; D1U5, AJ 530, 1–10 July 1930, #2486 of 1930. For domestic servants, see AJ 410, 1–14 February 1925, #89 of 1925.

66. Names have been changed in conformity with privacy laws. Simone Roulet's paternity suit went from the civil tribunal of Toulouse, where she lost her case, to the appeals court in Bordeaux, which decided in her favor on 7 March 1927, to an annulment of the appeals court's

decision at the Cour de cassation in 1930. Information about Simone Roulet can be found in Arch. Paris, Fonds 8.Mermet/89/1, D10 J16, liasse 775 (23700) and from Dalloz, *Recueil périodique*, 1927, pt. 2, *Cours d'appel et tribunaux*, 81–84, which provides information about the appeal along with legal commentary. Her lawyers gave Josette's birth date as 3 February 1925, with Roulet's legal recognition on 21 February 1925. The Dalloz publication gives the birth date as 3 May 1925, with legal recognition on 21 May 1925.

67. Simone Roulet's father never enters the picture. Because Simone Roulet's mother had a different surname, it is probable that Mme de Salviac was divorced and reverted to her maiden name (*nom de jeune fille*), as was the custom, and that Simone Roulet bore the name of her father.

68. *Le Matin*, 4 September 1925, 1G and 9 September 1925, 1G, 2A; Savatier, *La Recherche de la paternité*, 57–58.

69. BMD, DOS 347 PAT, document 48. In 1935, Mlle Dunau was equally fortunate in her paternity suit against Didant, who had advised her to use some pharmaceuticals to end the pregnancy. The judge ruling in her favor decided that advice to abort constituted an avowal of paternity—but in this case there was also evidence of concubinage. Arch. Paris, AJ 4215, 20–31 December 1933, #1460 of 1935. For other examples of letters advising abortion as evidence of paternity, see Arch. Paris, DU5, AJ 4034, 1–9 December 1928, #1265 of 1927, case dismissed 3 December 1928; D1U5, AJ 4215, 20–31 December 1935, #4063 of 1935; D1U5, AJ 710, 9–17 March 1937, #5344.

70. *Le Matin*, 25 February 1925, 1B.

71. *Le Matin*, 4 April 1925, 3D. This was one of the rare instances of *recherche de maternité*.

72. Article 323 reads: "... si l'enfant a été inscrit, soit sous de faux noms, soit comme né de père et mère inconnus, la preuve de filiation peut se faire par témoins. Néanmoins cette preuve peut-être admise lorsqu'il y a commencement de preuve par écrit, ou lorsque les présomptions ou indices résultant de faits dès lors constans, sont assez graves pour déterminer l'admission."

73. Dalloz, *Recueil hebdomadaire*, 1936, 387–88.

74. *Le Matin*, 14 March 1924, 3E.

75. *La Française*, 21 April 1928, in BMD, DOS347.PAT, document 23; Pach, *Recherche de la paternité par l'examen des groupes sanguins*, 66, 75.

76. Dalloz, *Recueil périodique et critique de jurisprudence*, 1936, pt. 2, p. 41.

77. BMD, DOS 347 PAT, document 45, from *Gazette du Palais*, Cour d'appel de Paris, 21 October 1935.

78. Arch. Paris, D1U5, AJ 710, 9–17 March 1937, #26 of 1936, judgment of 16 March 1937.

79. Arch. Paris, D1U5, AJ 100, 1–20 January 1906, #40 of 1905, judgment of 5 January 1906.

80. BMD, DOS 347 PAT, document 49, from the *Gazette du Palais*, 8 February 1936.

81. Arch. Paris, D1U5, AJ 250, #1255 of 1916, judgment of 7 July 1916. See also D1U5, AJ 390, 1–15 February 1924, judgment of 9 February 1924, "Nullité de reconnaissance de l'enfant adultérine."

82. Marin, *L'Abandon de famille*. At this time Marin was vice president of the Chamber of Deputies.

83. Sohn, "Les Rôles féminins dans la vie privée," 33, 231.

84. Anderson, "How Well Does Paternity Confidence Match Actual Paternity?" 513–20.

85. Savatier, *La Recherche de la paternité*, 217–37, 243; BMD, DOS 347 PAT, document 40, Cour de cassation decision of 21 June 1935.

86. Maria Vérone, "Aux colonies: La Recherche de la paternité," *L'Œuvre*, 31 October 1928, both in BMD, DOS 347 PAT, document 21. For recherche de paternité in the French colonies, see Pedersen, " 'Special Customs,' " 43–64.

87. Nye, *Masculinity and Male Codes of Honor*, 9.

88. Foucault, *The History of Sexuality*, 1: 64, 83, 87, 147–48; quotations from 147, 124, and 83.

89. McLaren, *The Trials of Masculinity*.

Five • Families Dismantled and Reconstituted, 1880–1940

1. Nye, *Masculinity and Male Codes of Honor*, vii, 9, chap. 4; Foucault, *The History of Sexuality*, 1: 64, 83, 87, 147–48. See also Carbon, *Le Désaveu de paternité*, 20–22.

2. If an adulterous wife was still living with her husband, her husband did not usually win his case of paternity disavowal. The records of the judgments of the AJ civil tribunal, Arch. Paris D1U5, discussed in "A Note on Sources" in the first footnote of Chapter 4, contain cases of *désaveu de paternité*.

3. *Le Matin*, 9 March 1925, 2B. At the time of the newspaper account, Gaveau was awaiting trial. His fate is unknown. For another case, see *Le Matin*, 22 February 1923, 1D.

4. Arch. Paris, D1U5, AJ 4034, 1–9 December 1928, #4332 of 1926.

5. Arch. Paris, D1U5, AJ 10 August 1900, #3980 of 1898, decision of 14 August 1900. In one instance, a man lost his case because the only evidence he presented was that his son looked like the local café owner. See Arch. Paris, D1U5, AJ 4034, 1–9 December 1928, #3317 of 1928.

6. Arch. Paris, D1U5, AJ 120, 1–30 April 1907, #3541 and 3542 of 1905, judgment of 23 April 1907. One man had been separated from his wife for twenty-five years, and during that time, she had had seven children. He disavowed them all. Arch. Paris, D1U5, AJ 120, 1–30 April 1907, #392 of 1907, judgment of 9 April 1909.

7. Arch. Paris, D1U5, AJ 710, 9–17 March 1937, #3678 of 1935, judgment of 9 March 1937, and #5954 of 1934, judgment of 12 March 1937. The right to bear the patronymic is important because it constitutes a form of property.

8. Arch. Paris, Requêtes d'adoption dans le Chambre du Conseil du Tribunal civil de la Seine, 1277 W, judgment of 30 November 1928, CE57841.

9. In these marriages, the adulterous couples had not been criminally accused of adultery and therefore could marry; in some instances, the woman had been legally separated for years, and her first husband had just disavowed paternity of the child.

10. Arch. Paris, D1U5, AJ 250, 1–31 July 1916, #1318 of 1915, judgment of 4 July 1916; D1U5, AJ 287, 1–8 January 1920; AJ 291, 1–10 March 1920; AJ 370, 18–31 January 1923; AJ 390, 1–15 February 1924; and AJ 410, 1–14 February 1925; Dalloz, *Recueil périodique et critique de jurisprudence, de législation et de doctrine*, 1921, 25–26, for Savatier's comments; Maria Vérone, "Les Enfants illégitimes devant la loi," *La Française*, 29 March and 5 April 1924, in BHVP, Fonds Bouglé, Articles de journaux, boîte 8, thèmes.

11. Medick and Sabean, eds., *Interest and Emotion*.

12. The best analysis of this law and all it implies for gender relations and the culture of the late nineteenth century is Schafer, *Children in Moral Danger.*

13. Two now-classic studies of the development of the welfare state are Ewald, *L'État providence,* and Hatzfeld, *Du Paupérisme à la sécurité sociale.* For more recent work, see Accampo, Fuchs, and Stewart, eds. *Gender and the Politics of Social Reform in France.*

14. Donzelot, *The Policing of Families.* Although Donzelot overemphasizes the social control mechanism of the state's "tutelary apparatus," he provides a useful presentation of the state's intended involvement in families, especially those of the poor.

15. Halpérin, *Histoire du droit privé,* 220.

16. Schafer, *Children in Moral Danger,* chap. 3.

17. Sources for the cases of deprivation of paternal authority are the dossiers of the Parquet de la Seine, Déchéance de la puissance paternelle, 1898–1901 and 1905–1908, Arch. Paris, D3 U7/2 and U7/3. Owing to privacy rules forbidding the use of names, I have used only the initial and the dossier number.

18. Garrioch, *Neighborhood and Community in Paris,* and Roche, *The People of Paris.* Garrioch underscores the complementarities of neighborhood and family in bringing up children, noting that neighbors often helped the family (p. 60). They could also work against the parents or family for the protection of the children.

19. Arch. Paris, D3 U7/2, Déchéance de la puissance paternelle, 1898–1901, dossier #1707. Richard S. Hopkins discovered maps indicating that Charles slept about a block away. See Hopkins, "Engineering Nature."

20. Arch. Paris, D3 U7/3, Déchéance de la puissance paternelle, dossier #2998 (1907).

21. Arch. Paris, D3 U7/3, Déchéance de la puissance paternelle, dossier #3363 (1908).

22. Arch. Paris, D3 U7/3, Déchéance de la puissance paternelle, dossier #3000 (1907) and dossier #2757 (1906). The case was investigated and came before the court twice. Neither time was the daughter taken from the father. Fathers were deprived of their paternal authority in cases of proven sexual abuse. See, e.g., 1907 dossier #3085. For family disputes, see dossier #1686 of 1901 and esp. dossier #1713 of 1901.

23. Arch. Paris, D3 U7/3, Déchéance de la puissance paternelle, dossier #2692 (1906). For a case in which the children were separated, a grandmother took the oldest boy, and Assistance publique took the others, see dossier #2531 (1905).

24. Arch. Paris, D3 U7/2, Déchéance de la puissance paternelle, dossier #854 (1898–1901).

25. Arch. Paris, D3 U7/3, Déchéance de la puissance paternelle, dossier #26851 (1906) and dossier #2862 (1907).

26. Arch. Paris, D3 U7/3, Déchéance de la puissance paternelle, dossier #2711 (1906). From 1792 to 1907, the age of majority was twenty-five years for men and twenty-one years for women; after 1907, it was twenty-one for both men and women until 1974, when it became eighteen for both.

27. Arch. Paris, D3 U7/2, Déchéance de la puissance paternelle, dossier #1713 (1898–1901).

28. Arch. Paris, D3 U7/2, Déchéance de la puissance paternelle, dossier #1701 (1898–1901). The records do not specify how the story ends; in such cases, it is likely that authorities made no changes. Alice probably kept her children.

29. See, e.g., Arch. Paris, D3 U7/3, Déchéance de la puissance paternelle, dossier #3399 (1909) and dossier #2714 (1906).

30. Arch. Paris, D3 U7/2, Déchéance de la puissance paternelle, 1898–1901, dossier 1686.

31. Arch. Paris, Fonds 8.Mermet/89/1, D10 J16, liasse 775 (23700). These details of Simone Roulet's life come in part from her lawyer, Georges L. Hoffmann, *avocat à la cour*, "Note en délibéré à Messieurs les Président et juges composant la Chambre du Conseil Première Chambre du Tribunal civil de Toulouse" (n.d.). The other source of information from Roulet's lawyer is the document addressed to Monsieur le Procureur de la République près le Tribunal civil de la Seine on 9 July 1943. Sources for Mme de Salviac's position come from her lawyer's brief of 25 June 1943, when she filed charges to deprive Simone Roulet of her *puissance paternelle* under article 21 of the law of 24 July 1889.

32. Godelier, *L'Énigme du don*; Mauss, *The Gift*.

33. Blau, *Exchange and Power*, 63.

34. Mauss, *The Gift*, ix; 32–33; Lévi-Strauss, *The Elementary Structure of Kinship*, xxxiii, 37; Lallemand, *La Circulation des enfants*, 32–33, 74–76. Because those adopted were adults, this somewhat awkward term "adoptee" is more accurate than "children," and adopters did not always function as parents.

35. Sand, *Indiana*, 231.

36. Balzac, *Ursule Mirouët*; Lucey, *The Misfit of the Family*, 7–13; Gutton, *Histoire de l'adoption*, 138.

37. Dalloz, *Recueil général des lois et arrêts: Table alphabétique 1791 à 1850*, 2: 91–96.

38. Ibid., 93.

39. Sirey, *Recueil général des lois et des arrêts*, 554. The year of birth is given only as year XI in the revolutionary calendar.

40. Dalloz, *Répertoire de législation de doctrine et de jurisprudence*, 304–5.

41. Data for this paragraph are derived from Gutton, *L'Histoire de l'adoption*, 138–45. Only seventy adoptions were legalized between 1837 and 1840, with thirty-seven of those adoptions of natural recognized children.

42. Lallemand, *La Circulation des enfants*, 48. Anthropologists such as Mauss and Lévy-Strauss have explored the circulation, often by adoption, of children among kin and within the community in a variety of societies. More recently Suzanne Lallemand, relying on the theories of Mauss and Lévy-Strauss has described models of informal adoption throughout Africa and Oceania.

43. AAP, Fosseyeux, liasse 647, Assistance à l'enfance—Agence de Saint-Calais, 1819–1885, Correspondence de l'Assistance publique à Paris aux préposés à Saint-Calais (cartons 1–5), e.g. letter of 3 December 1854, carton 2. Starting in the 1830s, the director of the hospitals and hospices in Paris, and after 1849 the director of l'Assistance publique in Paris, who had paternal authority over the abandoned children of Paris, inquired of their agents in the countryside who had received those children whether a degree of affection existed between foster parents and the children. There is no evidence that a foster parent ever left an inheritance to an abandoned child from l'Assistance publique.

44. Lallemand, *La Circulation des enfants*, 48, 60. In France, *recherche de maternité* was always permitted and a mother who abandoned her child prior to 1923 could always reclaim that child, but often had to pay the state for the costs of rearing the child.

45. AAP, Fosseyeux, liasse 647, Correspondence de l'Assistance publique à Paris aux préposés à Saint-Calais, cartons 3 and 5 (20 April 1861 and 9 March 1872) 5.

46. Gager, *Blood Ties and Fictive Ties;* Fauve-Chamoux, "Beyond Adoption," 1–13; Knibiehler and Fouquet, *L'Histoire des mères,* 135.

47. In addition to state-run foundling homes in most major cities, orphanages abounded, most run by religious orders and private charities. There were at least twenty orphanages in Paris alone. Lecour, *Manuel d'assistance,* 104; *Manuel des œuvres et institutions religieuses et charitables de Paris,* 27, 31–34, 44–45, 54, 63.

48. Dalloz, *Recueil périodique et critique,* 1923, pt. 4, 257–62; id., *Recueil hebdomadaire de jurisprudence,* 1936, 9; Halpérin, *Histoire du droit privé,* 228.

49. Gutton, *L'Adoption,* 151.

50. This section of the chapter on adoption during the 1920s and 1930s is based primarily on an analysis of the extant adoption records of the Requêtes d'adoption dans le Chambre du Conseil du Tribunal civil de la Seine for the years 1925 to 1936, conserved at Arch. Paris, Côte 1277 W. To obtain the statistics, I sampled 10 percent of those records for the years 1928–36. There were between 1,000 and 1,500 decisions on adoption for the entire period between 1924 and 1941, with only ten for the years 1924 and 1925, and none for 1927. I have only used the people's initials under the terms of my permission to see these files.

51. Paul Allard, "Voulez-vous un enfant? La maternité à l'essai," *L'Œuvre,* 25 July 1932, in BHVP, Fonds Bouglé, coupures de presse, articles de journaux, boîte 8, thèmes.

52. Cadoret, *Parenté plurielle,* 33; Bouvier, *Le Lien social,* 58–128.

53. Blanche Vogt, "Vous qui n'avez pas d'enfant... Adoptez un pupille de l'Assistance publique," *L'Intransigeant,* 20 November 1926, in BHVP, Fonds Bouglé, coupures de presse, articles de journaux, boîte 8, thèmes. An article on adoption dated 12 February 1937 by Alice Jouenne stressed children's need for protection, food and education. See Fonds Bouglé, articles de journaux, boîte 5, thèmes-enfants.

54. Vogt, "Vous qui n'avez pas d'enfant"; Allard, "Voulez-vous un enfant?"

55. Ibid.

56. Arch. Paris, 1277 W, judgment of 3 December 1930, EK49244.

57. Arch. Paris, DU5, Tribunal civil, Mineurs, 1934. Similarly, Antoinette P., never married and fifty-one years old at the time of adoption, had taken care of all of young Violette's needs for nine years, starting six months after Violette was born and abandoned to the Assistance publique in April 1923. Arch. Paris, 1277 W, judgment of 13 January 1932, EC17741.

58. Arch. Paris, 1277 W, judgment of 20 December 1933, EA18081.

59. Vogt, "Vous qui n'avez pas d'enfant."

60. Arch. Paris, 1277 W, judgment of 15 June 1933, case number missing.

61. Arch. Paris, 1277 W, judgment of 1 April 1936, ML32979. Similarly, see judgment of 2 November 1932, LS04516. All cases of adoption of an abandoned child through *l'Assistance publique* and an agency, such as the Section on Adoption of L'Entr'aide des femmes françaises, are similar. The couple received the child as an infant and adoption was finalized generally within a range of two to twelve years later. See also judgment of 6 June 1934, CM89269,

62. Arch. Paris, 1277 W, judgment of 29 October 1930, AK3733. See also HL86071 of 15 May 1929; KK61959 of 5 June 1929; L47640 of 10 June 1931.

63. Vogt, "Vous qui n'avez pas d'enfant."

64. Arch. Paris, 1277 W, judgment of 9 April 1926, 648–24.

65. Arch. Paris, 1277 W, judgment of 14 January 1931, HA01463. There was no change over the decade in the extant adoption records; among those adopting abandoned children were bankers, engineers, industrialists, accountants, *propriétaires*, and financially well off widows. See also judgment of 22 July 1925, 2690–24 where a couple in their mid fifties (he was an industrialist) adopted a 12-year-old girl whom they had raised since her birth in 1913, when she was abandoned at the foundling home in Beauvais. In 1935, André S., a 41-year old engineer, with his wife consenting, adopted two unrelated abandoned children not legally recognized by their birth mothers. One was a boy born in March 1929, whom the adopting parent received in July of that year, and the other a girl born in 1930, whom the adopting parents received within months of her birth. The adoption agency L'Adoption française facilitated both these adoptions on the same day. See judgments of 30 January 1935, CP98352 and CP98353. The childless widow of a former bank director benefited from a sufficient fortune to enable her to provide for a child. She took in an abandoned young boy of unknown parentage when he was ten years old, the year after her husband died, to overcome loneliness, or because her husband had objected to adoption, or just from love. The boy was with her for just two years when she filed adoption papers, but she "always surrounded him with the most affectionate care." Arch. Paris, 1277 W, judgment of 12 November 1931, HH49720. See also judgment of 28, LS03008, judgments of 3 May 1933, MM15260 and MM15263, judgment of 23 October 1935, KR35117. These few cases typify several others.

66. This was not significantly different from motives for adoption that Kristen Gager has found in early modern Paris. Gager, *Blood Ties and Fictive Ties*, 91.

67. Arch. Paris, 1277 W, judgment of 19 December 1934, HV49719. See also judgment of 31 October 1934, CS65855.

68. AP 1277 W, judgment of 25 November 1925, #2285–25. In another instance, a couple in their mid forties adopted his illegitimate nephew, whom they had raised for eighteen years. Judgment of 22 February 1928, CK63491.

69. Arch. Paris, 1277 W, judgment of 7 November 1928, EP09690.

70. Arch. Paris, 1277 W, judgment of 1 July 1931, LS70669. In another situation, following the death of his wife, Henri G. continued to live with his three minor children, whom he tried to support, but soon consented to his childless brother and sister-in-law, aged forty and forty-one, legally adopting the youngest of these children, his seven-year-old daughter. His brother, a master mechanic, "lived in a fortunate situation, quite superior to that of the child's father." Arch. Paris, 1277 W, judgment of 4 April 1928.

71. Arch. Paris, 1277 W, judgment of 22 April 1931, AH96085. Another unmarried uncle, a *propriétaire*, the comte de S., adopted his nephew, born in 1914, whom he had raised for eighteen years, since the age of three months when his mother had died. By the time of the adoption in 1932, the adoptee's father was also dead. Judgment of 23 November 1932, KK932205.

72. Arch. Paris, 1277 W, judgment of 6 June 1934, KL52578.

73. Arch. Paris, 1277 W, judgment of 28 May 1930, PC48908.

74. Arch. Paris, 1277 W, judgment of 8 February 1928, AC10382

75. Arch. Paris, 1277 W, judgment of 27 June 1928, AP4212; judgment of 13 June 1928, LL18942; judgment of 20 June 1928, LH36240; judgment of 15 October 1930, CM3951; judgment of 23 May 1928, KP12206.

76. Arch. Paris, 1277 W, judgment of 14 January 1931, EK11962. Another aunt, a 56-year-old childless widow whose husband had died in the war, adopted her two nieces in 1931. She had raised them for eighteen years since the death of their parents. Judgment of 25 March 1931, AH67250. Mme P., childless, propertied, divorced, and not remarried, adopted her nephew after her sister had died in 1923, leaving a 5-year-old boy. He had lived with his aunt since then. His father had disappeared. Judgment of 6 July 1932, KP30897.

77. Arch. Paris, 1277 W, judgment of 28 November 1928, LP22388. There are many instances when the relationship is unknown. In November 1928, a childless couple adopted four-year-old Jeannine S., born to Pierre and his wife Renée. Renée had died in 1926 and Pierre, who did not remarry, consented to the adoption of his daughter, Jeannine. Furthermore, the adopting couple had raised Jeannine since her birth and had always "taken care of her needs, shown her the strongest affection, and have considered her exactly as their own daughter." Judgment of 26 November 1928, AP65647. For a similar case see 1277 W, judgment of 19 July 1935, EA29448. See also 1277 W, judgment of 1 April 1936, EP45254.

78. Arch. Paris, 1277 W, judgment of 28 November 1928, ES66905.

79. Arch. Paris, 1277 W, judgment of 24 October 1928, LS79725.

80. Arch. Paris, 1277W, judgment of 2 April 1930, KA18360. In 1933, the 66-year-old widow Jeanne B., a concierge, whose only son had died without leaving any children, adopted the 17-year-old son of a domestic servant, whom she had taken care of since he was very young. See judgment of 22 February 1933, CS64283. Not dissimilarly, a nurse, Marie L., a 49-year-old single woman, adopted Micheline O. in 1934, when Micheline was seven. Marie L. had cared for Micheline since her birth in 1927. The mother, who had legally recognized the child, had died in 1931, and her express wish had been that Marie L. adopt Micheline. See judgment of 19 December 1934, LV38767.

81. Arch. Paris, 1277 W, judgment of 4 March 1925, 41–25.

82. Arch. Paris, 1277 W, judgment of 28 October 1925, 1642–25. Occasionally, stepchildren believed that they were the biological children of the stepfather. See judgment of 11 July 1928, M54839. In 1936, one year after his wife's death, 62-year-old Joseph P. adopted her three children by her first marriage. Joseph P. had taken care of these children and had "acted as a father" to them since his marriage to their widowed mother in 1913. All three of the adoptees were married, and the youngest was thirty at the time of adoption. See judgment of 22 January 1936, CA46005. For similar situations, see CP25686 of 1 June 1932 and LN3553 of 19 December 1934.

83. Arch. Paris, 1277 W, judgment of 23 November 1932, AS45219. In another instance, a wife adopted her deceased husband's adult children by his first marriage after their mother had also died. Arch. Paris, 1277 W, judgment of 19 December 1934, C53676.

84. Arch. Paris, 1277 W, judgment of 27 June 1928, AE95059.

85. Arch. Paris, 1277 W, judgment of 26 December 1928 LP80954. The records did not indicate whether the natural daughter had a Vietnamese mother.

86. Arch. Paris, 1277 W, judgment 18 July 1928, LS94411.

87. Raynaud, "Adoption," 249–52. As late as 1968, authorities called the "birth" parents "blood" parents, retaining the importance of blood ties.

88. The anthropologists Lallemand, Mauss, and Lévi-Strauss describe several reasons for adoption in ancient societies, many of which are appropriate for modern France. Lallemand,

La Circulation des enfants, 74–76; Lévi-Strauss, *La Pensée sauvage*, 86; Lévi-Strauss, *The Elementary Structure of Kinship;* Mauss, *The Gift.*

89. Rogron, *Code civil expliqué.*

90. Arch. Paris, 1277 W, judgment of 25 March 1931, AH67250.

91. Carbonnier, *Droit civil*, 2: 347. His words echo those of some redactors of the Civil Code two centuries earlier.

Six • Paternity and the Family, 1940 to the Present

1. Pollard, *Reign of Virtue;* Koos, "Engendering Reaction"; Koos, "Gender, Anti-Individualism and Nationalism," 639–73: Koos, "*'On les aura!'*: The Gendered Politics of Abortion," 21–22; Childers, *Fathers, Families, and the State.*

2. Dalloz, *Encyclopédie juridique*, 1–41.

3. Décret-Loi du 29 juillet 1939 relatif à la famille et à la natalité françaises in the *Journal officiel*, 23 July and 5 August 1939. It was modified by decrees of 16 December 1939 and 24 April 1940 and by the laws of 18 November 1940, 15 February 1941, and 3 February 1942. See Renaudin, *La Famille dans la nation;* Garcin, *Révolution sociale par la famille.*

4. For the Family Code under Vichy, see Drouhet, *L'Évolution juridique des allocations familiales;* Jarlot, *Le Code de la famille;* Childers, *Fathers, Family, and the State*, 40. The Code de la famille did not replace the Napoleonic Civil Code but supplemented it, incorporating ideas of welfare that had been operating piecemeal for the previous seventy years.

5. The Family Code and subsequent decrees specified that the recipient family had to be French, which usually meant that the father had to be a French citizen. New immigrants were not entitled to family allowances or birth bonuses. During the Vichy years, writers used the word "race" to connote an aspect of being French. It usually meant white and Catholic or Protestant, not Jewish or from the colonies. Vichy welfare programs also neglected the wives and families of over one million prisoners of war. Fishman, *We Will Wait*, xii.

6. In Western European industrial societies, especially in England and Germany, discourses about work were dominated by the ideal of a family wage and a male breadwinner model in which the man entered the labor force and earned wages to support his family. This model infrequently applied to France, where women's wage contributions to the family economy were more generally acknowledged. For example, in England, welfare and family subsidies went to the husband/father to provide for his family; in France, welfare for children went directly to the mothers. Vichy became an exception. Fuchs, *Gender and Poverty*, 110–14; Pedersen, *Family, Dependence, and the Origins of the Welfare State*, 5–20, 289–354, 386–88.

7. Penfentenyo de Kervéréguin, *Le Manuel du père de famille.*

8. Pollard, *Reign of Virtue*, 63; Paxton, *Vichy France*, 167; Gildea, *Marianne in Chains*, 100.

9. Blandine Grosjean, "Que tout enfant ait accès à son histoire," interview with Ségolène Royal, ministre déléguée à l'enfance et à la famille, *Libération*, 17 January 2001; "Le Vertige des origins," *Nouvel Observateur*, 14–20 December, 2000, 114–18; Lefaucheur, "Pères absents et droit au père," 11–17.

10. Pollard, *Reign of Virtue*, 65.

11. The case studies for this section are among the more than two dozen involving family law contained in the archives of one Paris law firm that deposited its records from the 1920s

through the 1950s at the Archives de Paris. See Fonds 8.Mermet/89/1, D10 with numbers of the specific carton and liasse following. To comply with authorization to access these files, I have changed all names.

12. Arch. Paris, D10 J34, liasse 816, dossier 22510. His letters but not hers were in the file.

13. For examples, see Chapter 4 above and Arch. Paris, D1U5, Tribunal civil, AJ 287, 1–8 January 1920, decision of 3 January 1920; AJ 370, 18–31 January 1923, #1940 of 1921, judgment of 18 January 1923. See also D1U5, AJ530, 1–10 July 1930, January 1928, judgment of 1 July 1930; D1U5, AJ 550, 1–14 May 1931, #5112 of 1928, judgment of 12 May 1931; and D1U5, AJ 710, 9–17 March 1937, #2495 of 1934, decision of 12 March 1937.

14. Arch. Paris, D10 J32, liasse 783, dossier 22926.

15. The many letters retained by Jean-Pierre Ponelle, which he gave to his lawyer, provide details of their lives.

16. For the context of daily life in France during the war years, see Veillon, *Vivre et survivre*, and Gildea, *Marianne in Chains*.

17. Mégève is in the mountains of the Haute-Savoie.

18. Veillon, *Vivre et survivre*, 83–85. Paxton, *Vichy France*, 53.

19. Pollard, *Reign of Virtue*, 65. Some of the best literary examples of adultery can be found in Guy de Maupassant's novel *Bel-Ami* (1885) and Émile Zola's *Pot-Bouille* (1882).

20. Arch. Paris, D10 J32, liasse 811, dossier 23514. He was posted to an area in the Charente roughly 500 kilometers from Paris. It would have been easier for him to travel between Paris and Tours.

21. In 2004, Renée Kahan was listed in the Paris telephone directory as living at the same address she had in 1940. My agreement of confidentiality prevented me from contacting her.

22. Pollard, *Reign of Virtue*, 63–64.

23. Farmer, *Martyred Village*; Fishman, *We Will Wait*; Gildea, *Marianne in Chains*, chaps. 5, 10 and 12.

24. Information on the Drossard-Montand paternity suit is derived from several sources. See, e.g., Craig Whitney, "Beyond the Grave, DNA Haunts Yves Montand," *New York Times*, 12 March 1998; interview with Drossard in *Paris Match*, 12 March 1998; and Anne Chemin, "Le Corps d'Yves Montand sera exhumé pour un test d'ADN," *Le Monde*, 8 November 1997, 10.

25. Montand had one adopted and one biological child whom he legally recognized; they shared his $3.7 million estate.

26. Carbonnier, *Droit civil*, 2: 300; Dalloz, *Recueil périodique et critique*, 1939; Malaurie and Aynès, *Cours de droit civil*, 266, 360–64; Cornu, *Droit civil*, 404, 408.

27. Rubellin-Devichi, "Le Droit, les pères et la paternité," 165.

28. Delumeau and Roche, *Histoire des pères et de la paternité*, 383.

29. Hunt, *The Family Romance*.

30. Duchen, *Feminism in France*, chaps. 1 and 3; Vincent, "A History of Secrets?" 127; Prost, "Public and Private Spheres," 209. Prost estimates that 17 percent of "couples who married in 1968 and 1969 were already living together" and "by 1977 that figure had increased to forty-four of every hundred" (p. 81). The sociologist Louis Roussel places the proportion lower; his data also indicate that over 20 percent of couples lived together before marriage, with children born within marriage. Roussel, *La Famille incertaine*, 7–8, 68, 74, 85, 90–94.

31. Berthet, *Les Obligations alimentaires,* 50, 111–12, 202–3; Labrusse-Riou, "Les Problèmes de la paternité," 117; Malaurie and Aynès, *Cours de droit civil,* 368; René Floriot, "Le Statut des enfants naturels et adultérins" *Le Monde,* 27 April 1971, 25; Delumeau and Roche, *Histoire des pères et de la paternité,* 324–25. The Law of 1972 was technically Act 72–3, but since it modified the Civil Code, it is convenient to refer to it as a law. With this law, the phrase *enfants adultérins* (adulterine children) disappeared from legal language. I have found this term odious and throughout this book have substituted the phrase "children of adultery," however awkward it sounds. For further details on the laws of 1972 and 1993, see Carbonnier, *Droit civil,* 2: 298–323; Cornu, *Droit civil,* 402–16; www.legifrance.gouv.fr, Civil Code, article 342 (accessed 13 May 2007).

32. Carbonnier, *Droit civil,* 2: 302.

33. Labrusse-Riou, "Les Problèmes de la paternité," 117; Malaurie and Aynès, *Cours de droit civil,* 368.

34. *Père subsidant* was a new term indicating a father who provided for the child materially with child support but did not have paternity judicially declared. The phrase derives from the French *subsides,* meaning aid or allocation. *Subsides* became the preferred term, replacing *alimentation.* See Malaurie and Aynès, *Cours de droit civil,* 371–72.

35. Malaurie and Aynès, *Cours de droit civil,* 370. Roughly 200 years earlier, the noted legal scholar Jean-François Fournel argued for this arrangement.

36. The percentage not paying child support, or paying irregularly, ranged from 30 percent to 60 percent, depending on the survey data. Berthet, *Les Obligations alimentaires,* 90–94. A 1972 survey indicated that men regularly provided the subsidies (a *pension alimentaire*) only in 36 percent of the cases. Roussel, *La Famille incertaine,* 175.

37. The French text reads: "La paternité hors mariage peut être judiciairement déclarée. La preuve ne peut en être rapportée que si'il existe des présomptions ou indices graves." Article 340 has several sections detailing the course of action and providing for divisibility of paternity between subsides and attribution of a name and parental authority. See www.legifrance.gouv.fr/code (accessed 14 May 2007).

38. Berthet, *Les Obligations alimentaires,* 83–90, 202–3, 222, 226. Since 8 March 1982 (International Women's Day), qualified mothers who were not receiving the child support that courts had awarded them, or who chose not to file paternity suits, were eligible for benefits from the Caisse d'allocations familiales, or Family Allowance Fund.

39. Carbonnier, *Droit civil,* 2: 298.

40. Ibid., 291–99.

41. Rubellin-Devichi, "Le Droit, les pères et la paternité," 175–76.

42. Ibid., 165.

43. Dekeuwer-Défossez, "Le Contentieux de la famille naturelle," 133.

44. Delumeau and Roche, eds., *Histoire des pères et de la paternité,* 361, 381–85, 393–98, 430–34, 445–58. In this volume, Françoise Hurstel and Geneviève Delaisi de Parseval proclaim the end of the paterfamilias with the legislation of 4 June 1970 that changed *puissance paternelle* to *autorité paternelle,* which was followed closely by that of January 1972 on filiation.

45. "Les Députés s'interrogent sur le droit pour l'enfant de connaître ses origins," *Le Monde,* 30 April 1992, 10.

46. J.-L. S., "Seul le RPR s'est opposé au projet de loi sur la famille et les droits de l'enfant," *Le Monde*, 18 May 1992, 8.

47. Scott, *Parité!* chap. 5.

48. Loi no. 99–944 du 15 novembre 1999 relative au pacte civil de solidarité. Article 515–8, *Journal officiel de la République française*, Lois (16 November 1999), 16959–62. Through the third degree of consanguinity included parents and children, grandparents and grandchildren, siblings, aunts, uncles, nieces and nephews.

49. Ibid., articles 6 and 7.

50. Lucey, *The Misfit of the Family*, 13.

51. The Civil Code (title 5, chap. 1) frequently refers to *époux* and not husband and wife; title 5, chap. 6, also refers to "des devoirs et des droits respectifs des époux."

52. *Le Monde*, 17–18 September 2006, 1, 10. In this instance and in n. 54 below, the information in the article appearing in *Le Monde* was derived from data in "La Situation démographique en 2004. Mouvement de la population," INSEE, *Résultats société*, n. 55, available at www.insee.fr/fr/ppp/ir/sd2004/dd/pdf/sd2004_brochure.pdf (accessed 22 September 2007). A survey of 2004 indicated that "57 percent of all Frenchmen and 75 percent of those under 35 believe that gay couples should be allowed to marry. That compares with only 24 percent in the United States." Elaine Sciolino, "Losing Its Nonchalance, France Feuds over Gay Vows," *New York Times*, May 20, 2004. Royal lost the election in April 2007, and during the campaign waffled on her position toward same-sex marriages. She and her partner have since separated.

53. *International Herald Tribune*, 10 July 1997, 3.

54. *Le Monde*, 17–18 September 2006, 1, 10. Data derived from "La Situation démographique en 2004," cited in n. 52 above.

Epilogue

1. *Le Monde*, 9 November 2006, 3.

2. Alessandra Stanley, "So Who's Your Daddy? In DNA Tests, TV Finds Elixir to Raise Ratings," *New York Times*, 19 March 2002, § C1, 6; Mireya Navarro, "Painless Paternity Tests, but the Truth May Hurt," *New York Times*, 2 October 2005, § 9, 1–2, shows how one does not have to be poor for a man to have paternity tests and find out that he is not the father. As in the late eighteenth and early nineteenth centuries, some lawyers now accuse the women of "father shopping" in naming the man most able to support the child.

3. Tamar Lewin, "In Genetic Testing for Paternity, Law Often Lags Behind Science," *New York Times*, 11 March 2001, §1, 1, 19.

4. Andrea F. Siegel, "Ruling Alters Idea of Mother," *Baltimore Sun*, 17 May 2007, www.baltimoresun.com/news/local/bal-te.md.appeals (accessed 18 May 2007). I wish to thank Henry Tom, my conscientious editor at the Press, always supportive of his authors, who went far above and beyond the call of duty and sent me this link.

5. Forth, *The Dreyfus Affair*, 9; Nye, *Masculinity and Male Codes of Honor*, esp. chap. 4.

6. *Le Monde*, 10–11 June 2001, 7.

7. John Bowe, "An Extended Nuclear Family? Gay Men, Lesbians and the Kids They Are Making and Raising, Sort of Together," *New York Times Magazine*, 19 November 2006, 66–73, 80, 116–18, 121.

8. *New York Times*, 24 March 2002, § 1, 8. These data, however, should be considered critically. In some census data, cohabiting couples are considered in the same category as married couples; other data consider a mother unwed if her name on the child's birth certificate differs from that of the father, ignoring the fact that some legally married couples have different surnames.

9. Foucault, *The History of Sexuality*, 1: 88.

10. Scott, *Parité!* 1–2, 5.

11. Nye, *Masculinity and Male Codes of Honor*, 9.

12. Foucault, *The History of Sexuality*, 1: 106.

13. Bourdieu, *The Logic of Practice*, 147–49; Rauch, *Crise de l'identité masculine*, 140.

14. Elaine Sciolino, "L'Amour Has Little to Do with l'État," *New York Times*, Week in Review, 21 October 2007, 1.

WORKS CITED

- *Archival Sources*
  - ARCHIVES DE L'ASSISTANCE PUBLIQUE (CITED AS AAP)

Fosseyeux, liasse 647, l'Assistance à l'enfance—Agence de Saint-Calais, 1819–1885

  - ARCHIVES NATIONALES DE FRANCE (CITED AS AN)

BB18

  - ARCHIVES DE LA VILLE DE PARIS ET DÉPARTEMENT DE LA SEINE (CITED AS ARCH. PARIS)

DU5 Tribunal civil de Paris, Registres mineurs, Registres 1ère Chambre, 1920–1940
D1U5 Tribunal civil de Paris, Registres Assistance judiciaire, 1870–1940
D3 U7/2 and D3 U7/3, Parquet de la Seine, Déchéance de la puissance paternelle, 1898-1901, 1905–1908
1277 W Requêtes d'adoption dans le Chambre du Conseil du Tribunal civil de la Seine, 1925–1936.
Fonds Mermet

  - BIBLIOTHÈQUE HISTORIQUE DE LA VILLE DE PARIS (CITED AS BHVP)

Bouglé Collection

  - BIBLIOTHÈQUE MARGUERITE DURAND (CITED AS BMD)

- *Newspapers*

Le Matin
Gazette des tribunaux (cited as GT)
Le Temps

- *Published Primary Sources*

Acollas, Émile. *Droit et liberté, l'enfant né hors mariage. Recherche de la paternité.* Paris: Sausset, 1865.

———. *Les Enfants naturels.* Paris: Librairie de la Bibliothèque nationale, 1871.

Actes du Congrès féministe international de Bruxelles [4–7 August 1897]. Brussels: Bulins, 1898.

Adresse à la Convention nationale, au nom d'une infinité de pères & mères chargés de familles, & dont plusieurs sont à la veille d'être ruinés par des enfans nés hors le mariage. N.d. Newberry pamphlet series, FRC 131.

Amblard, Jacques. *De la séduction.* Thesis, Université de Paris, Faculté de droit. Paris: A. Rousseau, 1908.

Amiable, Louis. *De la preuve de la paternité hors mariage: Étude de législation.* Paris: Chevalier Marescq, 1885.

Annat, Philippe. *De la recherche de la paternité naturelle.* Thesis, Université de Paris, Faculté de droit. Paris: Giard & Brière, 1898.

Azema, Michel. Convention nationale. *Rapport et projet de loi sur l'adoption, présenté à la Convention nationale, au nom du comité de législation.* Paris: Imprimerie nationale, 1793.

Balzac, Honoré de. *Ursule Mirouët.* 1841. Paris: Gallimard, 1981.

Baret, Paul. *Histoire et critique des règles sur la preuve de la filiation naturelle en droit français et étranger.* Paris: A. Marescq, 1872.

Baudin, Jean-Baptiste Armand. *La Recherche judiciaire de la paternité naturelle et la loi du 16 novembre 1912.* Paris: Société anonyme d'imprimerie, 1913.

Berlier, Théophile. Convention nationale. *De l'adoption: Idées offertes à la méditation de ses collègues.* Paris. Imprimerie nationale, 4 June 1793.

———. Convention nationale. *Opinion du citoyen Berlier, Député de la Côte d'Or à la Convention nationale sur les droits à restituer aux enfants nés hors du mariage, jusqu'à présent appelés bâtards lue au Comité de législation.* Paris: Imprimerie nationale, brumaire an II.

Bernard, Marie-Paul. *Histoire de l'autorité paternelle en France.* Paris: Montdidier, 1863.

Berthe, Léon-Noël, and Michel de Langre, eds. *Maximilien Robespierre: Les Droits et l'état des bâtards. Lazare Carnot: Le Pouvoir et l'habitude. Discours inédits prononcés devant l'Académie d'Arras les 27 avril 1786 et 25 mai 1787.* Arras: Académie des Sciences: Lettres et Arts, 1971.

Bonjean, Georges. *Enfants révoltés et parents coupables.* Paris: Armand Colin, 1895.

Bonzon, Jacques. *La Recherche de la paternité.* Preface by Mme Charles D'Abbadie D'Arrast. Vals-les-Bains: Aberlen, 1905.

Bordeaux, Henry. *La Crise de la famille française.* Paris: Flammarion, 1921.

Boret, Paul. *Histoire et critique des règles sur la preuve de filiation naturelle en droit français et étranger.* 1892.

Bourgeois, Charles. *La Recherche de la paternité et les projets de réforme actuels.* Paris. L. Larose & L. Tenin, 1912.

Boverat, Fernand. *Patriotisme et paternité.* Paris: B. Grasset, 1913.

Brun, François. *La Recherche de la paternité, commentaire théorique et pratique de la loi du 16 novembre 1912, suivi d'un essai de législation comparée.* Preface by Louis Martin. Paris: Marchal & Godde, 1913.

Brunetière, Ferdinand. "La Recherche de la paternité." *Revue des Deux-Mondes*, 12 September 1883.

Cadet, Ernest. *Le Mariage en France: Statistique et réformes. Études morales sur la société contemporaine.* Paris: Guillaumin, 1870.

Caillol, Aimé. *La Loi de 1912 sur la recherche de la paternité devant la doctrine et la jurisprudence.* Montpellier: Mari-Lavit, 1934.

Cambacérès, Jean-Jacques Régis de. Convention nationale. *Projet de décret sur les enfants nés hors du mariage présenté au nom du Comité de législation.* Paris: Imprimerie nationale, n.d.

———. Convention nationale. *Nouveau rapport sur les articles d'appendice du titre IV du livre 1er concernant les enfants né hors le mariage, présenté au nom du Comité de législation.* Paris: Imprimerie nationale, 9 brumaire an II.

———. Convention nationale. *Rapport fait à la Convention nationale sur le premier projet du Code civil.* 9 August 1793. Paris: Imprimerie nationale, n.d.

———. Convention nationale. *Rapport et projet de décret sur les enfants naturels, présentés au nom du Comité de législation (4 juin 1793).* Paris: Imprimerie nationale, 1793.

———. Convention nationale. *Rapport sur le Code civil, fait au nom du Comité de législation, dans la séance du 23 fructidor, an II (9 September 1794).* Paris: Imprimerie nationale, an II.

———. Corps législatif. *Projet de Code civil présenté au Conseil des Cinq-Cents au nom de la Commission de la classification des lois.* Paris: Imprimerie nationale, messidor an IV (June 1796).

Carbon, Émile. *Le Désaveu de paternité.* Thesis, Université de Montpellier, Faculté de droit. Montpellier: Firman & Montane, 1925.

Carité, Maurice. *Le Père de famille et le foyer.* Paris: Éditions du temps present, 1941.

Chevalier, Georges. *La Recherche de la paternité naturelle en droit français (étude sur la loi du 16 novembre 1912).* Poitiers: G. Roy, 1917.

Cinquin, François, *Étude sur la déclaration judiciaire de paternité naturelle.* Lyons: Phily, 1912.

Coirard, Louis. *La Famille dans le Code civil (1804–1904).* Thesis, Université d'Aix-Marseille, Faculté de droit. Aix-en Provence: Mahaire, 1907.

Coissac, Paul. *De l'interprétation par la jurisprudence des cas dans lesquels la recherche de la paternité naturelle est autorisée par la loi du 16 novembre 1912.* Thesis, Université de Paris, Faculté de droit. Paris: Pierre Bossuet, 1931.

Congrès international de la condition et des droits des femmes. Tenu les 5, 6, 7, et 8 septembre 1900 à l'Exposition universelle au Palais de l'Économie sociale et des Congrès. Paris: Imprimerie des arts et manufactures, 1901.

Considérant, Victor-Prosper. *Exposition abrégée du système phalanstérien de Fourier.* Paris: Librairie socìetaire, 1845.

Coulet, Paul, and Albert Vanois. *Étude sur la recherche de la paternité.* Paris: Marescq, 1880.

Coulon, Henri. *De la condition des enfants naturels reconnus dans la succession du leurs père et mère. Commentaire de la loi du 25 mars 1896, législation antérieure, travaux parlementaires, doctrine, législation étrangère, formules.* Paris: Marchal & Billard, 1896.

———. *Le Divorce et l'adultère. De l'abrogation des lois pénales en matière d'adultère.* Paris: Marchal & Billard, 1890–1893.

———. *De la réforme du mariage.* Paris: Marchal & Billard, 1900.

Coulon, Henri, and René de Chavagnes. *La Famille libre.* Paris: Flammarion, 1913.

Crémieu, Louis. *Les Preuves de la filiation naturelle non reconnue.* Thesis, Université de Paris, Faculté de droit. Paris: n.p., 1907.

Cussac, André. *Les Preuves de la paternité naturelle.* Lille: H. Morel, 1912.

Dabert, Jean. *De la responsabilité civile du séducteur.* Thesis, Université de Paris, Faculté de droit. Paris: H. Jouve, 1908.

Dalloz. Jurisprudence générale. *Les Codes annotés, additions au nouveau Code civil, 1 octobre 1907–1 octobre 1920.* Paris: Jurisprudence générale Dalloz, 1921.

———. *Encyclopédie juridique: Répertoire de droit civil.* Vol. 1. Paris: Dalloz, 1992.

———. *Recueil général des lois et arrêts: Table alphabétique (1791 à 1850).* Vols. 1 and 2. Paris: Jurisprudence générale Dalloz, 1857.

———. *Recueil hebdomadaire de jurisprudence.* Paris: Jurisprudence générale Dalloz, 1925, 1935, 1936.

———. *Recueil périodique et critique de jurisprudence, de législation et de doctrine.* Paris: Jurisprudence générale Dalloz, selected years from 1825 through 1936.

———. *Recueil périodique et critique. Quatrième partie. Lois et décrets, rapports et discussions législatives.* Paris: Jurisprudence générale Dalloz, 1912.

———. *Répertoire de législation de doctrine et de jurisprudence en matière de droit civil, commercial, criminel.* Paris: Jurisprudence générale Dalloz, 1846.

———. *Supplément au répertoire méthodique et alphabétique: paternité et filiation.* Vol. 12. Paris: Jurisprudence générale Dalloz, 1893.

———. *Table alphabétique des 22 années du recueil périodique de jurisprudence, de législation et de doctrine (1845 à 1867).* Paris: Jurisprudence générale Dalloz, 1867.

———. *Table alphabétique des dix années (1867–1877).* Paris: Jurisprudence générale Dalloz, 1877.

———. *Table alphabétique (cinquième) de cinq années du Recueil Dalloz (1927 à 1931).* Paris: Jurisprudence générale Dalloz, n.d. (1932).

———. *Table alphabétique (sixième) de cinq années du Recueil Dalloz (1932 à 1936).* Paris: Jurisprudence générale du Dalloz, n.d. (1937).

———. See also *Recueil Dalloz Sirey de doctrine de jurisprudence et de législation.*

Daubié, Julie-Victoire. *La Femme pauvre au dix-neuvième siècle.* Vol. 3: *Condition professionnelle.* 2nd ed. Paris: Ernest Thorin, 1870.

Dejob, Lucien. *Le Rétablissement de l'adoption en France.* Thesis, Université de Paris, Faculté de droit. Paris: A. Pédone, 1911.

Delzon, Louis. *La Famille française et son evolution.* Paris: Armand Colin, 1913.

Demolombe, Charles. *Traité de l'adoption et de la tutelle officieuse; de la puissance paternelle.* Paris: A. Durand, 1861.

Desloges, Louis. *Des enfans trouvés, des femmes publiques et des moyens à employer pour en diminuer le nombre.* Paris: Desloges, 1836.

Deuxième Congrès international des œuvres et institutions féminines, tenu au Palais des congrès de l'Exposition universelle de 1900. 4 vols. Paris: Charles Blot, 1902.

Douarche, Aristide. *Les Tribunaux civils de Paris pendant la Révolution (1791–1800)*, Documents inédits recueillis avant l'incendie du Palais de Justice de 1871 par Casenave, conseiller à la Cour de cassation. 2 vols. Paris: Librairie Léopold Cerf, 1905.

Drouhet, Pierre. *L'Évolution juridique des allocations familiales*. Paris: Édition social française, 1943.

Dubois, Francis Félix. *Les Fiançailles et promesses de mariage en droit français*. Thesis, Université de Rennes, Faculté de droit. Angers: A. Burdin, 1897.

Dumas, Alexandre, *fils*. *La Dame aux Camélias*. In *Théâtre complet*, vol. 1. Paris: Calmann Lévy, 1903.

———. *Les Femmes qui tuent et les femmes qui votent*. Paris: Calmann Lévy, 1880.

———. *Le Fils naturel*. In *Théâtre complet*, vol. 3. Paris: Calmann Lévy, 1893.

———. *La Recherche de la paternité. Lettre à M. Rivet*. Paris: Calmann Lévy, 1883.

Dumas, Dr. A. *L'interdiction de la recherche de la paternité et l'avortement provoqué criminellement*. Extract from the *Écho médical des Cévennes*. Nîmes: Imp. coopérative "la Laborieuse," 1903.

Dupanloup, Félix. *Le Mariage chrétien* (1869). 15th ed. Paris: Douniol, 1908.

Duruskam, Jean. *Mœurs de magistrats*. Paris: les principaux libraires, 1905.

Étude critique sur la puissance paternelle et ses limites d'après le Code civil. Paris: L. Larose, 1898.

Esquiros, Alphonse. *Paris, ou les sciences, les institutions et les mœurs au XIXe siècle*. 2 vols. Paris: Paul Renouard, 1847.

Fatoux, Raymond. *La Juridiction correctionnelle du tribunal civil en matière de recherche de la paternité. Compétence exceptionnelle résultant de l'article 3 de la loi du 16 novembre 1912*. Paris: Jouve, 1922.

Fenet, Pierre-Antoine. *Recueil complet des travaux préparatoires du Code civil*. 15 vols. Paris, 1827.

Fleury, Pierre. *Des causes de la dépopulation française et de la necessité de réorganiser les services d'assistance et d'hygiène*. Paris: Geuret, 1888.

Fournel, Jean-François. *Traité de l'adultère considéré dans l'ordre judiciaire*. Paris: J.-F. Bastien, 1778.

———. *Traité de la séduction considérée dans l'ordre judiciaire*. Paris: Demonville, 1781.

France. Assemblée nationale. *Journal officiel de la République française, Débats parlementaires. Débats du Sénat. Documents parlementaires de la Chambre des députés. Lois et décrets*. Paris: *Journal officiel*, 1871–1940.

———. Laws, statutes. *Le Code de la famille*. Décret-loi du 29 juillet 1939, modifié et complété par les Décrets-Lois des 16 Décembre 1939 et 24 avril 1940; les lois du 18 novembre 1940, du 15 février, du 29 mars, du 17 novembre 1941 et 3 février 1942. 5e édition, 1942. Paris and Vichy: Comité central des allocations familiale, 1942.

Fuzier-Herman, Édouard. *De la protection légale des enfants contre les abus de l'autorité paternelle*. Paris: A. Marescq aîné, 1878.

Gaillard (Abbé), Adolphe Henri. *Recherches administratives, statistiques... sur les enfans trouvés, les enfans naturels en France*. Paris: Th. Leclerc, 1837.

Gallardo, Ricardo. *L'Institution du mariage putatif en droit français*. Paris: Librairie sociale et économique, 1939.

Garcin, William. *Révolution sociale par la famille.* Vichy: Fédération française des associations de famille, 1942.

Garcin, William J., and Henri David. *La Famille.* Vichy: n.p., 1944.

Génestal, Robert. *Histoire de la légitimation des enfants naturels en droit canonique.* Paris: Ernest Leroux, 1905.

Gide, Charles. *La Recherche de la paternité.* Lyon: Société d'éducation et d'action féministes, 1905.

Gide, Paul. *Étude sur la condition privée de la femme dans le droit ancien et moderne.* Paris: L. Larose & Forcel, 1885.

Gigot, Albert. *La Séduction et la recherche de paternité.* Paris: Au Secrétariat d'Économie sociale, 1904.

Giraud, Léon. *Des Promesses de mariage: Étude historique et juridique.* Paris: F. Pichon, 1888.

———. *La Vérité sur la recherche de paternité.* Paris: F. Pichon, 1888.

Gouges, Olympe de. *Écrits politiques.* 2 vols. Paris: Côté femmes, 1993.

Guérillon, Ernest. *De l'Action en désaveu de paternité.* Paris: Marchal & Billard, 1900.

Guibal, Jean. *La Famille dans la Révolution nationale.* Paris: Éditions Fernand Sorlot, 1940.

Guides et Documents du Musée social. *Guide pratique des lois sociales. L'Aide à la famille, L'Aide aux travailleurs.* 2nd ed. Paris: Musée Social, 1943.

———. *Guide pratique des lois familiales.* Paris: Musée Social, 1946.

Guillot, Adolphe. *Le Jury et les mœurs.* Paris: Chaix, 1885.

Haussonville, Gabriel-Paul-Othenin d'. *Salaires et misères de femmes.* Paris: Calmann Lévy, 1900.

———. *Socialisme et charité.* Paris: Calmann Lévy, 1895.

———. *Socialisme d'état et socialisme chrétien.* Paris: *Revue des Deux Mondes,* 1890.

Jarlot, Georges. *Le Code de la famille: Préoccupation nataliste ou politique familiale?* Le Puy: Éditions Xavier Mapus, 1943.

Lambrechts, Hector. *Six projets de loi sur la recherche de la paternité.* Extract from the *Revue catholique des institutions et du droit.* Grenoble: J. Baratier, 1895.

Lecour, Charles-Jérôme. *Manuel d'assistance. La charité à Paris: des diverses formes de l'assistance dans le département de la Seine.* Paris: P. Asselin, 1876.

Lefebvre, Charles. *La Famille en France, dans le droit et dans les mœurs.* Paris: M. Giard, 1920.

———. *Cours de doctorat sur l'histoire du droit matrimonial français,* 3 vols. Paris: L. Larose & L. Tenin, 1906–13.

Legouvé, Ernest. *Histoire morale des femmes.* 1848. 5th ed. Paris: Didier, 1869.

Legrand, Louis. *Le Mariage et les mœurs en France.* Paris: Hachette, 1879.

Lévy, Édouard. *Traité pratique de la légitimation des enfants naturels simples, incestueux ou adultérins.* Paris: Recueil Sirey, 1926.

Lhospied, Henry. *Étude sur la recherche de la paternité en droit comparé.* Paris: A. Rousseau, 1914.

Lhostis, Pierre. *La Recherche de la paternité naturelle.* Rennes: Dubois, 1898.

Magnaud, Paul. *Les Jugements du Président Magnaud, réunis et commentés par Henry Leyret* Paris: P.-V. Stock, 1900.

———. *Les Nouveaux Jugements du président Magnaud*. Paris: Schleicher frères, 1903.

Manuel des œuvres et institutions religieuses et charitables de Paris. Paris: Librairie Poussielgue frères, 1867.

Marin, Louis. *L'Abandon de famille: Proposition de loi déposée à la Chambre des Députés le 20 février 1923*. Paris: Édition de la Ligue française pour le droit des femmes, 1923.

Martial, Lydie. *Action du féminisme rationnel. Union de pensée féminine. Un vœu important. L'enseignement de paternité à la caserne et dans les écoles de l'État*. Alençon: Vve F. Guy, 1909.

Mas, Henry. *De l'action en désaveu de paternité*. Toulouse: C. Marqués, 1906.

Masson, Émile. *La Puissance paternelle et la famille sous la Révolution*. Paris: A. Pedone, 1910.

Mauveaux, Julien. *De la recherche du père en tant que géniteur*. Paris: Marchal & Billard, 1900.

Mayet, Maurice. *La Recherche de la paternité, état de la question d'après les derniers travaux parlementaires en France et les législations étrangères*. Paris: A. Rousseau, 1899.

Millet, Albert. *La Séduction*. Paris: A. Cotillon, 1876.

Naquet, Alfred. *Religion, propriété, famille*. Paris: Poupart-Davyl, 1869.

Netter, Yvonne. *Le Code de la femme*. Paris: Éditions du progrès civique, 1926.

Oudot, Charles François. (Député de la Côte d'Or) *Convention Nationale. Essai sur les principes de la législation des mariages privés et solennels, du divorce et de l'adoption qui peuvent être déclarés à la suite de l'Acte constitutionnel*. Paris: Imprimerie nationale, 1793.

Pach, Jean. *Recherche de la paternité par l'examen des groupes sanguins*. Medical thesis. Paris: Jouve, 1934.

Pelletier, Madeleine. *La Désagrégation de la famille*. Paris: G. Sauvad, n.d.

———. *Le Féminisme et la famille*. Paris: La Solidarité des femmes, n.d.

———. *La Femme en lutte pour ses droits*. Paris: V. Giard & E. Brière, 1908.

Penfentenyo de Kervéréguin, Hervé-Alphonse-Marie de (vice-amiral). *Le Manuel du père de famille*. Preface by Marshal Philippe Pétain. Paris: Flammarion, 1941.

Perard, Raoul. *De l'influence de la paternité et de la filiation sur l'incrimination et la pénalité*. Thesis, Université de Paris, Faculté de droit. Paris: A. Rousseau, 1906.

Perrot, Michelle, ed., *From the Fires of Revolution to the Great War*. Vol. 4 of *A History of Private Life*. Translated by Arthur Goldhammer. Cambridge, Mass.: Harvard University Press, Belknap Press, 1990. Originally published as *Histoire de la vie privée: De la Révolution à la Grande Guerre* (Paris: Seuil, 1987).

Perruchot, R. *Résultats de la loi du 16 novembre 1912 sur la recherche de la paternité*. Paris: Sirey, 1931.

Poittevin, Gustave. *Les Théories de M. Alexandre Dumas fils sur la recherche de la paternité*. Angers: Dedovres, 1887.

Ponsolle, Paul. *La Dépopulation: Introduction à l'étude sur la recherche de la paternité*. Paris: L. Baillière & H. Messager, 1893.

Ponvert, Paul. *De la recherche de la paternité*. Marseille: E. Blévy, 1899.

Pothier, Robert-Joseph. *Œuvres complètes de Pothier*. Vol. 10: *Traités du contrat de mariage, de la puissance du mari*. Vol. 21: *Traité des successions*. Vol. 22: *Traité des propres*. Vol. 23: *Traité des donations entre vifs*. New ed. by Saint-Albin Berville. Paris: Thomine & Fortic, 1821–24.

———.*Traité du contrat de marriage. Avec des notes indicatives des changements introduits par la nouvelle législation et par la nouvelle jurisprudence*, par M. *** Avocat. Vol. 1. Paris: Letellier, 1813.

Poughon, Louis. *De la séduction, envisagée au double point de vue civil et pénal.* Thesis, Université de Paris, Faculté de droit. Paris: Crés, 1911.

Pouzol, Abel. *La Recherche de la paternité.* Paris: V. Giard & E. Brière, 1902.

Raicovicianu, Nicolae G. *La Loi du 16 novembre 1912 et l'action en déclaration de la paternité naturelle.* Paris: E. Duchemin, 1913.

La Recherche de la paternité. Conférence faite à la loge "La Fraternité vosgienne" O** d'Épinal par un F** de l'Atelier. Épinal: Imprimerie nouvelle, 1906.

Recueil Dalloz Sirey de doctrine de jurisprudence et de législation. Recueil périodique 1840. Paris: Bureau de la jurisprudence générale du Royaume, 1840.

Renaudin, Philippe. *La Famille dans la nation.* Paris: Commissariat général à la famille, 1943.

Riche, Daniel. *Le Mari modèle.* Paris: La Renaissance du Livre, 1917.

Richer, Léon. *Le Code des femmes.* Paris: E. Dentu, 1883.

———. "La Recherche de la paternité par Alexandre Dumas *fils*." *Le Droit des femmes*, no. 378 (21 September 1890).

Ricqlès, Émile-Heyman de. *La Recherche de la paternité.* Paris: A. Rousseau, 1901.

Rivet, Gustave. *La Recherche de la paternité.* Preface by Alexandre Dumas *fils*. Paris: Dreyfous, 1890.

———. *Le Châtiment.* Play presented in 1879 at Théâtre Cluny. Paris: M. Dreyfous, 1879.

Rivière, Louis. *De la recherche de la paternité naturelle.* Angoulême: Coquenard, 1901.

Roca, Stanislas. *Les Fiançailles ou promesses de mariage.* Thesis, Université de Montpellier, Faculté de droit. Montpellier: G. Firman, Montane, & Sicardi, 1908.

Rogron, Joseph-André. *Code civil français expliqués par ses motifs, par des exemples et par la jurisprudence.* Paris, 1838. Rev. eds. 1877 and 1885.

Rouast, André. *La Famille dans la nation.* Paris: Presses universitaires, 1941.

Roué, Paul. *Le Code des femmes: Droit des femmes dans le droit français.* Paris: L'Édition médicale française, 1901.

Rousseau, Jean-Jacques. "A Discourse on a Subject Proposed by the Academy of Dijon: What Is the Origin of Inequality Among Men, and Is It Authorized by Natural Law?" In *The Social Contract and Discourses*, ed P. D. Jimack. Translated by G. D. H. Cole. London: Orion Publishing Group, 1996.

Roussel, Nelly. *Quelques lances rompues pour nos libertés.* Paris: Giard & Brière, 1910.

Salzes, Gaston. *Recherche judiciaire de la paternité naturelle et la loi du 16 novembre 1912.* Thesis, Université de Montpellier, Faculté de droit. Montpellier: Firmin & Montane, 1920.

Sand, George. *Indiana.* 1832. Translated by Eleanor Hochman. New York: Penguin Books, 1993.

Savatier, René. *La Recherche de la paternité: Étude pratique de législation et de jurisprudence.* Paris: Dalloz, 1927.

Schuster, Charles. *De la paternité et de la filiation en droit international privé.* Paris: E. Duchemin, 1899.

Sécretan, Henri-F. *La Population et les mœurs.* Paris: Payot, 1913.

Simon, Jules. *L'Ouvrière*. Paris: Hachette, 1861.
Smith, Adam. *The Theory of the Moral Sentiments*. 1759. Reprint. Edinburgh: Hay, 1813.
Steinhard, Georges. *Des conséquences civiles de la séduction*. Thesis, Université de Paris, Faculté de droit. Paris: Barnéoud, 1907.
Strauss, Paul. *L'Enfance malheureuse*. Paris: Charpentier, 1896.
———. Commission de la Dépopulation. Sous-commission de la mortalité. *Rapport général sur les causes de la mortalité*. Melun: Imprimerie administrative, 1911.
Theuriet, André. *Paternité*. Paris: E. Dentu, 1894.
Torina, Martin de. *Mère sans être épouse pour la France et pour soi-même*. Paris: Chez l'auteur, 1917.
Toulouse, Édouard. *Les Conflits intersexuel et sociaux*. Paris: Fasquelle, 1904.
———. *La Question sexuelle et la femme*. Paris: Fasquelle, 1918.
Vaïsse, Gabriel. *De l'inexécution de la promesse de mariage et des ses conséquences juridiques*. Thesis, Université de Paris, Faculté de droit. Paris: L. Larose, 1901.
Variot, Gaston, Dr. "Conférence sur l'allaitement." *Revue philanthropique* 12 (1902).
Vernet, Madeleine. *Études sociales: La Paternité*. Poligny: Imprimerie Alfred Jacquin, 1906.
Vérone, Maria. *La Situation juridique des enfants naturels*. Paris: Éditions de la Ligue française pour le droit des femmes, 1924.
Vincent, François Eugène. *L'Interdiction de la recherche de la paternité*. Lyon: Pitrat, 1891.
Violette, Maurice. *La Recherche de la paternité: Commentaire de la nouvelle loi adoptée définitivement par le Parlement le 16 novembre 1912*. Paris: Giard & Brière, 1913.
Wahl, Albert. *La Recherche de la paternité d'après la loi du 16 novembre 1912*. Paris: Sirey, 1913.

• *Secondary Sources*

Accampo, Elinor. *Blessed Motherhood, Bitter Fruit: Nelly Roussel and the Politics of Female Pain in Third Republic France*. Baltimore: Johns Hopkins University Press, 2006.
Accampo, Elinor A., Rachel G. Fuchs, and Mary Lynn Stewart, eds. *Gender and the Politics of Social Reform in France, 1870–1914*. Baltimore: Johns Hopkins University Press, 1995.
Adler, Laure. *Secrets d'alcôve: Histoire du couple de 1830 à 1930*. Paris: Hachette, 1983.
Allen, Ann Taylor. *Feminism and Motherhood in Germany, 1800–1914*. New Brunswick, N.J.: Rutgers University Press, 1991.
Applebaum, Stanley. *French Satirical Drawings from "L'Assiette au Beurre."* New York: Dover, 1978.
Anderson, Kermyt G. "How Well Does Paternity Confidence Match Actual Paternity? Evidence from Worldwide Nonpaternity Rates." *Current Anthropology* 47, no. 3 (June 2006): 513–20.
Ariès, Philippe, and Georges Duby, general eds. *A History of Private Life*. Vol. 4: *From the Fires of Revolution to the Great War*, ed. Michelle Perrot. Vol. 5: *Riddles of Identity in Modern Times*, ed. Antoine Prost and Gérard Vincent. Translated by Arthur Goldhammer. Cambridge, Mass.: Harvard University Press, Belknap Press, 1990–94. Originally published as *Histoire de la vie privée* (Paris: Seuil, 1987).
Arnaud, André-Jean. *Essai d'analyse structurale du Code civil français: La Règle du jeu dans la paix bourgeoise*. Paris: Librairie générale de droit et de jurisprudence, 1973.

———. *Les Origines doctrinales du Code civil français.* Paris: Librairie générale de droit et de jurisprudence, 1969.

———. "La Référence à l'école du droit naturel moderrne: Les Lectures des auteurs du Code civil français." In *La Famille, la loi, l'État: De la Révolution au Code civil,* ed. Irène Théry and Christian Biet. Paris: Imprimerie nationale, 1989.

Audoin-Rouzeau, Stéphane. *L'Enfant de l'ennemi (1914–1918): Viol, avortement, infanticide pendant la Grande Guerre.* Paris: Aubier, 1995.

———. *La Guerre des enfants, 1914–1918: Essai d'histoire culturelle.* Paris: Armand Colin, 1993.

Augé, Marc, ed. *Le Père: Métaphore paternelle et functions du père: L'Interdit, la filiation, la transmission.* Paris: Denoël, 1989.

Aux sources de la puissance, sociabilité et parenté: Actes du colloque de Rouen, 12–13 novembre 1987, [organisé par le] Groupe de recherche d'histoire de l'Université de Rouen. Edited by Françoise Thelamon. Mont-Saint-Aignan: Publications de l'Université de Rouen, 1989.

Bard, Christine. *Les Filles de Marianne: Histoire des féminismes, 1914–1940.* Paris: Fayard, 1995.

Bardet, Jean-Pierre, ed. *La Première fois, ou Le Roman de la virginité perdue à travers les siècles et les continents.* Paris: Éditions Ramsay, 1981.

Bart, Jean. "L'Individu et ses droits." In *La Famille, la loi, l'État: De la Révolution au Code civil,* ed. Irène Théry and Christian Biet. Paris: Imprimerie nationale, 1989.

Battagliola, Françoise. "Mariage, concubinage, et relations entre les sexes, Paris 1880–1890." *Genèses* (January 1995): 68–96.

Baudrillard, Jean. *De la séduction.* Paris: Galilée. 1979. Reprint. 1992.

Bénabent, Alain. *Droit civil: La Famille.* 4th ed. Paris: Éditions Litec, 1991.

Berlanstein, Lenard R. *Daughters of Eve: A Cultural History of French Theater Women from the Old Regime to the Fin-de-Siècle.* Cambridge, Mass.: Harvard University Press, 2001.

———. "Illegitimacy, Concubinage and Proletarianization in a French Town, 1760–1914." *Journal of Family History* 5 (1980): 360–74.

Berthet, Paul. *Les Obligations alimentaires et les transformations de la famille.* Paris: L'Harmattan, 2000.

Bertin, Célia. *Femmes sous l'occupation.* Paris: Stock, 1993.

Blau, Peter M. *Exchange and Power in Social Life.* New York: John Wiley, 1964.

Bock, Gisela. "Poverty and Mother's Rights in the Emerging Welfare States." In *A History of Women,* vol. 5: *Toward a Cultural Identity in the Twentieth Century,* ed. Françoise Thébaud. Cambridge, Mass.: Harvard University Press, 1994.

Boswell, John. *The Kindness of Strangers: The Abandonment of Children in Western Europe from Late Antiquity to the Renaissance.* New York: Pantheon Books, 1988.

Boudouard, Laurence, and Florence Bellivier. "Des droits pour les bâtards, l'enfant naturel dans les débats révolutionnaires." In *La Famille, la loi, l'État: De la Révolution au Code civil,* ed. Irène Théry and Christian Biet. Paris: Imprimerie nationale, 1989.

Bourdieu, Pierre. *The Logic of Practice.* Translated by Richard Nice. Stanford, Calif.: Stanford University Press, 1990.

———. "Les Strategies matrimoniales dans le système de reproduction" *Annales: Économies, Sociétés, Civilisations* 27 (1972): 1105–27.

Bouvier, Pierre. *Le Lien social.* Paris: Gallimard, 2005.

Brinton, Crane. *French Revolutionary Legislation on Illegitimacy, 1789–1804.* Cambridge, Mass.: Harvard University Press, 1937.
Brive, Marie-France, ed. *Les Femmes et la Révolution française: Actes du colloque international, 12–13–14 avril 1989,* [organisé par l']Université de Toulouse–Le Mirail. 3 vols. Toulouse: Presses universitaires du Mirail, 1989.
Butler, Judith. *Excitable Speech: A Politics of the Performative.* New York: Routledge, 1997.
———. *Gender Trouble: Feminism and the Subversion of Identity.* New York: Routledge, 1990.
———. *Precarious Life: The Power of Mourning and Violence.* New York: Verso, 2004.
———. *Undoing Gender.* New York: Routledge, 2004.
Cadoret, Anne. *Parenté plurielle: Anthropologie du placement familial.* Paris: L'Harmattan, 1995.
Carbonnier, Jean. *Droit civil.* Vol. 1: *Les Personnes;* vol 2: *La Famille.* Paris: Presses universitaires de France, 1955. Reprint, vol. 1, 1996, vol. 2, 1999.
Certeau, Michel de. *The Practice of Everyday Life.* Translated by Steven Rendall. Berkeley: University of California Press, 1984. Originally published as *Arts de faire*, vol. 1 of *L'Invention du quotidien* (Paris: Union générale d'éditions, 1980).
Childers, Kristen Stromberg. *Fathers, Families and the State in France, 1914–1945.* Ithaca, N.Y.: Cornell University Press, 2003.
Commaille, Jacques. *Misères de la famille, question d'état.* Paris: Presses de la Fondation nationale des sciences politiques, 1996.
———. *Les Enjeux politiques de la famille.* Paris: Bayard, 1998.
Cornu, Gérard. *Droit civil: La Famille.* 7th ed. Paris: Montchrestien, 2001.
———. *Vocabulaire juridique.* Paris: Association Henri Capitant, 1992.
Cova, Anne. "Droits des femmes et protection de la maternité en France, 1892–1939." 5 vols. Thesis, Institut universitaire européen, Florence, 1994.
———. *Maternité et droits des femmes en France: XIXe–XXe siècles.* Paris: Anthropos, 1997.
Davis, Natalie Zemon. *Fiction in the Archives: Pardon Tales and Their Tellers in Sixteenth-Century France.* Stanford, Calif.: Stanford University Press, 1987.
Debré, Jean-Louis. *La Justice au XIXème siècle: Les Magistrats.* Paris: Librairie académique Perrin, 1981.
Dekeuwer-Défossez, Françoise. "Le Contentieux de la famille naturelle." *Revue française des affaires sociales,* special issue: *Pères et paternité* (November 1988): 129–39.
Delaisi de Parseval, Geneviève. *La Part du père.* Paris: Seuil, 1981.
Delumeau, Jean, and Daniel Roche, eds. *Histoire des pères et de la paternité.* Paris: Larousse, 1990. New ed. 2000.
Demars-Sion, Véronique. *Femmes séduites et abandonnés au XVIII siècle: L'Exemple du Cambrésis.* Paris: ESTER [Études scientifiques et techniques pour l'enseignement et la recherche], 1991.
Desan, Suzanne. *The Family on Trial in Revolutionary France.* Berkeley: University of California Press, 2004.
———. "Reconstituting the Social after the Terror: Family, Property and the Law in Popular Politics." *Past and Present* 164 (August 1999): 81–121.
De Singly, François, and Franz Schultheis, eds. *Affaires de famille, affaires d'état: Sociologie de la famille.* Jarville-la-Malgrange: Éditions de l'est, 1991.

Dhavernas, Odile. *Droits des femmes, pouvoir des hommes*. Paris: Seuil, 1978.
Dickinson, Edward R. *The Politics of German Child Welfare from the Empire to the Federal Republic*. Cambridge, Mass.: Harvard University Press, 1996.
Donzelot, Jacques. *The Policing of Families*. Translated by Robert Hurley. Baltimore: Johns Hopkins University Press, 1997.
Duchen, Claire. *Feminism in France: From May '68 to Mitterand*. London: Routledge, 1986.
———. *Women's Rights and Women's Lives in France, 1944–1968*. London: Routledge, 1994.
Dupâquier, Jacques, and Antoinette Fauve-Chamoux. "La Famille." In *Histoire des droites en France*, ed. Jean-François Sirinelli, vol. 3: *Sensibilités*. Paris: Gallimard, 1992.
Ewald, François. *Naissance du Code civil: An VIII–an XII (1800–1804)*. Paris: Flammarion, 1989.
———. *L'État providence*. Paris: Grasset, 1986.
Fairchilds, Cissie C. "Female Sexual Attitudes and the Rise of Illegitimacy: A Case Study." *Journal of Interdisciplinary History* 8 (Spring 1978): 627–67.
Farge, Arlette. *Fragile Lives: Violence, Power and Solidarity in Eighteenth-Century France*. Translated by Carol Shelton. Cambridge, Mass: Harvard University Press, 1981.
Farmer, Sarah. *Martyred Village: Commemorating the 1944 Massacre at Oradour-sur-Glane*. Berkeley: University of California Press, 1999.
Farr, James R. *Authority and Sexuality in Early Modern Burgundy, 1550–1730*. New York: Oxford University Press, 1995.
———. "Parlementaires and the Paradox of Power: Sovereignty and Jurisprudence in Rapt Cases in Early Modern Burgundy." *European History Quarterly* 25 (1995): 325–51.
Fauve-Chamoux, Antoinette. "Beyond Adoption: Orphans and Family Strategies in Pre-Industrial France." *History of the Family* 1, no. 1 (1996): 1–13.
Fillon, Anne. *Les Trois bagues aux doigts: Amours villageoises au XVIII siècle*. Paris: Lafont, 1981.
Fishman, Sarah. *We Will Wait: Wives of French Prisoners of War, 1940–1945*. New Haven, Conn.: Yale University Press, 1991.
Foriers, Paul, and Chaim Perelman. "Natural Law and Natural Rights." In *Dictionary of the History of Ideas*, vol. 3. New York: Charles Scribner's Sons, 1973.
Forth, Christopher E. *The Dreyfus Affair and the Crisis of French Manhood*. Baltimore: Johns Hopkins University Press, 2004.
Foucault, Michel. *The History of Sexuality. An Introduction*. Vol. 1. Translated by Robert Hurley. New York: Random House, Vintage Books, 1990.
Frey, Michel. "Du mariage et du concubinage dans les classes populaires à Paris (1846–1847)." *Annales: Économies, Sociétés, Civilisations* 33 (July–August 1978): 803–29.
Fuchs, Rachel G. *Abandoned Children: Foundlings and Child Welfare in Nineteenth-Century France*. Albany: State University of New York Press, 1984.
———. *Gender and Poverty in Nineteenth-Century Europe*. Cambridge: Cambridge University Press, 2005.
———. *Poor and Pregnant in Paris: Strategies for Survival in the Nineteenth Century*. New Brunswick, N.J.: Rutgers University Press, 1992.
Gager, Kristin Elizabeth. *Blood Ties and Fictive Ties: Adoption and Family Life in Early Modern France*. Princeton, N.J.: Princeton University Press, 1996.

Garaud, Marcel, and Romuald Szramkiewicz. *La Révolution française et la famille*. Paris: Presses universitaires de France, 1978.

Garrioch, David. *Neighborhood and Community in Paris, 1740–1790*. Cambridge: Cambridge University Press, 1986.

Gaudemet, Yves. *Les Juristes et la vie politique de la IIIe République*. Paris: Presses universitaires de France, 1970.

Gildea, Robert. *Marianne in Chains: In Search of the German Occupation, 1940–1945*. London: Macmillan, 2002.

Gleyses, Chantal. *La Femme coupable: Petite histoire de l'épouse adultère au XIXe siècle*. Paris: Imago, 1994.

Godelier, Maurice. *L'Énigme du don*. Paris: Fayard, 1996.

Grimmer, Claude. *La Femme et le bâtard: Amours illégitimes et secrètes dans l'ancienne France*. Paris: Presses de la Renaissance, 1983.

Grogan, Susan K. *French Socialism and Sexual Difference: Women and the New Society, 1803–44*. London: Macmillan, 1992.

Gutton, Jean-Pierre. *Histoire de l'adoption en France*. Paris: Publisud, 1993.

Haase-Dubosc, Danielle. *Ravie et enlevée: De l'enlèvement des femmes comme stratégie matrimoniale au XVIIe siècle*. Paris: Albin Michel, 1999.

Haase-Dubosc, Danielle, and Eliane Viennot, eds. *Femmes et pouvoirs sous l'Ancien régime*. Paris: Rivages, 1991.

Halpérin, Jean-Louis. *L'Impossible Code civil*. Paris: Presses universitaires de France, 1992.

———. *Histoire du droit privé français depuis 1804*. Paris: Presses universitaires de France, 1996.

Hanley, Sarah. " 'The Jurisprudence of the Arrêts': Marital Union, Civil Society, and State Formation in France, 1550–1650." *Law and History Review* 21, no. 1 (2003): 1–40.

Hanna, Martha. "A Republic of Letters: The Epistolary Tradition in France during World War I." *American Historical Review* 108, no. 5 (December 2003): 1338–61.

———. *"Your Death Would be Mine": Paul and Marie Pireaud in the Great War*. Cambridge, Mass.: Harvard University Press, 2006.

Hatzfeld, Henri. *Du paupérisme à la sécurité sociale, 1850–1940*. Paris: Armand Colin, 1971.

Heuer, Jennifer Ngaire. *The Family and the Nation: Gender and Citizenship in Revolutionary France, 1789–1830*. Ithaca, N.Y.: Cornell University Press, 2005.

Hopkins, Richard S. "Engineering Nature: Public Greenspaces in Nineteenth-Century Paris." Ph.D. diss., Arizona State University, 2008.

Hunt, Lynn. *The Family Romance of the French Revolution*. Berkeley: University of California Press, 1992.

Hurstel, Françoise. "L'Affaiblissement de l'autorité paternelle: La Notion de 'carence' des pères au 20ème siècle." *La Pensée* 261 (1988): 35–49.

———. *La Déchirure paternelle*. Paris: Presses universitaires de France, 1996.

Kalifa, Dominique. *L'Encre et le sang: Récits de crimes et société à la Belle Époque*. Paris: Fayard, 1995.

Kelley, Donald R. *Historians and the Law in Postrevolutionary France*. Princeton, N.J.: Princeton University Press, 1984.

Kent, Susan Kingsley. *Gender and Power in Britain, 1640–1991*. New York: Routledge, 1999.

Kertzer, David I., and Marzio Barbagli, eds. *Family Life in the Long Nineteenth Century, 1789–1913.* Vol. 2 of *The History of the European Family.* New Haven, Conn.: Yale University Press, 2002.

Klejman, Laurence, and Florence Rochefort. *L'Égalité en marche: Le Féminisme sous la Troisième République.* Paris: Éditions des femmes, 1989.

Knibiehler, Yvonne. *Les Pères aussi ont une histoire.* Paris: Hachette, 1987.

———. "Le Rôle des pères à travers l'histoire." *Revue française des affaires sociales,* special issue: *Pères et paternité* (November 1988): 31–39.

Knibiehler, Yvonne, and Catherine Fouquet. *L'Histoire des mères du Moyen-Age à nos jours.* Paris: Montalba, 1980.

Koos, Cheryl A. "Engendering Reaction: The Politics of Pronatalism and the Family in France, 1919–1944." Ph.D. diss., University of Southern California, 1996.

———. "Gender, Anti-Individualism and Nationalism: The *Alliance Nationale* and the Pronatalist Backlash against the *Femme moderne,* 1933–1940." *French Historical Studies* 19, no. 3 (Spring 1996): 639–73.

———. "*'On les aura!*': The Gendered Politics of Abortion and the *Alliance Nationale Contre la Dépopulation,* 1938–1944." *Modern and Contemporary France* 7, no. 1 (1999): 21–34.

Labrusse-Riou, Catherine. "Les Problèmes de la paternité sous les aspects du droit civil." *Revue française des affaires sociales,* special issue: *Pères et paternité* (November 1988): 109–18.

Lallemand, Suzanne. *La Circulation des enfants en société traditionnelle: Prêt, don, échange.* Paris: L'Harmattan, 1993.

Landes, Joan. *Women and the Public Sphere in the Age of the French Revolution.* Ithaca, N.Y.: Cornell University Press, 1988.

Lefaucheur, Nadine. "Des bâtards aux filles mères, ou du modèle angélique au modèle patriotique." In *La Famille, la loi, l'État: De la Révolution au Code civil,* ed. Irène Théry and Christian Biet. Paris: Imprimerie nationale, 1989.

———. "Maternity, Family, and the State." In *A History of Women,* vol. 5: *Toward a Cultural Identity in the Twentieth Century,* ed. Françoise Thébaud. Cambridge, Mass.: Harvard University Press, 1994.

———. "Pères absents et droit au père." *Lien social et politiques* 37 (1997): 11–17.

———. "En l'absence du père." *Informations sociales* 49–50 (1996): 56–67.

Lenoir, Remi. *Généalogie de la morale familiale.* Paris: Seuil, 2003.

Lévi-Strauss, Claude. *The Elementary Structure of Kinship.* Translated by James Harle Bell and John Richard von Sturmer. Boston: Beacon Press, 1969.

Lévy, Marie-Françoise, ed. *L'Enfant, la famille et la Révolution française.* Paris: Olivier Orban, 1990.

Louis, Marie-Victoire. *Le Droit de cuissage: France, 1860–1930.* Paris: Éditions de l'Atelier / Éditions ouvrières, 1994.

Lucey, Michael. *The Misfit of the Family: Balzac and the Social Forms of Sexuality.* Durham, N.C.: Duke University Press, 2003.

Luhmann, Niklas. *Amour comme passion: De la codification de l'intimité.* Paris: Aubier, 1982.

Mainardi, Patricia. *Husbands, Wives, and Lovers: Marriage and Its Discontents in Nineteenth-Century France*. New Haven, Conn.: Yale University Press, 2003.

Malaurie, Philippe, and Laurent Aynès. *Cours de droit civil. Vol. 3: La Famille*. 4th ed. Paris: Éditions Cujas, 1993.

Margadant, Jo Burr, ed. *The New Biography: Performing Femininity in Nineteenth-Century France*. Berkeley: University of California Press, 2000.

Marmier, Marie-Pierre. *L'Adoption*. Paris: Armand Colin, 1972.

Martin-Fugier, Anne. *La Bourgeoise: Femme au temps de Paul Bourget*. Paris: Grasset, 1983.

———. *La Vie élégante, ou, La Formation du Tout-Paris*. Paris: Fayard, 1990.

Maugue, Annelisse. *L'Identité masculine en crise au tournant du siècle*. Paris: Rivages, 1987.

Mauss, Marcel. *The Gift: Forms and Functions of Exchange in Archaic Societies*. Translated by Ian Cunnison. Glencoe, Ill.: Free Press, 1954.

Maza, Sarah. *Private Lives and Public Affairs: The Causes Célèbres of Prerevolutionary France*. Berkeley: University of California Press, 1993.

McLaren, Angus. *The Trials of Masculinity: Policing Sexual Boundaries, 1870–1914*. Chicago: University of Chicago Press, 1997.

Medick, Hans, and David Warren Sabean, eds. *Interest and Emotion: Essays on the Study of Family and Kinship*. New York: Cambridge University Press, 1994.

Messu, Michel. *Les Politiques familiales du natalisme à la solidarité*. Paris: Éditions ouvrières, 1992.

Moses, Claire. *French Feminism in the Nineteenth Century*. Albany, N.Y.: State University of New York Press, 1984.

Mossuz-Lavau, Janine. *Les Lois de l'amour: Les Politiques de la sexualité en France de 1950 à nos jours*. Paris: Payot, 1991.

Muel-Dreyfus, Francine. *Vichy et l'éternel féminin*. Paris: Seuil, 1996.

———. "La Volonté d'un homme." In *Histoire des pères et de la paternité*, ed. Jean Delumeau and Daniel Roche. Paris: Larousse, 1990. New ed., 2000.

Mulliez, Jacques. "'*Pater is est . . .*': La Source juridique de la puissance paternelle du droit révolutionnaire au Code civil." In *La Famille, la loi, l'État: De la Révolution au Code civil*, ed. Irène Théry and Christian Biet. Paris: Imprimerie nationale, 1989.

Murat, Pierre. "La Puissance paternelle et la Révolution française: Essai de régéneration de l'autorité des pères." In *La Famille, la loi, l'État: De la Révolution au Code civil*, ed. Irène Théry and Christian Biet. Paris: Imprimerie nationale, 1989.

Nicoleau, Patrick. "De la preuve judiciaire de la paternité naturelle: La Fille-mère, l'enfant abandonné et le séducteur au XIXe siècle en France." Thesis, Université de Bordeaux I, 1984.

Nord, Philip. *The Republican Moment: Struggles for Democracy in Nineteenth-Century France*. Cambridge, Mass.: Harvard University Press, 1995.

Nye, Robert A. *Crime, Madness and Politics in Modern France: The Medical Concept of National Decline*. Princeton, N.J.: Princeton University Press, 1984.

———. *Masculinity and Male Codes of Honor in Modern France*. New York: Oxford University Press, 1993.

Offen, Karen. *European Feminisms, 1700–1950*. Stanford, Calif.: Stanford University Press, 2000.

Okin, Susan Moller. *Justice, Gender, and the Family.* New York: Basic Books, 1989.

Olender, Maurice, and Jacques Sojcher, eds. *La Séduction.* Colloque de Bruxelles. Paris: Aubier, 1980.

Pateman, Carol. *The Sexual Contract.* Stanford, Calif.: Stanford University Press, 1988.

Paul-Levy, Françoise. *L'Amour nomade, la mère et l'enfant hors-mariage XVI–XXème siècle.* Paris: Seuil, 1981.

Paxton, Robert O. *Vichy France: Old Guard and New Order, 1940–1944.* New York: Columbia University Press, 1972.

Pedersen, Jean Elisabeth. "Legislating the Family: Gender, Population, and Republican Politics in France, 1870–1920." Ph.D. diss., University of Chicago, 1993.

———. *Legislating the French Family: Feminism, Theater, and Republican Politics, 1870–1920.* New Brunswick, N.J.: Rutgers University Press, 2003.

———. "'Special Customs': Paternity Suits and Citizenship in France and the Colonies, 1870–1912." In *Domesticating the Empire: Race, Gender, and Family Life in French and Dutch Colonialism,* ed. Julia Clancy-Smith and Frances Gouda. Charlottesville: University Press of Virginia, 1998.

Pedersen, Susan. *Family, Dependence, and the Origins of the Welfare State: Britain and France, 1914–1945.* New York: Cambridge University Press, 1993.

Phan, Marie-Claude. *Les Amours illégitimes: Histoires de séduction en Languedoc, 1676–1786.* Paris: Éditions du Centre national de la recherche scientifique, 1986.

———. "Les Déclarations des grossesse en France (XVI–XVIII siècles)." *Revue d'Histoire moderne et contemporaine* 22 (1975): 61–88.

———. "La Séduction impunie, ou La Fin des actions en recherche de paternité." In *Les Femmes et la Révolution française: Actes du colloque international, 12–13–14 avril 1989,* [organisé par l']Université de Toulouse–Le Mirail. Toulouse: Presses universitaires du Mirail, 1990.

Picq, Françoise. "Par-delà la loi du père: Le Débat sur la recherche de la paternité au Congrès féministe de 1900." *Les Temps modernes* 34, no. 391 (February 1979): 1199–1212.

Pollard, Miranda. *Reign of Virtue: Mobilizing Gender in Vichy France.* Chicago: University of Chicago Press, 1998.

Prost, Antoine. "Catholic Conservatives, Population and the Family in Twentieth-Century France." In *Population and Resources in Western Intellectual Traditions,* ed. Michael S. Teitelbaum and Jay M. Winter. Cambridge: Cambridge University Press, 1989.

———. "L'Évolution de la politique familiale en France de 1938 à 1981." *Le Mouvement social* 129 (October–December 1984): 7–28.

———. "Public and Private Spheres." In *A History of Private Life,* vol. 5: *Riddles of Identity in Modern Times,* ed. Antoine Prost and Gérard Vincent. Translated by Arthur Goldhammer. Cambridge, Mass.: Harvard University Press, Belknap Press, 1991.

Rauch, André. *Crise de l'identité masculine, 1789–1914.* Paris: Pluriel, 2000.

Raynaud, Pierre. "Adoption." In *Encyclopaedia Universalis,* vol. 1. Paris: Encyclopaedia Universalis France, 1968.

Reddy, William M. *The Invisible Code: Honor and Sentiment in Postrevolutionary France, 1814–1848.* Berkeley: University of California Press, 1997.

———. "Marriage, Honor, and the Public Sphere in Postrevolutionary France: *Séparations de Corps*, 1815–1848." *Journal of Modern History* 65 (September 1993): 437–72.

Reid, Roddy. *Death of the Family: Discourse, Fiction and Desire in France*. Stanford, Calif.: Stanford University Press, 1994.

Reynaud, Pierre, ed. *Histoire du droit de la famille*. Vol. 5. 2nd ed. Paris: Encyclopédie juridique Dalloz, 1992.

Rhoades, Michelle K. "Renegotiating French Masculinity: Medicine and Venereal Disease During the Great War." *French Historical Studies* 29, no. 3 (Spring 2006): 293–327.

Roberts, Mary Louise. *Civilization Without Sexes: Reconstructing Gender in Postwar France, 1917–1927*. Chicago: University of Chicago Press, 1994.

———. *Disruptive Acts: The New Woman in Fin-de-Siècle France*. Chicago: University of Chicago Press, 2002.

Roche, Daniel. *The People of Paris: An Essay in Popular Culture in the 18th Century*. Translated by Marie Evans. New York: Berg, 1987.

Ronsin, Francis. *Le Contrat sentimental: Débats sur le mariage, l'amour, le divorce, de l'Ancien régime à la Restauration*. Paris: Aubier, 1990.

———. *La Grève des ventres: Propagande néo-malthusienne et baisse de la natalité en France, 19e–20e siècles*. Paris: Aubier Montaigne, 1980.

Rossel, André. *Le Bon juge*. Paris: Armand Colin, 1983.

Roussel, Louis. *La Famille incertaine*. Paris: Odile Jacob, 1989.

Rousselet, Marcel. *Histoire de la magistrature française des origines à nos jours*. 2 vols. Paris: Plon, 1957.

Royer, J. P., R. Martinage, and P. Lecocq. *Juges et notables au XIXè siècle*. Paris: Presses universitaires de France, 1982.

Rubellin-Devichi, Jacqueline. "Le Droit, les pères et la paternité." *Revue française des affaires sociales*, special issue: *Pères et paternité* (November 1988): 161–87.

Sabatier, Pierre. *La Déchéance de la puissance paternelle et la privation du droit de garde*. Paris: Montchrestien, 1982.

Salvage-Gerest, Pascale. *L'Adoption*. Paris: Dalloz-Sirey, 1992.

Schafer, Sylvia. "Between Paternal Right and the Dangerous Mother: Reading Parental Responsibility in Nineteenth-Century French Civil Justice." *Journal of Family History* 23 (April 1998): 173–90.

———. *Children in Moral Danger and the Problem of Government in Third Republic France*. Princeton, N.J.: Princeton University Press, 1997.

———. "When the Child Is the Father of the Man: Work, Sexual Difference and the Guardian-State in Third Republic France." *History and Theory* 31, no. 4 (1992): 98–115.

Schnapper, Bernard. *Voies nouvelles en histoire du droit: La Justice, la famille, la répression pénale (XVI–XXème siècles)*. Paris: Presses universitaires de France, 1991.

Scott, Joan Wallach. "Feminist Family Politics." *French Politics, Culture and Society* 17, no. 3–4 (Summer–Fall 1999): 20–30.

———. *Only Paradoxes to Offer: French Feminists and the Rights of Man*. Cambridge, Mass.: Harvard University Press, 1996.

———. *Parité! Sexual Equality and the Crisis of French Universalism.* Chicago: University of Chicago Press, 2005.

Segalen, Martine. "Le XIXe siècle: Le Manteau des jeunes filles (La virginité dans la société paysanne)." In *La Première fois, ou, Le Roman de la virginité perdue à travers les siècles et les continents,* ed. Jean-Pierre Bardet. Paris: Éditions Ramsay, 1981.

Sharp, Walter Rice. *The French Civil Service: Bureaucracy in Transition.* New York: Macmillan, 1931.

———. *The Government of the French Republic.* New York: Van Nostrand, 1938.

Sohn, Anne-Marie. "Between the Wars in France and England." In *A History of Women,* vol. 5: *Toward a Cultural Identity in the Twentieth Century,* ed. Françoise Thébaud. Cambridge, Mass.: Harvard University Press, 1996.

———. *Chrysalides: Femmes dans la vie privée (XIX–XXe siècles).* 2 vols. Paris: Publications de la Sorbonne, 1996.

———. "Les Rôles féminins dans la vie privée à l'époque de la Troisième République: Rôles théoriques, rôles vécus." 5 vols. Thesis, Université de Paris I, 1993.

Souty, Georgina, and Pascal Dupont. *Destins de mères, destins d'enfants.* Paris: Odile Jacob, 1991.

Stora-Lamarre, Annie. *La République des faibles.* Paris: Armand Colin, 2005.

Surkis, Judith. *Sexing the Citizen: Morality and Masculinity in France, 1870–1920.* Ithaca, N.Y.: Cornell University Press, 2006.

Szramkiewicz, Romuald. *Histoire du droit français de la famille.* Paris: Dalloz, 1995.

Talmy, Robert. *Histoire du mouvement familial en France, 1896–1939.* 2 vols. Paris: Union nationale des caisses d'allocations familiales, 1962.

Thébaud, Françoise. "The Great War and the Triumph of Sexual Division." In *A History of Women,* vol. 5: *Toward a Cultural Identity in the Twentieth Century,* ed. Françoise Thébaud. Translated by Arthur Goldhammer. Cambridge, Mass.: Harvard University Press, Belknap Press, 1994.

———. "Le Mouvement nataliste dans la France de l'entre-deux-guerres: L'Alliance nationale pour l'accroissement de la population française." *Revue d'histoire moderne et contemporaine* 32 (1985): 276–301.

Théry, Irène, and Christian Biet, eds. *La Famille, la loi, l'État: De la Révolution au Code civil.* Paris: Imprimerie nationale, 1989.

Thompson, Victoria. *The Virtuous Marketplace: Women and Men, Money and Politics in Paris, 1830–1870.* Baltimore: Johns Hopkins University Press, 2000.

Traer, James F. *Marriage and the Family in Eighteenth-Century France.* Ithaca, N.Y.: Cornell University Press, 1980.

Tuck, Richard. "The 'Modern' Theory of Natural Law." In *The Languages of Political Theory in Early-Modern Europe,* ed. Anthony Pagden. Cambridge: Cambridge University Press, 1987.

Veillon, Dominique. *Vivre et survivre en France, 1939–1947.* Paris: Payot, 1995.

Vigarello, Georges. *A History of Rape: Sexual Violence in France from the 16th to the 20th Century.* Translated by Jean Birrell. Malden, Mass.: Polity Press, 2001. Originally published as *Histoire du viol: XVIe–XXe siècle* (Paris: Seuil, 1998).

Vincent, Gérard. "A History of Secrets?" In *A History of Private Life*, vol. 5: *Riddles of Identity in Modern Times*, ed. Antoine Prost and Gérard Vincent. Translated by Arthur Goldhammer. Cambridge, Mass.: Harvard University Press, Belknap Press, 1991.

Vovelle, Michel. *La Révolution et l'ordre juridique privé: rationalité ou scandale? Actes du colloque d'Orléans 11–13 septembre 1986.* 2 vols. Paris: Presses universitaires de France, 1988.

Wishnia, Judith. "Natalisme et nationalisme pendant la première guerre mondiale." *Vingtième Siècle*, no. 45 (January–March 1995): 30–39.

Index

abandoned children, 28, 76, 95, 102, 112, 143, 208, 226

abduction (kidnapping), 19, 72, 75, 120, 121, 260

abortion, 121, 142–143, 165, 172, 187, 246; advice as evidence of paternity, 187–189

Académie de Médecine, 143

Académie française, 77

accouchement sous x, 246, 280

Acollas, Émile, 95, 117

adoption, 48–51, 217–237; of abandoned children, 222–223, 227; of adults, 218, 233; and affection, 224, 228; agencies, 226–227; benefits to adoptee, 228–235; and birth mother, 228–229; and birth parents, 236; changes in Family Code, 242; changes in laws, 235–236, 270; and Civil Code, 48–51, 221, 223; and constructing families, 43–47, 223–238; upon death of biological mother, 231–232; denied to homosexual couples, 273; informal, 41–43, 217–221; and inheritance, 218, 221–222, 231; and kinship ties, 43, 218, 220, 223, 230–233, 235; legalization of child adoption, 200, 218, 223–226; legislative debates on, 223; nullification of, 219; *plénière*, 235, 270; as a result of World War I, 223; and the Revolution, 41–47; by single persons, 50, 227, 232–233; *simple*, 235; as a solution to childlessness, 225; of stepchildren, 233–234

adultery: children of, 205, 258; in the Civil Code, 55; decriminalization of, 259; and the Gardener's Law, 246; and honor, 204–205; responsibility for child support, 258; of men, 29, 137–138, 140, 154, 156, 179, 206; and moral order, 206; during the Old Regime, 29; and recherche de paternité, 91–92; of women, 55, 137, 154, 156, 201, 203, 252–253, 258

Algeria, 250

Allgemeines Landrecht. *See* Prussian Code

Alliance nationale pour l'accroissement de la population. *See* National Alliance for Population Growth

allocations familiales, 242–244

Alsace, 196

ancien régime. *See* Old Regime

Appeals Court (*Cour d'Appel*). *See* Court of Appeals

Arnaud, André-Jean, 4, 6, 55

L'Assiette au Beurre, 99, 124–136

Assistance judiciaire: law of, 84; use of, 100, 149, 168

assistance publique, 112, 172–174, 210–216, 221, 238; and adoption, 226–230

Auclert, Hubertine, 150

L'Aurore, 96

Austria, 174

author of the pregnancy (genitor), 1, 10, 16, 20, 25, 51, 64, 69–70, 73, 82, 162–163, 172–173, 193, 197, 242, 246, 261–262

Avril de Sainte-Croix, Ghénia, 301n14

Azema, Michel, 44–45, 229

Balzac, Honoré de, 218

Beaumarchais, Pierre-Augustin Caron de, 283

Bègles (Gironde), 274

Belgium, 196

Belleville, 210
Bérenger, René, 117–118, 144, 151, 208
Bergier, Antoine, 52
Berlier, Théophile, 31–32, 34–35, 38, 44, 48
Bigot, Alexis, 41
birth bonuses, 243–244
Blois (Ordinance of), 18
blood tests and types, 163, 197, 258–259, 261, 264; as proof in paternity suits, 191–192
blood ties, 42–48, 172, 194, 197. *See also* family; kinship
Bonaparte, Napoleon. *See* Napoleon I
Bonapartists, views on paternal authority, 80
Bonzon, Jacques, 149
Bourdieu, Pierre, 5
Brochard, Dr. André-Théodore, 143
Bürgerliches Gesetzbuch (BGB). *See* German Civil Code of 1896
Burgundy, 62
Butler, Judith, 107

Caisse de la maternité, 150–151
Calais, 173
Cambacérès, Jean-Jacques Régis: and adoption, 38–39, 44–46, 48–49, 229; and drafting the Civil Code, 48–49; and legislation, 33–35; and the nation, 38–39; 44–46; and natural law, 31, 34, 52, 137; on individual rights, 38–39; 44–46, 48–49, 52, 137, 229
Canon law, 18, 30, 43, 55, 122
Carbonnier, Jean, 238, 261, 266
Cartel des gauches, 190
Castelsarrasin, 73
Catholicism, 94, 117, 123; on aid to unwed mothers, 244; and conjugal family, 10, 79, 80; on consensual unions, 121; and paternal authority, 80; on paternity searches, 121, 152; on seduction, 121
Cazot, Jules, 118–119
Certeau, Michel de, 5
Chabot, François, 41
Chamber of Deputies, 109, 120–122, 137, 140, 150–151
charitable organizations, 166; religious, 223. *See also individual organization names*
Château-Thierry, 96, 98
Chauvin, Jeanne, 148

Chéliga, Marya, 148
child abuse, 212–215, 217
childbirth: belief in a woman's word, 16, 20, 23, 27; expenses, paid by putative father, 19, 25, 34, 41, 187, 264–265, 305n71
child custody, 192, 211, 213, 215, 230; during Vichy, 249–255
children: abandoned, 28, 76, 95, 102, 112, 143, 208, 226; affection for, 210; and citizenship, 30–34, 271; also endangerment of, 207; protection of, 155, 157, 169, 208, 211, 222, 242, 245, 256; rights of, 30–34, 39, 42, 137, 145, 149, 152, 271, 276; as victims, 146, 148. *See also* abandoned children; children, natural; rights: children's
children, natural, 31–32; adoption of, 219–220; assimilation with legitimate children, 30, 174, 276; filiation of, 10, 153–154, 173, 179, 191; financial responsibility for, 16, 23, 63, 80, 84, 113, 258; inheritance, 153, 170, 179, 191, 306n87; legal recognition of, 30, 35–36, 84, 95, 124, 153–154, 176, 193–194, 206, 228, 260, 291n34, 309n6; legitimation of, 171, 172, 260, 275, 300n10; rights of, 37, 44, 47, 121, 137, 143, 153. *See also* paternity: responsibility of; rights: children's
child support, 10, 70, 86, 96, 118, 123, 136, 143, 163–164, 167–168, 170, 175–176, 183, 186, 221, 249, 258, 260, 266, 305n71; in broken engagements, 100, 109, 111; as separate from filiation, 176
Civil Code, 12, 16, 37–56; on adoption, 44–47, 218, 221, 223; and adultery, 201, 260; child's right to support, 260; civil registration of births (article 60), 53; and contract law, 70; and damages (article 1382), 70; definition of paternity (article 312), 63, 201; framing of, 47–57; and inheritance, 153–154; legitimation and recognition of natural children, 30, 34–36, 300n10 (*see also under* children, natural); and marriage, 54; and morality, 54, 158; and paternal authority, 54, 207; and paternity searches (recherche de paternité, article 340), 52–55, 64, 72, 84; and property, 47, 159; reasons for changes, 142, 144; redactors of, 44–45, 52, 294n71; revisions of article 340 recherche de paternité in 1912, 113, 117, 123, 136–139, 302n30; revisions of arti-

cle 340 recherche de paternité in 1972, 260–262; revisions of article 340 recherche de paternité in 1993, 264, 266. See also *dommages-intérêts*; paternity suits
Civil Tribunal (*Tribunal Civil*), 91, 100, 115
Clemenceau, Georges, 96
Code de la Famille. See Family Code of 1939
Code Napoléon. See Civil Code, Penal Code
cohabitation, 12, 164, 303n39; as proof of paternity, 122. See also consensual unions, *concubinage notoire*
Commissariat of Police, 215
Committee on the Reform of Marriage, 115, 301n14
community: and broken marriage promises, 175; and men's honor, 204–205; and private lives, 155. See also *concubinage notoire*, paternity suits, witnesses
compensation. See *dommages-intérêts*
concubinage. See consensual unions
concubinage notoire, 125, 138, 156, 168, 176, 180, 192; definition of, 164, 181–183; evidence of, 181; as proof of paternity, 122, 164, 167; as socially acceptable, 157, 164; and witnesses, 165, 168, 182, 209
Congrès général des sociétés féministes. See General Congress of Feminist Societies
Conseil d'État. See Council of State
Conseil national des femmes françaises. See National Council of Frenchwomen
consensual unions, 95, 100, 107, 119–123, 160, 167, 178, 195, 214; acceptance of, 138, 156–157, 164, 239, 259–260, 270–271, 277, 281, 283; and adoption, 237; as civil contracts, 272; as families, 157, 196, 271; heterosexual, 165, 241, 272; as immoral, 165; and the poor, 165; same-sex, 11, 241, 272; as social disintegration, 165; during Vichy, 243–244. See also cohabitation; *concubinage notoire*
Constant, Benjamin, 53
contraception, 165, 185, 281
Corps législatif, 47
Coulon, Henri, 146
Counsel of Five Hundred, 47
Council of State, 47–48
Cour de cassation, 61, 182–183, 186; landmark decisions of, 73–74, 90–93, 117

Court of Appeals, 61, 82, 87, 91, 100, 188
courts. See Civil Tribunal; *Cour de Cassation*; Court of Appeals; *dommages-intérêts*; gendered narratives; paternity suits; women: decisions to go to court
Couturier, E., 99, 136
creditur virgini parturienti, 23, 27–28, 139
Crémieux, Adolphe, 62
crime: juvenile, 145; misdemeanors, 17; paternity searches as prevention of, 142–144
Criminal Investigation Department. See *Sûreté, Police de*

Daladier, Edouard, 242
damages, court-ordered. See *dommages-intérêts*
Dame aux Camélias, La (Dumas), 115
Daumier, Honoré, 76–77
déchéance de la puissance paternelle. See deprivation of paternal authority
déchéance maternelle. See maternal authority: deprivation of
Declaration of the Rights of Man and Citizen, 32, 152
Declaration of the Rights of Woman and Citizen, 33
déclarations de grossesse. See pregnancy declarations
degeneration, 142–143
délit, 83, 92, 116
Démar, Claire, 79
depopulation, 9, 122, 143, 169, 173, 218, 223, 242–243
deprivation of paternal authority (*déchéance de la puissance paternelle*), 207–217. See also under paternal authority
Deroin, Jeanne, 79, 147
Desan, Suzanne, 47
désaveu de paternité. See disavowal of paternity
Deuxième Congrès international des oeuvres et institutions féminines. See Second International Conference of Feminine Organizations and Institutions
Dijon, 183
disavowal of paternity (*désaveu de paternité*), 172, 201–207; and divorce, 205; grounds for, 203; irreversibility of, 205; procedure for, 202–203; witnesses, 204. See also under paternity

divorce, 203, 237, 269; and disavowal of paternity, 205; during Vichy, 249, 252, 254
DNA (deoxyribonucleic acid), 163, 197, 264, 266; as proof of paternity, 257–259
doctors, testimony of, 215
domestic servants, 21, 26, 88, 182–183, 311n52
dommages-intérêts (Civil Code article 1382), 24, 27, 39–41, 59, 69–80, 92, 96, 161, 167, 305n71; as consequence of a broken marriage promise, 19–20, 69–72, 74–75, 80, 100, 175–179; legal grounds for, 81–82; and the PACS, 273; principles of, 175; in seduction, 39, 82, 106
Droit des femmes, Le, 151
Drossard, Anne-Gilberte, 257
Drossard, Aurore, 257
Dubois, Jacques, 40
Dumas, Alexandre, *fils*, 114, 139, 152, 159
Durand, Marguerite, 147, 149

Enfants assistés, 222
enfants de la patrie, 53
enfants moralement abandonnés, 207
engagement. See marriage promise
Enlightenment, 31
Entr'aide des femmes françaises. See Society for the Mutual Aid of French Women
European Court for the Rights of Man, 274
European Union, 282

family: adoptive, 107; and birth bonuses, 244; and the Catholic Church, 79; and the Civil Code, 45–51, 53–54, 58, 79; conjugal, 45, 79, 107, 112, 153, 156, 206, 208, 238, 241, 243, 256, 281; and consensual unions, 107, 258–259, 271; construction of, 155, 200, 254; dysfunctional, 210; and honor, 29, 71, 100; idealized, 196, 201, 256, 281; and individual, 158; non-conjugal, 258; patriarchal, 272; and property, 16, 104, 124, 137–138, 285; protection of 180; reconstituted, 200, 219; same-sex, 273; and the state, 142, 158
Family Code of 1939 (*Code de la famille*), 242–247; changes in adoption, 242
family council, 213, 231
family planning movement, 266
fatherhood: and affection, 11, 97, 162–164, 181, 225; biological, 162–164, 206; in the Civil Code, 53; glorification of, 245; legal, 267. See also paternity
feminist leagues, 147–151. See also *individual association names*
feminists, 82, 136, 158, 174, 196; and adoption, 225–226; and childcare, 79; and marriage, 79; and paternal responsibility, 147; and paternity searches, 13, 79, 146–151, 284; and *recherche de maternité*, 147
Femme libre, La, 79
Figaro, Le, 96
filiation, 10, 64, 106, 118, 121, 148, 154, 163, 167–168, 177, 238, 260, 268, 275; definition of, 296n7
Fils naturel, Le (Dumas), 76, 114
Finance, Ministry of, 252
First Republic, 44, 57–58, 138, 152
Foreign Legion, 193
foster families, 53, 208, 211, 214, 217–218, 221
Foucault, Michel, 6–8, 187, 202, 285
foundling homes, 95, 222, 226
Fourierism, 79
Fournel, Jean-François, 17, 23
France, Anatole, 96
Franco Prussian War, 8, 220
French Revolution, 12, 27, 30–36, 40, 43–44, 47, 55–57, 139, 218, 223, 282–283
French Union for the Rescue of Children (*Union française pour le sauvetage de l'enfance*), 211
French Women's Union (*Union féminine française*), 166
Fronde, La, 147

Gardener's Law (*Loi du jardinier*), 246–247
Gavardie, Edmund Dufaure de, 117–118
Gazette des Tribunaux, 88, 100, 280, 296n2
gendered narratives, 85, 101, 166, 198, 240; in judicial proceedings, 25–26, 62–63, 68, 89, 93–94
General Congress of Feminist Societies (*Congrès général des sociétés féministes*), 147
Gentile, Antoine, 50
German Civil Code of 1896, 140–141
Germany, 8, 172, 174, 196, 242, 249–251, 256, 282
Gouges, Olympe de (Marie Grouze), 33, 146

grandparents, 212–216, 218, 230, 250–251
Great Britain, 56, 116, 141, 148, 215, 282, 284
guardianship. *See* child custody
Guillier, Pierre-Ernest, 144

Haut Comité de la population, 242
Henri II, edict of, 20–21
Histoire morale des femmes (Legouvé), 77
honor: and adultery, 204; and children, 173; and community, 20, 103, 204; in courtrooms, 26; defense of, 26, 204–205; family, 20, 22, 29, 71, 101, 168; and male bloodline, 202; men's, 28, 53, 103, 113, 139, 156, 158, 202, 204; and paternity, 281; and paternity disavowal, 202–207; and property, 158; and sexuality, 158; women's, 20, 24, 25–26, 81, 92, 102, 139–140, 166
Hôtel-Dieu, 43
Hugo, Victor, 146

illegitimate children. *See* children, natural
Indiana (Sand), 218
infanticide, 28, 95, 99, 121, 142–143, 246
inheritance: and adoption, 46, 218, 221–222, 231; and adultery, 156; and bloodlines, 197, 202; and class, 51; and natural children, 153, 170, 179, 191, 306n87; and paternity, 179; and paternity suits, 170; rights of, 25, 106, 118, 121, 153–155, 273. *See also* rights: children's
Interior, Ministry of, 62
International Congress on the Condition and the Rights of Women (*Congrés international de la condition et des droits des femmes*), 148, 150
International Red Cross, 216
Ireland, 284
Italy, 56, 196, 282

judges, 16–17, 70; appointment of, 61–62, 162; careers of, 96; challenges to the Civil Code, 60; judicial activism, 60, 63, 107; latitude in decisions, 10, 40, 160, 163, 176, 179, 181–182, 267; and moral order, 195; power of, 10, 26, 60, 73, 94, 109, 196, 262, 265; and public policy, 240; on the responsibility of adulterous men, 179; and rights, 106. *See also* Civil Tribunal; *Cour de cassation*; Court of Appeals; rights
July Monarchy, 74
jurisprudence, 5, 59, 70, 154, 156, 179, 195, 197, 219, 223; social use of, 106; during Vichy, 249

Kergomard, Pauline, 150
kidnapping. *See* abduction
kinship, 200–201, 211, 214, 217, 255; and adoption, 230–233. *See also* community; family

La Noue, Jeanne Caulnier de, 19
Lambrechts, Hector, 152
Larmartine, Alphonse de, 76
Lariboisière Hospital, 174
League for the Protection of Abandoned Mothers (*Ligue pour la Protection des mères abandonnées*), 166, 226–227
Le Chapelier, Isaac-René-Guy, 32
Legislative Assembly, 19, 120
Legislative Committee, 38
Legouvé, Ernest, 77
letters, as proof of paternity, 87–88, 96, 110, 138, 160, 167, 169, 171, 180, 183–184, 187, 253
Let Us Save Mothers and Babies (*Sauvons les mères et les bébés*), 166
Ligue pour la Protection des mères abandonnées. *See* League for the Protection of Abandoned Mothers
Locke, John, 31, 70
Louis-Philippe, 62
Loysel, Antoine, 11, 15, 156, 163–164, 241, 272
Lucey, Michael, 3

magistrates. *See* judges
Magnaud, Paul, 96–97
Mamère, Noël, 274
Margueritte, Paul and Victor, 115, 125, 136
Marin, Louis, 194
Martin, Louis, 150
marriage, 206; cost of, 113; legitimation of children, 245. *See also* adultery; children, natural; family: conjugal
Marriage of Figaro, The (Beaumarchais), 283
marriage promise (engagement), 19, 24, 96, 98, 161, 182; in the Civil Code, 54; as civil contract, 19–20, 24, 69–72, 74, 176; consequences for breaking, 20, 69–70, 80, 97, 100,

marriage promise (engagement) (*continued*) 176–178, 259 (see also *dommages-intérêts*); grounds for breaking, 20; and honor, 74; legal, 274. *See also* paternity suits

married men, 177; and adultery, 179; exempt from paternity searches, 118, 121, 139–140, 258–259; and responsibility for extranuptial children, 177–179

masculinity, 158, 172, 204, 237, 281; and paternity, 173; and seduction, 65

maternal authority: and adoption, 229; deprivation of (*déchéance maternelle*), 215–216

Matin, Le, 173, 188, 190, 280

Mauss, Marcel, 217

Mégève, 250–251

men. *See* paternity; paternal authority; fatherhood; married men; honor

mère au foyer, 225

Millet, Albert, 115

Misérables, Les (Hugo), 76

Misme, Jane, 174

Montand, Yves, 257–258, 264

Montesquieu, Charles de Secondat, baron de, 32

morality: as grounds for damages, 87; men's, 119, 143; sexual, 85, 158; women's, 25–26, 53, 80, 97–98, 111, 120, 122, 155, 162, 181, 222

moral order, 54, 105, 208

motherhood: affection, 161; fidelity of as proof, 138; glorification of, 245; virtues of, 225. *See also* mothers; mothers, unwed

mothers, 104, 198, 240; rights of, 123, 275; unwed, 8, 51, 174, 199, 205, 220. *See also* women; paternity suits

Mourier, Louis, 174

Mussolini, Benito, 173

Napoleon I, influence on Civil Code, 48–50

Napoleonic Code. *See* Civil Code

National Alliance for Population Growth (*Alliance nationale pour l'accroissement de la population*), 243

National Convention of 1793, 36–38, 40–46; 122, 145, 154–155, 229

National Council of Frenchwoman (*Conseil national des femmes françaises*), 151

National Revolution (Vichy), 255

natural children. *See* children, natural

Natural law, 31–32, 34–38, 56, 70, 94, 107, 151, 156

Naquet, Alfred, 119

Neuwirth Law of 1967, 259

Nord, Philip, 95

Normandy, 90

Nye, Robert, 8, 197, 202

Occupation (1940–1944), 247–250, 253–256

Old Regime, 12, 16–30, 42, 44, 52, 57, 118, 122, 152, 197

Ordinance of Blois, 18

orphans, 41, 43–47, 171, 218, 221, 224, 226, 231

Oudot, Charles-François, 31–32, 44, 45

PACS (*Pacte civil de solidarité*), 272–274, 276

Palais de Justice, 76–77

parental authority (*autorité parentale*), 270

parental responsibility. *See* children, natural: financial responsibility for; child support; paternity: financial responsibility of; paternal authority

Paris Commune, 220

paterfamilias, 8, 58

pater is est, as definition of paternity, 38, 156, 275

paternity: and adultery, 263; avowal of, 160, 183; biological, 2, 162–164, 197, 202, 213, 238, 264, 268, 278; defined by affection for child, 194, 197, 264, 278; definition in marriage, 205; denial of, 172–173, 200, 254; deprivation of, 200, 207–217; desired, 192–193, 215, 265, 268; disavowal of (*désaveu de paternité*), 38, 201–207; divisibility of, 64, 72, 76, 79, 83, 106, 118, 152, 163, 176–187, 197, 241, 260, 263, 267–268; and *dommages-intérêts*, 263; duties of, 53, 145, 181, 245; and financial responsibility of, 25, 27–28, 72, 87, 95, 98, 109, 152, 163; and honor, 173, 202; and inheritance, 179; judicially declared, 12, 123, 154, 162, 173, 182, 263; in jurisprudence, 179; in law, 179; legal recognition of, 81, 84, 117, 163; men's insistence on, 192–193; outside of marriage, 179; proof of, 24, 36, 38, 110–111, 119, 122, 138, 163, 184–185, 194–195, 264–265; responsibility of, 69, 80, 84, 86, 93, 125, 136, 148, 151, 161, 196; rights of, 151; social, 202; and visitation rights, 263, 271;

voluntary, 12. *See also* letters, as proof of; paternity suits
paternal authority (*puissance paternelle*), 12, 42–43, 94–95, 100, 172–173, 194, 198, 217, 267, 277; and the Catholic Church, 80; community testimony, 209; defined in practice, 162; deprivation of (*déchéance de la puissance paternelle*), 137, 207–217, 237, 270; disavowal of, 137, 201–207, 237; and mothers, 207
paternity suits (*recherche de paternité*), 1, 72, 109, 242, 254, 258; advising abortion as evidence of, 188–189; behavior as evidence, 163, 176, 180–181, 185, 192, 194–195, 199; blood groups as proof of non-paternity, 191–192; brought by adult children, 189–191; brought in bad faith, 120–121, 125, 136, 139–140, 185; for child support, 163–164, 167–168, 170, 175–176, 178–179, 181, 183, 186, 194; concubinage as evidence, 160, 164–165, 176–178, 180, 182–183, 185, 188, 193, 261; for damages, 175–179; death of putative father, 170–172; definitions of accepted evidence in, 157, 160–162, 176, 261, 264; and depopulation, 143; exemption from, 118, 121, 139–140, 177; feminist views on, 13, 79, 146–151, 284; for filiation, 148, 163, 166–168, 170, 173, 175–176, 177, 179, 186, 196, 197; forbidden in the Civil Code of 1804, 30, 38–39, 84; grounds for after 1912, 120, 124, 139, 248; and inheritance, 170, 266; judicial process, 26, 167–168, 261, 264, 266–267; legal changes in 1972, 260–262; legal changes in 1993, 264, 266; letters as evidence in, 87–88, 96, 110, 180, 187, 261; and literature, 76, 114–115; men's defense, 92, 162, 168, 192, 262; physical resemblance as proof, 191–192, 264; proposals to permit, 114–125; provisions of law of 1912, 160–162; reasons for permitting, 142, 302n30; revisions of 1972, 260–262; and socialists, 271–272, 274; during Vichy, 247; witnesses, 112, 165, 180–182, 185–186, 248
pater potestas, 239
patriarchal family, 3, 37, 54, 60, 238, 241, 269, 278
patronymic, 171, 216, 235, 269–270
Penal Code, 67, 72, 115, 118

pension alimentaire. *See* child support
père subsidant, 263–264, 267
Pétain, Philippe, 246–247
Pognon, Maria, 149–150
Poor Law Amendment Act, 141
Portalis, Jean-Étienne-Marie, 48, 55
Portugal, 141, 282
Pothier, Robert-Joseph, 19
pouponnières, 174
Préameneu, Félix-Julien-Jean Bigot de, 52, 55
pregnancy declarations (*déclarations de grossesse*), 20–23, 25, 27–28, 32, 40
press, popular, 83, 98, 124–136, 279–280
primes de naissance, 242
privacy, right to, 109, 123, 155
pronatalism, 169, 172, 188, 242–245
property: and the Civil Code, 159; and families, 137–138; and paternity, 186; rights of legitimate children, 113. *See also* inheritance
prostitution, 25–26, 80, 120, 198, 215
Prudhomme, René François Armand, 136
Prussian Code, 56–57
public order, 179, 193, 195
public policy, 169
Pufendorf, Samuel von, 31
puissance maritale, 54, 259
puissance paternelle. *See* paternal authority
pupilles de la nation, 224

quasi-délit, 83, 92, 116

Radicals, 121, 122, 123
Raison d'État, 144, 284
rape, 66, 72, 117, 120–121, 172, 187, 261; punishment for, 67
rapt, 17–19
rapt de séduction, 17–19, 72
recherche de maternité (article 341), 140, 147, 189–190, 198
recherche de paternité. *See* paternity suits
reparations, sought/granted. *See dommages-intérêts*
reproductive technologies, 268–271
republicans, 82, 94
Revolution, legislative debates on paternity, 30–39; 12 brumaire II, 34, 39
Richer, Léon, 147

rights: children's, 2, 30, 32, 121, 137, 143, 145, 153, 152, 209, 271, 276; of conjugal families, 113; of father's, 30, 34, 279; individual, 13, 16, 31, 34, 37–39, 58, 64–65; men's, 74–75, 106, 113, 137, 152, 155, 238, 282; of mother's, 123, 275; of parents, 209; privacy, 109, 123, 155; property, 104; women's, 33, 105, 137, 155, 275. *See also* children: rights of; women
Rivet, Gustave, 120–122, 137–138, 143–144, 146, 151, 164, 275
Robespierre, Maximilien, 28, 43
Roland, Pauline, 79
Roman law, 29, 38, 42, 275
Rousseau, Jean-Jacques, 7–8, 37
Roussel, Nelly, 149–150
Roussel, Théophile, 208
Royal, Ségolène, 274

Saint-Simonians, 78–79
Sand, George, 79, 218
Sarkozy, Nicholas, 286
Savatier, René, 186, 192
scandal, fear of, 68, 83, 107, 110–113, 117–120, 122, 139–140, 148, 168, 191
Sciolino, Elaine, 286
Scott, Joan Wallach, 75, 106, 165, 284
Second Empire, 80–95
Second International Conference of Feminine Organizations and Institutions (*Deuxième Congrès international des oeuvres et institutions féminines*), 148, 306n81, 306nn84–85
Second Republic, 61–62
seduction, 16, 92; as civil offense, 70; as criminal misdemeanor, 17; definitions of, 65–67; fraudulent, 66–69, 74, 83, 85, 92–100, 107, 116–117, 120, 123, 161, 176–177; and gendered narratives, 62–63; and judges, 17; and marriage, 117, 121; and paternal responsibility, 63; and rights of men, 75; and tort law, 100, 106
Sembat, Marcel, 150
Senate, 109, 118, 122, 139, 144, 146, 150, 156
sexuality, 164, 252; and class, 186; double standard, 201; men's, 36, 155, 173, 263; of single mothers, 173; women's, 8, 13, 255; and women's fidelity, 202; workingwomen's, 26, 112, 139, 165–166
Signoret, Simone, 258

Simon, Jules, 80
Smith, Adam, 47
socialists, and debates on paternity searches, 121–123
social order, 142, 145, 157, 271
Society for the Mutual Aid of French Women (*Entr'aide des femmes françaises*), 226–227
Solidarité des femmes. *See* Solidarity of Women
Solidarity of Women (*Solidarité des femmes*), 147
Spain, 141, 196, 282
stepparents, 212, 237
Strauss, Paul, 140, 144, 150, 196
Sûreté, Police de, 209

Tassaert, Octave, 76–77
Thermidor, 28, 37
Thibaudeau, Antoine-Claire, 48
Third Republic, 7, 14, 112; and adoption 220; and the Catholic Church, 283; fear of depopulation, 242–243; legislative debates on recherche de paternité, 114–123, 136–152; pronatalism of, 242–243; and solidarism, 195; and Vichy, 249, 252, 254–255
tort law: and broken marriage promises, 177; and paternity, 106; article 1382, 74; for seduction, 100. *See also dommages-intérêts*; seduction
Tristan, Flora, 79
Tronchet, François-Denis, 49

Union féminine française. *See* French Women's Union
Union française pour le sauvetage de l'enfance. *See* French Union for the Rescue of Children
United States, 116, 250, 278–280, 282
Ursule Mirouët (Balzac), 218

Valée, Oscar de, 86
Variot, Gaston, 142
Veil Law of 1975, 259
Vérone, Maria, 125
Vichy, 14, 242–247; and censorship, 251, 255; custody, 249–253; divorce, 249, 252, 254; fatherhood, 249, 251; and Jews, 249–250

Vigneron, Paule, 148
Vire, 90
Viviani, René, 147, 150
Volquin, Suzanne, 86

welfare, 2, 137, 208, 211, 266, 272, 281. *See also* assistance publique
wet nurses, 95, 112, 180–181, 208, 221
witnesses: in paternity disavowal, 201–207; in paternity suits, 112, 165, 167, 180–182, 186, 209
women: and citizenship, 104–105, 136, 159, 165, 196, 259; as biological mothers, 197; control over their bodies, 156; decisions to go to court, 75–80, 100–107, 166–169, 266–267, 279; indigenous, 196; and marriage, 117; morality of, 25–26, 53, 80, 87, 97–98, 111–112, 122, 155, 162, 181, 222; as mothers, 104, 166, 198, 240; and power, 104, 109, 198; as victims, 18, 23, 26–27, 104, 107, 136. *See also* motherhood; rights, mothers
World War I, 169–172, 175, 281; and adoption, 223–224
World War II, 216, 242

Yonne, 186

Zangiacomi, Joseph, 74